Janet & David
Apia 1/18/88

A Simplified Dictionary of Modern Samoan

R.W. Allardice

Polynesian Press

First published 1985 by
POLYNESIAN PRESS
334-336 Ponsonby Road Auckland 2 New Zealand
in association with Wesley Bookshop, Apia, W. Samoa.

Cover design by Fatu Feuu
Typeset by Jacobson Graphic Communications Group
Printed by Woolmore Printing

The publishers gratefully acknowledge the support of the Australian Government through the South Pacific Cultures Fund, and the New Zealand Maori and South Pacific Arts Council.

ISBN 0 908597 02 9

To Miriam

Contents

Preface

This dictionary has been prepared in response to a growing need, both in Samoa and overseas, for a simplified Samoan-English dictionary suitable for use by students and others.

It is in no way intended to replace the scholarly and comprehensive dictionary compiled by Prof. G. B. Milner (Oxford University Press). Rather, it is hoped that this dictionary will encourage students to make full use of the splendid material in Milner's work.

The present writer is greatly indebted to Prof. Milner; the Rev. George Pratt, who compiled the first dictionary in 1862 (Malua Printing Press, W. Samoa); and the Rev. Spencer Churchward, author of "A Samoan Grammar" (Melbourne 1951).

Students of Samoan are further directed to C. C. Marsack's "Samoan", for a clear introduction to the study of the language. (Teach Yourself Books).

Heinemann's "New Zealand Dictionary" is also most helpful with its clear meanings of English words and its simple guide to pronunciation.

Acknowledgements

I am pleased to acknowledge the generous assistance of a number of Samoans; teachers, ministers, chiefs and orators who, with their wives, have acted as consultants during the researching of this present work. The medical staff of the National Hospital in Western Samoa has been most helpful in checking contemporary medical terms.

In addition, a number of others have unwittingly contributed to the project. These include bus and taxi drivers, workmen, students, housewives and shop assistants.

The editors of the several weekly Samoan newspapers and regular church journals have also provided a source of contemporary terms, as have the local radio announcers.

To them all I am most grateful.

I am further indebted to Fr. P. M. Ryan whose Revised Dictionary of Modern Māori has provided the model for this Samoan Dictionary, and to Mrs. Koke Aiono (University Lecturer) and the Rev. Vaiao and Mrs. Erolini Eteuati of Wesley College, Faleula, for checking the typescript.

R. W. Allardice
Misi Alatise

How to use the Dictionary

This dictionary has been designed to assist the reader to obtain information as easily as possible.

Whilst the English to Samoan section is straightforward in that the entries are arranged in alphabetical order, the Samoan to English section is slightly more complicated. Each entry begins with the "base" or "headword" followed, where appropriate, by the listing of words derived from, or directly related to the "headword".

e.g. **muli:** – come last, rear
mulimuli – follow
fa'amuli – stay behind
mulilua – adultery
mulivae – heel

Where several "headwords" have the same spelling but different meanings they are listed separately and numbered.

e.g. **mama**$_1$ – masticate, chew
mama$_2$ – leak
mama$_3$ – ring
mama$_4$ – mother, mummy

Thus, when a reader is checking a Samoan word it will be necessary to first locate the "base" or "headword", and then run down the list following the main entry.

List of Abbreviations

The dash (__) indicates that the "head-word" is being used without repeating the spelling in each case.

art.	article
A.S.	American Samoa
bet.	between
ch.	chief
colq.	colloquial
C.C.C.S.	Congregational Christian Church Samoa
ea.	each
ea.oth.	each other
e.g.	for example
fig.	figuratively
ft.	foot, feet
gen.	generally
h. ch.	high chief
i.e.	that is
impol.	impolite
incl.	inclusive
indef.	indefinite
interj.	interjection
joc.	jocular
L.D.S.	Latter Day Saints (Mormon Church)
Meth.	Methodist Church
o. a.	one another
o. s.	oneself
oth.	other
O.T.	Old Testament
part.	particle
pass.	passive
ph.	phrase
pl.	plural
pol.	polite word
prn.	pronoun
R.C.	Roman Catholic Church
S.	Samoa, Samoan
s.	see
sm.	small
s.o.	someone
s.th.	something
v.	very
w.	with
w.o.	without
W.S.	Western Samoa

SAMOAN to ENGLISH

Aa

a$_1$	(indicates the possessive) – used with "a" nouns, belonging to
a$_2$	an emphatic suffix e.g. *e moni a'oe*
'a	when, for, because
ā$_1$	very, indeed, just, only
ā$_2$	be like what, be how e.g. *'ua ā mai 'oe?* How are you? *e ā pe 'ā?* How about?
a'a	root
a'afia	involved
a'a	(*a'asia*) to kick (pl. *fea'a*)
'a'a	be obstinate
'a'ai	village, town, city
'a'ala	be sore (throat)
'ale	(*'a'ale*) hasty, rash
'a'alu	be thick (mixture)
'a'ami, **'ami'ami**	fetch
'a'amu	make fun of
'a'ano	flesh, kernel, heart of the matter
'a'ao$_1$	(pol.) limb, bring, present
'a'ao$_2$	be conceited
'a'apa	reach for
'a'asa	be red hot, ardent
'a'asi	(*'āsia*) scratch deeply
ta'asi	scratch carelessly
'a'ati	gnaw
'a'atia	bite off
'a'ato	exactly
a'au	reef
'a'au	(pl. *feausi*) swim
'ausaga	group of swimmers
'a'ava	pungent, sultry
'avasia	smart sting
fa'a'a'ava	be fermented
'ā'ā	bread baked twice, answer stubbornly
a'e, a'ea'e	climb, go up (hill)
'ae	but
'ae'ae	take for granted
'a'e	(pl *fe'a'ei*) climb (tree)
'a'e'a'e	climb
ae maise	especially
'aeno	land crab
'āeto	eagle
afa	agree, wild almond
afā	storm, gale, hurricane
afātia	storm bound, caught in a storm
'afa$_1$	sennit, fishing-line
'afa$_2$	half, be fit
'afa kasi	half-caste
afafine	daughter (of a man)
afaga	place for beached canoe
'afaga	tight (of clothes), look abnormal (clothes, lips)
'āfai	if
āfāina	be hurt, in danger
e lē āfāina	it does not matter
'afato	grub
afe	thousand
	lift, turn over, tuck in, hem, turn aside, call in to a house
fa'aafe	light refreshment, invite into a house
afega	corner, turn
afemoe	to rest (of the dead)
āfea	when (of future)
āfei	line, lining
afi	fire, motor, car engine
afitusi	box of matches
afiafi	afternoon, evening
afī	bundle of fish, package, parcel
afifi	bundle, wrap
afio	to come (h.ch.) (pl. *āfifio*) reside, dwell, be present, presence (also used of God)

afioga	*lana afioga*, his lordship, gracious words
afioʻaga	residence
afisāvae	(pol.) groin
ʻafisi	carry under arm, on hip
ʻafisiga	load carried under arm
afo	fishing line
āfolau	long S. house
āfu	sweat, perspire, be heated (cooking) wither, waterfall
ʻafu$_1$	cover, draw sheet over body
ʻie afu	sheet
ʻafu$_2$	gift of fine mats
afua	begin
afuafua	(pol.) to become pregnant, conceive an idea
afulu	be over-cooked
aga$_1$	conduct, behaviour, culture
agāga	soul, spirit
faʻa-le-agāga	spiritual
agaalii	behave like a chief
agaalofa	be generous
agaleaga	unkind
agalelei	be kind
agamalū	gentle, meek
agamāsesei	troublesome
agamaulalo	humble
aganuʻu	custom(s) culture
agapiʻopiʻo	sly, crooked conduct
agasala	sin, offence
agatonu	correct behaviour
agavaʻa	suitable, ability, experience
agavaivai	gentle
agavale	treat unkindly, left-handed
aga$_2$	to face, set out for
agaʻi	set out for, against
agaaga	rebellious
feagai	face, be opposite, happen at same time, be in agreement
feagaiga	agreement, contract, covenant, testament, pastor
faʻafeagaiga	relations
agaʻese	(pol.) knife, axe
agaiotupu	(pol.) carpenter, builder
agatonu	(pol.) kava, equal
aga$_3$	span
ʻāgelu	angel
agi	to blow (wind)
agiagia	flutter (flag)
ago	design, invent
agoagoga	plan
ai$_1$	who
ai$_2$	there, hereby, who, which, that
āi	row (trees etc), sew, seam
ʻai$_1$	eat (pl. *ʻaʻai*), bite, grip
ʻaina	edible, eroded
ʻaiga	meal, feast
feʻainaʻi	eat quickly, quarrel
ʻaiate	coward
ʻaiavā	presentation of food
ʻaipā	glutton
ʻaipupula	look hopefully at food
ʻaisago	eat with relish
ʻaitagi	funeral feast
ʻaiʻū	unwilling to share food
ʻaiuli	play up to, make a fuss of, support a dance
ʻai$_2$	score (games), points, runs etc.
ʻai$_3$	from
ʻai$_4$	*ʻai lava,* probably
aʻi	with which, with
āiā	be entitled to, interfere
aʻiaʻi	pure, genuine, complete, absolutely
aiaiga	arrangement
ʻaifanua	emigrate
ʻāiga	family, related, home
ʻailao	twirl a knife, acknowledge a gift
ʻailoga	it is doubtful, unlikely, probably not.

'aimālō grab, snatch
'ainā inhabited
'ai'oi implore, beg
'aiou request food out of turn (impol.)
'aipula beg for food, money etc.
'aisa ice
pusa'aisa refrigerator
aisakulimi ice cream
'aiseā why
'aisi to ask for, beg.
'aitālafu borrow, debt
fa'a'aitālafu on credit
'aivao run wild (animals)
ala$_1$ path, road, track, way, method, cause of, reason for
alalaupapa bridge
alana'i take along
ala'alo side-track
alafa'a'apefa'i stairs, steps
alasopo overland track
atāasu chimney
alatanu highway
alau'amea railway line
alāva'a boat channel
alāvai canal
ala$_2$ be awake, awaken
alaala sit and talk at night
alaalafaga evening fellowship, residence, village
alaalafagamau (pol.) grave
fa'aala wake s.o.
alapō be awake at night
alausu early morning start
ala$_3$ scratch
'ala$_1$ incident, event
'ala$_2$**, 'a'ala** be sore (eyes and throat)
fe'alasi to smart
alala dry sticks for fire
'alāfau cheek
ālaga leg (pig, cow, etc.)
'alaga call out (pl. *ālalaga*) shout, public announcement, bestow a little
alagāupu saying, proverb
ālai cheeky
alaisa rice
alamea poisonous fish (crown of thorns)
alamū to speed along
alani reason for
'alauni money allowance
'alava stringy, fibrous, weal (skin), c'nut fibre strainer
'ale be hasty, unimportant event etc.
'alefa alpha (Greek letter)
'alei to divorce
tusi'alei divorce certificate
'aleu mistake, error
aliali be visible, appear
fa'aali show, display, reveal, tell
fa'aaliga notice, display, exhibition, revelation
'ali wooden head-rest
ālia creek
'alia double canoe
ali'i chief, lord, gentleman (pol. for man, boy)
ali'itia to have important guests
'alisi cicada, cricket
'alititai sea-bed
'alitivai river-bed
alo$_1$ smooth or soft side (pol.son, daughter) able to bear children
alo$_2$ be engaged in, to face
aloalo to fan
ālo row, paddle, fish for bonito
āloalo lagoon, keep paddling
'alo shun, turn away from
fa'a'alo'alo be devious
fe'alo'alofa'i dodge a responsibility
āloa'ia treat with courtesy
fa'aalo salute
fa'aaloalo courtesy, respect
'aloiafi sparks
alofa love, affection, greetings, to do a favour, friendly
alofa tunoa divine grace
alofa-mutimutivale divine mercy
alofagia shown affection
fealofani love for one another
alofa'aga love
alofi sit in a circle for a discussion

alofilima	palm of hand
alofivae	sole of foot
alomatū	partly dry
‘ālope	fox
‘alou	pus
‘aloua	contain pus
alu	(pl. *ō*) go, be spent (money)
alumia	be in demand
alualu	run after s.o.
fa‘aalu	drive, propel, spend
fealua‘i	go to and fro
‘alu	dregs
‘alu‘alutoto	clot of blood
‘aluga	pillow, cushion
alumini	aluminium
ama	outrigger, (joc.) wife, husband
‘amana‘ia	keep in mind, take notice of
‘āmata	to begin, start.
‘āmataga	beginning
‘āmene	Amen
āmio	conduct, behaviour, manners, habits (also *āmioga*)
āmiolelei	good conduct
āmiotonu	just, righteous
āmiolētonu	unjust, unrighteous
āmiovalea	be stupid, foolish
āmiomio	to go about
amituataliga	stuff the mouth with food
amo	yoke, carrying-stick, to carry
‘amoti	trigger of a gun, to fire
amu	thick (of speech)
‘amu	coral
‘amu‘amu	branching coral
‘amu‘ia	fortunate, blessed
‘āmulī	after death, in last days
‘amusia	mocked (s.*‘a‘amu*)
ana$_1$	his, hers (used w. “a” nouns)
ana$_2$	cave, cabin (boat), boot (car)
ana$_3$	prefix indicating past
anafea	when
analeilā	earlier today
anamua	in former times
fa‘aanamua	old fashioned
anapō	last night
anataeao	this morning
‘ana	if
‘ana lē seanoa	had it not been for
‘ana‘ana	obey
‘anagatā	durable, long lasting
‘anagōfie	perishable
‘anapogi	to fast
ane$_1$	along, aside (use after verb)
vaeane	by your leave
ane$_2$	white ant
aneanea	to be ancient (of a mat)
‘anei	it is likely, probably
‘anereueta	hundredweight
ānesi	harness
aniani	onion
anini	hitch up
‘aniva	Milky Way
ano$_1$	crater
ano$_2$	pay attention, listen
ano$_3$	plant used for yellow dye
anoano	a lot, quantity
‘āno‘ano	be respectful
‘ānogase	lean meat, tender
anu	(pl. *feanu*) spit, spittoon
anusaga	spittle
‘anufe	worm, caterpillar
‘anusā	you would think
ao$_1$	day, daylight
āoina	be overtaken by daylight
ao$_2$	cloud
aoa	cloudy
ao$_3$	(pol.) head
Ao o le Mālō	Head of State
aoao	supreme, over all
ao$_4$	collect
aofia	be assembled, assembly
aogātupe	collection of money
aofa‘i	sum, total
aofa‘iga	amount
aotele	gather valuable items (fine mats)

ao$_5$	it is essential, must
a'o	teach, learn
ā'oga	school
ā'oga maualuga	high school
a'oa'o	teach, educate, student of theological college
faiā'oga	teacher
ā'oa'o	grow straight
a'oa'i	reprove, admonish
fa'aa'oa'o	imitate
fa'aa'oa'oga	example
'a'o	but, while
'a'ole'i	before
āoa	banyan tree, cavity, cage
'ao'ao	armpit
aoauli	midday, noon
aogā	use, useful, value, valuable
fa'aaogā	to use
fa'a-le-aogā	cancel, invalidate
'Aokuso	August
'apa	tin, can, roofing-iron
'apa memea	copper, brass
'apa'apa	fin, mudguard, wing (plane)
'apa'au	wing (bird)
'apatā	flap wings, take off
apeape	be short, scarce
'apefa'i	ladder
Aperila	April
api	(pol.) be lodged, staying
'api	exercise book, note book
'apili	cling to, stick to
'apo	get ready, catch, observe closely
'apo'apo	take care of
'āpō	hurry up
apoapoa'i(ga)	give good advice, exhortation, homily
'apogāleveleve	spider, web
'aposetolo	apostle
'apulu	(pol.) sickness of h. ch.
'apulupulua	sticky
'aputi	ear of corn, pod.
'āreto	bread (Bible)
'ārio	silver (Bible)

asa(ga)	ford, wade through a ford
'asa	be fruitless
asamo	ask for raw vegetables
'āseta	acid
aseva	clumsy
asi, asiasi	visit
asiasiga	visit, inspection
'asi	c'nut shell scraper
'āsini	ass, donkey
'asino	be certain, fixed. (used in negative)
āsiosio	swelter, whirlwind, water-spout
aso	day, date, food for visitors etc.
asoā	be lengthy
asō	today
'aso	thin rafter
'asoa	(pol.) necklace
'asosi	persist, insist
asu$_1$	ladle, scoop, bale out.
asu$_2$	smoke
asuasu	column of smoke
fā'asu	smoke (fish etc.), fumigate
namuasua	smoky
ata$_1$	shadow, reflection, copy, picture, photograph, film
fā'ata	mirror, x-ray
atavili	movies, cinema
ata$_2$	dawn
ata$_3$	hearts (cards)
'ata	laugh (pl. *fe'atani*)
'atagia	laughed at
'ata'ata	smile, grin
fa'a'ata	amuse
ātaeao	tomorrow
'ātalī	in next world, hereafter
atali'i	son (of a man), (pol. *alo*)
atamai	(pl. *ātamamai)* clever, intelligent, wise, wisdom
atapa'ia	(use in negative) tender, painful to touch

ate	liver
ati$_1$	pull up by roots, build up a stonewall
atiina‘e	build up, develop
ati$_2$	pierce, go through, penetrate, fetch fire
‘ati	bite
‘atia	(worm) eaten, riddled
ma‘ati	be sharp
atigi	shell of, empty container
atigi-lima	finger nail, thimble
atigū	make faces
atili	increasingly
ato$_1$	to thatch (roof), throw
ato$_2$	alto (music)
‘ato	basket, luggage
‘atopa‘u	suit-case
‘atotupe	purse, wallet
‘ātoa	complete, all present, whole
fa‘a‘ato‘atoa	make whole
atofa	appointed (day) fixed
atomika	atomic
‘atone	wild nutmeg (usually *‘akone*)
‘ātonu	perhaps, maybe
atu$_1$	(verbal directive) away from, out
atu$_2$	row (chairs), range (hills)
atulaulau	whole world, earth
atumotu	group of islands
atunu‘u	a country
atu$_3$	bonito
atu$_4$	worry
atuatuvale	alarm
‘ai fa‘aatuatuvale	greedy
fa‘aatuatuvale	upset, disturb
Atua	God
atualala	embalm
atualoa	centipede
atule	mackerel
au$_1$	go on, flow on, current, reach
o le pepe lē au	premature baby
aulia	to have reached (pol.) beheaded

auaumālie	progress gradually
auaua‘i	one by one, in turn
fa‘aau	take over
fa‘aauau	continue to speak
feauga	be in harmony, meets the occasion
auaso	take daily turns
au‘iluma	advance
au‘itua	lose ground
augamālie	fitting, timely
augātupu	succession of kings
augavale	perishable, reluctant
au$_2$	carry (in the hand)
auau	select by hand
au‘ili‘ili	thorough
au$_3$ **auau**	be fond of
au$_4$	liver (e.g. pig)
au‘ona	gall bladder, bile
au$_5$	needle, tattooing comb
au$_6$	to be without
aunifoa	without teeth
aunu‘ua	exiled, banished
a‘u	I, me
‘au$_1$**, ‘aumai**	bring
‘auina	(pl. *‘a‘auina*) send
‘au$_2$	stalk, shaft, axle, handle, weapons
‘aufana	bow
‘aufaga	climbing strap
‘aulama	c‘nut leaf flare
‘aupolapola	coarse fan
‘ausa‘alo	c‘nut scraper w.seat
‘autā	bell clapper
‘āu‘upega	weapons, equipment
‘au$_3$	prefix indicating length etc.
‘auala	road
‘auala-laupapa	bridge
‘augutu	rim
‘āuiti	isthmus
‘aupā	wall, fence
‘autafa	side
‘autū	foundation, ditch
‘auvae	chin, jaw
‘auvai	river bank
‘au$_4$	prefix indicating clusters, bunches etc.
‘aufa‘i	bunch of bananas

ʻauivi skeleton
ʻaupeau waves, billows
ʻau$_5$ team, army, side with, company of
ʻauʻau be working with
faʻaʻauʻau show favour to
ʻaufaʻatasi co-operate
ʻaufaʻatau customers
ʻaufaifaʻatoʻaga farmers
ʻaufaigaluega work force
ʻaufaipese choir
ʻaufitafita army
ʻauiʻa shoal of fish
ʻaukilikiti cricket team
ʻaumāga group of untitled men
ʻaumaimoa spectators
ʻautasi be unanimous
ʻauvaʻa crew
ʻaʻu meet, join up, reach, attend
ʻaua don't! do not, should not
ʻaua neʻi let us not . . .
ʻauā because, for, on account of
ʻauai join with, share in
aualofa lament, gift at a death
āualuma ladies or daughters of the village who have finished school (pol.) penis
ʻauʻau (pol.) have a bath, ridge pole
ʻauʻaumamā be clean, well kept, innocent
ʻauʻauna to serve, servant
auē alas! oh!
ʻaufaga climbing loop (for c'nuts)
ʻaufua juggling
āuga symptoms of illness
augani take an oath, beseech
ʻaui wrap, cover
ʻauleaga ugly (people)
ʻaulefu ugly (people)
ʻaulelei handsome (man)
auli pure
ʻāuli iron (clothes)

auma whirlpool, breakers
aumā to be used for what purpose?
ʻaumaʻia sickly
aumatuā orphaned
ʻaumatua sow (pig)
aumau dwell, sojourn
ʻaumea colleague, friend
ʻaumeamamae bridal party
aumoe a suitor, one who courts a girl
ʻaunese ounce
ʻauomala be unsuccessful, bad luck
ʻauomanū be successful, good luck
auoso scramble, clamber
aupito indicates superlative e.g. *aupito poto* most intelligent
ʻaupū be hollow
ʻaupui splash in water (game)
ʻauro gold
ausa steam, vapour, smoke
ausage few in numbers, weak
ʻausi do better than another
ausigo bend down (on all fours)
ʻāusiusi spotless
ausulu go quickly
autago feel about, grope
autalo re-weed
autaunonofo polygamy
ʻaute hibiscus
āutiapulā short of taro tops
autilo peep
ʻautū centre around
ava passage in reef
āvā wife
āva respect, honour
ʻava$_1$ kava, (shrub, drink) orator's cup
ʻava$_2$ beard
ʻavaalalo beard
ʻavaaluga moustache
ʻavaʻe take up, put up, pick up

āvaga	elope
'avane	bring along, serve, hand over
avanoa	gap, space, room for, opportunity, vacant, be available
'avatu	give, take
'avau	bawl, speak loudly
ava'avau	shout
'avauga	brawl, fight
'ave$_1$	give, carry, hand to, send
'a'ave	spread, box one's ears, gesticulate, swift
fe'avea'i	transport to and fro
'ave'ese	take away
'ave fa'amalosi	force, compel, kidnap
'ave fe'au	messenger
'ave sa'o	take straight to s.o.
'aveta'avale	driver
'ave$_2$	ray of sunshine, sunbeam, tentacle
'āvei	strap, cord
avi	sexually attractive
'āvoka	avocado pear

Ee

e	verbal particle, *e lima vaa* – five boats. A "call" – *Maria e*! by (agentive)
'e	you (sing)
ē$_1$	(ph.) they who
ë$_2$	loud laughter
'ē	shout, call
ea	raise, elevate, come to surface, free, release
fa'aea	uphold
fa'aeaina	honoured, respected
'ea$_1$	used with a question *o ai 'ea 'oe*? – who are you?
'ea$_2$	air, atmosphere, climate
e'e$_1$	be raised, propped up, defer to
fa'ae'e	raise, prop up, go aboard (pol.) come, arrive
e'e$_2$	be scalded (of chicken, pig), to remove feathers etc.
'e'ē	scream, squeal, play (instrument)
'e'ela	be bleary, watery (eyes)
'e'eva	feel weak
efuefu	dust, powder
'efu'efu	grey
'eka	acre
'ekālēsia	church, church member
'ēkisi	x, sign of x
'ekueta	equator
'ela	miss the target
'ele	reddish soil, stone
'elea	rusty
'ele'ele	earth, soil, ground, dirt (pol.) blood
'ele'elea	dirty
elefane	elephant
'elei	put pattern on bark cloth (*siapo*)
'eletise	electric, electricity
'eli$_1$	dig
'eliga	digging
'eli$_2$	sharp pain
elo	offensive smell
'emo	blink, flash, twinkle, (eye)
'emo'emo	blink etc
fe'emo'emoa'i	flick
'ena, 'ena'ena	light brown (pl. *'e'ena*)
'ene	tickle

'epikopo	bishop
'ese	(pl. *'ese'ese*) be different, foreign, wrong, strange, unusual, queer, fat
'ese'esega	difference
fa'a'esea	isolated
'ese lava	extraordinary, distinct
Eseta	Easter
esi$_1$	drive away –banish
esi$_2$	pawpaw, papaya
eto	lick
fa'aeto	put tongue out
'etu	limp, hobble
'eu	flick away, brush off, scratch for food
eva	stroll for pleasure, sit about
evaga	sitting, walking for pleasure
evaeva	sit up late talking

Ff

fā$_1$	four
fāsefulu	forty
fā$_2$	be hoarse, husky
fā$_3$	decision, considered opinion
fā te a'u	I thought, I supposed
fā$_4$	stalk, stem (taro etc.)
fa'a	(prefix) to cause, make, be like etc. (See note under "Brief Grammar")
fa'ale	(double prefix)
fa'aleaiga	domestic
fa'alelotu	religious
fa'aleogalua	medium
fa'aletupu	royal
fa'alē	(prefix with negative)
fa'alēmigao	rude
fa'alēmāfaufau	thoughtless
fa'alētonu	uncertain
fa'aafu	to make perspire, sweat
fa'aagaaga	to set aside, reserve *O le Peresitene fa'aagaaga* President elect
fa'a'ala'ala	make frivolous remarks
fa'a'ale'ale	fascinating
fa'ali'i	wilful
fā'alo	ceiling, salute
fa'aaluma	clown
fa'a'autagata	womb
fa'aeteete	be careful, handle with care, cautious, beware
fa'aeteetegatā	tender, delicate, fragile
fa'afāilā	with thumb and one finger only
fa'afaileleina	guard jealously, train properly, nurse carefully
fa'afana	re-cook, warm up
fa'afatu'ulu	grudge
fa'afāufau	nausea
fa'afeao	stand beside s.o., aide
fa'afefea	(also *fa'apefea*) How?
fa'afetai	thanks, be grateful, also "no thank you"
fa'afiti	deny
fa'afitiga	denial
fa'afonokarafi	short-hand
fa'afuase'i	sudden(ly)
fa'afuata	carry on back, carry child against shoulder
fa'afuga	(pol.) hair cut
fa'agagafu	be in the offing
fa'agaugau	nod, droop
fa'agēgē	ill at ease, uncomfortable
fa'a'ī	larynx, throat
fa'aili	to blow, band, orchestra, (whistle)

fa‘a‘inaelo	be slovenly, coarse, make dirty
fa‘aipoipo(ga)	marry, wedding
fa‘akolosisi	make a fuss about a little food (usually *fa‘atolosisi*)
fa‘ala‘a	stranger, outsider
fa‘alala	be oiled (of body)
fa‘alau‘ava	caller at kava ceremony
fa‘alāva‘au	(pol.) be killed
fa‘alausoso‘o	ceaselessly
fa‘alavelave	accident, important event etc.
fa‘alialia	vain, show-off
fa‘alifu	S. food (taro and c'nut cream) joc. for woman
fa‘ali‘i	wilful, rage, wooden gong
fa‘alili	tease, provoke
fa‘aloloto	be greedy
fa‘aaluma	clown
fa‘alupega	traditional words pertaining to each village etc.
fa‘ama‘au	(pol.) show, reveal
fa‘amaela	burst with laughter
fa‘amāepaepa	sit solemnly, silently as a lady
fa‘amaga	open (mouth)
fa‘amaise	show sympathy
fa‘amalomaloā	be irritating
fa‘amanu	shriek, yell
fa‘amanū	to praise
fa‘amaoina	be deceived
fa‘amāsei‘au	deflowered
fa‘amatua	gift of fine mats from grandchildren
fa‘ama‘uma‘u	(pol.) put up with
fa‘ameo	disappointed, complain
fa‘anoanoa	be sad, mourn, regret
fa‘anoi	ask permission
fa‘a‘ofu‘ofu	be deep, cup-shaped
fa‘aolo	entreat, plead
fa‘a‘ona‘ona	too salty
fa‘a‘ono‘ono	make angry, provoke
fa‘aonoū	be on watch for
fa‘apalapala	yield to, give in to
fa‘apale	tolerate, put up with
fa‘apālupē	lack of energy, weary
fa‘apaupau	heathen
fa‘apea	think, suppose, imagine, assume, to speak to s.o., thus, like this, likewise
fa‘apeapea	excuse, pardon, leave as it is
fa‘apefea	how? what about?
fa‘apenā	(also *fa‘apelā*) like that, similar
fa‘apēnei	like this
fa‘apolopolo	earmark, set aside, first-fruits
fa‘apōpōaitu	speechless
fa‘apuna	poised ready to pounce, squat to conceal o.s., bring to the boil
fa‘asā‘au	hitch up
fa‘asala	very high note, high pitch (s. *sala*)
fa‘asalāvei	trip up, double-cross
fa‘aSamoa	S. custom, S. way of life, S. language
fa‘asasa	bear towards
fa‘asau	w.o. sheet or shirt, be bare (torso)
fa‘asausauga	(pol.) night assembly
fa‘asaulala	be demanding
fa‘asauea	be slow in action, speech, etc.
fa‘asausili	be arrogant, overbearing
fa‘asavala	endless, infinite
fa‘asegosego	screw up the eyes, cross-eyed
fa‘aseisei	move a little side-ways
fa‘asēlegā	saunter, walk idly
fa‘aseuapa	lie side-ways
fa‘asevaseva-loaina	be ostracized, outcast
fa‘asiasia	frown, scowl, be haughty

fa‘asifo	bow head in apology
fa‘asino	show, indicate, direct, refers to
fa‘asisi	act indirectly
fa‘asi‘ulā	raise eyebrows, be haughty
fa‘asivili	civilian
fa‘asoa	portion out, call the kava cups
fa‘asoasoa	distribute
fa‘asola	kill outright (colq), release
fa‘aso‘oso‘o	notify
fa‘asū	discuss thoroughly
fa‘asūlusulu	run for one’s life
fā‘ata	aim, point (also mirror)
fa‘atagā	pretend
fa‘atagataga	have something ready
fa‘atāiō	shout, yell
fa‘ata‘iti	cut hair short (man)
fa‘atāla‘ese	avoid, dodge
fa‘atalalē	be careless, negligent
	bear in mind
fa‘atalatala	careless
fa‘atamala	parable, proverb (s.
fa‘ata‘oto$_1$	*ta‘oto*)
	to lie down
fa‘ata‘oto$_2$	by force
fa‘atātā	spoil, waste
fa‘ataumo‘oi	destructive,
fa‘atāutala	wasteful, be cruel, torture
	reluctant to do s.th.
fa‘atāutāu	disagree with,
fa‘ataute‘e	disobey
	walk hesitatingly
fa‘atautū	scorn, condescend,
fa‘atauva‘a	be of little importance, modest, humble
	disembowel
fa‘atiau	careless, negligent,
fa‘atitipa	(pol. open bowels)
	just, only, for first
fa‘ato‘ā	time
	ask for, beg
fa‘atoga	look sour,
fa‘a‘ū	displeased
fa‘a‘ū‘ū	long-face, sourly
fa‘ausuusu	go on, continue
fa‘avalemalosi	suddenly, sharply, act as an imbecile
fa‘avauvau	loneliness, sadness
fa‘avavau	eternal, everlasting
fa‘aveveveve	in disorder (clothes, hair)
fafa	carry on back, pick-a-back
fafā	Hades, under-world
fafaga	feed, charge a battery, provide daily meal
fafai	pull up taro, scrape bark (mulberry tree)
fafano$_1$	wash hands
fafano$_2$	born too early, miscarry
fāfātala	rumour
fafie	firewood, (A.S.) *lā‘au*
fafine	woman, female
fa‘afāfine	effeminate man
fafo	outside, out of doors, overseas
faga$_1$	trap, cage
faga$_2$	bay
fagaloa	inlet, gulf
fāgafao	pet animal
fagamanu	wild canna (flower)
fāgatua	wrestle
fāgogo	tale, story, imaginary
fāgota	to fish
fagu$_1$	bottle, tree (gourd)
fagufagu	wind instrument
fagu‘ele	earthenware pot
fagusausau	bottle of perfume
fagu$_2$ **fafagu**	to wake s.o.
uati fagufagu	alarm clock
fai$_1$	to do, make, say, tell, put on (shoes etc.) put in (install), mend. adopt (*tama fai*) adopted son, child, false (*nifo fai*) false teeth; to be used as (*fai ma . . .*)
faiga	method, style, system, treatment

faigā'ai feast
faigāmalō government
faigāmalaga travelling party
faigāmea entertainment
faigānu'u village affairs
faigā'oloa business enterprise
faigāuō friendship
fāifai a trait, way of doing things e.g. *fāifaimālie* – easy going, to tease
faifaiga deal with
fai'a'ai new settlement
fai'āiga live as one family, (pol.) sexual intercourse
faiā'oga teacher
faiaso be demanding
faiavā take a wife
fai'ese be strong, keen
fai'fa'atoaga farmer, agriculture
faifalaoa baker
faife'au minister of religion
fai fea'u wait on, serve
fai fili make an enemy
faigāluega work, worker
faigatā difficult, hard, be dangerous, serious
fa'afaigatā complicate
faigōfie easy, simple
fa'afaigōfie facilitate, make easy
failāuga orator, lay-preacher, speaker
failautusi secretary, clerk
faimanatu self-conscious (child)
faimasasa threaten, be a nuisance
faimea activity, work
faimea'ai cooking, a cook
faimeamāe'a thorough, efficient
faimeafitā feat
fai'oloa trader, merchant
faipaipa plumber (also *palama*)
faipē deaf
faipea continue
faifaipea now and always
faipese choir conductor
faipona point to mistakes, critic
faipule member of parliament, ruling group in village
faisoa put in pairs
faiso'o become tedious, repeated
faita'a take a lover (by a girl)
faita'aga fornication
faitala$_1$ gossip, tell tales
faitala$_2$ barbed
faitalia please o.s.
faitasi general, communal
faitasia opposed by everyone
faitau read, count, census
faitaulia reckoned, included
faitautusi reading
tusi faitau reading book
faitele public, general (use)
faitīfaga clown, actor
faitogafiti be cunning
faitogāla'au gardener, grow crops
faito'o (pol.) doctor
faiuila electrician (also *fai molī*)
fai'upu make remarks, speaker
faivale be of no account
fai$_2$ sting ray
fāia'e to grow, increase
fāiatu go away, decrease, die out
fāiifo decrease, decline
fāimai come up, increase, come from outside
fa'i banana
fā'i I thought
fāiā log bridge, family relationship
faiaga be dilatory, idle
fāi'ai$_1$ brain
fāi'ai$_2$ S. food (c'nut cream, bananas etc.)
faia'ia agree with
faia'ina defeated, beaten
fāifai insult
faigā difficult, intense
faila file, register, carpenter's file

failā unkempt (hair), protrude (as of ears)
failele nursing mother
fa'afailele to nurse
failele gau complication following birth
fa'ita I thought
fāisua clam
faitalia please oneself
fāitio criticize
faititili thunder
faitoto'a door, gate, entrance
faiva fishing, employment, skill
fala pandanus trees, woven mat
fala'aina pineapple
falafala old mat
falalili'i sleeping mat
falai fry, frying-pan
Faraile Friday
falala lean, at an angle
fālana'i repose, recline
falaoa flour, bread
fai falaoa baker
fale house
falefale afterbirth
fale afolau long S. house
fale'aiga restaurant
faleaitu comedy
falealuga roof
faleā'oga school
fale'ava hotel
fale'ese toilet
fale'esea isolated
fale falaoa bakery
fale fasipovi butcher shop
fale fetāfa'i portable canopy
fale gaosi mea factory
fale 'ie tent
fale inisinia engineering shop
fale la'itiiti toilet, latrine
falelauasi (pol.) bury (people)
falelaufao bush shelter
fale logo bell tower, steeple
fale ma'i hospital
fale fa'amasino court house
fale mata'aga museum
fale meli post office
fale moa fowl house
fale'oloa shop
fale pia brewery
fale puipui jail, prison
fale sā church (building)
fale su'isu'i tailor's shop
fale ta'avale garage
fale talavai dispensary, chemist
fale talimalō guest house, hotel
fale tele S. round house
fale tusi bookshop, library
fale tupe bank
fale tīfaga cinema, theatre
fale tiute customhouse
fale ualesi radio station
fale 'upolu (pol.) orator
fale vali house (concrete and plaster)
fale vao toilet
falelogi furlong
faletua (pol.) wife of chief, pastor etc.
fāliu turn around, look over shoulder, decline (of sun)
fālō stretch, reach for, tug, pull, debate
fālōlō stretch one's neck, covet
falute gather together, bundle of mats
fana shoot, gun, rifle, spray
fanafanua large field gun
fanagutuono revolver, pistol
fanai'a dynamite
fanalau thatching needle
fanameme'i catapult
fana pepa fire cracker
fana ta'avili machine gun
fanā mast
fāna'e rise (moon, tide)
fānau be born, birth
fānauga delivery, children of
fanafanau multiply, proliferate
fano past (of time), perish
fano'ele'ele eclipse of moon (also *gasetoto*)
fanoga (pol.) request
fanū very nearly
fanua land, field, after-birth, placenta

fa'afanua	map
fanuaoti	cemetery
fanuatanu	built up, reclaimed land
fao$_1$	nail
faovili	screw (also *sīkulū)*
fao$_2$	snatch, grab, rob
faomea	thief
fao$_3$	fill
fafao	pack, insert, enclose
faoaugutu	fill to brim
faotu'i	cram
faova'a	go on board
faō	lie face down
fa'afaō	upside down
Faraile	Friday
faresaio	pharisee (Bible)
fasa	delerious
fasi	beat, kill (animal)
fasioti	kill, murder
fāsipovi	meat
mafasi	cracked (skin)
fata	shelf, stretcher, litter, carry aloft
fatafata	chest
fatafaitaulaga	altar
fatāmanu	scaffolding
fātai	sit cross-legged
fati$_1$	tune, melody, will-power
fati$_2$	break (waves)
fatiātāma'i	hinder, bother
fatu$_1$	make up
fafatu	put something together w. hands, to garland
fatufatu	arrange in rows, pile up
fatu$_2$	compose (song etc.), invent, make up
fatufua	imaginary
fatupese	poet, song writer
fatu$_3$	heart (man), seed, grain, essence (fig.)
fatuga'o	kidney
fatutale	phlegm
fatua'i	consider
fau$_1$	hibiscus tree
fau$_2$	fibre used for tying, binding
fau$_3$	make, construct, build
fafau	bind, lash together
fāua	saliva
faualuga	over confident
fāufau	plan, arrange
faufaumau	be conservative
faula'i	heaped up
faulalo	advise, counsel
fāupu'e	heaped up
faupu'ega	heap, pile
fausa	bundle dried c'nut leaves for torches
fautasi	long rowing-boat
fautua	advise, intercede, recommend, advisor
fautuaga	advice, recommendation
fe	sometimes sign of plural e.g. *feinu* – drink; used with *a'i* e.g. *fealua'i*, indicates a "to and fro" action
fea	where?
feagaiga	covenant, testament, agreement, (pol.) minister of religion
fe'ai	fierce, savage
fe'alasi	to smart
feanu	spit
feasogi	kiss
feasua'iga	argument, combat
fe'au	business, errand, task, message
feauga	be in harmony
feausi	(pl.) swim
fe'e	octopus
fe'efe'ea	warts (on filarial limbs)
fefe	fear, be afraid, anxious, scared
fefete	expand, swell, baking powder, yeast
fa'afete	to bluff
fa'afefete	to leaven
fefeu	tough (meat), hard (subject)
fegalegalea'i	on good terms
feganavai	speak out
fela	turn inside out, (impol.) eyes
felavasa'i	across one another
fele	clubs (cards), flare (of dress)

felefele tangled, complicated
felela teaching brother (R.C.)
fememea'i at a loss, perplexed
feoloolo fairly good, not too bad
fe'ōma'i press around (people)
Fepuali February
fesagoa'i gossip
fesaua'i be tangled
fesili question, ask a question
tusi fesili catechism (Meth.)
fesoasoani help
fesufia'i consult together
fetaia'i meet with, encounter
fetāla'i think something over
fetani meet accidentally
fetaomi stream out (people)
fetāpa'i (pol.) meet one another
fetaui meet, agree, fit, match
fa'afetaui adapt, adjust
feti'i hang up in pairs
fetōa'i be hesitant, at cross purposes
feto'i abate, slacken, lessen
fetū star
fale va'ai fetū observatory
fetui cover burning wood w. stones
fetu'u to curse
feū hot (spice), burn the tongue, itchy (*ta'amū*)
feula to blow
fia$_1$ wish for, like to, need to
fa'afia pretend to
fa'afiapoto pretend to be wise
fia'ai hungry
fiainu thirsty
fia moe feel sleepy
fia ola cry for help
fia$_2$ how many, how much
fiafia enjoy, like, be happy, gladness, joy
fiafiaga entertainment
fifi small intestine
figota edible sea animals
fika arithmetic, sums, figures, solve, plan
filemū be quiet, peaceful, calm, gentle, peace, silence
fa'afilemū to silence, keep quiet, pacify
fili$_1$ pick out, select
filifili choose
filifiliga choice, selection
fili$_2$ plait, braid
filifili u'amea chain
filitasi hair done with single plait
fili$_3$ enemy
filigā perserverance
filo$_1$ to mix with
fefiloi to be mixed with
tusi fefiloi dictionary
filo$_2$ thread, cotton
fimālie gentle, mild, easily, quiet voice
finagalo desire, will, command, (pol.) opinion, suggestion, thought
finau argue, quarrel, argument
finauga quarrel, argument, competition, debate
finauvale fond of arguing
fisaga gentle breeze
fisi peel skin, shave off
fitā be difficult, strenuous, product of hard work
fitafita soldier
'aufitafita army
fiti flick, bounce, fly off (sparks)
fitiā be restless, rough
tafiti be restless
tāfiti turn somersault
fa'atafiti speed up (work), second last night dance
fitivale fight for breath
fitu seven
fiu to be tired of, bored with
fa'afiu aggravate, provoke
fiva fever
fofō S. massage, give medical treatment, a remedy
foma'i doctor
fō make starch, end of fishing group
foa break (rock, shell), hatch, skull wound

fa'afoaga	origin
foafoa	conch shell, trumpet shell, create
foaga	grindstone
fōa'i	give, gift
foe	oar, paddle
fa'afoe	steer, turn s.th.
foeuli	rudder
fo'e, fofo'e	to peel
fofoga	(pol.) face, and its parts
fa'afofoga	(pol.) to hear
fogafoga	(pol.) to sing
foga	head of hair
fogā	prefix, indicates a surface
fogā'ele'ele	ground
fogāfale	story, floor
fogātai	surface of sea
fogāva'a	deck
fogāvai	surface of river
fogi	blow (nose)
fo'i	come back, return, (also slightly, fairly)
fa'afo'i	return something, withdraw (words)
fefo'ifo'ia'i	go back and forth, unreliable
fola	strew, spread (also *fofola*) floor, level
māfolafola	flat
fa'amafola	open out, lay out
tafola	shallow water
fōlafola	announce publicly, proclaim, promise
fōlafolaga	announcement, promise
folau	voyage, travel by sea
folaulau	to sail
fole	pale, anaemic, look sick, shellfish
fōliga	to appear, take after, look like, appearance, features, (pol.) face, figure, form, shape
fa'afōliga	to make like
folo$_1$	swallow
folo patatō	swallow whole
folo$_2$	fish guts
fōma'i	doctor
fono$_1$	meet, meeting, council etc.
fono$_2$	mend, patch, fill, plug
fono$_3$	provide food for kava ceremony
fōnō	(pol.) call to s.o.
fotu	appear, blossom (trees)
fotua'i	come into view
fou$_1$	be new, fresh
fa'afou	renew, restore, repair
fou$_2$	get ready, prepare
foufou	sight passage in reef
fou$_3$	challenge
fouvale	revolt, rebellion
fua$_1$	just, only, to no purpose, by chance, freely
fua$_2$	fruit, flower, egg, products, produce, bear fruit
māfua	be caused by, due to
fuafua$_1$	abscess, pimple
fuaiala	section of a village
fuainumera	figures (arithmetic)
fuaitau	lines of a song, part of a speech
fuatino	physique
fuai'upu	sentence, verse
fuāla'au	fruit, pill, tablet
fuāmanava	testicle
fuāmoa	hen's egg, (colq.) nil
fuāuli	(pol.) taro
fua$_3$	measure, size, scales, weigh, survey
fuafua$_2$	plan, think out
fuafuaga	plan
fa'afualoa	live long
fuafiva	thermometer
fuapau	of same size
fuapese	choir conductor (also *fuataimi*)
fua$_4$	flotilla of boats, fleet
fuā	jealous
fu'a	flag, banner
fu'afu'a	common tree
fualau	gather sugar-cane leaf for thatch
fualeva	be a long time
fuāluga	over confident
fua'ō	sea bird (noddy)
fuata	crop (trees) breadfruit
fuata'i	resume, take up again
fuatasi	be the only one

fue$_1$	creeping plants
fue$_2$	fly whisk, whisk, beat, whip, skip
tafuefue	fan rapidly
fuefue	fan away flies
fu'e	put food from oven in baskets, fill (basket, bag)
fuga	flower, blossom
fugafugāmutia	grass seeds
fui	to water, sprinkle
fufui	put into water, (pol.) bake a pig
fuifui$_1$	dip
fuifui$_2$	stick together, cluster, bunch
fuifuilua	be paired
fuilauvī	gills (fish)
fula	swell, swelling
fuli	turn over, roll over
mafuli	fall over, lean towards
māfulifuli	wobble
tafuli	roll
fulialo	turn upside down
fulitua	turn one's back
fulu$_1$	feather
fulufulu$_1$	fine short hair, fur, wool

fulufulua	hairy
fulumata	eyelash
fulufulumata	eyebrows
fulufululele	be quick to anger
fulu$_2$	wash
fulufulu$_2$	wash body, clean (teeth), wash (dishes)
mafulu	slipshod
tafulu	carefree
fulū	influenza
funa	call to woman or girl
fune	core (fruit)
fusi	bind, lash together, bandage, girdle, belt, bundle of, championship
fufusi	too tight (clothes)
fusimau	hug, embrace
fusipa'u	belt, strap
fusiua	necktie
fusu	to box, fight w. fists
fusu'aga	boxing match
futi	to pull (weeds, hair), pluck
futi afu	pool below waterfall
futu	foot (measure)

Gg

gā'au	guts, intestine
pito gā'au	appendix
fa'aga'au	tyre, tube, hose
gāe'e	move, stir
fa'agāe'e	move, encourage, stimulate
fa'agāe'etia	enthusiasm
ga'ega'e	pant, short of breath
gaepu	be cloudy, muddy (water)
fa'agaepu	stir up (water)
gafa$_1$	fathom
tagafa	measure in fathoms
gafa$_2$	lineage, genealogy
gafatia	able to do s.th, able to afford
gafua	be free from restrictions

Aso Gafua	Monday
gāga'e	to rise, well up, eastward
gagaifo	a little to the west
gagana	language, to remark, comment
gāi'oi'o	wriggle, squirm
gālala	craving for water
gālemulemu	soft, limp, flabby (body)
gali	gnaw
galo	forget
galo nimo	forget completely
galo si'o	pretend to forget
fa'agalogalo	overlook
gālo	disappear, sneak away
galu	wave, breaker
galugalu	rippled sea

galue (pl. *gālulue*) work, cultivate
gāluega work, job
galuea'iina to be working, in operation
gao molar tooth, sore point (fig.)
ga'o fat, lard, grease, wax, cream (medical)
gā'ō (pol.) get ready
gaoā rocky, stony
gaogao taro eating insect
gāogao deserted, empty
gaoi steal, cheat, thief
gāoi ache, throb w. pain
ga'o'i throng, swarm
gaoiā fidget
gāoioi move, stir, be active
gaolo rattle, clatter
gaosā be untidy, overgrown (path)
gaosi prepare food, make
gapā to crack (whip etc.)
gapāpā crackling of firewood
gāpatia be burdened with
gapelu be weak, worn, with age
gase$_1$ be numb
moe gase fast asleep
gagase ache
fa'agase local anaesthetic
gase$_2$ dead, kill (animals)
gasē rustle
gasegase (pol.) to be sick
fa'agasegase feel unwell
gase'ele'ele eclipse (moon), also *gasetoto*
gāsese prepare food
gāsolo$_1$ be fast, swift
gāsolo$_2$ run, flow, gather together (people)
gāsologa course, flow
gasu rubbish, junk
gasū wet with dew or rain (bush)
gata$_1$ come to an end, terminate
gata'aga end
fa'agata set a limit, lop (tree)
gata$_2$ snake
gatā suffix, indicates "hard to do" etc.
malamalamagatā hard to understand
gātai a little towards the sea
gātaifale coastal waters
gatasi (walk) level with, abreast
gātasitasi be united
fa'agatasi level off, make even
gatete to shake, tremble
gau$_1$ break (bone, stick etc.), strain, sprain (limb) be swayed (of mind), relapse, lose one's money, bankrupt, give in to, defer to
gagau to break
magaugau brittle
gaualofa yield out of love
gaumata'u yield out of fear
gāupule give a counter-order
gau$_2$ chew
gau$_3$ fold
gaugau fold
fa'agaugau nod, droop
gaugāivi joint
gā'uta a little inland
gē hesitate, be embarrassed
gēgē a fat person
geno to signal with eyes or head
gese slow
gōfie suffix, indicating "easy"
faigōfie easy to do
gogolo surge (of people), sink, a deep rumbling noise, sound of rushing water
goto sink, set (of sun)
magotogoto unsteady (boat), boggy (marsh)
gū growl (dog)
gugu rheumatism, arthritis, gout
gūgū be dumb, silent
gulu make a hollow sound
tagulu to thump
tāgulu snore
gutu mouth, beak
gutuā insolent, impudent
gugutu boast

gutugutu	be swallowed by sea
fa‘agutu	bit, bridle, rein
fa‘agutugutulua	two-faced
gutulua	double-barrelled gun
gutuvale	speak indecently

Hh

h	This letter is mostly used in words of foreign origin
haena	hyena
haikomisi	high commissioner
Hakai	Haggai (Bible)
helikopa	helicopter

Ii

i$_1$	in, at, on, up, of
i$_2$	prefix with *matou*, *tatou* etc.
‘i	to (also *‘iate*)
ī	feel empty (stomach)
‘ī$_1$	yes (short form)
‘ī$_2$	here (*sau i ‘ī* - come here), (A.S) *i ga‘ī*
‘ī$_3$	squeal, squeak, yell, soprano
fā‘a‘ī	vocal cords, throat
‘ī‘ivale	shrill, high pitched
ia$_1$	he, his; she, her; it, its (sometimes *o ia*)
ia$_2$	one form of the passive
ia$_3$	indicates emphasis after verb (*sau ia* - come on)
ia$_4$	these (*o fa‘i ia* - these bananas)
ia$_5$	a warning call - *ia ‘oe*, look out!
ia$_6$	a form of "yes", that's it, etc.
‘ia	sign of command or wish *‘ia faia nei* - do it now
iā	used before many proper nouns- to, from, in, e.g. *iā Mati*, *iā Ioane* (in March, to John)
‘iā	command to start a race, reading etc.
i‘a	fish
i‘a manu	whale
i‘a sā	turtle
iai	to be, be present - *‘ua iai*, there is/are
Ianuari	January
‘iao	common bird
‘iata	yard (measure)
‘ia te	(used before some pronouns) *‘ia te outou* = your
‘iato	boom of outrigger
i‘e	bark cloth beater
‘ie	pandanus bush used for fine mats, cloth, sheet, linen, material, the wrap-round *lavalava*
‘ie‘ie	working clothes
fasi ‘ie‘ie	piece of rag
‘ieafu	bed sheet

'iesina	white shaggy mat
'ietōga	fine mat
'iē	be weary of
ifi$_1$	to smoke a pipe
ifi$_2$	tree, nut of same
ififi	small tree
ifilele	large tree used for timber and kava bowls
ifo	bow down, restrain, give in, make a formal apology
ifoga	apology
fa'aifo	descend
fa'aifoaluga	speak with nasal accent
igaga	whitebait
igāga	hereditary right, privilege
Igilisi	English
igoa	name, signature, the person in question (so and so)
fa'aigoa	to name
'i'i	meat, fish (to complete a meal)
'ī'ī	at a low ebb
ila$_1$	mark on skin, defect
ila$_2$	feel pain, be hurt
'i'ila	shine, glisten, sparkle, twinkle, glitter, dazzle
fa'a'i'ila	to polish, shine
ilā	over there
'ile	and, of course, then, there
ili$_1$	to blow (trumpet etc.)
fā'aili	to blow (whistle), band, orchestra, to whistle
ili$_2$	a fan (*tapili* – to fan)
'ili	saw, file
'iligāla'au	sawdust
'ili'ili	gravel, small pebbles
ilo$_1$	maggot
ilo$_2$	perceive, be aware of, sort out
iloga	be obvious, well known, be marked, sign, distinguishing mark
iloa	to see, notice, recognize, know
lē iloa	be unaware, not conscious, to lose, be lost
iloilo(ga)	investigate, investigation
fa'ailo	to signal, navigation aid
fa'ailoa	to show, make known
fa'ailoga	mark, sign, evidence, symbol, emblem, prize, postage-stamp
fa'ailogaina	commemorate, celebrate
feiloa'i	meet
feiloa'iga	reception, welcome
fa'afeiloa'i	introduce
iloa tino	recognize, know with certainty
'imoa	small bird, small fowl
ina$_1$ **– ina'ua**	when (past), after
ina 'o	while
–ina$_2$	verbal suffix indicating passive
fa'ailoaina	make known
'ina$_1$ **– 'ina 'ia**	so that, in order that
'ina$_2$	sea urchin
'inā$_1$	there, in that place, (A.S.) *na'inā*
'inā$_2$	sign of emphasis
'inā sau ia!	come!
'ina'i	eat vegetables with fish, meat
inati	share of food
'ina'inā	be too harsh
'inei	here, (A.S.) *na'i nei*
'ini	pinch, nip
'ini'ini	pick up with thumb and fingers
'inisi	inch
'inisinia	engineer
inoino	call sharply
'ino'ino	feel disgust, have revulsion, hate, contempt
'inosia	disgusting
inu	(*pl. feinu*) drink (*inumia* – pass)
inumaga	a draught, dose
inugāfi	breakfast, light refreshments
fa'ainu	water (an animal), (colq.) shout (a drink), a treat
'io	a form of "yes"
'io'io	cheep (of a chicken)

i‘oi‘o	wind string, rope, between fingers, hands, arm
‘i‘o	tuber, corm
‘i‘oimata	eyeball
‘ioe	yes, to agree, approve
i‘ofi	tongs
ipiniu	coconut cup (usually *ipuniu*)
ipu	cup, kava cup, bowl, dish
‘isa	word of annoyance
isi$_1$	other, next, another
nisi	some, some more, several, cheat (at marbles)
isi$_2$	split (wood etc.)
isilua	split in two
māisi	split, cracked
iso	be puzzled, baffled
isu	nose
isuisu	be inquisitive
isumamafa	have a cold
isumiti	sniff
isupē	mucus (nasal)
isumu	rat
ita	be angry, anger, dislike, hate
fa‘aita	to anger
feitaga‘i	be on bad terms, hate ea. other
itagōfie	unstable temper
‘ita	I
‘ite, ‘itea	be in sight
‘i‘ite	foretell, have a premonition
iti, itiiti	(pl. *iti*) be small, little
to‘aitiiti	few people
fa‘aitiiti	decrease, reduce
itū	side
itu‘āiga	kind, sort, people, tribe, sex
itūaso	time of day
itūlā	hour, clock, time
itūlagi	point of compass, direction
itūlau	page
itūmālō	district
itūpō	time of night
itūtaua	army
itūtino	part of body
itūvai	bank of river
i‘u	be finished, ended, happen finally
i‘uga	end, decision, conclusion
i‘ugāfono	resolution
fa‘ai‘u	to end
fa‘ai‘uga	conclusion
i‘uvale	be a failure
Iulai	July
Iuni	June
iunivesitē	university
iupelī	jubilee
iva	nine
‘iva$_1$	be lanky
‘iva$_2$	be sleepy
ivi	bone, limb
ivi‘aso‘aso	rib
ivifatafata	breastbone
ivifoe	shoulder-blade
ivino‘o	pelvis
ivitū	spine
‘ivi	be blind in one eye
fa‘a‘ivi	wink, signal someone
fa‘a‘ivi‘ivi	blink

Kk

k	This letter is usually associated with words of foreign origin, but not exclusively.
kalama	grammar
kalapu	club
kalasia	divine grace (R.C.)
kalasini	kerosene
va‘a kalasini	ketch, trading ship
kalauna	crown (coin), buckle
kale	curry
kālena	calendar
keleva	clever
kaleve	gravy

kālone gallon, drum (container)
kamupani company
kāmuta carpenter, builder
fa'akāmuta carpentry
kanala canal
kanesa cancer
kapeta carpet, linoleum
kapeteni captain
kapineta cabinet (government)
kapisi cabbage
kāponi carbon (also *karaponi*)
kāpoti cupboard
kariota chariot (Bible)
kasa gas
katapila bulldozer, tracked vehicle
kaupoe cowboy
kea care
keke cake
kerose gross
Kerisiano Christianity, Christian
fa'aKerisiano Christian (also *Kilisitiano* R.C.)
kelū glue
kesi (A.S) gasoline, petrol
kēsia cashier
kī key
kia gear
kiki kick
kilouati kilowatt
kina Papua N.G. coin
kināmoni cinnamon
kini guinea (coin)
kiona snow
kirikiti cricket
Kirisimasi Christmas
kisi kiss
kītara guitar
kītata (*tītata*) kettle
koasisi (also *kolosisi*) cold chisel
koale coal
kofe coffee
koke parrot
koko cocoa
kola collar
kolisi college
kolona colon
kolone colony
kolopā crowbar
koluse cross
koma comma
komesina commissioner
hai komisi high commissioner
komunisi communist
komisi commissioner (as in *hai komisi*) commission
komiti committee
komitiina to judge
koneseti concert
konesula consul
konitineta continent
kopala cobra
kopi copy
kosi gauze
kovana governor
kuata quarter, quart, stipend (clergy)
ku'ava guava
kuka kitchen, cook, cooking
kukama cucumber
kulimi cream, sauce
kuluku crook, rogue
kupita cubit (Bible), cubic
kusi goose

LI

la (used in possessive) e.g. *la lā tama* - child of theirs
lā$_1$ (used after verb) - then *e mata lā* - do you think then?
lā$_2$ (short form of *lā'ua*) - they
lā$_3$ (those) over there (pl. for *lelā*)
lā$_4$ sun
lāina exposed to sun, weak

fa'alā	to sun
lā$_5$	a sail
lā$_6$ **lālā'au**	branch (tree)
la'a	step, march
la'asia	step over, go beyond
la'ala'a	step by step
la'avale	error, slip
la'ai	to go over
lā'au	plant, shrub, tree, wood, apparatus, instrument, radio-set, gun
lā'au afi tusi	match
vai lā'au	medicine, drug
la'au su'isu'i	sewing machine
lā'ei	(pol.) clothes
lā'ei'au	be armed
fa'alā'ei'au	encourage
lafa	ringworm, bruised (bananas)
lafetoga	wart
lafi	to hide
lafitaga	shelter, hiding-place
lafo$_1$	throw, contribute money, post (a letter), state an opinion, remark, motion, proposal, gift of fine mats
lāfoga	subscription, collection, tax
lāfoa'i	throw away
lafolafo	a good delivery (speaker)
felāfoa'i	take alternate turns, tossed by waves
felafolafoa'i	debate, discuss
lafo$_2$	piece of land ready for planting
lalafo	clear the land, weed
lafo$_3$	rod used for thatch
lafu$_1$	herd, flock
lafu$_1$ **lafuā**	rough, unworked land
fa'alāfuā	to devastate
lafulafuā	be barren
lafulēmū	rich, fertile
lafu$_3$	(pol.) small pig
laga$_1$	startle, raise, rush
laga$_2$	lever up, raise up, take up
lāgā	spring up (of thoughts)
lagi$_1$	sky, heaven
lagi mamā	(pol.) good health etc. funeral ceremony
lagifa'atafa	(pol.) illness of high chief
lagiā	be cloudy
lagilagiā	be stormy, (pol.) h.ch's illness
fa'alagi	to use proper form of address
lagilelei	fine weather
lagimasoe	(pol.) be wounded, operated on
lagi$_2$	to sing (also *lagilagi*)
lāgisi	lighter, whale-boat, barge
lago$_1$	pillow, bolster, to support
lagolago(ina)	stand, props, support
fa'alagolago	to lean against
felagolagoma'i	to support ea. o.
lago$_2$	a fly
lago-meli	bee
lagona	to feel, perceive, to scent, suspect, be conscious, aware of, feeling, sense
la'i	west wind
lailoa	be tired
laina	line
laisene	licence
la'itiiti	(pl.) *lāiti* - small, little, be young
fa'ala'itiiti	reduce, diminish
lakapī	rugby
laki	luck, fortunate
lala	scum
lālā	branch - stick out
fa'alālāina	shake, brandish
lalaga(ina)	plait, weave
lālaga	coarse mat
lale	over there
lālelei	be beautiful (women)
lali	wooden drum
lalo	down, under
fa'alālolalo	humble oneself
lalovasa	(pol.) hydrocele
lama$_1$	candle-nut tree, torch (leaf), lamp-black, fishing by torchlight
lama$_2$	ambush, trap, watch for a chance

lāmo'i small (animals)
lāmolemole be smooth
lamu chew
lana his, her, its
lanu$_1$ colour
felanulanua'i be colourful
lanu$_2$ - fa'alanu wash off salt in fresh water
lanu$_3$ water (childbirth)
la'o have enough to drink
laoa$_1$ choke
laoa$_2$ orator's house
la'o'ai platter, tray, (pol.) communion table
lā'o'ai (pol.) village
laofie fine day
la'oifua (pol.) recover from illness
lāolao be wide open, open space
fa'alāolao finish, discuss thoroughly
lapa$_1$ flat coral
lapa$_2$ flat root (tree)
lapa$_3$ grater, rasp
lapalapa mid-rib (c'nut leaf etc.)
lapata'i warn
lapata'iga warning
lape$_1$ entertainment to encourage team-mates, rounders (game)
lape$_2$ slip, mistake in speech
lāpisi rubbish, refuse
lāpo'a be large (pl. *lāpopo'a*)
fa'alāpo'a enlarge
lāpotopoto round, spherical
fa'alāpotopotoga group, organisation etc.
lase, lalase scrape, clean (a sore)
lasi many, numerous
lata$_1$ my
lata$_2$ be close to, tame, near
fa'alata draw near, tame, betray
felata'i near by
latou they
lātū one in charge of work
lau$_1$ your
lau$_2$ prefix denoting "thinness" or "flatness"
lau'ele'ele land
laufono plank in a canoe etc.
laulelei smooth (surface), even
fa'alaulelei make smooth
laumanifi thin layer, film
laumata eyelid
laupepa sheet of paper
lautele broad, wide
fa'alautele widen
lau$_3$ leaf, thatch, blade (knife)
lalau in first leaf (new growth)
talau produce leaves
lauao (pol.) hair
laufala pandanus (for mats)
lau'ie pandanus (for finer mats)
lau'ava funeral feast
lauaitu wailing for dead
laufanua cultivated land
laufofoga (pol.) face
lāuga speech, sermon, preach
laugasēsē fern
laugatasi be even, plain, level
laugutu lips
laui'a fish cooked in coconut leaves
lāuiloa be well known (pol. *lāusilafia)*
lauitiiti narrow
laulā untidy hair
laulā'au leaf (plant)
laulau coconut leaf platter, table, to serve food
laulautasi presentation of food
laulaufaiva tongue
laulaufaiva 'ati lisp
laulausiva a dance
laulauvavale swear
laulaututū all stand
lauleaga rough, uneven (surface)
laulelei smooth, even (surface)
laulili'i asparagus fern
laulogo resound, echo
laumafola flat land
laumālie sign of approaching death
laumanifi thin layer
laumata eyelid

laumea dry leaf
laumeavale famine
laumei turtle
laumua capital (town)
launiu coconut leaf, (pol.) fishing rod
launonu *nonu* leaf, be soft, cowardly
lauolaola be lush, luxuriant (also *lauusiusi*)
lauoneone sandy
laupae scattered
laupaogo a pandanus
laupapa timber
laupepa sheet of paper
laupola coconut leaf thatch
lāusilafia (pol.) well known
lausului dry banana leaf for cigarette paper
lautalotalo ornamental plant
laufī tea, tea leaf
lautele wide, broad
lautogia be chosen for . . .
lauulu hair
lau'ulu breadfruit leaf
lau vai taro sucker
laufalī referee
lau'u$_1$ my
la'u$_2$ carry (a load), transport
fela'ua'i carry about
la'u$_3$ **lala'u** scratch
lā'ua them (those two)
lava$_1$ very, actually, indeed, thoroughly
tatau lava must
tusa lava exactly the same
lava$_2$ be enough, complete
fa'alava$_1$ make up deficiency
fa'alava$_2$ be across, cross-wise
felavasa'i to cross each other
lava$_3$ volcanic lava
lavā be able to, endure
lē lavā be tired, fatigued, (A.S.) *lē savā*
lavātia be capable, able to manage
lāvalava clothes
fa'alāvalava to clothe, present to carpenter
lavalima work
lave, lāvea to catch (on an obstruction), stumble, be concerned with
lavea be hurt, affected by, cut, hit, a wound
lāvea'i rescue, deliver from
laveia attained, achieved
lavelave be tangled
fa'alavelave a hindrance, accident, important event, danger, trouble etc. to disturb
fa'alavelavea caught up in a problem, hindered, be busy
fa'afelāvei interrupt
le the (def. article)
lē (ph.) he who, she who (pl. *ē*)
lē fea which
lē indicates negative (before verb, *lē mafai* – unable)
lea this, that, it
o ai lea? who is it?
ā lea? what about this?
leaga bad, damaged, unfortunately, evil, badly
fa'aleaga destroy, spoil, damage
leai no, be none, be lacking, absent
fa'aleai be little, not much
lelefu go out (fire)
lefulefu ash
tālefulefu ashtray
lefulefua (pol.) greeting to visitors
lefu be ugly
lega turmeric powder, yolk of an egg
legalegā mouldy
lei ivory, enamel
le'i not (emphatic), not yet
le'ile'i delicacy, choice food
leipa labourer *O le 'au leipa* Labour Party (also *Leipa Pati*)
leise lace
leitio radio, wireless

lelā	that (over there)
lele$_1$	(pl. *felelei*) fly
va‘alele	aeroplane
lelea	blown by wind
talele	blown down (tree)
taleleina	raise house blinds
lelelele	flutter
fa‘alele	make fly, speak boastfully
lele$_2$	that there
lelei	be good, good, well, properly
fa‘alelei	to make up, settle a difference
fa‘aleleiga	reconciliation
lemo, lelemo	duck or drown s.o.
malemo	to drown
fa‘amalemo	to drown
lēmū	slow(ly), gentle, quietly
fa‘alēmū	slow down
lenā	that
lenei	this
leo$_1$	voice, sound
lē leoa	silently
fa‘aleo	pronounce, hold in great esteem
leo tele	loud, loudly
leo$_2$	watch over
leoleo	be on guard, policeman
leoleoga	guard, defence, a watch
fa‘aleoleo	hold in reserve
leona	lion (also *liona*)
lepa	stagnant, still (water)
vailepa	pool, pond
lepaga	lying in wait
fa‘alepa	halt (canoes etc.)
lepe, malepe	be broken, smashed, wrecked (structures)
mālepelepe	smashed to pieces
talepe	break up
fa‘amalepe	smash
lepeti	break, tear down
lēpela	leper, leprosy
lesona, lesoni	lesson (school), Bible reading (church)
lētioa	doubtless, no wonder!
leu	touch something accidentally
leva	a long time (since), old, ancient

levaleva	not long since
fa‘alevaleva	prolonged, be delayed
fa‘aleleva	idle, tarry
lī	grin, set one's teeth
lia	nit (hair)
li‘a	feel apprehensive, (pol.) dream
lili‘a	feel giddy, unsteady, (pol.) embarrassed
lia‘i	strike a blow, pull up by roots
lialia‘i	wave (flag)
lialia	vermicelli
ligi, liligi	pour
maligi	pour, run
fa‘amaligi	cause to flow etc.
ligoligoa	be hushed
li‘i	be scattered in small fragments
lili‘i	be made of small segments
fala lili‘i	finely woven mat
lili$_1$	shiver, tremble, eager, angry desire
lili$_2$	lily
līlī	(pol.) banana
lilivau	gnash teeth
lilo	lost to view, hidden, concealed from understanding
fa‘alilo	hide, cover up
fa‘alilolilo	be secret, devious, furtive
lima$_1$	five
lima$_2$	hand, arm, upper limb, sleeve
limalima	speed up
limafōa‘i	generous
limala‘u	whine, grizzle
limalelei	be good at, skilled, generous
limamālosi	hard working
limamatua	thumb
limatago‘ese	(pol.) light-fingered
limatama	little finger
limatauagavale	left handed
limataumatau	right handed
limavale	mean, stingy
limu	mosses, seaweed etc.
limumea	fungus
limupata	seaweed (also *limusū*)
li‘o	circle, ring, encircle

fa'ata'ali'oli'o	to surround
lipi	(joc.) dead
lipine	ribbon
lipoi	(pol.) full house
līpoti	report (usually *rīpoti*)
lise	make haste
lisi	lease, rent, list
līsiti	receipt (usually *rīsiti*)
lītaea	retire (usually *rītaea*)
liu$_1$	alter, change, turn into
līua	be changed, turned aside
maliu	(pol.) die, death
taliu	return
liuliu	turn over and over
liliu	to turn
fa'aliliu	translate, convert
fa'aliliuga	translation
liuausa	evaporate
liusuāvai	melt, dissolve
liu$_2$	bilge - water
lo$_1$	with pronouns, *lo matou* etc. - our etc.
lo$_2$	used in comparative phrases - "*sili lo*" more than, better than etc.
loa$_1$	at once, immediately
loa$_2$	a long time since, be very old
loloa	vast
fa'aloaloa	extend, stretch out
loaloavale	middle finger
loa$_3$	grave (built up)
loa$_4$	tree (bixa) red-dye
loata	black ant
lofi, lolofi	surge, flood, be overcome
lōfitūina	inundated, overcome
loga	hiccup
logo$_1$	perceive, inform, tell
logologoā	famous
lologo	be silent, hushed
fa'alogo	to hear, listen, feel, pay attention
fa'alologa	feeling
fa'alogogatā	disobedient
fa'alogogōfie	obedient
felogona'i	consult each other
logolelei	good, favourable (news etc.)

logovale	bad, unpleasant (news etc.)
logonoa	deaf
logovi'i	be conceited
logo$_2$	bell, gong
loi$_1$	ant
lōia	overrun with ants
loi$_2$ **loloi**	cook w. c'nut cream
lōia$_1$	be surfeited with greasy food
loifa'i	bananas and c'nut cream
lōia$_2$	lawyer, solicitor
loitoi	dip
lo'ilo'i	(pol.) pig sty
loimata	tear
loka	lock
lola	roller
lole	sweets, lollies, candy
loli$_1$	sea cucumber
loli$_2$	lorry, truck
loli$_3$	be all set, ready
lolo$_1$	abandon, withdraw, be defeated
fa'alolo	give up (for someone else)
fa'aloloina	give into, indulge
lolo$_2$	overflow, flood (*lōfia)* (pass.)
lolo$_3$	be scented (oil)
lololo	be fat, rich (meat)
lolō	plunge, steep (in water etc.)
loma	soon to take place
lomi$_1$	massage, knead
lomi$_2$	print, (*fale lomi tusi* - printing works)
lomiga	printing, edition
lolomi	to print, plunge in water
lomitusi	typewriter
lona	his, her, its
lo'o	verbal particle indicating a continuing situation
lo'omatua	(pl. *lo'omātutua*), old woman, to be aged
lōpā	shiny red seeds
lōpoto	(pol.) women's illness
losi	strive, aspire to
losilosivale	covet

losoloso	flower cluster – c'nut only
lota	my
lote	fidget, fiddle with, handle
lotelote	handle
lotelotea	been dealt with
lotemātūtū	hit for no reason
loto$_1$	pool, stretch of deep water
loloto	be deep
loto$_2$	heart, feeling, will, to agree
lotoa	hot-tempered
felotoa'i	disagree
loto'āiga	loyal to family
lotoali'i	polite
lotofiafia	happy, jolly
lotofa'afetai	grateful
lotofa'apito	selfish
lotofuatiaifo	conscience
lotoleaga	jealous, envious
lotolelei	kind-hearted
lotomalie	agree, be in favour, with graciousness
lotoma'a'a	obstinate
lotomāfatia	downhearted
lotofa'amāgalo	forgiving
lotomalō	stubborn
lotomālosi	strong-headed
lotofa'amaoni	conscientious
lotomaulalo	humble
lotomau	strict, steadfast, determined
lotomitamita	proud
lotomomomo	broken-hearted
lotomomotu	callous, heartless
lotonaunau	earnestness
lotonu'u	patriotic
lotooti	reckless
latotele	brave, courageous
fa'alototele	inspire others
lotovāivai	be timid, give up
fa'alotovāivai	discourage
lotovale	envious, spiteful
lotovi'i	vain, conceited
fa'alotolotolua	of two minds, undecided
lotoā	paddock, enclosure, yard
lotoi	be in middle of
lotoifale	middle of house

lotu$_1$	act of worship, service, church, religion, religious
lotu$_2$	persevere
lotulotu	work very hard, work quickly
lotusa'i	nevertheless
lou$_1$	your
lou$_2$	hooked picking stick
feloua'i	pull in different directions
lo'u$_1$	my
lo'u$_2$	be bent, curved
lolo'u	bend
louā$_1$	rough (sea, weather), noisy
loulouā	(pol.) rough, be gravely ill
louā$_2$	in case
lua$_1$	you, your (dual)
lua$_2$	two
lualua	ambiguous
fa'alua	twice
fa'aluaina	be doubled
feluani	keep company (two people)
lua$_3$	pit, hole, mine
luai	spit, disgorge
lua'i	hole for planting taro etc.
lu'au	S. delicacy (coconut cream, taro leaves, salt water)
lue	shake, rock, nod
luelue	shake, sway
māluelue	sway (trees, boat etc.)
lufilufi	to share out
luga } ***lugā***	on, over, up (emphatic)
lūgā	in disagreement, inflamed, septic (boil)
lugaluga'i	to assemble (people)
lu'i	defy, challenge, dare
luko	wolf
lula	ruler
lulu	owl
lūlū	shake, sow, lottery
galulu	tremble, whirl, swish
lūluga	a shaking, sowing
lululu	very fat
lulu'u	take a handful
lu'utaga	a handful

luma$_1$	in front of, forward, front
lumā	(emphatic) in front
luma$_2$	loss of face, humiliation, shame
fa'aluma	to make a fool of s.o.
fa'alumaluma	taunting
fa'aaluma	clown
luma$_3$ - **fa'alumaga**	share of food taken home from a feast
lumā'ava	morning meal
lupe$_1$	pigeon, dove
fa'alupe	to set aside, be marked, to address
fa'alupega	ceremonial form of address
lupe$_2$	be pending
lupe$_3$	scar tissue (*lupea*)
lupepe	gather in large numbers
lusi	loose, waste
luti	oppressed by pain, trouble
lutitau	anxious to fight
lu'ulu'u	of all kinds
luva	louvre (window)

Mm

ma$_1$	used with negative *lē* - unable, *lēmafai* - unable to do . . .
ma$_2$	and, with
ma$_3$	away from, out of
mā$_1$	we (dual, he and I)
mā$_2$	for (*'ave mā'oe* = take for yourself)
mā$_3$	be ashamed
fa'amā	put to shame
mā$_4$	pure, healthy (blood)
mā$_5$ - **māina**	shine on, flash on
ma'a	stone
ma'ama'a	gravel, pebbles
ma'ama'anoa	clear of stones
ma'a afi	flint, detonator
ma'aalā	solid stone
ma'afa'amanatu	monument, memorial stone
ma'ala'a	loose stones
ma'atāua	precious stones, jewel, gem
ma'atusi	slate
ma'auila	electric battery
ma'a'a	hard to break
lotoma'a'a	obstinate
fa'ama'a'a	tense (muscles), harden
ma'ai	sharp, clever, smart
ma'ama'ai	sharp
fa'ama'ai	sharpen
ma'ale'ale	fragile, brittle
ma'alili	feel cold, shiver, cold (weather), a cold, chill
fa'ama'alili	to chill, cool
ma'alo	appear and disappear suddenly
mā'ama'a	ease off (rain)
ma'amulumulu	slacken, relax
ma'amulumuluia	grazed skin
ma'anumi	crease
ma'anuminumi	be wrinkled
fa'ama'anuminumi	to crumple
ma'au	(pol.) turn
mā'au	(pol.) gift (food)
ma'avā	ajar
mā'ave'ave	small branch (fruit tree only)
ma'ave 'ese'ese	subdivision of a lineage
mae$_1$	(pol.) stale, smell
mae$_2$	dry up, wither (pl. *mamae*)
maea	rope, cord
māe'a	finished, ready, complete, thorough
fa'amāe'a	terminate
maela	hollow sound, ring false (of laughter)
ma'elegā	eagerness, zeal

ma'ema'e	industrious
ma'emae'ā	(pol.) anger
maene	sinker (fishing)
ma'epu	curl over (paper, mats)
ma'eu₁	remarkable, surprising
ma'eu₂	make a mistake
mafa	pass, brow of hill
mafai	can, able to
lēmafai	refuse
mafaia	manage, obtain
māfalā	wide-spread (tree)
māfana	to be intimate, married
māfanafana	be warm
fa'amāfanafana	warm up, comfort, encourage
māfatia	very tired, exhausted, overcome, be hurt
māfatua	sneeze
māfaufau	consider, reflect, mind, brain, memory, sensible
māfaufauga	thought, memories, fancies
mafia	thick, excessive
māfiafia	be thick
māfine	woman, girl (term of affection)
māfo'e	torn, lacerated skin
mafu₁	stale, go bad, sour, mouldy (food), ferment
fa'amafu	home brewed liquor
mafu₂	cubes of taro in "*fā'ausi*" (S. food)
mafu₃	to heal (wound)
mafu₄	fatty part of pigeon
māfua	originate from, be the reason why
māfuaga	cause, origin, source
mafui'e	earthquake
māfuta	live, dwell with
māfutaga	friendship, fellowship
māfutamoeafiafi	to happen early at night
maga	fork (road, tree)
tamaga	go off at a tangent, change subject
māgamaga	many forks
fa'amaga	open (mouth)
fa'amāgai	sit astride
magaala	lane, branch road
māgafā	cross roads, four corners
magālafu	hearth
magālima	space between fingers
magāvae	space between toes
magagū	mutter, mumble
māgalo₁	be fresh (water)
māgalo₂	forgiven, absolved
fa'amagalo	to forgive
magamate	(pol.) bamboo, fishing rod
magemage	disease of foot
mageso	itch
māgiagia	be on edge (teeth)
mago₁	(pl. *mamago*) dry, dry up
fa'amago	to dry
mago₂	mango (fruit)
magoivi	waste away, be very thin
magumagu	dry, withered
mai	used with verb, indicates direction, "towards, from"
māi	salty, bitter (water)
ma'i	(pl. *mama'i*) be sick, ill, infection, disease, sickness, the patient, pregnancy
ma'ima'i	sickly
fa'ama'ilili	delerious, feverish
fa'amama'i	madly in love
ma'iaitu	illness due to "devil possession"
ma'i fofō	complaint to be massaged
ma'ilasi	sickly (child)
ma'ilili	shivering, convulsions
ma'imāliu	epilepsy
ma'imalū	(pol.) sore, ulcer
ma'imanatu	homesick, lovesick
ma'i māsina	women's "period"
ma'i masunu	erysipelas
ma'imutumutu	leprosy (also *lepela*)
ma'i pipili	poliomyelitis
ma'i-o-tāne	enlarged scrotum, hydrocele
ma'isua	boil
ma'itaga	(pol.) pregnancy
ma'itō	be pregnant
ma'i vasa	seasickness
maia	used for emphasis after verb

maiesetete majesty
mai fea? from whence?
maila mile
mā'ila scar
maile dog (also *'ulī*, *ta'ifau*)
māilei trap
ma'ilo small c'nut leaf platter
ma'imau wasted
fa'ama'imau to waste
māimoa look at, look on
'au māimoa audience, spectators etc.
māimoaga sight, view
maina explosive mine
ma'ina express surprise, admiration
ma'ini sting, smart, driving rain
mainiga –
lē mainiga not to mind
maio portion of a pig
mai'u'u finger nail (also *atigi lima – matiu'u*), claws
maka a mark, marker
māketi market
māketi i'a fish market
mala scourge, plague, tragedy, disaster, sickness, epidemic (animals)
mamala be severe
mālaia overcome by disaster, a curse, (pol.) dead,fire
malae open space, village green
malae ta'alo sports ground
malae va'alele airport
mālaelae prominently, openly
malafufula prepare food for unwelcome guests
malaga$_1$ ceremonial visit, journey, trip, travel, travellers, visitors
malaga$_2$ –
fa'amalaga chase away
malaga$_3$ –
fa'amalaga introduce a subject
malaise beating block (c'nut husks)
malala charcoal
mālala glow of burning charcoal
malama to dawn, day break, blaze up (fire)
mālama dawn, daylight
fa'amalama window
mālamalama daylight, sunlight, sunshine, light, be fine (day) be clear, understood, be conscious, grasp, enlightened, civilized, made of glass
fa'amālamalama light up, explain, clarify
fa'a –
mālamalamaga explanation
malamala wood chip, portion of a fish
male (pol.) be angry, cough
maleifua (pol.) wake up
malele (pl. *mālele*) ring out (sound) (pol.) speak, talk
fa'amalele speak w. authority
malelega (pol.) speech
malemo drown
malepe break up
malie$_1$ agree, approve, be ready, willing, to be satisfied w.food & drink, pleasure, satisfaction
malie lou loto (pol.) to decline
le malie dissatisfied, displeasure
fa'amalie soothe, placate, also to compliment
maliega will, consent
malie$_2$ shark
mălie$_1$ be amusing, funny, enjoyable, beautiful, sweet, pleasing
mălie$_2$ gently, slowly
mālifa slope
maligi to pour, spill
malili fall before mature (fruit)
malini a marine
mali'o land crab
malo$_1$ loin cloth
malo$_2$ droop
malō hard, firm, solid, stiff
malōlō muscular

fa‘amalō taut, tight
mālō$_1$ to win, victory, party in power, government, state, kingdom, republic
fa‘alemalo of the govt., political
mālō$_2$ valuable fine mat, collection of fine mats
mālō$_3$ bundle of kava roots for ceremony
mālō$_4$ a guest
malōtia to have guests
mālō$_5$ (exclamation) well done! good work!
fa‘amālō compliment, congratulate
maloā noisy, noise
mālōlō rest, adjourn, pause, break
mālōlōina be healthy, well again
fa‘amālōlō be on leave, retire, cure, heal
malosi hurt, painful
mālosi be strong (physically, taste), violent strength, power, force, violence
fa‘amālosi press on, force, rape
fa‘amālosia be strengthened
fa‘amālosi‘aga encouragement
fa‘amālositino physical exercise - P.T.
malu$_1$ shelter, take shelter, weather-proof (house)
fa‘amalu cover, shelter, umbrella
fa‘amalumaluga protection
malu$_2$ crowd, throng
malū$_1$ be soft, calm, bass (music)
fa‘amalū make soft, mash, smoothly, mattress
malū$_2$ fish basket
mālū$_1$ be cooling, soothing (external things) sweet, comforting, (pol.) peace
mālūlū be cold
fa‘amālū (pol.) have a bath, soothe, appease, pacify
mālū$_2$ broil (pol. breakfast)
māluali‘i imposing (person), dignity, poise
mālu‘ia have a nightmare
mālumalu$_1$ loom over, gloomy
mālumalu$_2$ temple, cathedral
mama$_1$ masticate, (pol.) chew
mama$_2$ leak
mama$_3$ ring
mama$_4$ mother, mummy
mamā clean, clear (of rubbish), pure, innocent
fa‘amamā wash, clean, strain, strainer
māmā$_1$ lung
māmāpala tuberculosis
māmā$_2$ light (weight), lightly (attitude)
fa‘amāmā lighten, reduce
māmāsagia v. light
fa‘amāmāsagia treat v. lightly
mamae$_1$ wither, dry up
mamae$_2$ close (of a friend)
‘aumeamamae bridal party
mamafa heavy, weighty, important, pressure, heaviness (of heart)
māfamafa fairly heavy
fa‘amamafa stress, emphasize
mamafatū too heavy
mamala greatly valued (food)
mamalu dignity, majesty, glory, honour, prestige, infuence, to be in force (e.g. law)
fiamamalu put on airs
fa‘amamalu to respect, honour, keep safe, protect, watch over
mamanu sennit bindings in decorative design, design, pattern (*siapo*)
mamao distant, wide of mark
mamapo show off
mamata -
niu mamata drinking c'nut, green c'nut
māmoe sheep
tama‘i māmoe lamb
mamulu slip out of . . .
fa‘amamulu let slip
mana power (supernatural)
mamana powerful, almighty

mānaia	(pl. *mānanaia*) attactive, beautiful, smart, beauty, leader of untitled men's group, chief's son
fa‘amānaia	dress up, be vain (of a man), show off, decorate, make beautiful
manamana	consider doing s.th.
mānamea	good, favourite friend
mana‘o	(pl. *mānana‘o*) want, desire, require, like
mana‘oga	wish, desire
manatu	think, feel lonely, thought, idea, opinion, point of an argument
mānatua	remember
mānatunatu	reflect, think about
fa‘amanatu	remind, commemorate
manatu fa‘apito	selfish
manatu – fa‘atauva‘a	despise
manatu fa‘atū	propose, proposal
manava	belly, waist
mānava	breathe, stand still, break off, stop for a rest
mānavaga	breathing
mane‘e	loose (stone etc.)
māne‘e	move along (persons)
māneta	magnet
manifi – mānifinifi	thin, temple (head)
fa‘amanifi	sharpen, thinly
manino	clear, limpid, transparent, be clear, obvious
māninoa	quiet, still
fa‘amanino	make clear, explain
manioka	cassava
maniti	shudder, feeling of horror
mano	express great numbers
manomānō	countless
mānoa	string, cord
manogi	smell, have a good flavour, scent
fa‘alēmanogi	not appetising, unpleasant aftermath
manu$_1$	animal, cattle, bird
fa‘amanu	bestial, animal-like, rude, ignorant
manufasi	edible flesh
manufata	(pol.) roast pig, v. big pig on litter
manulautī	target
manulele	bird
manusā	S. pigeon
manu siliva	silverfish
manu$_2$	pattern, design
mānu$_1$	come to surface
mānu$_2$	proclaim, announce, proclamation
manū$_1$	while, before, nearly
manū$_2$	good luck, fortune
manuia	be happy, lucky, successful
ia manuia	to your health (kava ceremony)
fa‘amanuia	bless, wish good luck
fa‘amanuiaga	blessing, good wishes
manu‘a	(pl.*mānunu‘a*) wound
manu‘anu‘a	multiple wounds
manukī	monkey
mānumālō	succeed, win, victory, success
mānumanu	covetous, envious, stingy, miserly
manunu	wither, in pieces
mao$_1$	(prefix) indicates distance
maoa‘e	advanced, superior
maoluma	far ahead
maosasa‘e	further East
maotai	further towards sea
maouta	way (far) inland
mao$_2$	do s.th. by chance or accident
‘ua mao le ‘upu	word said by chance
māoa	dense, thick (bush)
māofa	be amazed
māo‘i	real, genuine
fa‘amāo‘io‘i	be in earnest, properly
ma‘oi	favourite
maona	let up, calm down, abate (storm)
mā‘ona	(pl.*mā‘o‘ona*) replete, full up
fa‘amā‘ona	fill to capacity
maoni, fa‘amaoni	true, faithful, loyal, honest, earnest, serious

tusi fa'amaoni	certificate, proof, evidence
fa'amaonia	confirmed, approved, to make true, realize, be proved, testify
fa'amaoniga	proof
māopoopo	well wrapped, compact, solid, well organized
mā'osi	torn, scratched
maota	house of chief, palace
ma'oti	sharp, distinct
mapeva	sprained
mapo	dry & hard (taro), haughty
mapu$_1$	whistle
mapu$_2$	have a rest, relief
mapusaga	resting place
māpuea	take deep breath
māpusela	sigh, pant
mapu$_3$	marble
mapuitīga	restless, always in trouble
mapuna	strained (back)
masa	smell, stink, empty (canoe after bailing out)
masa'a	be spilt
māsae	be torn, a tear
māsaga	twins
māsaga tolu	triplets
masagi	rebound, fly up
masalo	opinion (w.o. certainty), think, suspicion
māsalosalo	suspect, be sceptical, suspicious
māsalosaloga	suspicion
māsalosalovale	suspect w.o. reason
māsani	accustomed to, acquainted with, used to, normal, custom, habit
fa'amāsani	become accustomed to . . .
masau	hurry, fast
fa'amasau	speed up
masei	slip, mistake
māsei	misfortune, trouble, worthless, inferior
māsesei	be on bad terms
māseiga	dispute, quarrel

masele	cease for a time (rain)
masepu	slip (foot)
masi	fermented b'fruit, biscuits
māsiasi	ashamed, shame, embarrassment
fa'amāsiasi	to embarrass
masi'i	move, move off
māsima	salt
fa'amāsima	to salt
māsina	moon, month, season (pol.) chief who has died
masini	machine, engine
masino	be known exactly
fa'amasino	investigate, enquire, try before a judge, judge, magistrate, umpire, referee
falefa'amasino	court house
fa'amasinoga	court case, trial
masiofo	wife of h. chief, queen
masisi	clitoris
maso	muscle
masoa	muscular
māsoā$_1$	starch
māsoā$_2$	indecent, obscure
masofa	collapse
māsū, masūsū	breathe hard, wheeze
masua	overflow
masui	be sore (arms) (pol. work)
mata$_1$	look like, look as if, may, might
mata$_2$	raw, uncooked
fa'amatamata	half-cooked, simple, naive
mata$_3$	eye, face, point, blade (edge), spring (water), mesh (net), glasses, goggles
matamata	spy, scout
mātamata	look at
fa'amata	be likely that, think, sharpen
fa'amātamata	to show around
mataafi	groove in fire stick
mata'aga	sight for sight-seers
māta'āiga	ready to help family
mataaitu	peep as a "peeping-Tom"
mataala	wakeful, alert, prompt

matafa‘a‘ū‘ū frown
matagā ugly, indecent
matagaoi steal
mātagōfie beautiful, lovely, glory
fa‘amātagōfie decorate, adorn, beautify
mataita look angry
mata‘ivi blind in one eye, cock-eyed
mātalasi manifold, varied
matalelei good looking
matalili‘i fine mesh
matamāmā appear easy
matamamafa appear hard
matamau generous, open-handed
matamoe drowsy
matamuamua cheeky, forward
matamuli shy, reserved (pol.) embarrassed, ashamed
mataola recover, get better
mata‘o‘omo deep-set eyes
matapa‘u burnt end of wick, candle
matape‘ape‘a greed
matapogi look frightening
matapogia to faint
matapoto clever, sharp witted
matapua‘a ugly
matatetē protruding eyes
matatiotio alert, watchful
matatoa look brave
matatu‘i‘ai greedy
matatupa blunt
mata‘ū stingy, mean
matau‘a envious
matavale offensive, look bad
matavalea slow witted
matā (prefix)
mata‘āiga extended family
matāfaga shore, beach
matāfaioi obligation, duty
matāfale house gable, caretaker of a title
matāgaluega section, department
matāmatagi quarter of the wind
matāsele noose
matāsusu nipple, teat
matātuai grating tool
matāua raindrop
matāuila electric light bulb
matā‘upolu E. wind
matā‘upu subject, theme, chapter, business, problem etc.
matāvaga separately
matāvao edge of forest
matāvai source of spring
matāvili bit (drill)
mātagā ugly, indecent
matagi wind
matai titled family head
mata‘i observe, notice, remark, admire
mata‘inumera a figure, number
mātaisau (pol.) craftsman, carpenter
mata‘itusi letter (A.G etc.)
mataitōga v. valuable fine mat
mataitū direct, govern, responsible
matala get free, loose, be open, sharp, keen (mind) tear, fray (clothes)
fa‘amatala explain, describe, release
e lē-mafa‘amatalaina inexplicable, mysterious
fa‘amatalaga explanation, description, statement
fa‘amatalaloto cheer up, comfort
fa‘amatala‘upu interpreter
matamata (pol.) kindling wood, kindle
matanana boast (of wealth etc.), brag, cry often (baby)
matataotao prong (spear)
matau$_1$ (pol.) adze, axe
matau$_2$ right side of canoe
mātau$_1$ observe, notice, weigh another's words, count
mātau$_2$ fish hook
mata‘u (pl.*mātata‘u*) fear, hold in awe
mata‘utia dreadful, awful
fa‘amata‘u frighten, threaten
matau‘a jealous, envious
mate$_1$ (pl.*mamate*) die (plants, animals)
tamate kill
fa‘amate kill (animal), put out fire

matelaina	weak w. hunger
matelipi	stone cold (fire)
mate$_2$	guess
matele	hurry, walk fast
mateletele	be over-hasty
mātele	concentrate, too much on one side
Mati	March, fig-tree (Bible)
matinitini	be v. painful
mati'uti'u	edge of toe, fingernail
matiu'u	toenail (person), claw (animal)
mativa	(pl.*mātitiva*) poor, poverty
mato	narrow gorge, inland precipice
matofi	c'nut fibres for sennit
matolutolu	crunchy
mātou	we, us, our (exclusive)
matū	towel, dry cloth
mātū$_1$	(pol.) dry o.s. after bath
Mātū$_2$	North
matua$_1$	(pl.*mātutua*) mature (fruit), be adult (people), older, dense, thick (bush), age
matua$_2$	loyal to, text (sermon), core (speech)
mātua	parent
mātuaoti	orphans
matuā	very, absolutely, quite, great
matuā'ie	work clothes
matuāmanu	old bird
matuāmoa	mother hen
matuā'ofu	old garment
matua'i, ta'i	very (colq.)
matuitui	sharp, pointed, acute pain
matu'u	heron
mātūtū	be dry
fa'amātūtū	to dry
mau$_1$	keep, retain, grip, hold fast, stick firmly, live, dwell, have plenty
maua	get, be caught, obtain, be found, win
tāmau	pass, approve (law)
māua'i	firm, steadfast
fa'amau	lock, bolt, secure, tighten, fasten, a button, buckle
maua'a	rooted
mauaga	strange behaviour
mauagatā	hard to get, rare
mauagōfie	easy to get, common
maugatā	mean
maugōfie	generous
mau'alofagā	have loop-holes (law)
maumauloto	determined
maumanatu	certain
maumea	rich, wealthy
mau'oloa	rich, wealthy
maupipi'i	cling to
mausalī	secure, unshakeable
fa'amausalī	make secure
maumausolo	live a wandering life, nomad, vagrant
mautāma'ia	caught in the act
mautino	sure, certain
mautinoa	to be sure, certain, convinced
mautonu	settle on, decide
mautotogi	be a tenant, pay rent
mautū	long lasting, fixed
māumaututū	firmly established
mautūlaga	valid
mau'upu	fluent
mau$_2$	evidence, testimony, motion, proposal
mau$_3$	rebellion, revolution
mau$_4$	(pol.) breast (woman)
maua	a kite
mā'ua	we (he and I)
maualuga	high, tall, altitude, height (pol.) b'fruit
fa'amaualuga	proud, proudly, pride, conceitedly, upwards
mauga	hill, mountain
maugā	mountainous
maui	ebb, recede, diminish
māui	go down, subside (swelling)
maulalo	low, deep, humble
fa'amaulalo	lower, be humble
mauli	emotions affecting solar-plexus
'ua segia le mauli	have a fright
ma'ulu	drip (rain, dew)
ma'ulu'ulu	drizzle
ma'umaga	taro garden
māumau	be wasted
fa'amāumau	waste, squander
māunu	bait, decoy

maupu'epu'e hilly, hill, mound
mausa favourite pastime
mavae pass, go by (time)
māvae s.th. left, inherited, be apart, separate, to part, separate, split, a crack
māvaega farewell, parting words, last wishes, will
māvaevae cracked
fa'amāvae to part, resign
fa'amāvaega farewell
māvava yawn
mave'u untidy (hair, clothes)
fa'amāve'uve'u ruffle
maveve cracked
Me May, annual church offering
mea thing, object, place, area, property, goods, animals, beasts, (pol.) genitals
o le mea lea therefore
meāfale furniture
mea'ai food
meaalofa gift, present
mea avanoa blank space
mea'ele'elea chores
mea'ese strange experience
meafa'apolopolo first fruits
meafaigāluega tools
meafaigatā hardship
meafono food
meafulunifo toothpaste
meainu drink
mealeaga (impol.) person of humble origin, child (of speaker)
mealelei special food, favourite
mealilo secret
meamalō solid (thing)
meā manū be fortunate
meamao accident, by chance
meamoni truth
meanamuleaga (pol.) tobacco
meaola animal, creature
meapu'eata camera
measā genitals (either sex), gift of fine mat from brother to sister
measesē error, mistake
measina (pol.) fine mat, family valuables
meata'alo toy
mea tatau ai food (pol.)
meatau weapon
meatāua treasure, valuable object, essentials
meatāumafa (pol.) food, tobacco
meatausami (pol.) food
meatonu truth, justice
meavā'ai glass, telescope
meamea suckling
tamameamea sm. child
meana'i (pol.) wife of carpenter or craftsman
meanē (ph.) *ne'i meanē* in case s.th. should happen, but, however
me'eme'e feel happy
me'i flinch, wince, draw back
meme'i stretch, pull, shrink, contract, shrivel, elastic
fana meme'i catapault
fa'ame'i shrug, wince
meia stunned
mele reject, throw away
fa'amele misuse, waste
mele'i husking stick, remove husk
meleke adze axe, food bowl, (colq.) America
'ofu meleke "T" shirt, singlet
meli honey, mail
melo, memelo$_1$ about to cry, whitish
melo$_2$ marshmallow
memea yellowish-brown w. age
'apamemea brass, copper
memu move lips w.o. speaking
meo disappointment
metala metal
miaga urine
mimi urinate
miga, mīgao respect, reverence, respectful
migi curl
migimigi frizzy
mīgoi move slightly, budge

mili	rub, seed bed
milimili	rub gently
miliona	million
milionea	millionaire
milo	twist (thread, rope etc.), keep company, associate with, mingle, dance
milosia	sprained, twisted
milomilo	twist, be perverse, (pol.) preparing food
minisitā	government minister
minute	minute (time), minutes (of a meeting)
mio	mix with, associate with
femiomioa'i	wander aimlessly (also *miomiō*)
misa	quarrel, fight
fa'amimisa	start trouble
misasā	R.C. mass
misela	measles
misimisi	smack
misialofa	click tongue in sympathy
misi$_1$	to miss
misi$_2$	title for European missionary
misionare	missionary
mita, mita'i	to boast of
mitamitaga	pride
mimita	proud, conceited
miti$_1$	sip, whiff, sucking noise
mitimiti	sip, suck, smack o's lips
mimiti	absorb, suck in
mitiafu	singlet
mitivai	blotting paper
miti$_2$	dream, nap, siesta
miti$_3$	food-c'nut cream and salt water
miti$_4$**, mimiti**	thin (legs etc.)
mitu	(children's talk) ghost, spirit
mo$_1$	for
mo$_2$	fat pig w. short legs
moa$_1$	chicken, hen, spinning top
moa$_2$	solar plexus, belly, middle
moa$_3$	mower (lawn)
moamoa	Christmas decoration, part of S.house
moana$_1$	deep sea, deep water
moanasausau	v. deep water
moana$_2$	be devastated (place)
moe	(pl.*momoe*) sleep, (pol.) sex, intercourse, orator's opinion
moega	bed
moena'i	adjourn (for night)
moemoe	go on sleeping, bud, new shoot (plant)
fa'amoe	put to sleep, give anaesthetic, fold up, cajole
fa'amoega	sheath, case, nest
fa'amoemoe	hope, trust, expect
fa'amoemoeina	expected
moefiti	sleep restlessly
moegase	sleep soundly
moe'i'ini	close o's. eyes tight
moeloa	oversleep, sleep in
moepupula	drowsy, half asleep
moesavali	walk in o's sleep
moetolo	attempt intercourse w.sleeping woman
moevavale	talk in o's sleep (also *moetautala*)
momo'e, mo'e	run
tamo'emo'e	trot
femo'ea'i	run to and fro
moemoenoa	restless, hard to control (children)
mogamoga	cockroach
moge	sm. body hairs
mo'i	true, genuine, real
moi'a'a	c'nut husk fibre
mōkesi	mortgage
mōlali	blunt
mole$_1$	smooth
molemole	worn out, worn down
fa'amolemole	please, to plaster
mole$_2$	choke
molemanava	weak w. hunger
fa'amolemanava	fast
moli$_1$	orange
molisaina	mandarin
fasimoli	soap
moli$_2$	take, send
momoli	convey, take
mōliga	escort, accusation, charge

mōlia be taken, sue, accuse, charge
molimau witness
molitino frank, forthright
molipō secret message of love, warning etc.
mōlī lamp
mōlīga'o candle
mōlīmatagi hurricane lamp
molīta'īālava'a lighthouse, beacon
momo, tamomo (pl.*momoi.*) broken remnants, crumbs
momomo dash to pieces, broken (heart)
fa'amomoiloto heart-breaking
mōmona rich - of shell fish
mona swarm
mōna as his, hers, its
moni$_1$ true
mea moni truth, fact, real, honest, sincere
fa'amaoni agree with, uphold, accredited, in full status
mono plug a sm. hole, caulk
monotaga contribution of food
monomono slip (into the hand), pass secretly to s.o.
momono cork, stopper
mo'o$_1$ admire, envy
mo'omo'o, momo'o long for
mo'omo'oga wish, desire
mo'o$_2$ gecko
mosimosi fresh-water shrimp, (colq.) s.th. small
moso'oi tree, flowers used to scent c'nut oil
moti scar
moto$_1$ fist, punch
moto$_2$ unripe (fruit etc.)
moto$_3$ end of kava round
motu$_1$ break (stick, rope, friendship)
motusia broken
motusi snap, break in pieces
momotu break off, snap off
fa'amotu break off, bring to an end
motu$_2$ island
atumotu archipelago
motu$_3$ crowd
mou vanish, disappear
mōu as yours, be yours
mō'u as mine, be mine
mū$_1$ burn, inflamed
mumū burn away, blaze
mūmū red, filariasis
fa'amū burn up
fa'amumū light (the lamp)
mūgālafu hearth
mūgōfie inflammable
mūsaesae blaze, long hours of the night
mūmūsalī scarlet
mūtinitini v.hot (sun)
mūmūvale blush, be flushed
mū$_2$ game of draughts
mua$_1$ be first, precede, winner, record
mua'i (prefix) indicates first
mua'i sau first came
muamua$_1$ come, go (first), go ahead of . . .
muamua$_2$ first, former, original
fa'amuamua put first
muā'auvae chin
muā'au van guard
muāgagana saying, proverb
muāgutu centre of mouth, snout, muzzle
muāulu forehead
muāvae kick w. toes, front of foot
mua$_2$ band, stripe, tape
mua$_3$ cheer
mu'a green (grass, leaves), immature, unripe
mu'amu'a tender, soft
muimui murmur, criticize behind o's back
muimuiga murmuring of discontent
muli come last, rear of s.th., haunch of pig (impol.) posterior (man) bottom, young, new. (*'o le teine muli* young, unmarried girl)
mulia'i (w. verb e.g. *mulia'i sau* = last to . . . come)
mulimuli follow, be done later, last

fa'amuli stay behind

mulilua commit adultery

muliulu back of head

mulivae heel

mulivai mouth of river

mulu$_1$ handle slowly

mulumea interfere

mulu$_2$ singe, burn hair off (pig only)

mumulu warm in front of fire

mulu$_3$ grumble, mutter, murmur

mulumulu wash face & hands

mumu to crowd, swarm

mūmū$_1$ inflammation & swelling due to filariasis

mūmū$_2$ red

mumua dolphin

mūmūfālō tug, wrestle

muna answer back to older person

musa hop, game of hopping

musele muscle

musika music

musu$_1$ sullen, obdurate, uncooperative, refuse, sulk

musuā sulky

musu$_2$ -

musumusu whisper

musumusuga whisper

femusua'i whisper to ea. oth.

musuvā whisper news from o. to another

muta end, finish

muta'aga end

mutia grass

mutimutivale pity, mercy

mutu cut off, truncated

fa'amutu to cut short, cut off pig's tail

Nn

na$_1$ he, she, it

na$_2$ verbal part. - past tense

nā$_1$ those, that (pl. of *lenā*)

nā$_2$ stop crying, be silent (sm. children)

fa'anā hush (child)

fa'anānā lull

nafai nearly

nai$_1$ several, some, a few

nai$_2$ from

naifi knife

nailoni nylon

nainai$_1$ no wonder

nainai$_2$ pick, choose

nameri leopard

namu$_1$ mosquito

namu$_2$ coral lime (for building)

nāmu to smell of, smell

nanamu scent, perfume

nāmuasua smoked

nana$_1$ cry frequently

nana$_2$ boast, brag

nanā hide

nātia hidden

fa'anānā be secret

nanea sufficient (food)

fa'ananea make enough for all

nānei presently, later on, this evening, tonight

nanu mispronounce own language, speak in foreign tongue

na'o only, just

na'ona just

nape put foot on thigh (sitting)

nasu mulch

nati$_1$ hurry

nanati hasten, urge

fa'anatinati speed up s.th

nati$_2$ nut (bolt)

natu rubbing stick for making fire

natura nature

na‘uā	very, exceedingly, too
naumati	be w.o. water
nauna	noun
naunau$_1$	very
naunau$_2$	desire, want, be eager for
naunauta‘i	long for
fa‘anaunauga	s.th greatly desired
naunautala	be curious, inquisitive
ne‘a	loudly (laughter)
ne‘e$_1$	extol, praise
nc‘etaga	praise
fa‘ane‘ene‘e	praise highly, extol
ne‘e$_2$	laugh happily
nefu	cloudy (water)
nenefu	blurred, dim (e.g. mirror)
fa‘anefu	make water cloudy by stirring
fa‘anenefu	vague, hazy
fa‘anefunefu	disturbed, agitated (water)
nei	these (pl. of *lenei*), now
ne‘i$_1$	not at all, on no account
ne‘i$_2$	for fear that, in case
neva	saunter, stroll
ni	(pl. of *se*) some, any
ni nai	a few
nifo	tooth, tusk, horn, (fig.) enemy.
fa‘anifo	tooth (cog), thread (screw)
nifoloa	evil spirit
nifo ‘oti	hooked dancing knife
nifopū	gapped teeth
ni‘i	spring up (plants), granulate (in a healing wound), pimples
nila	a needle, sting (insect)
nimo	vanish, disappear, slip one's memory
fa‘animonimo	obscure, mysterious
nini	rub in, smear (ointment etc.)
nini‘i	v. small, minute
niniva	giddy
ni‘o	sway, undulate (body), twirl, twiddle, coil
nipi	nib
nisi	some more, some other
niu	coconut palm
niu‘afa	long c'nut for sennit
niu le‘a	dwarf c'nut
niu mamata	drinking nut
niu masoā	sago palm
niu muli	fermented c'nut
niu piu	fan palm
niu vao	wild palms
niu popo	matured nut
noa$_1$	(suffix) indicates "no importance", "easy"
fa‘anoa	donc w.o. difficulty
noa$_2$	(pl. *noanoa*) tie, bind
noataga	bond, fastening
nonoa	tie s.th up
noanoaga	bondage
noanoatia	be bound
nofo	live, dwell, stay, remain, lodge, sit, hold matai title, be married
nofoia	occupied
nofoaga	dwelling, residence, seat, location (pol.) buttocks
nofoa‘i	sit, hold title
nōfoi	stay, sit (assembly)
nofoa	chair, seat, saddle
nofoa afi	railway, train
nofonofo	stay put, be idle
fa‘anofo	place, put, appoint, install
nofoāfono	sit in council
nofoali‘i	throne
nofoāpi	stay as a guest
nofofua	unmarried
nofogatā	difficult to live in
nofogōfie	pleasant, cheerful
nofopologa	live in bondage, enslaved
nofosala	guilty, convicted, serve a sentence
nofo sa‘o	sit straight, sit up
nofosauni	be prepared
nofotane	married (of a woman)
nofogātāne	marriage (of a woman)
nofotuāvae	to serve a matai, (pol.) untitled man
nofouta	be on one's guard
nofu	toad fish (poisonous)
nonō	borrow

nonu	tree & fruit (Indian mulberry)
nonufi‘afi‘a	Malay apple
no‘o	hip, (pol.) seat, posterior
nota	note (music)
nou – fa‘anounou	frown
no‘u	bent (body)
no‘utua	stoop
fa‘ano‘uno‘u	have a stoop, stoop
Novema	November
nuanua	rainbow
nu‘anu‘a	shrub (flowers used to scent c'nut oil)
numera	number, be numbered, arithmetic, sum
numi	tangled, complex, mixed up, get into a muddle, tuck, pleat (sewing)
fa‘anunumi	crumple, crease
fenumia‘i	mixed up
fenumia‘iga	confusion, disorder
nunu$_1$	ceremony after birth of first child
nunu alofa	love feast (Meth.)
nunu$_2$	surge (people)
nunu$_3$	washing (in starch making)
nusipepa	newspaper
nuti	broken in sm. pieces, smash, crush (also broken of heart)
nu‘u	village, home
fa‘anu‘upō	uncivilized, heathen, indecent
nu‘utūloto	islet

Oo

o$_1$	of
o$_2$	used w. certain pl. pronouns for "o" nouns
‘o$_1$	used to begin certain statements *‘O Samoa*, *‘O a‘u* etc.
‘o$_2$	an alternative to *‘ua* (verb particle) while, as
ō	pl. of *alu* and *sau*
feōa‘i	go about
‘ō$_1$	yes (in answer to call by name)
‘ō$_2$	there, over there, (A.S.) *i ga‘ō*
‘ō$_3$	zero, nought
oa	gunwale of boat
o‘a	to husk a c'nut
o‘aga	c'nut husks
o‘ao‘a	a stake
‘oa$_1$	lather, suds, soapy, frothy
‘oa$_2$	valuable goods, possessions, rich, fertile (land)
‘oa‘oa	rejoice inwardly
‘o‘a	tree (gives brown dye for siapo)
‘oase	oasis
‘oe$_1$	acknowledges a call, roll call
‘oe$_2$	you (singular)
‘o‘e	(pol.) knife
ōfaga$_1$	nest
ofaofata‘i	gather under wings (bird)
ōfaga$_2$	taro-tops for planting
‘ofe	bamboo, fishing-rod, (pol.) knife
o fea	where?
ofi	go through (a space), be room, to mate (animals)
fa‘aofi	insert, make s.th. go through
fa‘aofiofi	make one's way through a crowd
‘ōfisa	officer, clerk, official, office
fa‘a‘ōfisa	clerical work

ofo$_1$ be astonished, surprised, wonder at, astonishment, surprise
ofoofogia marvellous, wonderful
fa‘aofo surprise, amaze
ofo$_2$ offer
ofotū offer (spontaneously)
ofoa‘i ring out, lead (a song etc.)
ofoa‘iga start of a song
ofoalofa greeting
feofoa‘i greet one another
‘ofu$_1$ bundle of food (in leaves)
‘ofu$_2$ (pl.) *‘o‘ofu* garment, dress, clothes, to wear, be dressed
‘ofu‘ofu wrap food in leaves
‘ofutalitimu rain coat
‘ofuloto underwear, petticoat
‘ofutele overcoat
‘ofutino shirt
‘ofuvae trousers, shorts, slacks
‘ogā (prefix) indicates “main part”
‘ogā‘ele‘ele area of land
‘ogāfa‘i banana stem
‘ogāgase tender (meat), muscle
‘ogālā‘au trunk (tree), log
‘ogālima upper arm
‘agāmanava abdomen
‘ogāsami stretch of sea
‘ogātino trunk (body)
‘ogātotonu centre, middle
‘ogāumu oven, stove, cylinder (car engine)
‘ogāvae thigh
ōgatasi be in keeping with
oge famine, food shortage
fa‘aoge be starved
ogo serious, severe (injuries)
ogotia overcome w. heat, hunger etc.
ogoogo$_1$ poisonous, venomous, severe, harsh
ogoogo$_2$ a rattle
ōi groan, moan
‘oi exclamation of surprise
‘oi auē! expresses grief (also *‘oi ‘oi*)
‘ō‘ī creak, grind (teeth)
ōia doomed, condemned (people)
‘o ia he, she, it
okaoka! exclamation of shock, surprise, disbelief
‘ōkeni organ (musical)
‘okesene oxygen
‘Oketopa October
ola$_1$ live, be alive, life, recover from, live by, live on, grow, increase, give birth, remit, cancel (debt, punishment), end (a war) (Note: *ola, olaga* – pol.≡ *soifua, soifuaga* – (i.e. live, life)
olaga life, existence
olataga salvation, deliverance
olaola thrive (plants, enterprises)
fa‘aola save life, light, set alight, start (engine), pay back, refund, Saviour
fa‘aolataga salvation
olafanua (pol.) adze, axe, knife
olalelei work, function well
olamālosi thrive, do well
olamoamoā wretched, miserable
ola$_2$ basket (fish, clothes etc.)
‘ola$_1$**, ‘ola‘ola!** expression of surprise
‘ola$_2$**, ‘ola‘olā** soiled, smeared (plates)
ole beg, request
olega request
fa‘aoleole cajole, soothe (child)
‘ole$_1$ over there
‘ole$_2$ deceive, hoax
‘olegia deceived
fa‘a‘ole‘ole cheat
‘o le‘ā (verb particle) indicates future tense shall, will, about to, etc.
oli, olioli eager
‘oli‘oli rejoice, be glad, joy, gladness
‘oli‘olisaga (pol.) chief’s grave

'oli'olī	large fern
'ōlive	olive tree
olo$_1$	rub, grate, grind, carpenter's plane
oloia	worn down
olopala	crush, reduce to dust
olo$_2$	to coo (pl. *feolo*)
'olo$_1$	fort, shelter, tower, castle, wicket, stumps (cricket)
'olo$_2$	ready to leave (journey)
'oloa	goods, stock, supplies, riches, fortune, wealth, a business, (pol.) teeth, gift of fine mats (wedding)
fa'a'oloa	collect money
fa'a'oloaga	salary, stipend
'oloā	disease w. infection
'olo'o	(verb particle) indicates present continuous tense
'olomatua	(pl. *'olomātutua*) old woman
'olu 'olū	flabby
'oloto	soprano
oma	strap to control pig, dog
ōmea	clay, earthenware, china-ware
Omeka	Omega (Bible)
'omo	(pl. *'o'omo*) to have holes, dents, dent, hole, pot-hole, dip, depression
'omo'omo	pitted w. holes
mā'omo'omo	battered about
ona$_1$	to (when used w. verb e.g. *'ua mafai ona pese* – able to sing)
ona$_2$	so, then (when used with *"lea"*)
ona pau lea	that is all
ona$_3$	his, her, its (plural) used with "o" nouns
'ona$_1$	because, on account of
'ona$_2$	poisonous, septic, infected
'o'ona	sour, bitter, acid, strong (alcohol), (fig.) bitter (words), bitterness
fa'a'ona	poison
'ona$_3$	lower abdomen
'ona$_4$	plentiful (fish, game), eat sufficiently (also *mā'ona*)
'ōnā	drunk, intoxicated, poisoned
'ōnaga	drunkenness, poisoning
fa'a'ōnā	made drunk
onapō	times, days
onapō nei	present time, contemporary
onapō nā	in those days
fa'aneionapō	contemporary, modern, up-to-date
oneone	sand
oneonea	sandy
one	gunpowder
ono$_1$	six
onoono$_2$	peep through, round
ono$_3$	be fitting, suitable, fit for, proper
onomea	becoming, graceful, skilled
onopapa'i	be graceful
'onosa'i	patient, patience
o'o$_1$	reach, arrive, extend as far as, take place, happen
o'o mai	come to pass, arrival
o'otia	be moved, touched (feeling)
o'otaga	gift after a death etc.
o'oo'o	presumptuous, excellence, v. high (tide)
fa'ao'o	convey, pass on, carry out
fa'ao'olima	assault
fa'ao'osala	carry out a sentence, execute
o'o$_2$	germinating c'nut
'ō'ō$_1$	hollow, hollow sound, empty, loose
fa'a'ō'ō	loosely
'ō'ō$_2$	central portion of pig
'o'omi	(pl.*fetaomi*) squash, crush, press in, squeeze
'omia	crushed
ta'omi	squeeze, crush (tightly)

'ōmiga	pressure
'o'ono	bear down, strain, make a great effort, suppress (grievance etc.), make a wry face, grimace, push, work under strain
'onosi	tolerate, put up with
'o'osi	scratch (w. fingers)
'ōsia	scratched
'o'osiga	scratching
'osi'osiga	scribble
mā'osi	torn, ripped
opeopea	(pl. *ōpea*) float
ōpea	travel by sea
opo$_1$	hold, clasp (w. both hands)
opoopo	hug, embrace
opoopoga	load carried in arms
māopoopo	well wrapped, firm, compact, solid
fa'amāopoopo	take care of, organise
fa'aopoopo	add
fa'aopoopoga	addition, extension
opo$_2$	fully planted
oponi	support, strengthen
'oreva	vulture, raven
osaosa	be partly filled
osi	make an agreement, covenant, pay a forfeit, offer a sacrifice
osia	pledged
ositaulaga	priest
osilagi	wake (vigil)
osiosi	(pol.) dance
oso$_1$	jump, hop, dash, rush, break into, raid, destroy
so'ona oso	rash, thoughtless
osooso	jump up and down
fa'aoso	egg on, incite, excite
fa'aosofia	excite, arouse
fa'aosooso	tempt
fa'aosoosoga	temptation
osopuna	jump over
osotatau	know what to do
osovale	wander off the subject
oso$_2$	traveller's gift to hosts etc., provisions for a journey
tāoso	prepare food for journey, be mentally prepared
oso$_3$	rise (sun)
'oso$_1$	dig, digging stick, planting stick
'oso$_2$	jut out, project
ota$_1$	my
ota$_2$	pickled raw fish
otā	(pl. *ōtatā*) ripe (bananas)
fa'aotā	ripen artificially
ōtai	food (c'nut & molasses)
otaota	rubbish, refuse, (pol.) excrement
'ote	scold (pl. *fe'ōte 'otei)*
'otegia	scolded
'ote'ote	always scolding
oti	(pl. *feoti*) die (people), knocked out (boxing)
otifaō	die face downwards
fa'aoti	completely
otilāina	starve
otiola	be v. lazy
'oti$_1$	cut (pl. *'o'oti*), cut w. scissors etc.
'otiga	hair-cut
'oti'oti	trim
'oti$_2$	goat
'oto	pluck, pick (leaves), select (a subject etc.)
oto ma le sau	(pol.) for *lu'au*
'oto'oto	outline, summary
fa'a'oto'oto	summarize, briefly
ou$_1$	your, yours (second pers. sing.)
ou$_2$	to bark
ōu	(interjection) shame! oh!
o'u	mine
'ou	I (first pers. sing.)
'o'u, o'u'o'u	bulge
'oulua	you (second pers. dual)
'outou	you (second pers. pl.)
'ova	go over (fig.) v. good, excellent
ovasia	overseer, foreman
ovataimi	overtime

Pp

pa	(prefix) e.g. *patino* – personal
pā$_1$	burst, explode, break out (into song etc.)
fa‘apā	fire a gun, explode
pāpātoto	bloodshot, flow of blood
pā$_2$	fence, wall, food-tray
pāla‘au	wooden fence, hedge
pā$_3$	pearl-shell fishing lure
pā$_4$	barren, sterile (women)
pa‘a	crab (gen.)
pa‘a‘ā$_1$	dry, withered (grass etc.)
pa‘a‘ā$_2$	coarse, rude, rough
pā‘aga	friend, partner, partnership
pa‘agugu	crunch (also *pa gugu*)
pā‘auli	dark red-maroon
pa‘ave	braces (trousers)
pae	scatter, strew, spread out
paepae$_1$	scattered about
paepae$_2$	raised stone platform, pavement
pa‘e	bleach
pa‘epa‘e	(pl. *papa‘e*) white, pale, light-coloured
pa‘epa‘emā	snow-white
pa‘e‘e	thin, lean, scraggy (pl. *pā‘e‘e‘e*)
paega	formal food presentation
pa‘ela	fumble, fail (in an attempt . . .)
paelo	barrel, keg
pafuga	cheep, chirp (bird)
pagā	alas!
pagātia	afflict, trouble
pāga	ground used for a game, partner (dance etc.) opponent (e.g. boxing), boxing match
pāgalēmū	be safe
pāgamālie	satisfied, content, suit well
pāganoa	empty, silent, free, unoccupied, silence, chance
pago, papago	mean, stingy
pagoa	chance, opportunity
pāgotā	prisoner
fa‘apāgotā	put under arrest
pai	pie, pasty
pa‘i	touch
pa‘ia	be touched
pa‘ivalea	hurt accidentally
pa‘ia	holy, sacred
fa‘apa‘ia	bless, sanctify, dedicate
paiē	lazy
fa‘apaiē	sloth, sluggishness
pailate	pilot, pilot boat
paina	pint
paipa	pipe, valve, tube, tap, shower, tobacco pipe
pakete	bucket, pail
pala$_1$	rotten, decay, perish, swamp
palapala	earth, soil, dirt, mud, (pol.) blood
palapalā	muddy, dirty
fa‘apalā	leave s.th to rot, ferment
pala$_2$	children's disease – thrush
palā	rusty
pāla‘ai	(pl. *pāla‘a‘ai*) reluctant, cowardly, coward
palagatete	shaky, unstable
palagā‘ie	old clothing, material
palakarafa	paragraph
palalau	in abeyance
fa‘apalalau	place in abeyance
pālalū	flap (wings etc.)
palana‘i	pile up, beach a boat
palaniketi	blanket
palagā‘ofu	old dress
palapalaū	foot disease
palasi	fall, collapse
fa‘apalasi	plunge into, let fall, drop

palauvale (pl. *pālalauvale*) swear, curse, bad language

pale$_1$ garland, wreathed, be crowned

fa'apale to crown

paleali'i crown

pale$_2$ (pol.) rowing, paddling

palepale hold firmly, prop up, support (pol.) reply to a speech

palemene parliament

fa'apalemene parliamentary

pālemia premier, prime-minister

pāleni balance (money)

pālepō (pol.) arrive at night

palo$_1$ defeated

palopalo defeated often

palo$_2$ puzzle, riddle

palolo seafood delicacy (sea annelid)

pālota election, ballot, vote

palu mix, dilute, dissolve, grope for

paluni balloon

pālusami food (taro leaves, c'nut cream, salt water) (pol. for *lu'au*)

palutu hit

pālutu women's dance

pama palm tree

pānapa thrifty

pani$_1$ pan, pot

pani$_2$ bun

pani$_3$ hit, punch

panikeke pancake

papanu paint thickly, daub

panupanu daubed, smeared

pao interrupt, stop

pa'ō (pl. *pa'o'ō*) clash, clang, excessive noise, noise, beat (music)

pa'o'ō rattle, clatter

paoa power (electric), influence

paogo pandanus tree

paolo$_1$ relatives by marriage

paolo$_2$ shade, shady

fa'apaolo shade, protect, preserve

fa'apaologa porch

pā'ō'ō gills (fish)

paopao sm. outrigger canoe

pa'ōtonu direct hit

papa$_1$ board, plank, rock, make level, flatten

papā be rocky

papatū solid rock

papātua back of man, horse etc.

papāvao edge of forest

papa$_2$ dad, daddy (child's word)

papa$_3$ coarse floor mat

papa$_4$ brassiere

papā (pol.) sterile (women)

pāpa barber, hairdresser

pāpā high titles

papaga hole

papa'i reach

pā'ia reaches, goes up to

papala sore, ulcer, covered w. sores

papālagi white man, European

fa'apapālagi like a European, European custom & language

pāpatiso baptize

papatisoga baptism

papa'u shallow

pa'ulia be aground (boat)

papitema baptize (R.C.)

parakarafa paragraph

Parataiso Paradise

Paratiso Paradise (R.C.)

pasā bazaar

Pasefika Pacific ocean

Pāseka Passover (Bible)

Pasekate Easter (R.C.)

pasene percent

pāsese passengers, fare

pasi$_1$ pass by, pass (exam, law)

pasi$_2$ bus

pāsi be tired of s.th.

pāsika bicycle (also *uila*)

pasiketi-polo basketball

pāsio passion fruit

pata$_1$ butter

pata$_2$ be marked (blow,sting)

pata$_3$ – **papata** rough (mats, cloth)

pata$_4$ – **patapata** a rash, grow up well (children)

patatō bang (door etc.)
pātatō whole, food swallowed whole
patatū heavy, hollow sound
pate$_1$ bat (cricket), racket
pate$_2$ colourful plant-coleus
pate$_3$ harlot
pate$_4$ putty
pātē$_1$ sm. wooden gong
pātē$_2$ spathe of c'nut
pātele priest (R.C.)
pateta potato
pateto make lot of noise
pati$_1$ rush
pati$_2$ party (political)
pati$_3$ (pl. *pati*) clap
tapati clap together
patipati clapping
patiapatā hustle & bustle, noise of a dispute
patino personal, private
pato domestic duck
patō have swellings on glands
pato'i deep black, jet black
patu swelling, lump, tumour
patua swollen
patupatu bulge, protrude, lumpy
tipolo patupatu lemon
pau$_1$ end, stop, be limited to, be all, all over
fa'apau terminate
pau lava that's all, can't be helped
pau$_2$ **- tusa pau** exactly the same
paū stern, frightening, weird
pa'u skin, hide, leather, belt, tyre, rubber fore-skin, bark (tree)
pa'upa'u scab
pa'upa'ua mucus-like, gummy, (of eyes etc.)
fa'apa'u toast
pa'ū$_1$ (pl. *pā'u'u*) fall, drop (price), fail, fall on, devolve on (a duty), sale
fa'apa'ū reduce prices, cut down (a tree), throw o.s. down
pa'ū$_2$ (sing. & pl.) arrive (guests)
pa'ua'i to be used to
pāui (pol.) announce publicly
pa'ulua out of tune
pa'umātū dry land
pa'umutu promiscuous
pauna pound (weight)
pauni pound (money)
pā'upa'u to be few
pa'usisi place or spot (in a house)
pauta powder
pavao be in the forest
pē$_1$ indicates a question, *pēfia* – how many?
pē$_2$ (pl. *pepē*) die, be dead (animals), go out (fire, tide) be low tide, stop (engine), numb, paralysed (limb)
tapē kill, turn off engine, put out (light) also *fa'apē*
pē$_3$ approximately, about, probably
pea$_1$ follows verb to indicate continuity e.g. *fai pea* – keep on doing . . .
pea$_2$ pair (sheets etc.), suit (clothes), woman's two-piece costume (also *puletasi*)
pea$_3$ bear (also *urosa*), animal
pea$_4$ pear (fruit)
pe'a$_1$ flying-fox
pepe'a smell offensively, stink
pe'a$_2$ tattoo
pe'ā when, if (of future)
pe'āfai if
pe'ape'a propeller, ceiling fan
peau wave, billows
peaua agitated (sea)
pe'epe'e c'nut cream
pēfea trouble, accident
pefu dust
pefua dusty
pefupefua v. dusty
pei$_1$, **pē'ī** be like, look like, be as if

peisea'ī	look like, look as though
pei$_2$, tapei	crack (nuts)
peita'i	but, yet
peita'i ane	but, however, on the contrary
'ae peita'i	and yet, nevertheless
pēlā	as if, as though
fa'apēlā	like that
pele$_1$	darling, favourite, beloved, dear
fa'apele	make a pet of s.o.
pēlega	gift from parents to daughter, dowry
pele o tama	gift on behalf of a child
pelepelega	grief for loved one
fa'apelepele	be very dear
pele$_2$	edible shrub (leaves like spinach)
pelē	play cards, play (other games)
pelega	card game
pelesitene	president (also *peresitene*)
peleue	coat, jacket
pelogia	deceived
pelu	bush knife, sword (also *sapelu*)
pēmita	permit
pena$_1$	cut up (animals)
tapena	pack up
penaga	cutting up
pena$_2$	(pol.) to bathe
pēnā	like that
po'opēnā	v. probably
fa'apenā	be like that
penapena	(pol.) to wash
pene	penny
pēnei	like this
po'o pēnei	v. likely
fa'apēnei	be like this, similar to this
Penetekoso	Pentecost, Whit – Sunday *Penekosite* (R.C.)
peni	pen
peniutu	fountain pen
penina	pearl
penisilini	penicillin
penisina	chalk
penisini	petrol, benzine
penisiō	banjo
penitala	pencil
penu$_1$	grated c'nut
penu$_2$	frayed, tattered (garments & materials)
pepenu	stringy (dried fruit)
pepa$_1$	paper, bank-note, ticket, label, playing-card, licence, receipt, document
pepa malō	card, cardboard
pepa$_2$	pepper
pepe$_1$	butterfly
pepepepe	flutter
fa'apepepepe	hover
pepe$_2$	parts of a S. house where orators sit
pepe$_3$	baby, doll
pepelo	lie, be false
pelogia	deceived
peritome	(pol.) circumcise (Bible)
peritomeina	circumcised
perofeta	prophet
pese	(pl. *pepese*) sing, song, hymn
pesega	singing
pesepese	sing along
pesi	base (baseball)
pesipolo	baseball
pēsi	rage (as a storm), strike with violence (as an epidemic)
pēsia	caught in epidemic
pēsini	bowl, basin
peti$_1$	(pl. *pepeti*) fat (animals)
fa'apeti	fatten
peti$_2$	strike (with thrown knife)
peti$_3$	bet
peti$_4$	spades (cards)
peva	sea cucumber
pī$_1$	letter "P", alphabet
pī$_2$	wasp, hornet
pī$_3$	pea, bean
pī$_4$	make water (children)
pia$_1$	
piapia	foam, froth
piapiā	full of foam
piasua	food made w. arrowroot

pia$_2$ beer
piano piano, organ (musical)
pi‘i$_1$ wrestle (wrist wrestling)
pī‘iga wrestling match
pi‘i$_2$**, pipi‘i**$_1$ (pl. *fepi‘iti*) stick to, adhere to
mea pipii paste, adhesive
pipii$_2$ cling to, hold on, keep close to, be moored (boat)
pi‘itaga s.th. to cling to
pi‘ipi‘i stick to, sticky, tacky, curly (hair)
fa‘apipi‘i stick w. paste etc.
pī‘i lima fold one's hands
pī‘i tuli sit w. knees together
pi‘i$_3$ (pl. *tapi‘i*) raise (S. house blinds), shut tight (eyes)
pikopo bishop (also *epikopo*)
piki pick (tool), to pick
pili$_1$ be stuck fast
pili$_2$ lizard
pili$_3$ bill, account
piliati billiards, pool (game)
piliki brick
pilitati pilchards (fish)
pīnati peanut
pine$_1$ pin, hairpin, safety-pin, rowlock, badge, mark, symbol, peg
pipine secure w. pegs, mark out w. pegs
fa‘apine pin
pine$_2$ (used with *lē*)
le pine w.o. delay, soon
pīniki be pink, pink
pi‘o$_1$ (pl. *pipi‘o*) be bent, crooked, crafty, shifty
fa‘api‘opi‘o (walk) w. a limp, craftily, crookedly
fepi‘opi‘oa‘i zig-zag
pi‘o – pi‘oi slow-moving, tardy
pipi a shellfish
pīpī turkey
pipili lame, crippled
fa‘apipili lame, cripple
pisa make a noise, noisy
tapisa make a sound of revelry etc.
pisapisaō make a lot of noise
pisi$_1$ splash
pisia$_1$ be splashed, be infected, contaminated
pīsia$_2$ stained, splashed
pisipisi to lap
pipisi gush, spout, spray, spurt, squirt, be contagious, infectious
pisi$_2$ busy
pisinisi business
fa‘apisinisi business-like
pisupo corned beef
pito be next, come next, edge, border, extremity, point
fa‘apito put on one side, special, biased in favour of, be selfish, deal mainly with
piu (used with *leai)* no, none at all *e leai piu se isi* no one at all
po indicates a question "*po‘ua ‘uma?*" – is it finished?
pō$_1$ night, be dark, (pol.) blind
fa‘apō ambush
fa‘alepō (pol.) dream
pō‘ele‘ele pitch dark
pōmalaē be in ignorance
pō nanei this evening
pōpōloloa invisible (moon)
pōula indecent night dance
pōuligia night arrival
pōuliuli be dark
nofo fa‘apōuliuli de facto couple
pō$_2$ slap, clap (cupped hands)
pōpō slap, beat, pat
pō$_3$**, popō** pounce
pō‘ia pounced
pō$_4$ chamber pot
pō$_5$**, fa‘apō** bow (in hair, dress etc.)
po‘a male (animals)
poapoā smell of fish
poe buoy
po‘e, popo‘e worried, anxious
po‘epo‘e hesitate, be anxious, nervousness

pogai due to, caused by, origin, cause, stem, stump (tree)
pogaiisu nostrils, bridge of nose
pogaimata inner corner of eye
pogapoga worm
pogati stem, stump (tree)
pogi blurred, dim
pogia overtaken by dark
popogi night fall
pogipogi twilight
pogisā be dark, darkness
poi$_1$ food (c'nut cream & bananas)
poi$_2$ (pl.*poi*) timid, reluctant, respectful
poi$_3$ cut, slice (flesh)
poka poker (card game)
pola leaf blinds
polapola c'nut leaf woven litter
polavai c'nut leaf floor mat
polata (pol.) firewood
pole, popole worried, anxious, afraid of, worry, anxiety
polepolevale worry w.o. cause
popolevale fret, fuss
fa'apopole create anxiety
pole pole (of earth)
pōlepole be hasty, rash
polesi porridge
poletito verandah
polili plant same area twice, throw a stone
polo$_1$ (pol.) knife, cut into pieces (fish)
polo$_2$ ball, ball-bearings
polo$_3$**, pologa** slave
nofo pologa live in slavery
fa'apologaina repress (desire etc.)
pōloa'i command, order
pōloa'iga commandment, order
poloka block, lump, portion, to block, obstruct
polokaka block & tackle
polokarama programme
polotiki politics
pona node, knot, swelling, fault, weakness
pōnā full of knots (e.g. timber) be at fault
ponatia trip, stumble, upset, hurt (feelings)
ponapona full of knots
popona protrude, bulge
fa'apona knot, tie a knot
ponăivi bone
ponāua Adam's apple
ponaponāvae ankle bone
pone$_1$ child's game (blind man's buff?)
pone$_2$ pony, a fish
po'o$_1$ – "*e pei o le po'o*" = "quick as a flash"
po'o$_2$ (joc.) head
po'o fea where? wonder where?
Pope (colq.) Roman Catholic
Lotu Pope R.C. Church
popi (joc.) dagger, puppy
popo ripe c'nut, be well established
popoga to be pre-occupied
popoteā full of termites
posi boss, manager
posikati post card
pōsini boatswain (bo'sun)
poto (pl. *popoto*) clever, smart, intelligent, skilled, expert, learned, wise, wisdom, wise man
fa'afiapoto conceited, presumptuous
pōtoi ball, lump (dough, paste etc.)
pōtopoto assemble, gather together
pōtopotoga assembly, gathering
fa'apōtopoto gather together, collect
fa'apōtopotoga assembly, society
potu room
potu moe bedroom (etc.)
potutipitipi operating theatre
pou house post, pillar
pou o le isu septum
tapou prop up w. posts
poupou renew posts
tū poupou stand like a post
poutū main post in S. house
po'u sore
po'upo'ua covered w. sores
pōuliuli be dark, unenlightened, heathen, ignorant, darkness

fa‘apōuliuli darken s.th., illegitimate
fa‘apōuliuligia darkened, unenlightened
poumuli tree – valuable hardwood in S.
povi cow, cattle
pū$_1$ be holed, perforated, hole, pit
pupū have holes, gaps, blow holes
pūpū riddled w. holes
pū$_2$ c’nut shell
pū$_3$ conch, shell-trumpet, bugle (band instrument)
pua tree(s) – frangipani, gardenia
pua‘a pig
saipua‘a pigsty
fa‘apua‘a vulgar
pua‘i vomit
fa‘apua‘i make s.o. vomit
puanea remote, distant
puao mist, fog
puaoa misty, foggy
puapuagā disaster, affliction
puapuagātia afflicted, distressed
pu‘e (pl.) *tapu‘e* catch, clutch, grasp, arrest, capture, take a photograph
pu‘e, pu‘eina caught, captured
pu‘ega capture
pupu‘e treat medically
pu‘eia suffer an attack of fever
puga$_1$ white coral
puga$_2$ groin
pupuga inflammation of groin
pui‘āiga a related family
puimanava belly, abdomen
puipui surround, fence off, protect, defend, shield, prevent, put in brackets, register a letter, curtain, railing, fence
puipuiga protection, prevention
puke interjection to startle s.o.
fa‘apuke startle
pula$_1$ ripe
pula$_2$**, pupula** (pl. *fepulafi*), bright, luminous; look, stare, be able to see, have sight
pulapula look
fa‘apupula make shine, give sight to, explain clearly
pulapō luminous, phosphorescent
pūlato‘a gaze, stare
pula‘a wild taro
pula‘ū untattooed
pule$_1$ authority, power, right to decide, decision, ruling, director, principal manager etc. authorize, govern, control, direct, administer
pulega authority, power, government
pule‘aga area of responsibility
puleaoao supreme authority
pulenu‘u local government official, mayor
puletua party opposed to government
pule$_2$ title of six special villages in Savaii “*pule ma tumua* . . . ” See National Anthem W.S.
pule$_3$ shells, cowries etc.
pulepule plot
pūlepule spotted
puligi pudding
pūlou hat, headgear, cover (oven)
pūlou taumata cap
fa‘apulou to cover s.th.
pulu$_1$ b‘fruit gum, chewing-gum, rubber
puluti plug a leak
pulutia plugged
pulu$_2$ c’nut husk & fibre
pulu$_3$ bullet, pellet, bomb, lead
pulu$_4$**, pupulu** interpose, mediate, intercede, intercession
puluvāga mediator, advocate
pulupulu wrap round

pūlupulu wrap, shawl
pululima take care of
pulumu broom, brush
pulunaunau urge, ask earnestly
pulu'ō'ō bomb
pulupulusia (pol.) illness of h. chief
puna jump, leap, well-up, spring up (water), boil, a spring, gland
mapuna raise (dust etc.)
punapuna boil, bubble gently, jumping about
fa'apuna boil
punāfāua salivary glands
punāafu sweat glands
punatoto (pol.) excessive menstrual flow
punāvai spring (water)
pūnefu dust
pūnefua dusty
puni$_1$ blocked, clogged
pupuni block, bar, close, screen off, hide, curtain screen
pūnitia blocked
māpuni slam, close suddenly
tāpuni shut
puni$_2$ surround (also *punipuni*)
punimatagi wind-break, wind-bound
pūnitā interpose (to stop fight)
punou (pl. *pūnonou*) bow head, nod, bend
pupū be devoted to s.o.
pūpū rinse (mouth)
pupuvao tall grass, weeds
pusa$_1$ send out smoke, steam etc.
fa'apusa build up a fire
pusaloa comet
pusa$_2$ oven
pusa$_3$ box
pusa'aisa ice-box, refrigerator
pusa'apa tin trunk, carton of fish
pusatoso drawer
pusatū cupboard, wardrobe
pusi$_1$ eel
pusi$_2$ cat
puta$_1$ (pl. *puputa*) fat
fa'aputa fatten
putagaele be v. fat
puta$_2$ stomach
pute navel
puti, putiputi collect, gather up, hold on to
putu rows (lines), over-crowded
putuputu thickness
fa'aputu pile up, heap up, save up
fa'aputuga heap, fund
fa'aputuputu collect, gather, bunch together
pu'upu'u (pl. *pupu'u*) be short
fa'apu'upu'u cut short, shorten, abbreviate
fa'apu'upu'uga abbreviation
fa'apupu'u short, doubled up (body)
pu'u swallow (whole)

Rr

rane frog
rosa rose
rula ruler (also *vase*)

Ss

sa indef. pronoun - a
sā$_1$ (verb particle) indicates past tense
sā$_2$ set apart, sacred, forbidden, taboo, out of bounds
fa'asā forbid, make taboo, become a church member
fa'asāina prohibited
sā$_3$ (pol.) canoe, boat, vessel
sā$_4$ indicates extended kinship e.g. *'o le sā Malietoā* - the extended family of Malietoa
sā$_5$ your own (second person)
sa'a$_1$ be short-legged, dwarf
sa'a$_2$ hit out (w. leg, foot)
sa'alutu jolt
sa'alu'u shake about
sa'a$_3$ be emptied (container)
masa'a spilt
fa'amasa'a be shed
sasa'a (pl. *sa'ati*) pour out, empty
sasa'aina (pl. *sa'atia*) poured
sa'asa'a pour out (a little), spill
sa'a$_4$ haul in (line), (also *fufuti*)
sa'ā (pol.) adversity (fig.)
sā'afa mallet (to beat c'nut husks)
sā'afi (pl. *sā'afi*) to miss s.o. who is dead or absent
sā'afiga regret, long for s.o.
sā'afi'afi, sā'afi'afiga words spoken when deeply moved
sa'asa'a$_1$ (pol.) dance
sa'asa'a$_2$ be brief, short
sae$_1$ tear off (skin), to skin
māsae torn
māsaesae in rags
sasae tear, rip up
saesae tearing
sae$_2$ throw, hit, kick to start a game
sae$_3$ continue, press on
saesae furiously, with a roar (e.g. fire)
sa'e (pl. *sa'ei*) overturn (boat)
sasa'e cause to capsize, spread oven stones for cooking
māsa'esa'e apt to capsize
sa'esa'e$_1$ carry s.th by its ends (two people)
sa'esa'e$_2$ large reef crab
saele stride along w. arms swinging
sa'eu (pl. *sā'eu*) stir, scratch for food (chickens)
safue whip, beat
saga$_1$ face towards, attend to
fa'asagasaga continue facing . . .
fa'asagatau opposed to, rebel against
fesāga'i sit face to face
sagatonu lie evenly
fa'asagatonu set straight
fa'asagasagatonu keep o's balance
saga$_2$ flipper (turtle)
saga$_3$ dowry
sāga prefix, indicates "to go on", continue, persist in *sāgafiafia* - continue to be happy
sāgai (pol.) give one's attention to s.th.
sagole rummage, ransack
sai$_1$ sm. pig-sty
sai$_2$ twist of tobacco
sai$_3$ (pl. *sai*) bind, bandage
sāisai tie up, put shackles on
sāisaia, sāisaitia be bound
sāisaiga arrest
sai$_4$ ace (cards)
saienisi science
fa'asaienisi scientific
saienitisi scientist

sā'ili look for, search, seek
sā'ilia sought
sā'iliga search
sā'ili'ili seeking
sā'ili'iliga investigation
sā'ili matagi convalescence
sailini siren
saini sign
sainiga signing
sainigālima signature
saito wheat (Bible)
saka to boil
sakalameta sacrament
sakete skirt
sala$_1$ (verb particle) used before verb; - rather
sala$_2$ make a mistake, slip of tongue, at variance with, offence, fault
sala$_3$ be punished, fined, punishment, fine
fa'asala punish, fine, condemn, sentence
fa'asalaga punishment, sentence
fa'asalaga oti capital punishment
sala$_4$ cut (hedge etc.)
sasala trim
salasala slice surface
salafa wide, extensive
sālafalafa flat
fa'asalafa extend, expand
salaki salad (also *salati*)
salalau circulate, spread (stories etc.)
fa'asalalau scatter, broadcast, spread widely
uālesi fa'asalalau broadcasting
fa'asalalauga broadcast
Salamo Book of Psalms
salamō repent
salani surface, line surface of s.th.
salatua be doubtful, uncertain
sali$_1$ scoop up, give an undercut, skim
salisali scoop out (c'nut flesh)
sasali skim w. fingers etc. (cream, fat)
sali$_2$ adze for hollowing canoes (also *to'ū*)
sālo wipe w. fingers (e.g. forehead, plate)
sālosālo lick
salu sweep, rake, cut away, broom
saluina swept
salusalu sweep, cut into shape
sasalu drag one's feet, do s.th. slowly & deliberately
sama a medication. i.e. turmeric powder (*lega*) mixed w. oil
samasama yellow
sasama wan, yellow
sāmala hammer
sāmani salmon, summons
samanoa idle
samasamanoa empty-handed
sami sea
samilolo food (c'nut & salt water)
Sāmoa Samoa
Fa'asāmoa Samoan way - custom, tradition, culture
sana$_1$ his, her (indef.)
sana$_2$**, sanatoto** dysentery
sana$_3$ corn
sanasana Job's tears, necklace seeds
sanisani rejoice
sasani boast, flaunt
sanuisi sandwiches
sao$_1$ (pl. *sasao*) collect
saofia collected
saofaga collection of valuables
saogātupe collection of money
saofa'i (pol.) be assembled, sit up & talk, ceremony for installation of matai.
saofa'iga (pol.) gathering, assembly
sao$_2$ be saved, save oneself, be safe from
fa'asao save, preserve
fa'asaoina saved, salvation, preservation
fa'asaosao save up
sāogālēmū be safe, escape
sao$_3$ gain access to, get through
sāofia be through safely

saogatā be reached w. difficulty

sao$_4$ cleared, acquitted

sao$_5$ row (seats etc.)

sasao burst into flame, burn fiercely, erupt (volcano), rage (temper), spread (rash), blaze

saovale be wasted (heat)

sa‘o$_1$ right, correct, straight

sā‘o sit up straight

fa‘asa‘o correct, straighten (pl. *fa‘asasa‘o*)

fa‘asa‘oina straightened

fa‘asasa‘o tall, erect, stately

fa‘asa‘osa‘o (pol.) lie down

sa‘o$_2$ (pol.) senior title holder

sa‘oao (pol.) for *aualuma, taupou* and *aumāga*

sa‘otama‘ita‘i (pol.) village maiden

sāō thank you "*sāō fa‘alālelei*" "it is v. beautiful" (fine mat)

fa‘asāō (pol.) give thanks

saofa‘i sit still, sit up (pl. *saofafa‘i*)

sa‘olele have complete authority

sa‘oloto free, self-willed

sa‘olotoga freedom

fa‘asa‘oloto set free

fa‘asa‘olotoina freed

sao‘o rough, uneven

saosaoa be fast, quick, quickly, speed, rate of speed

fa‘asaosaoa speed up

sapai carry (w. arms under the object carried)

sapasapai carry, cradle

Sāpati Sabbath

sapatū fish (barracuda)

sapelu bush knife, (A.S.) *pelu*

sapini whip

sapo catch (ball etc.)

sapoga catch

saputu throb, pulsate, come in rapid succession

saputuvale pant

sasa$_1$ beat, thrash, slash, rod, cane, whip

sasa$_2$ saucer

sāsā$_1$ token, mark of recognition, sign, omen

sāsā$_2$ dance

sasa‘e$_1$ east, (A.S.) *gaga‘e*

sasa‘e$_2$ pole for spreading oven stones

sasala trim, cut (also used of scent, smell)

sasalapa tree – soursop

sasamu forage for food (dogs)

sasau$_1$ desire for sexual intercourse

sasau$_2$ (pl. *sausau*) cast (a line), lash out, flap, swing, a blow

sāusāu cast from side to side (rod)

sasi slip (tongue)

fa‘asāsisasi mispronounce

sata my (indef.)

sātauro cross

fa‘asātauro crucify

sati, sātia attacked (by pests)

sātini$_1$ sergeant

sātini$_2$ sardines

sau$_1$ your (indef.) second pers. sing.

sau$_2$ (pl. *ō*) come

masau range (of a gun etc.)

sau$_3$ fall in fine drops (dew etc.), dew

sautia damped, wetted

sausau sprinkle, dampen, be flecked, speckled, perfume, scent

sausauina dampened

sau$_4$**, sāua** be brushed, touched by, overshadowed, caught by fire

sa‘u my (indef. prn.)

saua umbrella fern

sa‘ua stop! hush!

sāuā cruel, cruelty

sāuāga act of cruelty

fa‘asāuā cruel

fa‘asāuāga persecution

sa‘ai ogre

sauali‘i (pol.) ghost, spirit

sauaso one day, later on

sau‘ātoa be in one piece, seamless

sauauli (pol.) pig-yard
sauga smell, odour (people & animals), smell of stale food
saugā give off a strong smell (people, animals)
sa'ulā sword-fish
sāuni (pl. *sāuniuni*) prepare, get ready
sāuniga church service, ceremony, arrangement
sāuniuniga arrangements
sāunoa$_1$ (pol.) speak (chief)
sāunoaga speech
sāunoa$_2$ be unkind, harsh
fa'asāunoa torment, torture
sāunoa$_3$ (pol.) play
sāusaunoa sing, dance
sausau deep (sea)
saute south
sautua (prefix) indicates number of times e.g. *sautuatolu* - threefold *sautualasi* - happen frequently
sava (pl. *sāvasava*) to soil
savali (pl. *sāvavali*) walk
tagata sāvavali pedestrians
sāvali messenger, ambassador
sāvaliga a walk, march
sāvalivali go for a stroll
fa'asavali make s.o. walk, exercise
fesāvalivalia'i walk around
save'u be in confusion
savili$_1$ breeze, fresh air
fa'asavili cool oneself, air, ventilate
savili$_2$ civilian
se (indef. article) a, an, one (pl. *ni*)
se isi any
so'o se tasi anyone
sē$_1$ (interj.) indicates impatience
sē$_2$ he who, one who
sē$_3$ stick insect
sē$_4$ lose one's way, go astray
sesē wrong, stray, fault, mistake
fa'asesē mislead, lead astray, distort (meaning)
fa'asesēina misled
fesēa'i go astray, lose the way
sē$_5$ (used with *a'e*) surpass, be outstanding
sē$_6$ sharp stomach pain (due to fear etc.)
sea$_1$ sea cucumber
sea$_2$ indef. form of "*lea*" - this
sea$_3$ chairman
seafā respond quickly
seanoa be present, available
ana lē seanoa had it not been for . . .
seāseā rare, seldom (happen etc.)
se'e slide, glide, slip, skid, wrench, dislocate
se'ese'e glide gently
se'ega gliding
māse'ese'e be slippery
fa'ase'e to make glide, ride the surf, deceive (by flattery), joke, a lean-to-extension of a house
sē'ea be straight (hair)
se'emū dragon-fly
se'eti sandy bank (river)
se'evae (pl. *se'evavae*) wear shoes, shoes, sandals
sefe a safe, be safe
sefulu ten
sefulua'i be tenth, a tithe (1/10th)
sega$_1$ bird
sega$_2$ glare
sesega glare, turn pale
segaia be dazzled
segasega with a glare
segavale turn pale
segi, sesegi wild, shy, to snatch
segia snatched, startled
sei flower worn in hair, friend
se'i$_1$ (verb part.) indicates wish, desire, request, let me, let us (w. first person) "*se'i o'u alu*" becomes *so'u alu* let me go

se‘i, se‘ia	until
se‘i iloa	I wonder, who knows?
se‘i$_2$	(pl. *tase‘i*) pull up, grab, snatch, jerk, draw a sword, draw a lottery
se‘ia	pulled up
se‘i$_3$	a square fishing net
seila	sailor
seilala	tree (flowers used to scent c'nut oil)
se‘iloga	it only needs, unless
sekone	second (time)
sela	out of breath, gasp, asthma
selā	indef. form of *lelā*
selau	one hundred
sele$_1$	catch w. rope & noose, tie up, tether (animal) snare for catching fish etc.
sele$_2$	cut one's hair, shave, slash
selesele	to harvest
seleselega	a harvest
seleulu	scissors
fa‘aselemutu	break off, interrupt
sēleni	shilling, money
selo	zero, very easy (to do)
selu	(pl. *seselu*) comb (also *seluselu*), a comb
sēmanū	almost, nearly, probably
seminā	seminar
semu	to snap (pig, dog, etc.)
sena	used to call older people
senā	indef. form of *lenā*
sene	cent
senei	indef. form of *lenei*
senetenari	centenary
seniturі	century
sepa	(pl. *sesepa*) squint
serafi	giraffe
Setema	September
setete	state
seti	to set, set (mats etc.)
setima	steamer, ship
setu	limp, hobble
seu$_1$ **taseu**	(pl. *seseu*), steer (boat, car) stir
seu$_2$	catch w. net (birds, fish etc.)
seua	caught
seuga	hunting
seuseu	"playing" a fishing line
seu$_3$	horn (animal)
se‘u$_1$	bird S. fantail
se‘u$_2$**, se‘use‘ua**	tousle (hair)
si	expresses affection *si toea‘ina* – dear old man
sia	this (a form of "*lea*")
si‘a	make fire by friction
si‘aga	implements for fire-making
siaki$_1$	cheque
siaki$_2$	jack, jack up
siama	germ
siamu	jam
siamupini	champion
siapo	bark cloth
si‘aula	(pol.) form of address to girl
si‘i$_1$**, tasi‘i**	(pl. *sisi‘i*), put up, raise, lift, move, promote, attack, wage war
si‘itia	removed
si‘itaga	lifting, promoting
masi‘i	move, move off
fesi‘ita‘i	moved around
si‘ilaulau	food presentation
si‘ilima	raise hands, surrender
si‘itā	raise a stick
si‘itaua	wage war
si‘ivaelua	gallop (horse)
si‘i$_2$	hold child in ones arms, on knee; sit on s.o's lap
sikā	cigar
sikareti	cigarette
sikauti	scout
sikolasipi	scholarship
sikoni	scone
sikuea	square
sikurū	screw
sila$_1$	steel
sila$_2$**, silasila**	(pol.) see, watch
sisila	look steadily
silafia	(pol.) know
sīlafaga	(pol.) view, sight
lāusilafia	(pol.) well known
fa‘asilasila	(pol.) make known, give notice

fa'asilasilaga (pol.) making known
fa'asisila look at s.th. hoping to be given it
fesilafa'i meet
fesilafa'iga reception, welcome
silailagi carbuncle, boil (above waist)
silailalo carbuncle, boil (below waist)
sili$_1$ be highest, top, great, principal, best, go beyond, stick out, protrude
"sili i lo" better than, preferable to, more than
"ua sili ona lelei" it is the best
silia more than
tupe silia profit (also *fa'asiliga*)
fesilia'i uneven
silimusa be in the lead
silisili main, principal, very great, supreme, almighty
silisili 'ese (God) Almighty
sili$_2$ (pl. *sili*) put s.th up
fa'asili place at the top, exalt, extol
siliga be too late for s.th., overdue, in vain, hopeless
sîliga pen-holder
silika silk
silipa slipper
simā cement, concrete
fa'asimā put in plaster
sina$_1$ a little, some
sina$_2$ (pl. *sisina*) be white, grey hair
sinā be white, grey
sinasina white
fa'asinasina whiten
sina$_3$ (pl. *sisina*) fall (like raindrops), drip
sinei form of *lenei* - this (denotes affection)
sini aim, target
si'o fenced, enclosed, surround, encircle, communion - rail, hand-rail
si'osi'o surround
si'oina, si'omia surrounded
sîoa dazzled, dumbfounded, in a trance
sioka$_1$ chalk
sioka$_2$ choke (car)
sioki jug
sipa slant, slope, at an angle, queer, eccentric (people)
fa'asipa tilt
sipai spy
sipaka spark, electric shock, spark-plug
sipi$_1$ jeep
sipi$_2$ zip-fastener (also *sipa*)
sipili methylated spirits, spirits
sipuligi spring (wire)
sipuni spoon
sipuni ti teaspoon
sipuni puligi desert spoon (also *sipuni fa'aleogalua*)
sisi$_1$ (pl. *tasisi*) raise, hoist, hang, turned up (lip), hanging
sisigāfu'a flag raising
sisi$_2$ sm. snails
sisi$_3$ hist s.o. w. a sibilant sound
sisi le moa chase the hen away
sisi$_4$ cheese
sisi$_5$ leak, escape
Sisifo West, (A.S.) *gagaifo*
sisipeni sixpence
sitepu steps, stairs
fa'asitepu terrace, tier, step
sîtiū stew
si'u, si'ui tip, extremity
si'usi'u tail (animal)
si'ufofoga (pol.) voice, accent, echo
si'ugutu corner of mouth
si'uleo accent, echo, murmur
si'umata corner of eye (also *pogaimata*)
fa'asi'usi'umata look out corner of eye
siva dance, dancing
so indef, "*so māua*" - one of ours
sō used with *'oe* - one of your own
soa friend, partner, in pairs

soagia	be paired, even, follow next after
fa'asoa	act as a go-between, act on behalf of
fesoasoani	help, assist, assistant, auxiliary, helper, assistance, R.C. Catechist
soāivi	ulna, fibula (bone)
soāmoemoe	leaf next to youngest leaf (plant)
soātau	armour bearer
soatau	large canoe
so'a	spike, transfix (w. spear etc.), hit, strike
soso'a	husk c'nuts, speak bluntly
soa'ai	steal food
sōesā	be annoying, (pol.) beard
sofa$_1$	(pl. *sosofa*) collapse
sofa$_2$	sofa, couch
sofesofe	food (yam & c'nut cream)
soga'imiti	youth recently tattoed
sogasoā	persevere, unyielding
sogi	(pl. *feasogi*) smell, scent, kiss
sosogi	sniff, smell
sogisogi	sniffing, smelling
sogo, sosogo	smell, stink (of urine)
soi	wild yam
sōia	do not!, don't!, stop!
soifua	(pol.) live, wish s.o. farewell
	(pol.) health
soifuaga	(pol.) life, living
soisoi	(pol.) laugh
sokalate	chocolate (also *sukalati)*
sola	(pl. *sosola*) run away, escape
sola'aga	escape
fa'asola	let out, release
fesolata'i	be on the run
sole	call to man or boy – son! boy! exclamation of astonishment – *'oi sole!*
soli	(pl. *fesoli*) tread on, trample on, violate, desecrate, break, transgress (law)
solia	trespassed
solisoli	tread on repeatedly
soliga	a massage (kneading by walking on muscles etc.)
solialofi	(pol.) cup-bearer
	(pol.) smouldering brand
solipaepae	(pol.) chicken
solipala	crush underfoot
soliali'i	(pol.) cup bearer
soli tōfaga	adultery w. chief's wife
solitulāfono	crime, law-breaker
solivalea	trespass
solo$_1$	(verb. suffix) around, all about
va'ai solo	look all around
solo$_2$	move forward, make progress, slide, slip, procession, parade, line, row, landslide, poem
sōloia	slipped, collapsed
sōloga	succession, dynasty
soloa'i	succeed to a title
solosolo	going along well
fa'asolo	make s.th. go along, continue, proceed, recite
fa'asologa	order, sequence, succession, continuation, drawing, sliding
fa'asolosolo	pass, proceed, pass from one to another, deal one by one
fa'asolofua	ignore, (pol.) excuse, forgive
fa'asolopito	successive, point by point
fesoloa'i	circulate
solo'ātoa	without a join

'ofu solo'ātoa	overalls
solo'iluma	slide forward, make progress, improve
solo'itua	slide back, regress, diminish
sololelei	be in good order, proceed normally, be at ease, comfortable
solomua	make first move, take the initiative
solomuli	reverse, move back, retreat
solo$_3$	wipe, dry (w. towel etc.), wipe out, cancel, towel, duster
sōloi	wipe
sōloia	cancelled, wiped out
solosolo	handkerchief
solota'ele	bath towel
solo$_4$	solo (music)
solofanua	horse
solofa	yield, give w collapse, subside
somo	gum (secreted by eyes)
somoa	gummy
sona	indef. form of "*lona*" – any of his, hers
soni$_1$**, sogi**	chop, cut up
soni$_2$	c'nut shell water vessel
so'o$_1$	any, anyone
so'o$_2$	often, frequently
so'o$_3$	join, splice, joint
so'oga	joint, articulation, splice
so'otaga	alliance, union
soso'o	(pl. *feso'ota'i*) be joined, connected, next to, adjoining, follow next
soso'oga	extension, annexe
so'oso'o	join up several things
fa'aso'o	join together
fa'asoso'o	extend, add to
feso'ota'iga	relationship, bond, communication, connexion
fa'afeso'ota'i	get in touch with
so'ofa'atasi	unite
so'ofa'atasiga	union
so'o$_4$	(pl. *soso'o*) take after s.o., resemble closely, follower, disciple, courtship
so'o$_5$	(pl. *soso'o*) completely covered
fa'aso'o	to cover
so'ona	(prefix) very, extremely, excessively, freely, indiscriminately
so'ona fai	exaggerate, overdo, rash, harsh, thoughtless
sope	lock or tuft (hair)
sopo	(pl. *sosopo*) go, travel across, go over, walk over, go right through, trespass, go too far, "overstep the mark"
sōpotofaga	(pol.) possess a sleeping woman
sōpo'aga	way across river
sōpoloa	omit, pass over
sōsaiete	society
sosi	sauce
sōsisi	sausage
soso$_1$	water, inedible (taro)
soso$_2$	crazy, demented
fa'asosososo	a fool
sōsō	draw near or back, move over
sosolo	spread, creep, crawl
fa'asosolo	cause to spread
sota$_1$	indef. form of "I"
sota$_2$	soda
sou$_1$	indef. form of "your" (second pers. sing)
sou$_2$	rough (sea)
sousou	rough, agitated
fesousoua'iina	tossed to & fro
so'u$_1$	indef. form of "my"
so'u$_2$	see "*se'i*"
sovalini	sovereign (coin)
sū	moist, watery (taro)
susū	wet, moisture
fa'asusū	water s.th.
sūsū	slightly wet, damp
fa'asūsū	sprinkle, dampen
sua$_1$	contain liquid, rise (tide), flow, be funny, amusing
ma'i sua	a boil

masua	brimful, abundant, blurt out a secret
masuasua	full to overflowing
masuagofie	easily spilt (secrets)
suasua	rising (tide)
fa'asua	make into soup, stew, soften a boil etc.
suāliu	bilge water
sualua	brackish
suamalie	sweet
suāpeau	rich stew (turtle)
suāsami	salt water
suāsusu	milk
suāu'u	oil
fa'asuāu'u	to oil
suāvai	fresh water, (pol.) contents of an oven, be liquid, watery, thin
mea 'ai suāvai	liquid foods
sua$_2$	(pol.) chief's daily meal, presentation of special food etc.
suata'i	includes green c'nut, siapo etc.
suataute	includes whole roast pig
sua$_3$	(pl. *tasua*) lever up, up root, dig up, root, thrust, butt, plough
suaga	rooting
suataga	thrust
suafa	(pol.) name
suati	up-root, dig up (suddenly)
suatia	dug up
su'e$_1$	(pl. *sū'e*) look for, try to find, search, explore
tasu'e	sit for (exam), compete (for prize)
su'eina	examined
su'ega	examination, search
su'esu'e	examine, investigate, study
su'esu'ega	investigation, inquiry
su'e$_2$**, susu'e**	(pl. *tasu'e, sueni*) open, uncover, lift up, raise (pol.) put food from oven in baskets
su'ena	lift
masu'e	be raised, curl over (sheets of paper etc.)
sufi	coax, wheedle
fa'asufi	question closely
suga	call to a girl
sui$_1$	(pl. *fesui, tasui*) change, replace, represent – act as representative of . . ., deputy, assistant, delegate, successor
suiga	change
fa'asui	instead, as a substitute
fesuia'i	exchange
fesuisuia'i	fluctuate, take turns, alternate
sui$_2$	add water to dilute . . .
suia	diluted
su'i	(pl. *susu'i*) thrust through, pierce, pin, sew, mend, darn, hem tack
su'i'ofu	tailor
su'iga	stitch
su'isu'i	be sewn, stitched
nila su'i su'i	sewing needle
su'isu'iga	sewing
suilapalapa	hip, thigh
suka	sugar
fa'asuka	sugar, sweeten
sula	speak sincerely, give thanks for gifts, speech etc.
sūlā	acknowledge
suli	heir
sulu$_1$	put on, wrap around o.s. (garments)
sulu$_2$	(pl. *tasulu*) put in, insert, wear, tuck in, slide, tuck dress under armpits (women)
suluina	tucked, put on
sulu$_3$	illuminate, light up, torch
susulu	shine (sun, moon), sunlight, glare
sulugia	lit up
sulusulu	shine on
fa'asusulu	shine light on to . . .
sulu$_4$	(pl. *sūsulu*) flee
sulufaga	R.C. feast day
sulufa'i	take refuge
sulufa'iga	refuge, sanctuary, R.C. Patron, Protector
sūlusulu	run for safety, as fast as possible

fesūlua'i	flee from place to place
sulu$_5$	fall headlong
suluga	fall
sulugātiti	waist
sului	dry banana leaf (used as cigarette paper)
sumepalo	cymbals (Bible)
sumu	Southern Cross, full toss (cricket)
sunu	(pl. *susunu*) burn up
susunuina	burnt up
masunu	singe, partly cooked food
sunusunu	scorch
sunu'i	thrust into, pierce, insert, stab
sunu'ia	stabbed etc.
suō	spade, hoe, shovel
suō asu	shovel
suō tipi	spade
suōtosina	plough
supa$_1$	paralysis, palsy
supa$_2$	dislocate, put out of joint
supa$_3$ - *supakako*	supercargo
supamāketi	supermarket
supo	liquid food, soup
pī supo	corned beef
susu	(pl. *fesusui*) suck, breast of a woman, milk
fa'asusu	suckle
matāsusu	nipple
susū	(pol.) come, go (chiefs)
susuga	(pol.) form of address
lau susuga	your honour, excellency
lana susuga	his honour, excellency

Tt

ta$_1$	prefix for certain verbs
ta$_2$	(prn.) I, in phrases e.g. *'ua ta fefe* - I'm afraid
tā$_1$	(prn.) dual - you and I
tā$_2$	(pl. *tatā*) strike, ring (bell), play (music) wash (clothes), hew, adze, bail out (bilge water), tattoo, cut, make (road), blow, stroke
taia	struck
tāga	felling (trees), washing (laundry), act of tattooing.
tātā	to tap
fa'atātā	cast a fishing-line
fetāa'i	beat about, strike o.a.
tātātuli	(pol.) awake s.o.
tātāvale	beat fast (heart etc.)
tāgāfiti	somersault, cartwheel
tagāmea	washing, laundry
tagati'a	game (darts)
tā'ofu	laundress
tālā'au	musician
tātatau	tattooist
tāva'a	canoe builder
tā$_3$**, tā e**	term of endearment, man to wife, favourite child
tā$_4$	tar
ta'a	(pl. *tata'a*) run freely, be loose, at large (animals), loose, rolling (e.g. stone) loose, unchaste (woman), lover, suitor
mata'a	come loose
fa'ata'a	set loose
fa'ata'aina	to be set loose
fa'ata'ata'a	play out a fishing line
tā'aga	herd, gang
ta'āiga	favour one's family
ta'afale	be loose in the house
ta'afili	roll about, wallow
ta'agaogao	be clear, empty (land) (also *ta'alaelae*) wasteland, be hairless
ta'alili	roar, boom, thunder

ta‘aligoligoa be silent, noiseless, lonely

ta‘ali‘o roundness

fa‘ata‘ali‘oli‘o circular, encircled

ta‘alise hurry

fa‘ata‘alise speed up, hasten

ta‘amala ill-fated

ta‘amanuia fortunate

ta‘amilo go round, make a tour of, circular, around

ta‘amiloga turn of a rope (etc.)

ta‘amilosaga turn (of a wheel), journey, tour, circulation, round (boxing), league, championship

fa‘ata‘amilo go around s.th.

fa‘ata‘amilosaga circumference

fa‘ata‘amilomilo coil round, go round in circles

ta‘anoa be loose, unstable

ta‘apaepae chicken

ta‘asē stray, go astray

ta‘asolo wander (mind)

ta‘atasi live alone

ta‘atele common, ordinary, prevalent

ta‘atua play truant

ta‘avale (pl. *tā‘avavale*) roll (ball, wheel etc.), cart, car, truck, taxi

tā‘avalevale roll over and over

ta‘avao wander in forest

ta‘avili turn (of wheel), rotate

ta‘avilivili continue to turn

ta‘ā fishing line

tā‘ā abound in fish

ta‘afi bark cloth, old bark cloth

ta‘ai (pl. *tā‘ai*) wind (e.g. thread on reel), roll

tā‘ai‘ai coil, curl

tā‘aiga roll, coil

tā‘ai everyone

tā‘ailua corporal (i.e. two stripes)

tā‘a‘ina drag, influence

ta‘ale kernel of unripe c'nut

ta‘alo play, playing

tā‘aloga game, sport

tā‘aloga sipeisi space games

fa‘ata‘alo play with

fa‘atā‘aloga lightly, w.o. strain

ta‘alolo ceremonial, group presentation

fa‘ata‘alolo proceed in a body

ta‘amū large edible tuber

ta‘ape disperse (also *ta‘ape‘ape*)

ta‘apepāpā (pol.) die (of chief)

ta‘atia (pl. *ta‘atitia*) lie, leave, leave alone

ta‘atiatia leave lying

fa‘ata‘atia lay down, lay aside, set out, state (opinion etc.)

tae$_1$ faeces, excrement

taea dirty, disgusting, filthy

taefe‘e octopus ink (also *taelama*)

taelago fly speck, freckle

taelagoa freckled

***taemanu**$_1$* animal droppings, dung

taepaloloa mildew

taetafe driftwood

***taetuli**$_1$* ear wax

tae$_2$ pick up, gather up, (A.S.) *ta‘alao*

tāea been collected

taena‘i gather up

taetae gathering up

ta‘e (pl. *ta‘ei*) break, smash (cups etc.), crack (nuts, c'nuts etc.)

ta‘ea, ta‘eina broken

tā‘ega broken pieces

ta‘eiga (pl. *tā‘eiga*) breakage

ta‘eta‘e breaking

tata‘e break, smash

ta‘eilili‘i smashed in sm. pieces

taeao morning, tomorrow (also refers to a memorable occasion)

taelasi interfere, meddle

ta‘ele keel, bottom

tā‘ele have a bath, bathe

tā‘elega bathing place, bath

fa‘atā‘ele to bath s.o.

taemanu$_2$ wild S. banana

taetuli$_2$ glow worm

tafa$_1$ flank, slope

tafatafa side, at the side of, beside

tafatafā 'ilagi	over the horizon
fa'atafa	step aside
fa'atafatafa	make way
tāfafā	four sided, square
fa'atāfafā	be square
tafalua	two sided, made of two pieces
tafatasi	be in complete agreement, unanimous
tafatō	v. steep, sheer (ravine)
tafatolu	three sided, triangle
fa'atafatolu	three sided, three cornered
tafa$_2$	(pl. *tatafa*) lance, incise (boil etc.)
tafaga	lancing
tafa$_3$	of light and shade, be visible, discernible
'o le tafa o ata	dawn
tafatafa	break of dawn
tafa$_4$, tatafa	begin to ripen
tafa$_5$	(pol.) be abated, mitigated
tafa$_6$, fa'atafa	be ill, indisposed
fa'atafafa	be unwell
tafa$_7$, fa'atafalia	blocked, *ua lē fa'atafaliale ala,* the road is blocked
tafā	battlefield
tafaga	(verb particle) too soon, prematurely
tafāga	bonito canoe (also *va'aalo*)
tafagaloa	be empty, clear
tafa'ifā	to hold four paramount titles in S.
tafale	seek someone's support
tafao	(pl. *tāfafao*) roam, wander, people on holiday, tourists, be idle (pol.) to hurt, (pol.) circumcise
tāfatafao	stroll about
tāfaoga	trip, tour, picnic
tafaovale	do no work, be idle
tāfasi	break into portions
tafe	(pl. *tatafe*) flow, run
tafea	carried away (current etc.), drift (pol.) die of h. ch.
tāfega	current
tāfeaga	exiles, castaways
tafetafea	drift
tatafe	flow swiftly (water)
fa'atafe	drain off water
fa'atafetafea	set adrift
fetāfea'i	circulate (e.g. blood)
tāfelēmū	flow gently
tafetoto	bleed
tāfetotoi	stream w. blood
tafēfē!	exclamation of surprise, fear
tafi$_1$	clear away, remove, expel, brush, rub off
tafia	removed
tafiga	removal, clearance
matafi	blow away, clear (clouds)
tatafi	(pol.) wash hands, clear the bowels (laxative)
tafitafi	brush
vai fa'atafi	laxative
tafito'elau	clouds blown away by the trade winds
tafi$_2$	razor, to shave
matātāfi	razor blade
tafolā	whale (also *i'a manu*)
tafu	(pl. *tatafu*) be alight, burn
tāfuna'i	bonfire
tāfuna'iga	burning up (weeds etc.)
fa'atafuna	place for burning rubbish
fa'atāfunaga	ruin, destruction by fire etc.
tafu'e	stump of tree
taga$_1$	(pl. *tataga*) remove, be allowed, permitted, lift a prohibition
tataga	a signal (bell etc.) announcing the lifting of a ban
mataga	let go, release one's grip, be freed, release, relax
matagataga	loose, slackened
fa'ataga	permit, allow, give s.o. leave
tusi fa'ataga	permit
fa'atagaina	permitted, allowed

fa'atagataga	prepare for action, take in case of need e.g. *pa'u fa'atagataga* – spare tyre
taga$_2$	bag, sack, pocket
taga'aluga	pillow case
taga o le malie	shark's stomach
tagā'ai	bird's crop
tagā'mimi	bladder, climbing plant (Black-eyed Susan)
tāga	gesture, movement
tagai	roll into a ball, coil
taga'i	(pl. *tāga'i*) be visible, (pol.) see, look, behold
tagataga'i	look (at)
tagata	man (i.e. human being), native
tagatā	many inhabitants, thickly populated
fa'atagata	statue
fa'a-le-tagata	human
tagata'ese	stranger
tagatānu'u	commoner, villager, citizen (also *tagatā fanua, tagatālautele*)
tagatāvao	peasant
tagata matua	adult
tagata mātutua	elderly people
fa'atagata matua	like an adult, grown up
tagāvai	insignia, badge, emblem (of war), oven (food), (also *suāvai* = oven)
tagi	(pl. *fetagisi*) cry, weep, make noise, ask for, beg, request, appeal, claim, petition (at law), case (law)
tagisia	was requested, wanted etc.
tāgisia	cry over illness
tāgisaga	crying, lamentation
tagitagi	jingle – high pitched
fa'atagitagi	ring (bell etc.), rattle
fa'amātagitagi	fret
tatagi	ring, sound of bell
tagiauē	wail, lament
tagifāno	walking & crying (also *tagi savali*)
tagimaiala	be absent when illness, death, occurs
tagitu'i	overcome by grief
tagivale	too ready to cry (children)
tāgivale	too demanding (adults)
tagikerī	dungarees
tagitagi$_1$	ornamental shrub
tagitagi$_2$	bird, scarlet robin
tagipalau	drum (also *talipalau*)
tagito'ia	lose heart, be faltering in speech, stunted
tago	(pl. *fetāgofi*) take, get hold of, touch, feel (w. hand)
tagofia	(pol.) be touched
tago 'ese	(pol.) light-fingered
tāgotago	feel for, touch & feel
tāgo'au	ready for action
tāgolima	well off, have resources
tagovale	(pol.) light-fingered, steal
tagovalea	be light-fingered
tagole	ransack, rummage
tāgulu	snore
tagutu	stump
tāgutugutu	stubble
tai	tide
'i tai	towards the sea
'i uta	inland
tailelei	have a good time
taileleia	fortunate, lucky
taimaui	ebb tide
taimasa	neap tide
taio'o	spring tide, v. high tide
taipupū	rocky coast w. blow holes
taitafola	lagoon
taivale	poor season (fish), have a bad time, unfortunate
tāi	(prefix) indicates nearly, almost
tāitāi	used with *lē* or *le'i*, meaning nowhere near, far from
ta'i$_1$	precedes numerals to indicate distribution e.g. *ta'ifia*? – how many each?
ta'ilua	two each, two at a time

ta'ito'alua (people) two, pairs
ta'i₂ lead, bring or serve (food), point, aim (gun), draw (net)
ta'ia, ta'iina led, brought etc.
tā'iga leadership, influence, setting (a course)
ta'ita'i lead, guide, carry (of hand luggage)
ta'iala guidelines, leader
ta'ita'i'au officer
ta'ita'i pese conductor, choir-master
ta'ita'iga guidance
tata'i lead, guide (person)
fa'ata'ita'i imitate, test s.th., try on (garment), practise
fa'ata'ita'iga imitation, test, trial, model, practice
feta'ia'i lead around
ta'ifau (pol.) dog
ta'ife'e to fish for octopus
ta'imua leader
fa'ata'imua give warning of a coming event
fa'ata'imuaga forewarning
ta'iola presentation of live food (e.g. pig)
tā'ivale lead s.o. nowhere
ta'ivalea out of control, w.o. a leader
ta'i₃ large sore (yaws)
taia mature tree w. hard core, heart wood
taiamita diameter
tāifa'i hand of bananas
ta'igāfi hearth
taigalēmū be auspicious (also *taigamālie)*
ta'ilo I don't know, who cares?
taimane diamond
taimi time, musical time, turn
ta'inamu mosquito net
tainane (phrase) who knows whether? even
tainifo gums
taisi₁ hit, strike
taisi₂ play dice
tā'isi package of food (taro, yams)
taisina outer ring of soft wood (trees)
tāivai grass cutting tool (hoop iron)
tala₁ unfold, undo, open out, take to pieces, dismantle, change (bank notes), draw out (money)
tala'a'ao walk, arrive
talaga stripping, dismantling
matala open, bloom (flowers)
mātalatala unfurl (sails)
tālā unfold and give away (fine mat)
tatala (pl. *talai*) unhitch, take off, open, undo, break, cancel, release, repeal, annul (law)
tatalaga release
talatala pay out (net) to space
talalautasi break up (ship)
talaloa come undone, reach to ankles (garment)
fa'atālaloa be in abeyance
tālalua open into two parts etc, to part (people)
talavai obtain medicine
fale talavai dispensary, chemist
talavou be young, youthful
tala₂ tell, news, story, account, statement, report, gossip, tale, legend, play, novel, reputation
talā be told, related
tala'aga history
tālatala talk, chat, discuss, confer, consult, be reported
tālatalaga discussion, conference, consultation
talatalaō cackle (hen)
talatalatasi give detailed account
fetalai speak (orators, God)
fetalaiga speech, (pol.) orator
tala'alelo worthless story, nonsense
tala'ese speak badly of
tala fa'afāgogo fiction
tala fa'aoti tell in detail
talafa'asolopito tradition, oral history

talafatu fiction, novel
talagafa recite a genealogy
talagāgafa recounting a genealogy
talagū speaking in low voices, murmur, discuss
talanoa (pl. *talatalanoa*) chat, make conversation, talk
talanoaina discussed
talanoaga discussion, conversation
fa'atalanoa discuss, talk about
talaoso blurt out
tala'oto'oto summarize, summary
talapipi tell in detail
talasolotua rumour
talatomua headline
talalausui exaggerate (also *tala vale*)
talatu'u traditional story (also *tala ta'oto*)
talavalea nonsense
tala$_3$ spike, prong, barb, spine, prickle, spur, thorn
talaia scratch, graze
tālatala rough - uneven
'o le pepa tālatala sand-paper
fa'atalatala stick out, protrude
fa'atālatala give a rough surface
talāmoli orange thorn
tala$_4$ rounded end of S. house
tala$_5$ indicates position - next to, near, behind, beyond
talātu ananafi day before yesterday
talātua the back of s.th.
tālā dollar
tālaelae deserted (usually *ta'a laelae*)
talafa side-whiskers
talafalu tree (used medicinally)
talafātai sea coast
talafeagai agree, be in accordance with, in keeping with, in harmony with
talai - ma'atalai hewn stone (Bible)
tāla'i summon, announce
tāla'iga announcement
tāla'i preach, propagate, boast, brag
tālaleu (pol.) oppose, relax, make s.o. comfortable
fa'atālaleu (pol.) stretch ones legs
talalī blaze up, flare up
fa'atalalī set on flame, set ablaze
talana'i pull up on beach (canoe etc.)
tālasua make fun of
talatama parent over-anxious for children
tālatū refuse to co-operate
tala'u'ula take advantage of s.o., beg, implore
tale cough
tale vivini whooping cough
tale'ū hacking cough
tāleni talent, ability
taleu move, touch
tali$_1$ (pl. *tatali*) wait
talia waiting
taliga keep s.o. waiting
talitaliga waiting
fa'atali wait, waiting
fa'atalitali expect, wait for
taliala be in wait
talimau stay and wait
talisoa await company
tali$_2$ (pl. *tali*) answer, reply, receive & give gifts, reciprocate, receive or welcome guests, a reply, welcome, answer, reception
talia be received, accepted etc.
taliaina be accepted, admit, agree
taliga reception, welcome
talitali hold s.th. up, support, overhead rack in S. *fale*
talitaliina be supported
fa'ataliga reception party
fetalia'i exchange of speeches
fetālia'i take turns in providing food
talifaufau special feast
taligatā unreceptive

talilelei	welcome
talileleia	welcomed
talimalō	receive & welcome guests
faletalimalō	S. house for guests, hotel, motel etc.
talimua	first to receive guests
talisapai	appreciate
talisapaia	trust, have confidence in . . .
talitāne	prostitute
talitonu	believe, trust
lē talitonu	disbelieve, sceptical
fa'atalitonu	convince
talitua	keep wickets (cricket)
talitupe	cashier
talitutū	answer back
taliuālesi	radio operator
tali$_3$	guard against, ward off, parry, stand up to, catch (in hands) (also *sapo*), shield, guard, protection
tatali	stand up to
tali'ele'ele	apron
taligalu	breakwater
talimatagi	wind break, windscreen
talipupuni	shield (also *talitā*), trophy (sport)
tali$_4$	(pol.) eat, eating
talialo	(pol.) eat (chiefs)
talialoga	(pol.) meal
taligāsua	(pol.) meal
tālimanava	(pol.) eat
tālisua	(pol.) have a meal
tālisuaga	(pol.) feast
tālisuaga a le Alii	Lord's Supper, Holy Communion
tāli	(prefix) nearly, almost
taliaga	lie on one's back, face upwards
fa'ataliaga	put on its back
talie	tree, tropical almond, hard wood for furniture etc.
taliē	a lot of laughter
taliēga	roar of laughter
talifau	beyond repair
taliga	ear, fungus
fa'ataligatuli	turn a deaf ear
talitaliuli	attendant, bodyguard, pilot fish
talitū	persist in carrying
talo$_1$ **tatalo**	(pl. *tatalo*) pray, prayer
tālosia	pray for, it is the prayer that . . .
tālosaga	entreat, implore, prayer, petition, request
tālotalo	hope, wish, hope & pray
talo$_2$	taro
taloa	have plenty of taro
taloloa	set of taro gardens
talomua	first fruits (gift)
talopa'ia	a district gift (like *ta'alolo*)
talotasi	feast for visitors, harvest together
tālo	(pol.) wave, signal, call, invite
tālotalo	waving
tālofa	general greeting - good day etc., expression of pity, sympathy e.g. what a pity! alas!
fa'atālofa	greet ea. other
talu$_1$	from, since
talu ai	owing to, because of, last, previous
talu$_2$**, talutalu**	new growth of weeds, growth of an idea (fig.)
talu$_3$	wooden hand-gong
tāluā	annoying, troublesome
fa'atāluā	be a nuisance
talusā	bring trouble, bad luck, haunted
tama$_1$	child (of a woman)
tama tāne	son
tama teine	daughter
tama$_2$	chief of high rank, boy, youth, knave (cards), male
tatama	incubate (eggs)
fa'atamatama	play like a child
tama'āiga	(pol.) title of ea. of four paramount S. chiefs
tamāli'i	chief, noble, gentleman of noble descent

fa'atamāli'i characteristic of a chief
tamafafine descendants of a woman, daughter of a woman
tamafai adopted child
tamafaitīfaga clown, actor, acrobat
tamafusu boxer
tamaitiiti (pl. *tamaiti*) child, childhood
fa'atamaitiiti childish
tamāloa (pl. *tamāloloa*) man, married man
tamameamea newly born child
tamāo'āiga be wealthy, wealth
fa'atamāo'āiga make rich, enrich
tamasā child of a man's sister
tamatāne descendants of a man
fa'atamatāne like a man
tamauli black skinned man, Negro
tamā father
fa'atamā treat like a father
tamā fai foster father
tama'i (indicates a small th.) e.g. *tama'i fale*, young (animal) – *tama'i pua'a* young, immature (tree)
tama'ilima finger (also *tamatama'ilima*)
tama'imata pupil of eye, eye ball
tamatama'ivae toe
tāma'i (pol.) war, calamity
tāma'ia be destroyed
fa'atāma'ia destroy, devastate
tama'ita'i lady, princess, (pol.) woman
tama'ita'i matua (pol.) elderly lady
tama'ita'i – fa'anofonofo (pol.) village maiden (also *taupou)*
tupu tama'ita'i queen, queen (cards)
tamalini tamarind tree
tamanu large tree used for timber
tane$_1$ skin diseases e.g. tinea
tanesusu chicken pox
tanetanea spotty skin
tane$_2$ tank (water etc.)
tane$_3$ ton (also *tonne*)
tāne husband, man, male

tanoa$_1$ (pol.) excuse, forgive
tanoa$_2$ (pol.) speak, talk, speech
tānoa wooden bowl (kava)
tānoa fai mea'ai food bowl
fa'atānoa cavity, hollow, reservoir
tanu (pl.*tatanu*) cover over, build up w. soil etc. bury
tanumia buried
tanuga raised surface (e.g. road), burial
tanuma'i covered over
tatanu strew
tao$_1$ cook, bake
taopa'u bake till crisp
taopa'ua baked w. skin on
taouli bake b'fruit in skins
tao$_2$ cover the oven, put a weight on, press down
taomua weighted down etc.
ma'ataopepa paper weight
taomaga weighted basket (c'nut husks)
taotao press down
tao'ofu waistcoat
tao$_3$ (pl. *tatao*) follow a trail
taomi troubles (one after another)
tāotao follow closely
taotua follow
taotaotua follow closely
tao$_4$ spear
tāofi$_1$ (pl. *tāofi*) hold, stop, detain, prevent, hold back, save, resist, check, remain, stay, support, brake e.g. *tāofi a le taavale* – the brakes of the car
tāofiofi restrain, moderate
tāofiofiga restraint, restriction
tāofi$_2$ opinion, view
tāofiga opinion, opposition
taotasi steady
ta'oto (pl. *tā'o'oto)* lie down, (pol.) be operated on
ta'otoga layout (pol.) operation
ta'oto'oto rest, recline
fa'ata'oto$_1$ lay down

fa'ata'oto$_2$ proverb, parable
fa'ata'oto le maliu autopsy, post mortem examination
fa'ata'otoga layout, outline, plan
ta'otogalelei well settled, comfortable, a matter settled satisfactorily (also *ta'otogāmālie*)
tapa$_1$ (pl. *tatapa*) ask for s.th.
tapatapa ask repeatedly
tapatautali beg to join a party
tapa$_2$ (pl. *tāpā)* tackle (e.g. football)
tapa$_3$ **tapatapa** fumble, grope for
tapa'a tobacco
tapa'au c'nut leaf mat, (pol.) chief, God
tāpafua (pol.) w.o. a kava title
tapaipu call titles (kava ceremony)
tapale box (the ears), water game
tapasā compass
tāpatapa oily
tapena tidy up, clear up, prepare, put on board (ship), load, pack up
tapenaina packed up etc.
tapili fan, wave
tāpili propeller, rudder, pectoral fins (fish)
tapioka cassava, arrowroot (also *manioka*)
tapo catch (s.th. thrown) (also *sapo*)
tapoleni tarpaulin
tapona S. game (*taponaga*)
tapu$_1$ forbidden
tapui be taboo
tapuiaina made taboo
tāpua'i support s.o., show positive good will, worship
tāpua'iga (pol.) act of worship, church service
taputapu strictly forbidden
tapula'a boundary, limit, maximum, full-score, pass-mark
fa'atapula'a set a limit
tapulima wrist
tapulima 'ofutino cuff-link
tapuvae ankle, pig's trotter
tapu$_2$ tub
tapua mouth of "no return" fish trap
tapulu area o solid tattooing (man), largest tattooing tool
taro taro (also *talo*)
tāseni dozen
'afa tāseni half a dozen
tasi numeral one, same, one only, single, someone, anyone, an agreement (*tasi le mea* one thing i.e. however)
'o le tasi tagata a certain man
soatasi alone, by oneself
fa'atasi collect, gather, be present at, join (persons) together
fa'atasi ma together with
fa'atasitasi assemble
fa'atasiga assembly, gathering
tasū clearing for a plantation
tata grab & pull violently, violent grab
tatā bail out, bailer
tātāgase profuse sweating
tatau$_1$ be fit for, right, proper, appropriate, necessary, have to, must, suitable
'o le mea tatau ai (pol.) food
fa'atatau adapt, apply, fit, arrange, make arrangements, plan, estimation, opinion, estimate
fa'atatauga plan
tatau$_2$ turn of tide
tatau$_3$ tattooing
tātō (pl. *tātotō)* boisterous (girls)
tātou (prn.) we, us (more than two)
tatū (pl. *tātutū*) stamp on ground

tau$_1$ (particle, indicates (1) possession of a characteristic) e.g. *e tau fe'ai le maile* – savage dog (2) location (3) habitat
e.g.
(2) *taulima* bracelet
taumata eyeshade
tautaliga earring
tauvae anklet
(3) taufale householder
taufanua commoner (usually *tūfanua)*
tautai master fisherman, ship's captain
fa'atautaia to direct, govern
tauuta landsman
tauvao hunter, bush dweller
tau$_2$ (particle, indicates continued activity)
taualo paddling, rowing
taualumaga progress, development
tau'ave take on, bear, carry
taufāifai jeer, scoff (also *fāifai*)
taufōnō call repeatedly for s.o.
taufusifusi in a clinch (boxing)
taulima keep on doing s.th., make a pet of s.th.
taumamao keep away
taumau adhere firmly
taunonofo practise polygamy, polygamy
taupese has a musical bent
tausisi$_1$ stick to, stay, remain, mark an opponent (game)
tautā$_1$ beat, slash, stick, goad
tautāina beaten etc.
tautago gropingly
tautamā excused from duties (a woman w. young children)
tautigā hard work, labour
tāutū persist, adhere firmly, continue to be . . .
tautua serve a *matai* (by untitled men), service, servant
tautuāvae (pol.) serve a *matai*
tauvala'au call for s.o.
tauvala'auga roll call

tau$_3$ (prefix) indicates an attempt to do s.th.
taugagana try to speak
taulu'ilu'i challenge, defy
taumafai try, attempt
taumafaiga attempt
taupale try earnestly, make a boat go faster
tauseu try to steer away
tausisi$_2$ try to hoist (flag)
tautā$_2$ try to dust (mat) etc.
tautū try to stand up
tau$_4$ reach, go to, come to
tauane come across, find
tauia found etc.
fa'atau$_1$ refer s.th. to another
taunu'u arrive, reach, land (plane), come true (hope, wish), materialize, arrival
taunu'uga end, destination, goal, effect, result
fa'ataunu'u convey, fulfil (desire etc.), bring to pass
fa'ataunu'uga accomplishment, fulfilment
tautonu hit target
tau$_5$ (particle) only, just, provided that e.g. *tau o 'oe ma a'u* – only you and me
tau$_6$ cost, count in, include, price, charge (also refers to a number of the same things *tau i'a* – string of fish)
taulia included in
tāua dear, precious, valuable, important, essential, importance, value
fa'atau$_2$
fa'atau mai buy
fa'atau atu sell
fa'atau'oloa trader, merchant
fa'ataua, fa'ataulia bought, sold
e lē mafa'ataulia it is invaluable
fa'atauga sale, shopping, buying
fa'atatau be worth, work, value
fefa'ataua'iga trade, barter, commerce

tau'ese count wrongly, miscalculate
taugatā dear, expensive
taugōfie cheap, inexpensive
taupō be numbered (days before event), look forward to
tautasi jointly, bought jointly
tautotogi buy w. money, pay by instalments
tau₇ fight, struggle against, fighting, battle, war
taua'ifusu to box, fight
taua'imisa quarrel, brawl
taua'i'upu dispute
fa'atau₃ provoke, debate between orators to decide on a speaker
fa'atauga shopping
fetaua'i fight with o.a.
taufagatua wrestle
taufagatuaga wrestling
taufao scramble for, snatch
taufaoa grabbed
fetaufaoa'i grabbing for food
tauivi struggle, wrestle with
taupepē fight to kill, struggle
tausiniō compete for
tagata tausiniō competitor
tausinioga competition, sports day etc.
tau'upu quarrel, argue
tau'upuga dispute
tauvā fight for, compete for
tauvāga competition
tau₈ season, climate, weather
taumafanafana summer
taumālūlū winter
tautuputupu spring
tau e āfu ai mea autumn
tau₉ (pl. *tatau*) anchor, moor
tauga (va'a) anchorage
taulaga harbour, port, town
tauva'a anchor
tau₁₀ (pl. *tau*) pick (leaves, flowers etc.), leaves used to cover S. oven
tauvela middle layer of oven leaves
tauveve outer layer of oven leaves
tau₁₁ indicates a wish that s.th. will eventuate e.g. *tau lava ina 'e sau* (I wish) that you would come
tau₁₂ particle indicates bunch, cluster e.g. *'o le taulua popo* a pair of c'nuts
tau₁₃ prefix indicating position
tauagavale left side
taualuga top, ridge, roof, cockscomb, a final dance
taufa'ai'uga conclusion, concluding period
taufa'ai'ui'uga extremity, very end
taugāgaifo be in West, set (sun)
taulotoa'iga middle, half-way
taumatau right side
taumua bows (boat)
matagi taumuaa'i head-wind
taumuli stern
matagi taumulia'i following wind
tausi'usi'u extremity
tausi'usi'uga most distant point, tip, topmost part
tautulua middle
tautuluaga middle
tau₁₄ tāla'i keep facing, straight at
taula'iga target, junction (roads)
fa'atau₄ make s.th. join or fit
fetāula'i join, converge
fetāula'iga meeting point
fetāula'igāla road junction
fetāula'igāva'a shipping centre
taugalelei be in good time
taugalēmū be in accordance with
taugamālie fit in, accord with, (pol.) be appropriate
tau₁₅ concerning, regarding, having to do with e.g. *mea tau va'a* things concerning ships
tau₁₆ (particle) nearly, almost, scarcely, more or less e.g. *ua tau'uma tupe* the money is almost finished
tau₁₇ hang

tautau hang up
tautauina hung up
tautauga hanging of s.th.
tautaulaga hook, peg, tobacco leaves hung up to dry
fa'atau₅ (pol.) b'fruit
fa'atautau hang (object, person), hang loosely, eaves (house)
taufu'a decorated w. flags
taulalo low hanging fruit
taulilo fruit hidden by leaves
taumamao fruit hanging furtherest away
tau₁₈ tatau wring out, strain (kava), milk (cow)
taulia (strained etc.)
tāuaga wringer, strainer
taufua wring out grated c'nut w.o. water
tau₁₉ (particle) indicates absolutely, completely e.g. *sa vili tau le uati* the watch was fully wound
tau₂₀ foredeck of bonito canoe
tāu (pl. tāu) connected by kinship
tāu'āiga branch of the family
ta'u tell, announce, mention, suggest, speak of
ta'ua be called, known as, be mentioned, tell, inform, report, denounce
ta'uga mention
ta'uta'u announce, mention frequently
ta'uta'ua wellknown, famous, reputation
ta'ugatā hard to pronounce
ta'ugōfie easy to pronounce
ta'uleagaina spoken badly of
ta'uleleia spoken well of
ta'umamāina declared innocent, acquitted
ta'usala blameworthy
ta'usalaina declared guilty, condemned
ta'utatauina well deserved
ta'utino declare, be frank
ta'utinoga pledge, assurance, declaration, confession, interview
ta'uvalea disgraced
ta'uvaleaina criticize, condemn
tā'ua (prn.) we two (incl.)
tau'a'ao (pol.) to present, make a gift
tauafiafi afternoon, evening shadow
tauagafau well mannered, polite (man)
tauagavale left-handed
tāu'ai throw stones
tauala blow from certain direction (wind), arise, spring up
taualaala go courting (man)
taualoa be respected, recognize
tauānau entreat, urge
tauānaua entreated
tauānauga entreaty
fa'atauānau press earnestly, earnest request
tauanave tree (used for dishes, boxes)
tāuaso be blind
tauati take place out of doors
tauau show tendency to go . . . (up, down etc.) within sight of, on the point of
tau'au shoulder
tau'ava a drinking party
tauāvale have no idea . . ., too dumb
tauemu mock, ridicule, jeer
tauemuga jeering, scoffing
fa'atauenu scoff, jeer
taufai (phrase) indicates involvement of many e.g. *'ua taufaitagi auē* many are wailing
taufale (pol.) intestines, bowels
taufe (double prefix) indicates plural & repeated activity e.g. *taufea'a* many kicks

taufe'ai (pl. *taufe'a'ai*) wild, savage
taufelefele have many branches (tree etc.)
taufetuli run
taufetuliga running race
taufetulituli trot
fetaufetulia'i run about
taufolo S. food (b.fruit, c'nut cream etc.)
taufui cluster of fruit
fuifui thickly clustered
taufusi swamp, marsh
fa'ataufusi boggy, marshy
tāuga basket of cooked food, gift of food
tautāuga gift of food
taugā a direct hit, hurt, wound deeply (fig.)
tāugā waste
fa'atāugā waste, be cruel, over-eat
taugaloloa wear ankle-length garment
taugāmata base of skull
taugauli become blackened, dark
taugutu keep telling s.o. what to do
taui repay, reward, retaliate, revenge, be punished, result, compensation
tauia repaid etc.
fetauia'i retaliate
taui ma sui take vengeance, revenge
ta'ui (pl. *tā'ui*) wrap up s.th., bundle, wrapping
ta'uia wrapped up etc.
taula₁ anchor
tāulaga anchorage
taula₂ used of priests in old S.
taulā branches
taulaga shake& lift (e.g. wind under eaves)
tāulaga offering (church), sacrifice (made by priest etc.)
taulagi (pol.) sing
tāulagi (pol.) be blind
taulāitu spirit medium
fa'ataulāitu witch, magician, magical, by magic
taulalo'ese poison s.o's mind
taulāmalama to spy
taulāmua have first place, leading, foremost
taulāsea bush doctor
taulata almost, nearly
taulau be realized, fulfilled (hopes etc.)
taule'ale'a (pl. *tāulele'a*) young man, youth, untitled man, one's youth
tāulia be dirty, (pol.) illness e.g. "*tāulia i le fala*" = the illness of the chief
taulote debate, discuss
tauloto know by heart, memorize, poem, poetry
taulotoina memorized
tauluulu leafy
tauluuluola grow luxuriantly (trees)
tāumafa (pl. *tāumamafa*) (pol.) eat, eat & drink
tāumafaina eaten
tāumafataga food, meal, feast
taumafai try, endeavour
taumalae be host, host
taumālie mild (mannered)
taumālua roll, sway (ship), hang in balance (problem)
taumālualua swaying a lot
taumanu flock of birds
taumate be uncertain, to guess
lē taumate certainly, no doubt
taumateina guessed, uncertain
taumāunu put bait (before fish)
taume spathe of c'nut tree (sheath)
taugāmoa game (like ride a cock horse)
taumoa lever
taunapa take care of, be fond of, pester
tauofoga offer, tender
tau'olo prepare for journey
taupati do one's best
tāupe hang-swing

tāupega a swing
tāupeupe swinging
fa'atāupe carry (suspended from a stick)
tāupepē fight to kill, fight to a finish
taupou ceremonial village maiden, virgin
taupule i le ola about to commit suicide
tāupule consult together, confer, arrange, organize
lē tāupulea undisciplined, lawless
tāupulega arrangement, retinue, attendants
taupulepule take counsel, make arrangements, plot
tausa'afia much approved of, popular, be regretted, missed
tausaga year
tausagā long time since, be v. old
fa'aletausaga annual
tausala$_1$ titled woman, lady, (pol.) girl
tausala$_2$ be charming, pleasant, well mannered (women) ("*tausala*" is used in describing "Miss Samoa" etc.)
fa'atausala properly
tausama'aga (pol.) h.ch's meal, wedding feast
tausamiga (pol.) special meal, feast, Holy Communion
tausani bird song, dawn chorus
tausi$_1$ take care of, look after, nurse, keep to, stick to
tausia cared for etc.
tausiga care, maintenance
fetausia'i help one another, mutual help
tausi$_2$ wife of orator
tausili climb (tree, rock etc.)
tausoa carry load on pole between shoulders of two men
tausua have sense of humour, be funny, be indulgent, easy
tausuaga joke, fun
tausuamatamuli be shy
tausuauigā sarcastic
tausūai be scandalized, take offence
tausūaiga scandal, stumbling - block
fa'atausūai scandalize, shock s.o.
tausulu torch
tautafa (pol.) abate, mitigate
tāutagata be conscious, be in control of oneself
tautala (pl. *tāutala*) speak, talk, discuss, refer to, reprimand, hire (e.g. *'o le pasi tautala* — a hired bus)
tautalagia talked about etc.
tautalaga speech, lecture
tautalatala much talking
fetautalatalā'i converse together
tautalaiti impudent, cheeky
tautapa praise a bridal couple
tautapaga chiefly praises
ta'uta'u a squall
taute (pol). eat, drink (h.ch.)
tautega repast, ch's meal
taute'e disagree with, disobey
tauteva walk unsteadily, stagger
tautili come quickly
tautino own, very own
tautō to swear (oath)
tautōga oath, declaration on oath
fa'atautō take oath of office
fa'atautōina swearing-in
tāuto'ai grope
tautolopa'ā get on in years, lose (in game)
tautū$_1$ serve (kava etc.)
tautū$_2$ under water rocks
tautū$_3$ fish w. rod, line, hook
tautua$_1$ stone adze, (pol.) tool
tautua$_2$ serve a matai
tautua$_3$ arrive late
tautuanā take good care of, be careful to do s.th.
tāutu'i curse, regret missing an opportunity

tāutu‘u$_1$ place something slowly (down etc.)
tāutu‘u$_2$ yield, be over-ruled
tauusoga relation by kinship
tauvale cause annoyance, be ill-fated (enterprise)
tavale$_1$ object to, oppose
tavale$_2$ marry below one's status
tāvini servant
te (verb, part.) indicates present or vague future e.g. *‘e te alu i fea?* where are you going?
tē bulge, protrude, stick out
tētē open eyes wide
fa‘atē stick out
tea$_1$ **tetea** albino
tea$_2$ (suffix) indicates white, pale (plants) e.g. *niutea* – "white" c'nut
te‘a$_1$ (pl. *tēte‘a*) pass, be separated, parted, dismissed, discharged, weaned, divorced
te‘aga dismissal
fa‘ate‘a expel, dismiss, banish, relieve (pain etc.)
fa‘ate‘aina expelled etc.
fa‘ate‘aga expulsion, dismissal etc.
te‘a$_2$ (pl. *tete‘a*) throw, bowl (cricket)
fa‘ate‘a bowl, bowler
te‘e (pl. *te‘ete‘e*) prop up, shore up, prop, support, be hostile, provoked, show off (A.S.)
tete‘e (pl. *tete‘e*) repulse, push back, reject, deny, oppose
tē‘ea opposed
tē‘ena object to, resist
fete‘ena‘i oppose one another
fete‘ena‘iga conflict
tega, tetega a ticklish, tingling feeling
tei affectionate term for one's sm. brother, sister, youngster
te‘i$_1$ rise (tide)
tete‘i put up (umbrella etc.)
te‘i$_2$ (pl. *tete‘i*) start, be startled, surprised, shocked, awake suddenly, surprise
te‘i ane (phrase) all of a sudden
fa‘ate‘i startle – give a fright
fa‘ate‘ia startled
fa‘ate‘ite‘i be unexpected
teinane in spite of, (also *tainane*)
teine girl, female
teine muli (pol.) unmarried girl, virgin
teine tausima‘i nurse
fa‘ateine be vain, show off
teiō sulphur (Bible)
teisi a little, somewhat
tele$_1$ (pl. *tetele*) be large, big, great, much, many, numerous, loud (voices), severe, serious, very, too, excessive, bulk of, quantity
tele na‘uā far too much
fa‘atele, fa‘atetele increase, enlarge, multiply
fa‘ateleina increased
fa‘atelega the increase
tele$_2$ (pl. *tatele*) to plane, carpenter's plane
tele$_3$**, tetele,** walk quickly, hurry
tele‘a‘i continuously
fa‘ateletele‘a‘i hurry
telegese (pl. *telegegese*) go slow, be slow (clock)
telelise go, walk faster
telemulu v. slow (A.S.)
televave (pl. *televavave*) be fast, speedy, rapidly
telefoni telephone
telefua (pl. *telefufua*) be naked
telekarafi telegraph, cable
telekarame telegram

telenoa (pl. *telenonoa*) (pol.) naked
telona tax collector, publican (Bible)
teme, tateme fidget, be restless
temeteme jump up & down (child), dance with a wriggle
temu$_1$ prize, reward (for winner)
temu$_2$ **temutemu** reluctantly
fa'atemutemu uncooperative
tene, tenetene dance a jig, jump up & down
tēnisi tennis
tepa (pl. *tetepa*) look at, glance
tepatepa continue looking
tepatasi glance
tepatāula'i look fixedly, stare
tepataumeasina behold (a beautiful object)
teritori territory
teropika tropics
Tesema December
tete tremble, shiver, quake, shivering, trembling etc. nervous fear
fa'atetetete quiver
tetemū (pl. *tetemumū*) tremble w. cold, fear, anger
teu put away, keep, pack, store up, save, deposit, save (money), tidy up, put in order, bury (dead), adjust, arrange, dress, decorate, welcome guests, bunch cut flowers
teua, teuina tidied etc.
teuga decorating
tēuga decorations, ornaments
teteu decorate, castrate, geld
teuteu decorate
teuteuga decoration
teumālo (pol.) welcome guests
teutupe treasurer, banker
teutusi envelope
teuila red ginger plant
teva$_1$ (pl. *tēteva*) walk out (in rebellious mood), strike
tēva'aga departure (in anger etc.)
teva$_2$ (pl. *teteva*) do poorly (bananas etc.)
teva$_3$***, tevateva*** stagger, stumble
tēvolo devil, demon
fa'atēvolo devilish, heathen
tī$_1$ shrub (leaves used in S. dress)
tī$_2$ tea, breakfast
iputī teacup
tia (pol.) grave, funeral cairn
tiamau tombstone, monument
ti'a dart (game of *tāgāti'a*), (pol.) speech, (joc.) head
tia'i (pl. *tatia'i*) get rid of, abandon, leave out, omit
tia'ia abandoned etc.
ti'ākono deacon
tiale shrub (gardenia), pig no longer breeding
ti'āpolo devil
tiapula taro-top for replanting
fa'atiapula plant taro-tops
ti'eti'e ride, sit astride, be placed upon, lie on, sit on (chair)
tī'eti'ega ride
fa'ati'eti'e be perched
tifa$_1$ soar, hover (birds)
tifatifa soaring, hovering
tifa$_2$ mother-of-pearl shell
tīfaga cinema, film show
fale tīfaga theatre, cinema
tīfiga ornaments (men & women)
tīgā be painful, sore, hurt, pain
tīgāina suffer, painful, serious, (pol.) labour
fa'atīgā hurt, offend s.o., have labour pains (woman)
fa'atīgāina be worried, troubled
fa'atīgatigā have slight pain
tīgālofa sympathize, sympathy, sorrow

tīgāfa‘atasi condole with
tīkite ticket
tila spar of S. sail, mast (also *fanā*)
tili hurry, urgent message
tilitili hurrying! hurrying!
tiliola run for one's life
tiliva deliver (letters etc.), delivery
tilotilo look, glance, peep, peer, cheat (in exam), survey, look over
tilofia surveyed etc.
fa‘atilotilo have an ulterior motive
fetilofa‘i glance, peer
tiloalalo steal a glance under one's eyelashes
tilotilomāsae find fault w. everything
tīma‘i encourage, exhort
tīma‘ina encouraged
tīma‘iga encouragement, exhortation
fetima‘i encourage ea. other
tīmata mend a net, a new ideà (fig.)
timu$_1$ to rain
tīmuga rain
timutō rainfall
timu$_2$ (colq.) boast
tina$_1$ closely packed, wedge
fetīna‘i closely packed
tina$_2$ backbiting
tina$_3$ **titina** (pl. *tinei*) put out, switch off (light), strangle, erase, rub out, wipe clean, stub out, crush, to stump (cricket)
tineia put out, strangled etc.
fetīneia‘i differ, disagreement, undermine o.another
tīnamū fire-extinguisher
tinā mother
fa‘atinā adoptive mother
tinae guts, entrails
tini$_1$ reach the goal, pass finishing line, finishing post, goal
tini$_2$ traditional poem
tinifu all women & children of one village
tiniō hurry, rush
tinitini clearly, brightly (sun)
tino$_1$ body, put on weight
fa‘atino carry out, practical
titino increase
tino‘ao ostentatious display, an affected walk
tino‘ese fat, corpulent
tinoiti small (people)
tinoitupe cash, coin, sum of money
tinoū be keen on . . .
tinovale thin, sickly
tino$_2$ openly expressed, appear, manifest
tino mai shape, appearance, fully, frankly
fa‘atino clarify
tio$_1$ a shell fish
tio$_2$ **tiotio** active, lively (of eye, body movements), energetic, ready to oblige, energy
tiovale look in all directions for no reason
tio$_3$ blame, find fault
fāitio criticize
tioa - e lē tioa no wonder, it is not to be wondered at
ti‘o use the bowels
tioata glass, pane, spectacles, lens
tioata-va‘ai mamao telescope
ti‘otala bird-kingfisher
tipa segment of orange, four-sided glass bottle
tipi (pl. *titipi*) cut, slice (flesh), operate, amputate, cut, scar
tipia, tipiina cut, sliced etc.
tipiga cutting
tīpiga surgical operation
foma‘itipitipi surgeon
mātipitipi sharp-edged
tīpiloma diploma
tīpolo lime (tree & fruit)
tīpolo patupatu lemon
tīpoti teapot
tiso diesel, diesolene
tīta‘e open a drinking c'nut
titi kilt, girdle of leaves, feathers etc.

fa'atiti put on girdle
titi'e begin to well up (anger, desire)
titipa lazy
tītō headlong, head-first
fa'atītō cast away – cause to fall headlong
tiu shark fishing w. bait & noose
tiutamala neglect
tiute duty, task, be on duty, customs duty, customs
fale tiute customs house
tō$_1$ to plant
totō (sing. & pl.) plant, cultivate
totōina planted, cultivated
togālā'au garden, plantation, orchard
togāufi yam garden
togāvao forest, bush
totōga planting, cultivation
tōfa'i plant bananas
tōtasi plant singly
tō$_2$ (pl. *totō*) reach for, withdraw money (bank)
tōina withdrawn
tō'ese take off, remove, subtract
tō'esea removed etc.
tō$_3$ (totō) put up, erect (house)
tōga fale erection of houses
togālauapi camp (also *to'agālauapi*)
tōlauapi camp
tō$_4$ (pl. *totō*) be pregnant, pregnancy
tōifale pregnant before marriage
tō māsaga two women pregnant together
fa'atōsaga mid-wife
tō$_5$ strainer (for making dye)
tō$_6$ levy (according to S. custom)
tō$_7$ (pl. *tō*) make over, give outright (land etc.)
tōina given
tō$_8$ sink, subside (land), subsidence
tō$_9$ (pl. *totō*) fall upon, come upon (of rain, misfortune)
tōfaō fall face down
tō$_{10}$ cast out, cut off (relative)
toa$_1$ (pl. *totoa*) brave, bold, warrior, a brave, hero
fa'atoatoa pretend to be brave
toa$_2$ rooster, cock
toa$_3$ ironwood tree, a marble
to'a$_1$ particle indicating human-beings e.g. *to'alua* two people
to'aitiiti few people, minority
to'alua spouse, pair of people
to'atasi individual, single person
to'atele many people, majority
to'a$_2$ (pl. *toto'a*) be still (liquids), settle down, calm, relief (pain), run aground (boat), stop (people)
lē to'a lose one's nerve, panic
to'ato'a calmly
toto'a be calm, steady, too thick (stew, kava etc.)
feto'ai bump against
to'afimālie, to'afilēmū quiet, peaceful
to'alēmū, to'amālie be relieved
to'aluga obstacle
toafa barren, treeless region, desert
to'aga (pl. *tō'a'aga*) be zealous, diligent
tōa'i agree reluctantly
tō'ai arrive
to'asā (pol.) be angry, anger, wrath
to'atāma'i (v. pol.) be angry, wrath
to'au yam vine
toe$_1$ (particle) indicates "again", "repeat" etc. (e.g. *toe sau* = come again) more, final, last (e.g. *'ole toe tama* = the last boy)

toe'aiga left-overs (meal)
toe faiga repetition, reconstruction
toe mālosi recover (illness)
toe tū resurrection
toe$_2$ remain, be left, remainder, remnant
toega remainder, balance
totoe remain, be left
toetoe v. nearly (happen)
fa'atoe, fa'atotoe to leave s.th.
toeitiiti almost, nearly
tōē (pl. only) laugh
tōēga shouts of laughter
to'e comb, crest (rooster)
toea'ina (pl. *toea'i'ina*) old man, be old, minister, elder (C.C.C.S.)
fa'atoea'ina like an old man
to'elau trade winds
to'ele to land, stoop low
fa'ato'ele lower someone's reputation
to'ese come down, sink
fa'ato'ese apologize
fa'ato'esega apology, confession
tofa oven stick
tōfā$_1$ (pl. *tōfafā*) sleep, form of address to an orator = *lau tofā* speech, opinion, fine mat
tofā mamao opinion of a chief, shrewdness, foresight
tōfaga (pol.) bedding, sleep
tōfā$_2$ parting salutation - goodbye, farewell
fa'atōfā say goodbye
fa'atōfala'ia (pol.) be decided upon, sanctioned
fa'atōfala'iga decision, conclusion
tōfa'i (A.S.) plunge into ground
tōfatumoana be absolutely lost
tofē steep, precipitous, ravine, precipice
tofi$_1$ split, cleave, divide, a chisel
mātofi be split
mātofitofi cresent-shaped
tofitofi divide, share out
tofitofiga breaking, sharing
tofi$_2$ assign, appoint, position, appointment, assignment
tofia appointed etc.
tofiga occupation, profession
tofitofi pick, choose
tofo test, sample, taste (food)
tofoga tasting
tofotofo test, provoke, make a trial, experiment
tofotofoga experiment
tofotofoga leaga temptation
tofu$_1$ dive, plunge
tofua to huff (at draughts)
tofugia huffed
va'atofu submarine
tofutofu dabble, plunge up & down
fa'atofu immerse, dip
tofu$_2$ (particle) indicates distribution, receive (i.e. each has a share) e.g. *ia tofu le tagata ma keke e lua* - let each man provide two cakes
tofusia allotted, shared
toga South
tōga, 'ie tōga fine mat
tōgafalea obtained by bribery or family influence
togafiti treat, give medical treament, attend to, fix s.th. up, remedy, device, scheme, prank, trick
togafitia treated etc.
fa'atogafiti trickery, dishonest dealing
togālauapi temporary shelter, camp
togi$_1$ make a mark, put on a sign, badge, carve (wood work etc.), mark (exam papers), dot, mark
togia marked, selected etc.
tōgiga$_1$ uniform
togitogi peck, dotted
togitogiga wear a uniform (also *togitasi*)

togi$_2$ (pl. *fetogi*) throw

togia thrown

fetogia'i throw to ea. other

taufetogi be in habit of throwing things

togi$_3$ **totogi** pay, contribute, donate, wages, pay, salary

togia be paid

totōgia paid for

tōgiga$_2$ contribution, donation

togiola redeemer, redemption

togipau charter (bus, ferry)

gāluega togipau contract work

togisala pay for sin of another, make amends, pay a fine

togi$_4$ prize

togo$_1$ mangroves

togo$_2$**. totogo** spring up again (plants)

togotogo growing again

toi tree (leaves used as soap)

to'i adze, axe, halve, split

to'ipua wooden b'fruit adze

to'ia be struck

to'ilalo be defeated, defeat

fa'ato'ilalo defeat, conquer, lower someone's prestige

fa'ato'ilaloina defeated etc.

tōio lengthwise (fish)

tolaulau announce, give out, read

toleni, koleni training

toli pick fruit (i.e. twist stem)

toliu turn septic

tolo$_1$ (pl. *fetolofi*) crawl, swarm, steal food (animals)

totolo creep, crawl, move along in a respectful, stooping posture

tolofia (pol.) stolen

fa'atotolo make child crawl

fetōlofa'i crawl about

tolo$_2$ drag, pull

tolo$_3$ mix, stir (certain foods)

tolo$_4$ put off, postpone, adjourn

fetōloa'i put off frequently

tōlopō postpone

tolopōina postponed

tolo$_5$ singe

tolo$_6$ sugar-cane

tolo$_7$ yam tuber

tolo$_8$ **tolovae** play a ball game w. feet

toloa grey duck

toloa'i litter, brood (domestic animals)

tolo'a'i set one's heart on, seek

tologa long lasting, hard wearing

tololī grating, grinding noise

tolopu (colq.) to drop it (also *kolopu*) – in rugby

tolotolo cape, headland, point

tolu three

fa'atolu three times

toma$_1$ ask for fine mat

totoma search for fine mats

tōma'aga request for fine mats

toma$_2$**,**

fetōma'i encourage ea. other

fetōma'iga encouragement

tōmatau (pol.) encourage, good advice

tomau (pol.) stay behind, remain at home

tomo drop, fall, slip (into water etc.)

fa'atomo make s.th. drop

tomua begin, introduce (a speech, etc.), preface, arrive first

fa'atomuaga introduction, preface

tomuli arrive last

tomumu mutter, grumble

tomumumumu growl

tona yaws (disease)

tonā have yaws

tonatonāfe'e pimple, wart (on an elephantoid limb)

tonu be exact, correct, right, just, agreed, resolved, decided, exactly, correctly, arrangement, plan, decision

fa‘atonu instruct, order, command, fix, put right, arrange, admonish, editor, director, assessor
fa‘atonuina corrected etc.
fa‘atonuga command, order, instruction
fa‘a-lē-tonu be uncertain, doubtful
to‘o punting pole, wife (joc.)
to‘oto‘o walking stick, staff (orator), orator, talking chief (A. S.)., Member of Parliament (W.S.) walk w.a stick, lean on a stick
to‘oto‘o ali‘i chief who speaks
toto‘o lean on
to‘olima press w. both hands
to‘otū forked hanging post
to‘otuli kneel
to‘oala abdominal pains
to‘oma‘a abscess on sole of foot
to‘omaunu hiccup, death rattle
to‘ona‘i main Sunday meal
Aso To‘ona‘i Saturday
tope be quick, fast, rapid
topetope hasty, hurried
fa‘atotope speed up
fa‘atopetope act v. quickly
topevale be hasty
topu‘epu‘e be fitful, spasmodic, act in fits & starts
tosi score, scratch
tositosi scrawl, scribble
fetosia‘i scribbling, scratching
toso pull, draw, heave, drag, rape, trawl (fish)
tosoa raped
tosoga pulling, etc.
tōsoga tug-of-war
totoso trail, drag
fa‘atosotoso be drawn out, dragged
tōtatau rebuke
tōta‘uta‘u be fitful, spasmodic (also *tōpu‘epu‘e*)
totini sock, stocking
tōtino true kin, own, private, special, particular
failautusitōtino private secretary
toto blood, bleed
fa‘atoto cause bleeding
totolua of mixed descent (people)
totoulia a contusion e.g. black-eye
totō belch
tōtō to shuffle (playing cards)
tōtōā (pol.) steal
totōa‘i to regret
toto‘ē crow (cock), crowing, cockscomb
to‘eto‘ē cackle (hen)
tōtōga internal organs, accessories, constituent parts
totonu inside, within, among, in the midst of, interior, in between
totonugalēmū centre of, middle of
toto‘o thick (liquids)
‘apa susu toto‘o condensed milk
fa‘atoto‘o thickly
tou (prn.) you (three or more people)
to‘u (pl. *feto‘ui*) grumble at, scold, answer back, cluck (chicken) speak whilst eating
to‘ū adze
to‘ulu (pl. *to‘u‘ulu*) fall, drop (leaves, fruit, hair)
tovā sit in between, intersperse with
tovale plead guilty
tū$_{1}$ stand, stand up, stand erect, be stationary, alight, settle (bird), pull up (bus), stand in s.th., stand by s.o., be placed, e.g. *tūlua* (second), firm, stable, existing, steep, sharp, customs, ways, posture, submerged rock
tūlia occupied, guarded
tūlaga position, location, status, rank, situation, platform, stage, pulpit, mark, print e.g. footprint, climbing notches in c’nut etc.

tūtū stand idly by
tūtūnoa w.o. just cause or reason
tūtūsolo thinly planted, sparse (trees etc.)
fa'atū (pl. *fa'atutū*) stand s.th. up, set upright, erect, set up, establish, leave standing, park a car, propose a motion, steer towards (boat), squat
fa'atūina stood up, established etc.
fa'atutū men's hair style
fa'atūtū go straight, direct
fa'atūlagaga arrangement
fa'atūfanua roughly
tū'a'ao (pol.) set foot on land, arrive
tūlau'ele'ele to land
tūloto central, in very middle
tūmamā cleanliness, hygiene, clean, hygienic, tidy
tūmātilatila stand proudly, stand instead of sitting i.e. impolite
tūmau cling to, stick to, abide by, firm, fixed, permanent, immortal, everlasting
a'oga tūmau boarding school
lē tūmau temporary
fa'atūmau make fast, firm
tūpaepae (pol.) chicken
tūpito stand at the end
tūsa'o be upright, vertical
tūtai sited towards the sea
tūvae set foot
tūvao start (speech etc.)
tūvaoga start, beginning
tū₂ eye disease - terygium
tua₁ back side of a thing, back (man, animal), also indicates at back of, behind, beyond, outside, overseas
ta'a i tua play truant
tuā over there, beyond
tuana'i be past, over, gone by (time)
tuatua thick (rope, cord)
fa'atua contributions to assist a family provide for a celebration etc.
fa'atuatua believe in, have faith in, rely on, trust, belief, faith
fa'atuatuaga hope, belief, one in whom others trust
fa'atuatuaina relied upon, trusted in
fa'atuatuana'i turn one's back, ignore
tuā'au beyond the reef
tuāfale back yard, space at rear of house
tuāfanua garden land beyond village, (pol.) *tuāmaota*
tuāgalu back-wash (wave)
tuaiti thin (cord, rope), fine (thread)
fa'atuaiti tall & lean (man)
tuālima back of arm
tuāmauga beyond the hill
tuāmata eyebrow
tuāniu mid-rib of c'nut leaflet
tuano'o stoop (also *tuano'u*)
tuāpā beyond, behind the fence
tuāpapa rock bound coast
tuapi'o hunchbacked, humpbacked
tuāpola behind the wall blinds
tuasivi ridge (hills, backbone), brow of a hill
tuasivi vae shin
tuātusi address
tuāua back of neck
tuāulu back of head
tuāvae back of leg
tuāvao deep inland
tua₂ (particle) indicates rows, layers, lines, thickness etc. e.g. *e tua tolu le laupapa* - the timber is three-ply
tua'ā (pol.) parent
tuā'a'ao (pol.) hand, give to s.o.
tuafafine (pl. *tuafāfine*) sister of a man
tuagane brother of a woman
tuai₁ be late, delayed, take a long time, later, lateness

tuatuai	slow
fa'atuai	delay, hold up
fa'atuatuai	ask for time, play for time, delay
tuai$_2$	grater
tuā'ie	working clothes
tualā	loin of pig for chiefly distribution
tualua	make two, double
tuania	be busy, occupied
tuano'a	difficulty, trouble, worry
tuā'oi	boundary, limit, neighbour, adjoin
tuā'olō	(pol.) pig-yard
tuā'oloa	strong S.E. wind
tuāta'afalu	(pol.) at back of a chief, illness
tu'e	edible part of crab, lobster
tufa	share, portion out
tufa'aga	share
tufatufaina	shared out, distributed
tūfanua	commoner
fa'atūfanua	uncouth, rude
tufi	gather in baskets (fruit)
tufu	pool, spring (fresh water)
tūfue	too soon
tufuga	craftsman, expert, carpenter, builder
fa'atufuga	(pol.) tools
tuga	maggot
tugatuga	mosquito larva
tūgā$_1$	be far advanced (of the night)
tūgā$_2$	in a tender part of body e.g. a boil
tūgā$_3$	be bruised (fruit)
tūgā$_4$	critical, insulting (remark)
tūgā$_5$	serious, grave (wound)
tugase	dried kava root
tui$_1$	(pl. *fetui*) stab, jab, prick, sting (insect), spur (horse), thread s.th. through, fork, bayonet, hypodermic syringe, injection, spur
tuia	pricked etc.
tūiga	injection
tuigālama	candle-nut torch
tuitui	goad, prick
matuitui	be sharp, pointed, acute (pain), hurtful (words)
tui$_2$	ceremonial title of paramount chief e.g. *'O le tui Manu'a*
tu'i$_1$	give a blow, punch, knock, hit, strike, hammer, beat, mash, blow up, bomb, blast, eat heartily (colq.), a blow, punch, pounder, pestle
tu'ia	struck
va'atu'ia	ship-wreck
tu'itu'i	pummel, hammer, nail down, knock (at door), pound, pulverize, a pounder, pestle
tutu'i	hammer (in)
fa'atu'iava'a	dangerous to boats (reef)
fa'atu'iavae	protruding - cause stumbling
fa'atu'i'ese	stand aside from, refuse to co-operate - object to, reject
tu'ifao	to hammer (nails)
tu'iipu	c'nut shell shark lure
tu'imomomo	smash up
tu'imōnoi	beat silently
tu'inini'i	pulverize
tu'ioti	knock-out blow
tu'ipala	mash
tu'ipē	strike dead (animals)
tu'itino	blame oneself
tu'i$_2$	fishing device
tuiga	ceremonial S. head-dress (*taupou* etc.)
tu'inanau	long for, yearn
tu'inanauvale	long for vain things
tuitui$_1$	special hair oil
tuitui$_2$	edible sea urchin
tu'itu'i$_1$	sm. stand for vegetables (used during peeling)
tu'itu'i$_2$	short supports between boom and outrigger (canoe)

tula$_1$	bald
tula$_2$	orator (high rank)
tulāfale	orator, talking chief (A. S.)
tulāfono	law
fa'atulāfono	pass a law
fa'atulāfonoina	become law
tula'i	(pol.) pass water etc.
tūla'i	stand up
fa'atūla'i'ese	drive away, expel
tūtūla'i	stand straight up
tūlāi'u	sacrum, coccyx
tulali	blunt (tools)
tūlau	seamless, in one piece
tule, fetuleni	press on, crowd around
tulei	(pol.) speak
tuleiga	(pol.) speech, talk
tūlei	push, shove
tūlemoe	drowsy, nod
tuli$_1$	(pl. *tutuli*) chase, expel, hunt, send off quickly, despatch
tulia	chased, dismissed
tuliga	expulsion
tūliga	hunt
tulituli	pursue unfairly
fetuliga'i	chase around
tuli'ese	drive away
tuli'esea	driven away
tuliloa	run after, pursue
tuliloaga	pursuit, chase
tulituliloa	pursue persistently
tulimanu	hunt (animals)
tulioso	run & jump in
tulitatao	harry
tuli$_2$	joint of the body, knee
tulilima	elbow
tulimanava	loin (also *tulialo*)
tulivae	knee
tuli$_3$**, tutuli**	be deaf
fa'ataligatuli	turn a deaf ear
tulimanu	corner, angle
tulimata'i	watch, scrutinize
tūlipe	tulip
tulitā	bladder complaint
tulitausi'a	make a row or din
tulolo	bend
tulou	expression of deference, please excuse me, pardon me
tulouna	apology for any inadvertent offence in a speech, "with all due respect"
fa'atulou	beg s.o's pardon
tulu, tutulu	leak (of a house), (pol.) cry
tului	put drops into . . .
tūluia	be dripped on
tulutulu	drip, (pol.) cry, eaves
tuluvao	rain drops from leaves
tului	add s.th. to, increase, addition, increment, supplement, interest (on money)
tulu'i	extend, prolong
tulu'iga	end
tulu'ipae	eaves
tuma$_1$	rap (w. knuckles)
tuma$_2$	tumour
tūmoa	banana shoot
tumu	(pl. *tutumu*) be full of, crowded, packed
tumua'i	crown of head
tumutumu	top, peak, height, zenith
tumutumuga	highest stage of s.th.
fa'atumu	(pl. *fa'atutumu*) fill, filler, funnel
fa'atumuina, fa'atumulia	filled
tumusāisai	filled to brim
tūmua	honorific title for orators of Lufilufi & Leulumoega
tuna	tuna (fish)
tūnoa$_1$	freely given or obtained
alofa tūnoa	divine grace
tūtūnoa	w.o. cause or reason
tūnoa$_2$	(pol.) kitchen
tunu	(pl. *tutunu*) broil, boil (also *fa'apuna*), grill, barbecue
tunua	boiled
tunupa'u	broil (chicken, fish)
tunuma	container for tattooing instruments
tupa$_1$	beach crab
tupa$_2$	swollen (filarial infection)

tūpapa ask for fish in an emergency
tupe c’nut disk (used in game of *lafoga*), money, knee-cap
tupea provided w. money
tupu$_1$ grow, arise, occur, happen, growth
tupuga ancestor, originate
tupu‘aga origin, descent, ancestors
tupulaga generation, young people
tupulaga fa‘atasi contemporary with
tātupu (pl.) young shoots
tutupu, tuputupu occur frequently
fa‘atupu make s.th. grow, raise, stir up, provoke, arouse, stimulate
fa‘atutupuina growth, development
fa‘atupuleaga trouble-maker
tupu$_2$ king, sovereign, monarch
tuputama‘ita‘i queen
tupua idol, riddle, (pol.) village
tusa (pl. *tutusa*) be the same, equal, be in accordance with, about, roughly, in any case
tutusa be the same, even, equal, regular
fa‘atusa$_1$ be like, comparable to
tala fa‘atusa fable, parable, illustration
fa‘atusa$_2$ likeness, image, picture
fa‘atusaina likened to
fa‘atusatusa compare, match
fa‘atusatusaga a comparison
tūsameme of no importance
tusapau identical, exactly the same
tūsaga an agreed contribution
tusi (pl. *tutusi*) point (w. finger), draw, write, letter, book, ledger
tusi fa‘amau registered letter (also *tusi puipuia*)
tusi fa‘ataga permit (also *pēmita*)
tūsia written, drawn
tusiga writing
tūsiga registration of, give notice of a marriage
tusitusi write, be striped
fetusia‘i correspond
tusiata drawing, painting, illustrated paper, magazine
tufuga tusi ata architect
tusi folau passport
tusigāigoa subscription list
tusigaata drawing, painting
tusigātala composition, essay
tusi i‘u, tusi pasi school certificate
tusitala writer, reporter, novelist
tuta arrive, land (ship & passengers)
tūtaga arrival
tuta‘ia hit, bang, faced with
fa‘atuta‘ia oppose (an idea)
tute groin
tūtogi ring-bark (tree)
tutu$_1$ (pl. *tatutu*) light (a lamp)
tutuina lit
tutuga lighting, to obtain lamp black from candle nuts
tutu$_2$ to beat paper, mulberry bark
tutua anvil (wooden) for beating bark cloth
tutū to fell, cut down
tutu‘a muscular, sinewy
tutūga special privilege
tu‘u (pl. *tatau‘u*) put down, let down, cut down, fell trees, leave, give up, let go, give, grant, hand over, put, place, decision, reward, result, (pol.) separate, divide
tu‘ufua empty, deserted, let go, leave alone
tu‘uga share (food)
matu‘u put down (load)
tu‘ugamau grave
tu‘ugā‘oloa treasury
tū‘uga race
tu‘ua leave, depart from, name given to senior village orator

ū‘ua break up for school holidays
ū‘uaga holidays
u‘ua‘i blame s.o. else
u‘uai‘ina blamed
u‘ua‘iga accuser
u‘una be overtaken
u‘utu‘u reach out, place, lower
u‘utu‘uga conditions, arrangements, custom, regulation
a‘ata‘utu‘u indulgent, lenient, overlook, ignore
utu‘u race, give up, abandon
etu‘u to curse
etu‘ua‘i blame, accuse one another
etu‘una‘i decline in turn (to do s.th.), entrust, commit, exchange valuables, blame o.a.
etu‘una‘iga pass responsibility to others
etu‘utu‘una‘i negotiate towards a compromise or reconciliation
tu‘uafu reach great age
ū‘u‘ala frivolous
tu‘ualuga (pl.) hills, highlands
tu‘u‘apa tinned, canned (food)
tu‘ufā‘aliali display, exhibit
tu‘ufa‘asolo pass on, hand down
tu‘ufa‘atasi unite, sum up, to pool
tu‘ufa‘atasiga combination, union
tu‘ufa‘apito reserve for . . .
tu‘ufau leave w.o. supervision (child)
tu‘ufua lay (hen), believe too readily
tu‘ufesili ask questions
tu‘ugalēmū unanimous (also *tu‘ugamālie*)
tu‘ugatā adamant
tu‘ugutu passed by word of mouth
tu‘u‘ilalo lower, reduce (reputation etc.)
tu‘u‘itua postpone (also *tolopō*)
tu‘ulāfoa‘i abandon, forsake
tu‘ulāfoa‘iina abandoned
tu‘ulalo prompt, egg on, prompter
tu‘ulima pass from hand to hand
tu‘umālepelepe go into desrepair
tu‘umālo (pol.) die, death
tu‘umāvaega fail to follow instructions
tu‘umuli retreat, retire, go back, departure
tu‘upāgātia be left, abandoned
tu‘upō fix, appoint a date
tu‘upōina appointed (time)
tu‘usa‘oloto free, release
tu‘utapula‘a set date, limit
tu‘utaula lie at anchor
tu‘utele do s.th. on a communal basis
tu‘utia‘i abandon (also *tu‘ulāfoa‘i*)
tu‘utō devote time to s.th.
tu‘uva‘a depart (by ship)
tu‘uvasega sort out
tu‘uvāvā intersperse
tuvae send message after message

Uu

ū$_1$ hold fast, grip e.g. pliers, bitc on, sting (insects) bite (food)
ūtia bitten
fa‘aū tighten, take a firm grip, wedge, spanner, pliers, vice
ūogo have painful sting
fa‘aūamo notch (in carrying stick)
ū$_2$ reed, reedcane, arrow
ū$_3$**, ūū** make a hollow sound, cooing (pigeon)
ū$_4$ turn, point towards

feūa‘i point, turn towards ea. oth.

‘ū$_1$ be bad (taro)

‘ū$_2$**, fa‘a‘ū** look sour, displeased

ua$_1$ neck

ua$_2$ (pol.) rain

uaga (pol.) rain, very wet, torrents

‘ofufa‘aua raincoat

uatea sun shower

u‘a$_1$ paper mulberry tree (for *siapo*)

u‘a$_2$**, u‘au‘a** describes taste and texture of taro

u‘a$_3$**, u‘au‘ā** wiry, sinewy

‘ua$_1$ (verb part.) indicates present or recent past tense, also used in narratives

‘ua$_2$ **‘ua‘ua** grunt

uaea wire, send a wire (cablegram)

uaealesi wireless, radio (also *uālesi*)

uafu wharf, pier, quay

uagagau (pol.) sickness (of o. self)

uāgalu series of heavy waves

ua‘i attend to, concentrate on, attention, concentration

uaina wine

uālesi wireless, radio, telegram

faleuālesi radio station

uālesi fa‘asalalau broadcasting

‘ua loa long-lasting

‘ua mau firm, stable

u‘amea metal, iron, steel

uati$_1$ prise up

uati$_2$ watch (on watch)

uati$_3$ watch, clock

uatogi club, war club

uaua sinews, ligament, vein, artery, pulse

uea dizzy (of head), (also *niniva*)

ufi$_1$ (pl. *taufi*) cover, put on a covering, cover, lid

ufitia covered

ufitaga cover, flap

ufiufi to cover

fa‘aufiufi cover up

ufiata (pol.) darkness, trouble

ufifatafata suit of armour, breastplate

ufilaulau table cloth, *siapo* used with a *“sua”*

ufimata mask

ufisau fine mat for chief woman mourner

ufi$_2$ yams

uga$_1$ (pl. *feuga*) pinch (a person)

ugaina pinched (also *feugaina*)

uga$_2$ borrow

uga$_3$ hermit crabs

ui$_1$ go along, go by way of, gain admittance

uia went along etc.

feuia‘iga circulation, procedure, movements

uiāuta go by land

uitua (pol.) ambush, attack from rear

ui$_2$ announce publicly, call w. loud voice

fa‘aui call, proclamation

ui$_3$ take down, off (peg etc.), remove a restriction

maui set aside (opinion), overruled

fa‘aui take off s.th., give away, concede a point, surrender

fa‘amaui give up, surrender, abandon

uimoto take, pick while still unripe

ui$_4$ **e ui ina** granted that, though, although, despite, in spite of

ui i lea nevertheless

uiga about, concerning, regarding, meaning, character, nature, manner, behaviour

uiga leaga bad habit, fault

uiga lelei quality, virtue

uigā barbed, sarcastic (remark)

fa'auiga put meaning into s.th., make a deduction from . . .
fa'auiga'ese put a bad construction on, make a false deduction
uiga'ese curious, odd, strange
uigalua ambiguous, double meaning
ui'i youngest of a family
uila$_1$ lightning, electricity
ma'a uila battery
uila$_2$ bicycle
uili wheel
uiō high pitched call, scream, yell
'uisikī whisky
ulugia (pol.) canoe
uivale careless toilet habits
'ukulele ukulele
ula$_1$ used in addressing a lady, madam
ula$_2$ to smoke (tobacco)
ulaina, ulaula smoking
feula blow onto, puff, breath
ula$_3$ make fun of, laugh at, mischievous, fond of practical jokes
ulagia laughed at etc.
fa'aulaula done in jest, for fun
ulavale (pl. *ulavavale*) play up, make trouble, be a nuisance
ula$_4$ lobsters, prawns
ulātai lobster
ulāvai freshwater prawn
'ula$_1$ garland, necklace, to wear around neck
'ulālei whale-ivory necklace
'ula$_2$ be deep red, crimson, joyful, red feathers on fine mat
ulaoge (pol.) axe, adze
uli$_1$ steer, drive (car), steering
ulia steered
uliga steering
fa'auli steer, drive, helmsman, steersman
ulimasao (fig.) proceed cautiously
uli$_2$**, uliuli** (pl. *uli*) black, dark (skin, hair)
fa'auliuli black cloud
uliulipaṭo'i jet black
ulitō (fig.) be stubborn
fa'auliulitō strong minded
ulī (pol.) dog
'ulo pot, pan, (A.S.)*'ogāumu*
ulu$_1$ (pl. *ulu*) go into, enter, enter a team in a competition, reach full score (game), set (tennis)
ulufia entered etc.
maulu dash in
fa'amaulu put on, get into (garment)
fa'aulu bring a case, enter (a plea), lodge (a claim), register, enter (in a book)
ulufafo go out
ulufale enter
ulufalega admission, entry (to a school etc.)
fa'aulufale require s.o. to come in
fa'aulufalega inauguration, official opening of a building
ulu$_2$ mend, darn (mat), repair thatch
uluina mended
uluga mending
uluulu fill in, patch leaky thatch
ulu$_3$ head, hair (also *lauulu*)
taulu lop off, cut off (palm leaf)
fa'auluulu be under the authority of . . .
fa'auluuluga most eminent person, height, peak, summit
ulugāli'i man & his wife, couple
ulugāmanu pair birds (male & female)
ululā top of sail
ulumatua first-born, eldest child
ulumoega bed, gift of mats to groom's family
ulupo'o skull, shaven head (shameful)

ulusinā grey, white-haired
ulusū base of c'nut leaf
uluto'i protruding forehead
ulutula bald-headed
ulu$_4$**, uluulu** (of trees, foliage etc.), dense, thick, bushy
uluola grow well, thrive (plants), increase (people, families etc.)
ulu$_5$**, uluulu** clear stones from hearth
ulu$_6$ swell, breakers caused by hidden rocks
'ulu breadfruit
'ulua rich in b'fruit
uluā serious
ulua'i (particle) indicates "first", early, primitive *'o le ulua'i va'a* the first boat
ului, uluia to egg on, incite
uluitino demon possessed, overpowered by an evil spirit
uluitinoina possessed
'uma be finished, done, over, all, entire, completely
fa'a'uma finish, conclude, bring to an end, terminate
fa'a'umaina finished etc.
fa'a'umatia kill, destroy, wipe out
fa'a'umatiaga destruction
'umala sweet potato
'umete wooden cooking bowl
'umi (pl. *'u'umi*) be long, tall
'umi'umi fairly long, tall
fa'a'umi'umi be lengthy, prolonged, make longer
umu stone ground oven, contents of an oven
umuumua covered w. soot, ashes
umufono presentation of food
umukuka cook-house, kitchen
umunamu lime-kiln
umusā gifts to carpenter on completion of a building
umusāga ceremony & feast to mark formal house opening
umutausama'aga food for wedding feast
una$_1$ scale (fish), tortoise-shell, piece of kava root
unā scaly
unafi to scale (fish)
unāi'a cataract (eye)
una$_2$ to remove taro-tops
'une lend
fa'a'une ask for loan, borrow
fa'a'unega loan
unīvesitē (also *iunivesitē*) university
uno'o be bruised, swollen
uno'oa bruised etc.
uō friend, be friends
fa'auō make friends
fa'auōina made friends
fa'auōga friendship
'uo short, thick log
uosi dancing, waltz
upe cling to, swing from
'upega net
āu'upega weapon (war)
'upeti printing board for bark cloth
'upu word, remark, statement
'ūpua talked about
fa'a'upu put into words
fe'upua'i wrangle, quarrel
fe'upua'iga quarrel
upu'atagia amusing, facetious
'upu'ese speak against s.o.
'upumamafa reproach
'upusi'i quotation
'uputu'u tradition, legend
urosa bear
usi$_1$ melt (fat), be ready (of liquid when strained), be tested, tried, dripping (fat), clear c'nut oil
fa'ausi food – cooked taro cubes & c'nut cream
usi$_2$ (pol.) listen, look, pay attention
usita'i obey
usiusita'i obedience
usi$_3$ keep, honour (an agreement), help, look after (family etc.)

usia looked after
usi$_4$ describes blue or green variety of plants, animals
'o le fugausi blue-green flower
uso$_1$ brother (of a man), sister (of a woman)
ūsoga brotherhood
usoali'i name of a group of matai
uso$_2$ umbilical cord
uso$_3$ pith
uso$_4$ (pol.) sm. kava roots
usoa half-cooked (food)
usu$_1$ rise & leave early in morning, meet, be in session (council etc.), make a formal call, reception
usuia left early, has met etc.
usuusu instigate trouble
usufono attend, take part in council, die (of an orator), a representative, delegate
usupō arise before daylight
usu$_2$ court, woo (a woman)
usuga courting
usugafa bring about a union of a man & woman
feusua'iga marriage alliance
usu$_3$ sing
usuina sung
usupese song leader
usui thrust (of a stick, spear)
usuia pester
usuusui push, thrust gently
ususū a yell (anger or joy)
ususūina whooping
uta$_1$ (indicates location) ashore, on the landward side
utā inland
uta$_2$ load, cargo
uta$_3$ beware of, opinion of an orator
utaga wise opinion, decision, wisdom
utauta, fa'auta consider carefully
fa'autagia try to understand
fa'autaga understanding, judgement, (pol.) decision, conclusion
fa'autauta be careful, consider carefully, care, prudence
feutaga'i considerately
utamamao shrewdness, foresight, wisdom
ute tail of a crab, (fig.) best part
utete a Jew's harp
'uti'uti be inadequate, unworthy (of o.s.)
uto float (fish net), bait tied to float
utu$_1$ fill (containers), fill (a pipe), pour into, load (gun)
utufia filled
utufaga sm. amount tobacco
utaga filling
feutufa'i distribute into different containers
utupūpū note carefully
ututau ammunition, cartridge, stick of dynamite
utu$_2$ bamboo fishing container
utu$_3$ search for & dig yams
utu$_4$ ditch, trench
ututaia (fig.) load of troubles
utu$_5$ be stopped, checked (blood, tears etc.), cease, stop (noise)
'utu$_1$ louse
'utua lice infested (hair)
'utufiti flea
'utufitia flea infested
'utu$_2$ a fungus disease
utupoto large tie beam (S.house)
'utu'utu (plant) water-rushes
utuvā happen at intervals
u'u oil, anoint, rub w. oil etc.
u'ua oily, stained w. oil
u'uga oiling
fa'au'u anoint, crown, bless, ordain, consecrate
fa'au'uga ordination, coronation, graduation ceremony (A. S.)

u'una'i push, propel, shove, encourage, persuade
u'una'iina pushed etc.
u'una'iga push, persuasion
'u'u (pl. *ta'u'u*) hold, grip, clutch
'ūmia gripped etc.
'u'uga a grip
'u'umau hold fast
'u'umauina held fast

Vv

vā$_1$ be divided, separated, estranged – on bad terms, space, distance between . . , relationship
fa'avā estrange, alienate
vā$_2$ (prefix) indicates distance, relationship
vāapiapi narrow
vāfeagai relation bet. people, things
vāfealoa'i rules of behaviour, etiquette
vālatalata close, near (to ea. o.)
vāmamao far from (ea. o.) – also *vāvāmamao*
vānimonimo sky
vātau on bad terms
vāteatea wide open sky
vātele wide
va'a boat, ship, vessel, craft
va'ava'a skeleton of a bird (w.o. wings)
fa'ava'a bind a book, frame a picture, cover, binding, frame
va'aafi motor boat, outboard
va'aalalo surface vessel
va'aalo bonito canoe
va'afolau sailing ship
va'akarasini motor boat, launch
va'alele aircraft
va'amaulu,
va'atofu submarine
va'amoso'oi raft
va'ataualo rowing boat
va'atele large vessel
va'a fa'atau fortune teller
va'ai (pl. *va'ai)* look at, look, sight
va'aia catch sight of, look after
vā'ai observe, scrutinize
va'aiga view, sight, look, appearance, supervision, spectacles, glasses
va'ava'ai act of looking, seeing, watching
va'ava'aiga supervision, care
fa'ava'ai open s.o's eyes
feva'aia'i look around
va'aifetū observatory, astronomer
vae$_1$, vavae divide, separate
vāea be removed, reduced in numbers
vāvaeina adopt a child
vāega section, division, part, portion, share, party of people, faction
vāevae divide, be careful (in a speech)
vāevaeina divided
māvaevae cracked
vaevaelua hesitant
fevaevaea'i be in disagreement
fevaevaea'iga disagreement
vaegā'au troops, army
vaegāmea fraction
vāeloto fly flag half-mast
vāelua divide in two
vāeluaina divided in two
vaeluaga half, middle
vāeluagalēmū one of two equal parts
vāeluāpo middle of the night
vāesefulu divide in ten
vae$_2$ lower limb, leg, foot
vāea, tavae kick

fa'avae	foundation, basis, constitution, fundamentals, principles, to found, establish, to have its roots in . . .
vāefā	four-legged, quadruped
vaematua	big toe
vaemutu	one-legged
vaeoso	be willing to help
vaepenisini	accelerator (car)
vaepi'o	lame, crooked leg
vaesape	walk on side of foot
fa'avaevaetulī	long-legged
vāe	used in polite expressions e.g. *vāe ane i le aofia* – with respect to all present
vaeseugā	(pol.) parted for a long time
vagai	face o.a., sit opposite
vagaia,- vagavagaia	surrounded
vāganā	except, unless
vai$_1$	water (usually freshwater), medicine, remedy, c'nut-gourd
vaia	watery
tavai	give water, medicine
vaivai	a puddle
fa'avai	soak in water, stay in water (for long time)
vaiaitu	bush medicine
vai'eli	well
vaifagaloa	bay, inlet
vaigase	local anaesthetic
vaiinu	drinking water
vailā'au	medicine, drugs, disinfectant, deodorant
fa'availā'au	develop a film
vailaumea	S. medicine
vailepa	pool, stagnant water
vailolo	(pol.) c'nut
vaima'a	stone jar
vaimanu'a	antiseptic
vaimāsima	epsom salts
vaimoe	general anaesthetic
vaimū	iodine etc. (*aiotini*)
vainini	lotion, liniment
vai'ona	poison
fa'avai'ona	to poison
vaipaipa	piped water (*vai ki A.S.)*
vaipuna	spring of water
vaisā	Holy Water (R.C.)
vaisalo	c'nut porridge
vaisapai	c'nut water bottle
vaisuāu'u	castor oil
vaitā'ele	bathing place
vaitafe	stream, river
vaita'i	irrigated garden
vaitale	cough medicine
vaitane	*tane* lotion
vaituloto	lake, pond
vaitusi	ink
vai$_2$	trick, trap, guile
vaia	cheat, trick
vāi	(prefix) indicates a space or interval between places, events etc.
vāi 'aiga	morning tea, afternoon tea etc.
vāiaso, vāiasosā	week
vāifale	relationship bet. neighbours
vāiiulā	period, time of the day
vāimāsina	season (also *tau*)
vāimea	spot, corner, place
vāipalolo	wet season
vāitā	half-hour
vāitaimi	interval, period
vāiniu	space bet. c'nuts
vāitausaga	season of the year
vāivae	space-between the toes
vāivao	bush separating two villages
va'iga	exaggerate
va'ili	look for, search
va'iliga	search
vā'ili'ili	extricate, question closely
vāivai	be weak, soft, tired, timid, faint-hearted, watery, light (colour), faint (sound)
fa'avāivai	relax (body)
va'iva'ia	thin, scraggly (hair)
vala$_1$	sm. piece of bark cloth
vala$_2$	reason
vāla, vālalua	be divided in two, forked path

vālatolu	be divided in three
vālatalata	be close
valavala	wide apart
vālavala	loosely woven (mat etc.)
vala'au	(pl. *vāla'au*) call, invite
vala'aulia	called, invited
vale$_1$	indicates "of no use", "in vain" e.g. "*e vale le faiva* - an unrewarding fishing trip
valevalenoa	barren (land)
vale$_2$	lunatic, madman, fool, imbecile
valea	mad, insane, stupid, dull-witted, foolishly
vālevale	dotage, stupidity
fa'avalea	be foolish, fooled, foolishly
valevale	shorn closely (hair)
vali	paint, plaster, whitewash, be built in cement etc., paint, dye, cosmetics, cement, concrete
valitā	asphalt
valifale	house painter
valiga	painting
valo$_1$, valovalo	chirp, twitter (birds, children)
valo$_2$, vavalo	prophesy, predict, foretell
valo'ia	foretold etc.
vālo'aga	prophecy, prediction
valo$_3$, vālovalo	yearn, feel heartache
valo'a	edible sea cucumber
valu$_1$	eight
valu$_2$	(pl. *vavalu*) scrape, grate, scratch
valusia	grated
valuga	grating, peeling
valusaga	peeling stand
vālusaga	vegetable peelings
valuvalu	scrape smooth, rub down, graze
valuāpo	mid night
valusi	make grazes
vane	make a cavity, mortise, carve, chisel
vaneina	carved etc.
vanevane$_1$ vavane	chisel, force open
vanevane$_2$	throb (w. pain)
vānisi	varnish
vanu	valley, ravine
vānuvanu	interspersed w. valleys
vao	bush, forest, weeds, tall grass
vaomago	straw, hay
vaoa	overgrown w. weeds
vao'esea	(pol.) be absent
vaofefe	sensitive plant
vaomāoa	virgin forest (also *vao matua*)
vaotā	bush, forest
va'o	(colq.) to eat
vasa	open sea, ocean
vāsagalēmū	middle
vāsagamālie	be moderate, of the centre
vasa'i	be spaced, occur at intervals, space of time, pause
vasāsui	ham
vase	draw, rule, ruler, hyphen, dash
vasega	ruling, drawing, class, form, body of people
fa'avasega	sort out, divide, separate into lots etc.
fa'avasegaina	sorted etc.
vaselini	vaseline
vasi	be awkward, clumsy
vāsivasi	clumsiness
vau, vavau	work, squeeze w. fingers
vaueli	vowel
vavae	cotton, kapok, fuse
vavai	pliable, flexible (things), lithe, supple (people)
vavala	break (of dawn), shown, revealed
vavale	glutinous, slimy, viscous, mucus, slime
vavao	prevent, restrain, curfew
vaoina	prevented
vāovao	hold back (progress etc.)
vaogōfie	docile, tractable
vāogatā	intractable, fractious
vāvāō	uproar commotion, disturbance

vavau the distant past, olden times
fa'avavau forever, eternal, eternity
vave$_1$ early, in good time, quickly e.g. *vave taunu'u* arrive early
vave$_2$ (pl. *vavave*) be quick, fast, speed, premature
vavevave rush
fa'avave hasten, quickly
vaveao dawn
vāvega miracle, wonder
ve'a common bird (banded rail)
veape verb
vela be cooked (food)
falaoa vela bread
fa'avela cook, grill
vevela be warm, hot, warmth, heat
vēlasia warmed, heated, scorched
fa'avevela heat, (pol.) pit of ripening bananas, (pol.) taro & yam ready for cooking
velavela hot, severe, fierce (famine, epidemic etc.)
fa'avēlavela have a fever
vele to weed
velevelega garden, plantation
velefuti weed w.o. pulling up roots
veli veil
velia veiled
velo$_1$ throw, hurl (spear etc.)
velosia thrown, speared
vēlovelo to spear fish
velo$_2$ antenna, feeler
velo$_3$ slide, push s.th. along
velovelo push gently
vesi, vevesi be agitated, bustle, excitement, confusion, disorder
vēsia confused etc.
fa'avevesi confuse, disturb, upset
fa'avēsivesi disturbance, incident

vete$_1$ to split, smash open
māvete be split
tavete break, cut
vevete open up a food bundle
vete$_2$ spoils of war, booty
veve top covering of S. oven
veveni plump
vī fruit tree (Otaheite apple)
vi'i praise, glorify, national anthem
vī'ia praised
vi'iga praise, hymn
vivi'i praise
vī'ivi'i compliment, congratulate
vi'ivi'iga,- fa'avi'ivi'i be flattering
fevī'ia'i praise ea. o.
vili spin (cotton, top, coin etc.), bore a hole, drill, revolve, strive, make a 'phone call, whirlpool
vilia spun etc.
vivili writhe
vilivili wheel, pedal (bicycle)
vilifatafata brace & bit
vilipā pump drill
vilivilitō run away in fright
viliuila electric drill
vina ask insistently (child) importune, pester
vine grapes, raisins, vine
vineta tree w. edible fruit
vīnika vinegar
vini fruit tree (Otaheite gooseberry)
vi'o form a curve, loop, circle, be coiled
tavi'o make into a curve etc.
violē purple, violet
vivini crow, crowing
volipolo volley-ball
vovo capable of doing s.th.
vōvoga use, point of doing s.th.
vulu wool

ENGLISH to SAMOAN

Aa

a, an se, le (pl. ni)
abandon tu'ulāfoa'i, tia'i, tu'u
abate fāiifo, maui (*of rain*)
abbreviate fa'apu'upu'u
abdomen manava, puimanava, (pol.) laualo
abduction 'ave faamālosi se tasi
abeyance tu'u fa'apalalau, fa'apafala
abide (live) māfuta, nofo
ability agava'a, tāleni
able mafai, gafatia, lavā
aboard i luga o le va'a
abode nofoāga, (pol.) afio'aga
abolish fa'a'uma, fa'agata
aboriginal tagata moni, tagata uliuli
abort fa'apa'ū le pepe, lēfaia
abound maua tele
about
(concerning) e uiga i
(almost) tāli
(approximately) e tusa mā, pē
above i luga o, i luga a'e o
abreast fa'alautata'i
abroad i nu'u 'ese, i nu'u mamao
abrupt se'i, fa'afuase'i
abscess fuafua
absent 'o le aunoa mā, e leai, lē 'auai
absent-minded loto galo
absolutely matuā, 'ato'atoa, a'ia'i
absorb (soak up) miti, mimiti
abundance mau, e tele
abuse fa'amele
accept talia
access sao
accelerate fa'asaosaoa
accelerator (car) vae penisini
accident mea mao, fa'alavelave fa'afuase'i, *(A.S.)* esikeni
accommodation mea e api ai
accompany ō fa'atasi ma
accomplish e mafai ona faia, 'uma, mae'a
accord
(of his own ___) lona lava loto
(in ___ with) feagai ma, tala feagai ma . . .
accordance
(in ___ with) talafeagai ma, e tusa ma
account (story) tala, fa'amatalaga
(___ in a store) 'aitālafu
(of no ___) fa'atauva'a
(on ___ of) 'ona 'o, auā
accountant tausi tusi tupe
accurate sa'o lelei lava, matuā sa'o, sa'o a'ia'i
accusation mōliga, mōliaga
accuse tu'ua'i, mōlia
accustomed to māsani ma, fa'amāsani
ace (cards) 'o le sai
ache tigā, gāoi, gagase
achieve mafai, maua
acid 'āseta
(___ taste) 'o'ona
acknowledge ta'uta'u, fa'ailoa
(___ a gift) 'ailao
acquaint fa'amāsani
acquaintance 'o le māsaniga
acquiesce e i'u ina loto i ai
acquire maua mai
acquit ta'umamā
acre 'eka
acrobat tama faitīfaga
across i le isi itū, fa'asālavei, fa'alava
(over there) i tuā
act āmioga, gāluega
(law) tulāfono
(___ of worship) tāpua'iga, saunigā lotu
action faiga, gāluega, gāoioiga
(out of ___) lē aogā

(prepare for ___)	fa'atagataga, mā 'ulu'ulu
(___ song)	pese fai taga, mā'ulu'ulu
activate	fa'agāoioi
active	gāoioi tele
activity	gāoioiga, gāluega
actor	tama faitīfaga
actress	teine faitīfaga
actual (real)	mea moni, moni lava
acute	matuitui, ogoogo
adamant	tu'ugatā, maua'i, lē finauaia
Adam's apple	ponaua
adapt	fa'atatau, fa'afetaui, fa'amāsani
add	fa'aopoopo, tului, fa'asoso'o
addition	fa'aopoopoga
additional	
(two ___ houses)	e lua isi fale
address	
(residence)	tuātusi
(speech)	lāuga, sāunoaga, fetalaiga
(form of ___)	fa'alagiga
adhere	pipi'i, taumau
adhesive	mea fa'apipi'i
adjoin	soso'o
adjourn	mālōlō, tolo
adjudicator	fa'amasino, pasi lauga
adjust	fa'afetaui, fa'asa'o, fa'atonu
administer	pule
administration	pulega
admiral	ta'ita'i o le fuāva'a, atimalala
admiration	sa'afi'afiga
admire	mata'i, fiafia i ai
admit	fa'aavanoa, fa'ataga, fa'aulufale
(agree)	'ioe i ai
admonish	a'oa'i, fa'atonu
adopt	
(___ a child)	fai ma tama fai
(___ a point of view)	talia se manatu
adorn	teuteu, fa'amātagōfie
adrift	tafea
adult	tagata matua
adultery	mulilua
advance	au'iluma, aga'i'i luma
advanced	mao a'e
advantage	itū lelei, fa'amanuiaga
adverb	soaveape
adversity	sa'ā, feuia'iga faigatā
advertise	fa'ailoa, fa'asalalau
advice	faulalo, faufautua, fautuaga, tōmatau
advise	faufautua, fa'atonutonu, fesoasoani, tōmatau, tīma'i
adviser	'o le fautua, fa'atonu
advocate	fautua, puluvaga
adze	to'i (pol.) 'aga'ese, 'ausulu, malau
(stone ___)	tautua, to'i ma'a
aeroplane	va'alele
afar	i mea mamao
affair	matā'upu, fe'au, faiga
affect	tau lavea, āfāina
affectation	fia mamalu, fa'alialia
affection	alofa
afflict	pāgātia, puapuagātia
affluent	tamāo'āiga, mau'oa, mau tupe
afford	gafatia
afloat	opeopea
afraid	fefe, lotovāivai, popole
after	ina'ua, 'ā'uma
afterbirth	falefale
afternoon	afiafi, aoauli
afterwards	mulimuli ane
again	toe
against	fa'alagolago i
(in opposition to)	aga'i, tau tete'e
age	'o le matua, tausaga
(for ages)	tausagā
aged (man)	toea'ina
(woman)	lo'omatua, olomatua
agent	sui
(property ___)	o lē fa'atau fanua ma fale
aggravate	fa'a'ono'ono, fa'afiu
agile	feosofa'i
agitate	vevesi, fa'anenefu
ago	talu ai, taimi ua mavae
agree	loto, lotomalie, 'ioe, taliaina, fetaui, feagai
agreement	feagaiga, maua se tasi, tonu
agriculture	fai fa'ato'aga, mea tau fa'ato'aga

aground	to'a, pa'ulia
ahead	i luma
aide-de-camp, (A.D.C.)	fa'afeao
ailing	'auma'ia
aim	sini, mea 'ua tausisi i ai
(__ a gun)	ta'i, fā'ata
air	savili, 'ea
aircraft	va'alele
airport	malae va'alele
ajar	ma'avā
alarm	atuatuvale
(sound the __)	ili pu
alarm clock	uatifafagu, uati tatagi
alas!	auē, pagā, tālofa e!
albino	tetea
alert	mataala, mata'alia
algae	limu
alien	mai fafo, 'ese, tagata 'ese
alienate	fa'avā, fai ma fili
alight (fire)	tafu, fa'aola
(bird)	tū
(passenger)	tū lau'ele'ele
alike	tutusa, fōliga i ai
all	'ātoa, 'uma, ona pau lea
allegiance	loto tautua
alliance	so'otaga
(marriage __)	feusua'iga
allot	fa'asoasoa, tufa, lufilufi
allow	fa'ataga, loto malie
allowance	alauni
all powerful	mamana
all right	'ua lelei, e lē āfāina
almighty	mamana, pule aoao, silisili 'ese
alms	fa'atōga i tupe
almost	tāi, tāli, tau, toetoe 'ā, tau lata, toeitiiti 'ā, semanū
aloft	i luga
alone (person)	to'atasi, na'o ia
along	ane, i tafatafa o
alongside	i tala ane o, i tafatafa o
aloud	leo tele
alpha	*(Bible)* 'ālefa
alphabet	pī
already	'ua 'uma ona fai

all ready	'ua sauni mea 'uma
also	fo'i
altar	fata faitaulaga, (R.C.) āletale
alter	liu, toe fai
alteration	toe faiga, suiga
alternate	fesuisuia'i, feauaua'i
although	e ui ina
altitude	'o le maualuga
alto (voice)	'ōloto
altogether	fa'atasi, 'uma
always	pea lava, i taimi 'uma, faifai pea
amaze	ofo, meia, māofa
ambassador	sāvali, amapasa
ambiguous	uigalua
ambition	naunau
ambulance	ta'avale a le fale ma'i
ambush	lama, fa'apō
amen	amene
amenable	lotomalie
amend	fa'alelei, toe teuteu
amendment	toe teuteuina
ammunition	ututau
among	i totonu o, i le vā o, fa'atasi ma
amplifier	fa'atele leo, masini fa'ateleleo
amount	aofa'iga, tau aofa'i
amputate	tipi motu (vae, lima)
amuse	fa'afiafia, fa'a'ata
amusement	fiafia, fiafiaga
amusing	mālie, 'atagia
anaemic	toto vāivai, fole
anaesthetic (general)	fa'amoe
(local)	fa'agase
ancestors	(pl.) tupuga, tupu'aga
anchor	taula, tauva'a, tu'utaula
ancient	leva, loa, fa'aanamua, anamuā
and	ma, i le, fa'apea fo'i
angel	agelu, agelo
anger	ita, (pol.) to'asā, to'atāma'i
(to __)	fa'aita
angle	tulimanu, pi'o
Anglican (church)	Lotu Egelani, Ekalesia Ageleane
angry	ita, (pol.) to'asā, to'atāma'i, ma'ema'eā

animal manu, mea, meaola, manuvaefā
ankle tapuvae
(__ bone) ponaponāvae
(__ length) talaloa
(__ length dress) 'ofu tātapuvae
anklet tauvae
annex soso'oga, 'o le fa'ase'e
annihilate fa'atāma'ia, fa'a'umatia
anniversary fa'amanatuga
announce ta'u, folafola, fa'ailoa, (pol.) pāui
announcement folafolaga, fa'aaliga
annoy fa'asoesā
annual fa'aletausaga
annul fa'alēaogā, tatala
anoint fa'au'u
another se isi, le isi
answer tali, mautali
ant loi, lōata, loipoto
antagonize faifili
antenna
(fish etc.) velo
(T.V.) enatena
anthem (gen.) pese
(national) vi'i o le tupu, vi'i o le fu'a
anticipate aloalo
antiseptic vai manu'a, vaimū
anus māliuga, alāfe'au
anxiety, anxious o le fā'atu, popole
any se, ni, so'o se, se isi
anyhow tusa lava
anyone so'o se isi, so'o se tasi
anything so'o se mea
anywhere soo se mea
apart 'ese'ese, māvae, valavala
apartheid fa'anofo 'ese'ese (e.g. *S. Africa*)
aperient vai fa'atafi
apex pito i luga, tumutumu
apiece ta'itasi
apologize fa'ato'ese, ifo
apology fa'ato'esega, ifoga
apostle aposetolo
apostrophe koma liliu, gau
apparatus lā'au, tōtoga
apparent iloa tino, fōliga ma . . .
apparition fa'aaliga
appeal tagi
appear aliali mai, fōliga mai, fotua'i mai, peisea'ī
appearance fōliga, tino mai, va'aiga
appease fa'amālū
appendix
(organ) pitoga'au
(to a book) vāega fa'aopoopo
appetite fia 'ai
applause patipati
apple 'apu
appliance mea faigāluega, togafiti
application 'o le fa'aaogāina, fa'atatau, tālosaga
apply
(ointment etc.) nini
(for a job) su'e se gāluega
(put on) tu'u
(be appropriate) tatau, onomea
appoint tofi, fa'anofo, tōfia, atofaina
appointment tofiga, tofi
apportion tufa, lufilufi, fa'asoa
appreciate lagona, talisapai, talifiafia
apprentice nofo a'oa'oina i se tasi faiva
approach fa'alatalataane, sōsō ane
appropriate feagai lelei, onomea, (pol.) taugamālie
approve malie i se mea, fa'amaonia, 'ioe i se mea, tausa'afia
approximately e tusa 'o __
April Aperila
apron tali'ele'ele
arbitration fa'amasinoga
arch lo'u, faitoto'a
archbishop epikopo sili
archipelago atu motu
architect tufuga tusi ata
area ogā'ele'ele
argue finau
argument finauga, manatu, feasua'iga
argumentative finauvale
arise tupu, alu a'e, tauala, māfua
aristocratic fa'atamāli'i
arithmetic 'o le fika, numera

ark va'a (o Noa) etc.
arm lima, 'ogālima (pol.) 'a'ao
(to __) fa'a'ā'upega, fa'ala'ei'auina
armchair nofoa fa'alagolago
armful opoopoga
armpit 'ao'ao
army 'au, vaegā 'au, 'aufitafita, itūtaua, 'autau
around ta'amilo
arouse fafagu, fa'aosofia le loto
arrange teu, fa'atatau, tāupulepule, faifa'atatauga
arrangement tonu, fa'atatauga, tu'utu'uga, faigātonu, tu'ugātala
arrest pu'ega, pu'efa'apāgotā, ave fa'apagotā
arrive o'o, tō'ai, taunu'u, tuta
arrogant fa'asausili
arrow ū, ūfanafana
arrowroot māsoạ̄
art faiva, tusiata
artist tusiata
artery uaua, alātoto
arthritis gugu
article (thing) mea
(story) tala
articulate fa'aleo
articulation fa'iga, gaugāivi, fa'aleoga
artificial mea fai
(__ teeth) nifo fai
as (__ if) e pei, peisea'ī
(__ soon as possible) i le vave 'ua mafai
ascent 'o le a'e
ashamed mā, māsiasi, (pol.) matamuli
ashes lefulefu
ashore i uta, pa'u matū
ashtray tālefulefu
aside ane, i autafa
(set __) fa'a'ese, tu'u'ese
ask fesili, tapa, taga, 'aisi, fa'atōga
(__ earnestly) pulunaunau
(__ pardon) fa'atulou, fa'ato'ese
(__ repeatedly) vinavina
(__ permission) fa'anoi
(__ for food) 'aipula, 'aipupula, 'ai'aiga
asleep moe, (pol.) tōfā (pl. momoe, tōfafā)
aspect itū
asphalt vali tā
ass 'āsini
assassinate fasioti
assault (attack) fasi tagata, fa'ao'olima
assemble (collect) ao, aofa'i
(meet together) fa'apotopoto
(fit together) fafatu
assembly fa'atasiga, fa'apotopotoga, aofia
(Legislative __) Fono Faitulāfono
assessor fa'atonu
assign tofi, tu'u mai
assist fesoasoani
assistant tagata fesoasoani
associate 'au fa'atasi, miomio
association fa'alāpotopotoga, sosaiete
assume tau'ave, fa'apea
(I assumed) fā te a'u
assure ta'utino atu, mautinoa
asthma sela
astonish fa'aofo, ofo, māofa
astray sē, fesēa'i, ta'asē
(lead __) fa'asesē
astride fa'amāgai, ti'eti'e
astronaut 'ave va'asipeisi, 'ave va'a o le vāteatea
astronomer va'ai fetū
at i, iā
(__ once) nei loa, nei lava
ate 'ai, (pol.) tāumafa, (pl. 'a'ai, tāumamafa)
atmosphere 'ea, atemosifia
atomic atomika
attach noa, nonoa, pipi'i, soso'o, fa'aopoopo, auau
attack osofa'iga, osoga, fa'apō, si'i le taua
attain maua, laveia
attempt taumafaiga, taumafai
attend
(be present) 'auai, fa'atasi, usufono
(pay attention) fa'alogologo)

(__ to s.th) tausi, fai
attendant agai, fa'afeao
attention ua'i, fa'alogo
(stand to __) tū fa'amalō
attitude uiga
attract tōsina
attractive mānaia, lālelei
auction fa'atautu'i
August 'Aokuso
audible logo, lagona
audience 'aufa'alogologo, 'aufa'afofoga
aunt tuafafine o le tamā, uso o le tinā
auspicious (occasion) taeao fou, taigamālie, aso 'ula
author tusitala, lē na tusia . . .
authority pule, pulega
authorize pule, fa'atonu, fa'amaonia, fa'ataga
automatic gāluea'iina e ia lava, 'otomeki
autumn tau e afu ai mea
available avanoa
(no longer __) lē toe maua
avenge taui, taui ma sui
avenue ala
average e māsani ai, tūlaga māsani
avocado pear avoka
avoid 'alo 'ese, fa'atala'ese, te'ena
await fa'atali, nofo fa'amoemoe
awake ala, iloa, mālamalama
awaken fafagu
award foa'i, fa'ailoga
(wages __) totogi pulea e le mālō
aware iloa, lagona
away atu, 'ese
(right __) nei lava
awe mata'u
awful mata'utia
awkward valea, vasi, limavalea
awoke sa ala, te'i
axe to'i, (pol.) aga'ese, matau, meleke
axle 'au

Bb

baby tamameamea, pepe, tama'i meaola
bachelor tamaloa nofofua
back (the __) tua, papātua
(__ of) i tua o
(turn one's __) fulitua
(to support) fa'alagolago, palepale
backbite muimui
backbone ivitū
background i tua
backward (person) tele gese le māfaufau
(direction) i tua
backyard i tuāfale
bacon fasipua'a fa'aasu
bad leaga, vale
(__ food) mafu
(not too __) feoloolo lava
(too __) tālofa e
baffle fa'avevesi
bag taga
baggage 'ato
bail (water) tatā, asu
(legal) tupe fa'amau
bait māunu
bake tao
baker faifalaoa
bakery fale faifalaoa
baking powder 'o le fefete
balance (money) tupe totoe, pāleni
(__ s. th.) fa'asagasagatonu
balcony poletito i luga, fogāafeafe
bald tula
bale taga
ball polo, potoi
balloon paluni
ballot pālota

bamboo ‘ofe
banana fa‘i
(bunch) ‘aufa‘i
(hand) taifa‘i
(leaf) laufa‘i
(cigarette paper) sului
(ripe __) fa‘i otā, fa‘ipula, (A.S.) fa‘ipala
band (musical) fa‘aili
(people) ‘au
(stripe) mua
(elastic) pa‘u meme‘i
bandage fusi
bandit tagata faomea
bang pā
banish fa‘ate‘a, fa‘aaunu‘ua, tuli‘ese
banishment aunu‘ua, tāfeaga
banjo penisiō, ‘ukulele
bank (river) ‘auvai
(money) fale tupe
(__ note) tupe pepa
(__ teller) tala tupe
bankrupt gau, pa‘ū le kamupani
banner fu‘a
banquet tāumafataga
banyan tree āoa
baptize pāpātiso, (R.C.) papitema
baptism pāpatisoga
bar (soap) fāsimoli
(prevent) pupuni, tāofi
barb tala, lave
(barbed wire) uaeatuitui, pāuaea
barbarian fa‘alenu‘upō
barbecue pāpikiu
barber ‘o le ‘otiulu, pāpa
bare (torso) fa‘asausau
(land) ta‘alaelae, toafa, lēvaoa, lāolao
(__ one’s teeth) lī
bareback ti‘eti‘e fua
barefoot e lē se‘evavae
bargain mea taugōfie
(to __) fetu‘una‘i
barge lāgisi, lānisi *(also launch)*
bark (tree) pa‘u
(dog) ou
(__ cloth) siapo, tapa
barley karite *(Bible)*
barrel paelo
barren (land) lafulafuā, toafa
(women) pā
barter fefa‘ataụa‘iga (e aunoa ma tupe)
base (foundation) fa‘avae
(baseball) pesi
baseball pesipolo
bashful mā, matamuli
basin pēsini, ‘apa fafano
basis fa‘avae
bask (in sun) fa‘alā le tino
basket ‘ato, ola
basketball pasiketi polo
bass (voice) malū
bast (tree) fau, u‘a
bastard ‘ela‘ela
bat (animal) pe‘a
(cricket) pate, tā
bath tā‘ elega, tā‘ele, (pol.) ‘au‘au, fa‘amālū
bathe tā‘ele (pol.) ‘au‘au, fa‘amālū
bathing costume ‘ofu tā‘ele
bathroom potu tā‘ele
batter (cooking) paluga
(beat) talepe, mā‘omo‘omo
battery ma‘auila
battle taua
(__ field) tafā o le taua
bawl ‘avau, tagi leotele
bay fagaloa
(__ horse) solofanua mūmū
bayonet tui
bazaar pasā
be (verb) e, ‘ua, na, sa, ‘o etc.
beach matāfaga
(__ a canoe) talana‘i, palana‘i
beacon fa‘ailo o le ava, molī ta‘ialāva‘a
beak (bird) gutu
beam (timber) lā‘au tāfafā
(light) ‘ave o le lā
(smile) mata fiafia tele
bean pī
bear (animal) urosa, pea
(carry) tau ‘ave
(__ a child) fanau
(__ fruit) fua
beard ‘ava, ‘avalalo, (pol.) soesā
beast mea, manu
beat (music) pa‘ō, taimi

(to __)	tā, sasa, fasi, pōpō, tu'i, tavete
(heart __)	tātā
beaten (lost)	fa'ato'ilaloina, faiaina
beautiful	mānaia, lelei tele, malie, mātagōfie, lālelei
beautify	fa'amānaia
became, become	avea ma, fai ma
because	'auā, ona 'ua, talu ai, (colq.) leaga
beckon	tālo, genogeno
becoming	
(of dress)	onomea
bed	moega, ulumoega
bedding	'ie moega, (pol.) tōfaga
bedroom	potu moe
bee	lago meli
beef	fasi povi
(corned __)	pīsupo
beer	pia, 'ava mālosi
beetle	'āvi'ivi'i
before (time)	'a'o le'i o'o 'i
(place)	i luma o
beforehand	muamua
beg	ole, 'aisi, tagi
(__ pardon)	fa'atulou
beggar	tagata fa'atoga i mea, tupe etc., tagata 'aisi, paka
begin	'āmata
(originate)	āfua
beginning	'āmataga
begrudge	lotovale
behalf (of)	fai ma sui o
behaviour	āmio, faiga, uiga
(correct __)	agatonu, vāfealoa'i
behind	i tua o, i tala atu o
behold	taga'i, fa'auta
being (human __)	tagata ola
(for the time –)	mo lenei vāi taimi
belch	totō, tōtō'a'ava
believe	talitonu, fa'atuatua
bell	logo
(__ tower)	fale logo
belly	manava, puimanava, (pol.) alo, laualo
belong	e ona e ana, e o latou etc.
beloved	pele, fa'apelepeleina
below	i lalo ifo
belt	fusi, fusi pa'u
bench	nofoa 'umi
(carpenter's __)	laulau kamuta
bend (a __)	afega, pi'oga
(to __)	punou, lolo'u, fa'alo'u
beneath	i lalo ifo
benefit	aogā, maua se aogā
benighted	pogia, pōuliuli
benzine	penisini
(__ lamp)	molī penisini
berth (bed)	moega i se va'a
(to __)	'ua pipi'i le va'a
beseech	augani, matuā ole atu
beside	i tafatafa o
besides	i le ma lea
best	sili, silisili ona lelei
bestial	āmio fa'amanu
bet	peti
betray	fa'alata
betrothed	fa'amau, faufautane *(Bible)*
better (__ than)	e sili le . . . i lo le . . .
(feeling __)	feoloolo
between	i le vā o, totonu
beware	uta, fa'aeteete, 'ia 'oe!
bewilder	fa'avevesi, lē 'āsino
beyond	i tala atu o
(__ reef)	i tuā'au
bias	fa'a'au'au, fa'apito
Bible	Tusi Pa'ia
bicycle	uila, pāsika
motor-bike	uila afi
bid	tauofoga
(__ farewell)	fa'atōfā
big	tele, lāpo'a, tino 'ese (man)
bile	au'ona
bilge (water)	liu, suāliu
bill (account)	pili
(parliament)	tulāfono
(bird)	gutu
billiards	piliati
billow (wave)	peau
bind	noa, fusi, saisai
(lash)	faufau
(__ a book)	fa'ava'a
bird	manu, manulele
(__ nest)	fa'amoega, ōfaga
(__ song)	tausani
birth	fānauga, (pol.) ola
birthday	aso fānau
biscuit	masi

bishop	‘epikopo, ‘epikopō
archbishop	‘epikopo sili
bit (piece)	fāsi mea
(drill)	matāvili
bite	‘ai, ‘ati, ū
bitten	ūtia
bitter	māi, ‘o‘ona, matuitui
bitterly (cry __)	tagi auēuē
black	uliuli (pl. uli)
blackboard	laupapa a‘oga
blackout	mata pogia
blacksmith	faiu‘amea, tu‘iu‘amea
bladder	tagāmimi
blade	lau, mata
(shoulder __)	ivifoe
blame	tu‘ua‘i, fāitio, sā‘i
blameless	lē pōnā
blank	e leai se mea, fua, mea avanoa
blanket	palanikete, ‘ie vulu
blast	pā, tu‘i
blaze	afi sasao, mūsaesae, mūtinitini
bleach	fa‘apa‘epa‘e i le lā
bleed	toto, tafetoto, pāpātoto
blemish	ila
bless	fa‘amanuia, fa‘apa‘ia
blessing	fa‘amanuiaga
blight	ma‘i ‘ese‘ese o lā‘au
blind	tauaso, (pol.) pō,
(__ in one eye)	mataivi
(house __)	pola, pupuni
blind man’s buff (game)	pone
blink	‘emo
blister	pā (i le pa‘u)
block (wood)	‘ogālā‘au
(blocked)	poloka, punitia
blood	toto, (pol.) ‘ele‘ele, palapala
bloody	totoā, tafetotoi
bloodshot	pāpātoto, mūtoto
bloom	fugālā‘au, fua, fuga
blossom	fuga, fōtuga, fotu mai
blot (stain)	maka ‘ele‘elea, pīsia
(soak up)	fa‘amitivai
blotting paper	mitivai
blow (strike)	tu‘i, sasau
(wind)	agi
(nose)	fogi
(breath)	feula
(trumpet)	ili, fā‘aili

blowhole	pupū
blown (by wind)	lelea
blue	lanumoana
blunt	matatupa
blur	fa‘anenefu
(vision)	nenefu
blurt (out)	talaoso
blush	mūmūvale
boar	pua‘a po‘a
board (timber)	laupapa
(committee)	komiti
(a ship)	alu i luga o le va‘a, tu‘u va‘a
(live)	nofo mautotogi
boarding-school	a‘oga nofo mau
boast	mita‘i, mitamitavale, gugutu
boat (gen.)	va‘a, (pol.) sā
(cruise ship)	‘o le meli
boatswain (bo’sun)	posini
bob (up & down)	ma‘alo
body	tino, vasega
(ruling __)	‘o le pule
bodyguard	talitaliuli, leoleo
bog	taufusi
(to __)	goto vae, uili etc.
boggy	magotogoto
boil (ulcer)	ma‘i sua, sila‘ilagi, sila‘ilalo
(to __)	puna, saka, tunu
boiler	‘ogāumu
bold	toa, lototele
bolster	lago
bolt (door)	fa‘amau
(run)	tamo‘e lē pulea
(nut & __)	fao fai nati
bomb	pulu mālosi, pōmu, pulu‘ō‘ō
(nuclear __)	pōmu niukilia
(to __)	tu‘i
bond	feagaiga, noataga
bondage	nofo pologa
bone	ivi, ponāivi
bonfire	tafuna‘i
bonito (fish)	atu, (pol.) i‘a mai moana
bonnet (baby)	pūlou pepe
(car)	ufi o le afi
bonus	tupe fa‘aopoopo fua, toe (A.S.), ponesi
book	tusi, api

bookie (colq.) tagata tali peti
book-keeper tausi tusi tupe
bookshop fale tusi
boom (noise) ta'alili
(canoe) 'iato
boot (foot) se'evae 'u'umi, puti
(car) ana
border tua'oi, pito
bore (drill) vili
(annoy) fa'alavelave mai, fai so'o, fa'afiu
bored fiu, lē lavā
born fānau
(__ prematurely) fanau lē au
borrow fa'a'une, nonō, aitālafu
bosom fatafata
boss posi, pule
both 'uma le lua, to'alua
bother fa'atigā, fa'alavelave, popole
bottle fagu, tipa
(to __) utufagu
bottom
(of s.th.) muli
(of sea) alititai
(of the heart) ta'ele o le fatu
bounce (ball) fiti
bound (tied) noanoatia
boundary tua'oi, tapula'a
boundless fa'alētua'oia, lētua'oia
bounds mea 'ua pau mai ai
bouquet 'o le teu fugālā'au
bow
(weapon) 'aufana
(ribbon) fa'apō
(__ down) punou, ifo, (pol.) fa'asifo
(canoe) taumua
bowels gā'au, (pol.) taufale
bowl pēsini, ipu, tanoa, (pol.) 'umete
(cricket) fa'ate'a
bow-legged vae'o'ofu, vaesape
box (gen.) pusa
(fight) fusu
boxer tama fusu
boxing fusu'aga
boy tama, taule'ale'a
boy scout sikauti
brace (tool) vilifatafata
(support) tāofi

bracelet taulima
braces pā'ave
brackets
(writing) puipui
(wall __) tāofi
brackish (water) sualua
brain fāi'ai, māfaufau
brake (car) tāofi
branch
(tree) lālā
(family) tāu'āiga
(road) magaala
brand itū'āiga (*also* afi)
brandish fa'alālā
brass 'apamemea
brassiere (bra) papa
brave lototele, matatoa
brawl misa, 'ava'avau, tau'upuga
brawny malōlō
bread falaoa (vela), areto (Bible)
breadfruit 'ulu, fuata, (pol.) maualuga
breadth lautele
break
(smash) talepe, malepe
(snap) gau
(glass etc.) ta'e
(rope, wire) motu
(law) solitulāfono
(__ up-school) tu'ua (le a'oga)
(waves) fati
(into sm. pieces) nuti
(__ of day) tafa o ata
breaker(s) (sea) galu
breakfast 'aiga o le taeao, tī o le taeao
breakwater taligalu
breast susu, fatafata
breastbone ivi fatafata
breath mānavaga
(puff) feula
(out of __) sela
breathe mānava
(__ quickly) mapusela
breed
(to __) fanafānau
(kind) itū'āiga
breeze savili, fisaga
brew fa'atū le pia
brewery falepia

bribery	togāfalea, fa'atosina
brick	piliki
bridal party	'aumeamamae
bride	teine fa'aipoipo
bridge	alalaupapa
(__ of nose)	pogaiisu
bridle	fa'agutu
brief	
(short)	pu'upu'u, sa'asa'a
(legal)	fa'atonuga
briefcase	tama'i 'atopa'u, atota'ita'i
bright	
(shining)	susulu, pupula, 'i'ila
(of colours)	mālosi
(person)	poto tele, matapoto, atamai
brilliant	
(people)	ma'eu, a'ia'i, uiga'ese
(things)	'i'ila
brim	lau, augutu
(__ full)	masua
bring	'aumai
(__ to an end)	fa'a'uma, fa'amotu
(__ back)	fa'afo'i
brisk	tiotio, gāoioi vave
bristly	save'u
brittle	magaugau
broad	lautele
broadcast	fa'asalalau
broil	tunu, tunupa'u, (pol.) lalagi
broken	mālepelepe, ta'e, gau etc.
(__ off)	motu
brood (chickens)	toloa'i
(to __)	taumusu
brook	ālia
broom	salu, pulumu
broth	supo
brother	
(of a man)	uso
(of a woman)	tuagane
(R.C. __)	Felela
brotherhood	usoga
brought	sa'aumaia
brow (head)	muāulu
(hill)	mafa, tuasivi
brown	'ena'ena (pl. 'e'ena)
bruise	totoulia, uno'o
(of fruit)	tugā
brush	pulumu, palasi
(to __)	tafi, tafitafi mamā
brutal	fa'asāunoa
bubble	punapuna
buck (horse)	feosofa'i
(money)	tālā (A.S.) (colq.)
bucket	pakete
buckle	fa'amau fusi, kalauna
bud	fuga (ae le'i matala), moemoe
budge	migoi
budget	tupe fa'atatauina
bug	meaola nini'i
bugle	pū (ilitasi)
build	fai, fau, atiina a'e
(__ a fire)	fa'apusa, tafu
(__ up with soil)	tanu
builder	tufuga, kamuta, (pol.) agaiotupu, mātaisau
(master __)	matai tufuga
building	fale, atiga
bulb (electric)	matāuila
bulge	patupatu, 'o'u'o'u, ponapona
bulk	'o le tele (o se mea)
bull	povi po'a
bulldozer	pulutosa, katapila
bullet	pulu fana
bump (into)	feto'ai
bumper bar (car)	tali fa'alavelave
bumpy (road)	'omo'omo
bun	pani
bunch	
(fruit)	fuifui, 'aufa'i
(flowers)	teu fugālā'au
bundle	fusi, taui, afī, 'ofu, tā'isi
(__ fine mats)	'au'afa
bunk	moega
buoy	poe
burden (load)	'āvega
(be burdened)	gāpatia, māfatia
burial	tanuga, (pol.) falelauasiga
burial place	fanua tanu, fanua oti
burn	mū, tafu, susunu
(of heart)	o'otia
(tongue)	feū, mū
burr	fuga pipii
burst	pā
(__ into)	osofa'i
bury	tanu, teu, (pol.) falelauasi

bus	pasi
bush	vao, togāvao
bush knife	pelu, sapelu, naifi
bush medicine	vaiaitu
bushy	felefele, uluulu
business	fe'au, faiva, faigā'oloa, pisinisi, matā'upu
bust (body)	fatafata, susu
bustle	vevesi, fa'atopetope
busy	fa'alavelavea tele, pisi, matuā fa'asaga i fe'au
but	'ae, 'a'ua, 'a'o, peita'i, meanē, tasi le mea
(all __)	vāganā
butchery	fale fasipovi
butt (end)	muli
(to __)	sua
butter	pata, fa'apata
butterfly	pepe
buttocks	muli, (pol.) nōfoaga
button	fa'amau
(__ hole)	pū fa'amau
buttress	te'e, lagolago
(__ root)	lapa
buy	fa'atau mai
buyer	tagata fa'atau mai
buzz	ū (o le pī etc.)
by	i, mai, e
(by and by)	toeitiiti
(beside)	i tafatafa o
by-pass (to __)	'alo'alo
by-path	ala'alo

Cc

cabbage	kapisi
cabin	potu (va'a, va'alele, loli)
cabinet	
(government)	kapineta
(cupboard)	pusa tū
cable	maea u'amea, uaea telekarafi
cackle	talatalaō, to'eto'ē
cage	faga (o se manu), āoa
cairn	ma'a fa'amanatu, tia
cajole	fa'aoleole, sufi
cake	keke
calamity	asovale, mala, (pol.) tāma'i
calculate	fuafua
calculator	masini fai fika
calendar	kālena
calf (cow)	tama'i povi
(leg)	atevae
call	ui, uiō, vala'au, 'alaga
(__ on telephone)	vili
(roll __)	tauvala'auga
(__ in)	afe
(to name)	ta'u, igoa iā
calm	to'amālie, filemū, toto'a
(__ sea)	malū le sami
came	sa sau, o'omai, taunu'u
camel	kāmela
camera	mea pu'e ata
camp	togālauapi
can	
(able)	mafai
(tin)	'apa
canal	alāvai, kanala, vaita'i
cancel	sōloia, lē o'o, titina, tatala se feagaiga
cancer	kanesa
candidate	tagata ofo
candle	molī ga'o
candle nut	lama
candy	lole
cane (beat)	sasa
(reed)	ū
(sugar __)	tolo
canna (flower)	fagamanu
canned-food	mea'ai tu'u'apa
cannibal	'ai tagata, sāu'ai
cannon	fanafanua *(also artillery)*
cannot	e lē mafai
canoe (gen.)	va'a, (pol.) sā, paopao

(double __)	‘alia
(bonito __)	va‘aalo
canopy	falefetāpa‘i, fale‘ula
canvas	‘ie māfiafia, kapoleni
cap	pūlou taumata
capable	lavātia, vovo, agava‘a
capacity	fua, mālosi, agava‘a
cape (land)	tolotolo
(dress)	pūlupulu
capital	
(punishment)	fa‘asalaga oti
(__ city)	laumua, a‘ai
(money)	tupe fa‘avae
(__ letter)	mata‘itusi tele
capsize	sa‘e, faō le va‘a
captain	kapeteni
(vice __)	sui kapeteni
capture	pu‘e, maua
car	ta‘avale
caravan	kalaveni
carbon	kāponi, karaponi
carbuncle	sila‘ilagi, sila‘ilalo
carburettor	kapuleta
card	pepa malō
(playing __)	pepa o le pelē
(pack of __)	fusi pepa pelē
cardinal	katinale
care (for)	tausi, fa‘aeteete, va‘ava‘ai
(prudence)	fa‘autauta
(don’t __)	e lē kea, lē amana‘ia
carefree	tafulu
careful	fa‘aeteete, tautuanā
careless	fa‘atamala, fa‘atalalē, fa‘atitipa
carelessly	so‘ona fai, lē fa‘aeteete
caretaker	leoleo fale
cargo	uta
carol	pese Kirisimasi, vi‘iga o le Kirisimasi
carpenter	kamuta, tufuga, (pol.) agaiotupu, mātaisau
carpentry	fa‘akamuta
carpet	kapeta
carriage	ta‘avale
(transport)	fela‘ua‘iga
carry	‘ave, tau‘ave, la‘u
(__ on)	fai pea
(under arm)	‘afisi
(with yoke)	amo
(on stretcher)	fata
(on one’s back)	fa‘afuata
(w. both hands)	sapai
(__ off w. force)	‘ave fa‘amālosi
cart	ta‘avale toso
(to __)	fela‘ua‘i
cartwheel	tāgāfiti
case	
(box)	pusa
(bag)	‘ato pa‘u
(in any __)	e tusa lava pē
(legal __)	tagi
(in __)	ne‘i, meanē
cash	tupe mo‘i, tino i tupe
cashier	talitupe, kēsia
cask	paelo
cassava	manioka
cast	lafo
(__ a fishing line)	sasau
(__ a glance)	usi le silasila
(__ away)	tia‘i, lafoa‘i
cast adrift	tāfeaga
castle	‘olo
castor oil	vaisuāu‘u
castrate (cattle)	launiu, (pol.) fofō, fa‘amamā
casual	so‘ona faia
cat	pusi
catalogue	lisi fa‘asolo o mea ‘ese‘ese
catamaran	‘alia
catapult	fanameme‘i
cataract	unāi‘a
catarrh	isu mamafa
catastrophe	mala tele
catch	sapo, maua, pu‘e, ‘apo
(door __)	fa‘amau
(caught on s.th.)	lāvea
catechism	‘o le tusi fesili (Meth.)
catechist	leoleo (Meth.), fesoasoani (R.C.)
catechumens	‘ausā‘ili
caterpillar	‘anufe, katepila
category	itū‘āiga, vasega
cathedral	mālumalu
Catholic	Katoliko, Pope
cattle	povi, manu papalagi
caught	pu‘ea, mautāma‘ia
cauliflower	kolifalaoa
caulk	mono, puluti
cause	ala, mafuaga, pogai
causeway	alapae, tanuga

caution	fa'aeteete, lapata'iga
cave	ana
cavity	āoa, 'ono, vane, pū o le nifo
cease (of tears, blood)	utu, 'uma, gata
ceaseless	fa'alausoso'o, fai pea, pea lava pea
ceiling	fā'alo
celebrate	fa'amanatu, fa'afiafiaina, fa'ailogaina
celery	selalī
cell (gaol)	potu
cellar	potu i lalo o le fale
cement	simā
(__ sheet)	'apa simā
cemetery	fanua oti
census	faitau aofa'i o tagata, tusigāigoa
cent	sene
(per cent)	pasene
centenary	senetenari
centimetre	senitimita
centipede	atualoa
central	tūloto
centre (core)	'autū, 'ogātotonu, totonugālemū
century	seniturі
ceremony	sāuniga
(funeral __)	lagi
certain	mautino, mautinoa
(a __man)	'o se tasi tagata
certainly	e lē taumate, lava
(__ not)	e matuā leai lava
certificate	tusi fa'amaoni
(school leaving)	tusi i'u, tusipasi
chafe	mili, mafo'e
chain (metal)	filifili u'amea
(to __)	nonoa
(__ of mountains)	atu mauga
chair	nofoa
chairman	sea, ta'ita'i fono
chalk	penisina, sioka
challenge	lu'i, tete'e, fou
chamber pot	pō
champion	siamupini
chance	
(opportunity)	avanoa
(by __)	tupu fua, mao
change	
(alter)	fesuia'i, sui, liliu
(money)	tupe totoe
(__ a bank note)	tala
channel	alāvai, alāva'a, ava
chaos	so'ona gaogao, matuā fenumia'i
chap (lips etc.)	māvaevae
chapel	fale sā la'itiiti
chapter	matā'upu
char (burn)	mū (ae le'i mū 'uma)
character	uiga, uiga moni, āmio
charcoal	malala
charge	
(attack)	osofa'i, tau
(accuse)	mōliga
(__ a battery)	fafaga le ma'auila
(account)	tusi fa'a 'aitālafu
chariot	kariota
charity	alofa
charm	uiga fa'afiafia
charming	tauagafau, tausala
chart	fa'afanua
charter	
(rules)	tusi fa'avae
(hire)	togipau
chase	tuliloa, tuli
chasm	vanu loloto
chassis	fa'ava'a o le ta'avale
chastise	'ote, sasa
chastity	āmio mamā
chat	tālatala, talanoa
cheap	taugōfie
cheat	fa'a'ole'ole, tilotilo
check (cheque)	siaki
(stop)	tāofi, utu
(verify)	iloilo, su'esu'e, fa'atonu
cheek (face)	'alāfau
cheeky (rude)	tautalaitiiti, ālai
cheep	'io'io
cheer	mua, 'alaga fiafia, fa'amanuia
cheerful	fiafia, mata'ata'ata
cheese	sisi
cheesecloth	'ie valavala
chemicals	vai mālolosi
chemist	tagata tala vai
(__ shop)	fale tala vai
cherish	fa'apēlepēle
cheroot	
(S. cigarette)	tapa'a Samoa (sului)
chest (body)	fatafata

(box) pusa
chew lamulamu, (pol.) mama
chewing-gum pululole
chicken tama'i moa, (pol.) ta'apaepae
chicken-pox tane susu
chief
(principal) sili, sa'o
(title-holder) ali'i, tamāli'i, tui, (pol.) tama, tapa'au
(leader) ta'ita'i
chief's son mānaia, (pol. sa'o 'aumāga)
chiefly fa'atamāli'i
child tamaitiiti
(of a man) fanau
(of a woman) tama
childbirth fānauga
childhood aso fa'a-tamaitiiti
childish fa'atamaitiiti
chill ma'alili
chime tagi
chimney alaasu
chin 'auvae
china (plates etc.) ōmea
chip (wood) malamala
(__ into shape) tā
chirp (chicken) valovalo
chisel tofi
(cold __) tofi u'amea, koasisi
(to __) vane, vavane
chocolate sokalate, sukalati
choice (i.e. nice) le'ile'i (*of food*)
(decide) filifiliga
choir 'aufaipese
(__ master) ta'ita'i pese
choke (car) sioka
(to __) titina, titiva
(__ w. food) laoa
(suffocate) mole
choose filifili
chop soni, tātā, tatu'u
(meat) fasimāmoe
choppy (sea) gutugutu, sousou, si'i si'i
chores gāluega 'ele'elea
chorus tali (o le pese), tini
Christ Keriso, Kilisito (R.C.)
Christian Kerisiano, Kilisitiano
Christmas Kirisimasi
Church 'ekālesia, lotu
(building) fale sā, mālumalu
cicada 'ālisi
cigar sikā
cigarette sikareti
(cigarette-lighter) afi penisini
(packet __) fusi sikareti
cinema faletīfaga
cinnamon kināmoni
circle li'o
(__ around) fa'ata'amilo
circuitous fa'ata'amilo
circular fa'ata'ali'oli'o
circulate (blood) fetāfea'i
(go about) fe'avea'i, fesoloa'i
circumcise tefe (pol.) tafao, fa'amamā; peritome (Bible)
circumference fa'ata'amilosaga
citizen tagatānu'u, sitiseni
city 'a'ai, laumua
civilian fa'asavili
civilized tagata mālamalama, fa'a Kerisianoina
claim āiā, tagi
clam fāisua
clamp fa'aū
clan 'au'āiga
clang pa'ō
clap pati, pō, tapati, patiapti
clapper (bell) 'autā
clarify fa'amanino, fa'amālamalama, fa'atino
clash pa'ō, pā
class vasega
classify fa'avasega
classroom potu a'oga
clatter gaolo, pa'ō'ō
claw mati'uti'u vae/lima, maiu'u
clay ōmea
clean mamā, tūmamā
(to __) fa'amamā, fufulu
clear (view) manino, mālamalama
(away) teu, fa'amamā, tapena, tafi
(empty) ta'alaelae, ta'agaogao, fa'atu'ufua
cleave tofi
cleaver (b'fruit) to'i pua
cleft (in ground) mato

clergy vasega o faife'au
clerk failautusi, 'ōfisa
clever atamai, poto, matapoto, keleva
click tagitagi
(__ tongue) misialofa
cliff tofē, mato, pupū
climate tau, 'ea
climax tumutumu
(in dancing) taualuga
climb (up) a'e, 'a'e, (pl.) fe'a'ei
(down) fa'aifo, aluifo, ifoifo
climbing strap 'āufaga
clinch (boxing) taufūsifusi
(__ a deal) fai feagaiga
cling pipi'i, tūmau
clip (cut) 'oti'oti
(paper __) fa'amau pepa
cloak pūlupulu
clock uati, itūlā
(it is six o'clock) 'ua tā le ono
clog pupuni, poloka
close$_1$ (near) lata
(__ together) vālatalata, vāvālalata
close$_2$ (shut) tāpuni, fa'apau
(__ umbrella) fa'amoe
(__ eyes) moe'i'ini
clot (blood) 'alu'alutoto
cloth 'ie, fasi'ie'ie
clothe fa'alāvalava, fa'a'ofu
clothes 'ofu, lāvalava, (pol.) lā'ei
clothing lāvalava, lā'ei
cloud ao
(rain __) taufānu'u
(black __) fa'auliuli
cloudy aoa, 'auaoa, lagiā
(__ water) gaepu, nefu
clown fa'aāluma, tamafaitīfaga
club (weapon) uatogi
(group) kalapu, sosaiete
(cards) fele
cluck to'uto'u
clue mea molimau, mea fa'asino, fa'amaoniga
clump (of trees) pupulā'au
clumsy vasi, valea, aseva, soso
cluster (fruit) fuifui
clutch pu'e, 'u'u
(car) kalasi
coach (passenger) pasi
(to __) faia'oga, fa'akoleni
coagulate to'a, 'alu'alutoto
coal koale
coarse
(food, materials) patapata, malō
(manners) lēmigao, pa'a'ā
coast talafātai
coastal waters gātaifale
coat peleue
(__ hanger) tautau 'ofu
(__ of paint) valiga
(to __) nini
coax fa'asufi
cobra (snake) kopala, gata fe'ai
cobweb apogāleveleve
coccyx tūlāi'u
cock toa
cockle pae, pipi, tugane
cockroach mogamoga
cockscomb taualuga (o le toa), toto'ē
cocoa koko
coconut niu (pol.) vailolo, mu'a
(grated __) penu
(__ cream) pe'epe'e
(__ husk) pulu
(__ leaf) launiu
(__ milk) sua o le niu
(__ oil) sua, usi, suau'u, ga'opopo
(__ shell) atigi pū
(ripe __) popo
coffee kofe
coffin pusa oti
cohabit (pol.) fai'āiga, usu
coil tā'aiga
(to __) ta'ai, i'oi'o, tagai, fa'ata'amilomilo
coin tinoitupe, tupe
coincide feagai ma
cold mālūlū, ma'alili
(sickness) mālūlū, ma'alili, isu mamafa, falū
coleus (flower) pate
collapse sofa, masofa, palasi, solofa
collar kola
colleague 'aumea
collect ao, potopoto, fa'atasi, sao, putiputi
collection

(money) āogātupe, lāfoga, mē, saogātupe, tusigāigoa
(goods) aotelega, saofaga
college kolisi
collide feto'ai
colon kolona
colour lanu
column pou, laina, solo
comb selu, to'ē o le moa
(tatoo __) au
combat feasua'iga, tautete'e
combine tu'ufa'atasi
come sau (pl.) ō mai; (pol.) susū mai, maliu mai, afio mai, tala'a'ao mai
(__ in) ulufale mai
(__ on) fa'avave!
(__ to) toe mālamalama
(__ back) fo'i mai
comedian tama faitīfaga, fa'aaluma
comedy tala fa'atausuaga, fale aitu
comet pusaloa, kometi
comfort fa'amāfanafana
comfortable mālū, nofo lelei, tu'u faitalia, nōfogōfie
comic (paper) nusipepa fa'atamaiti
comma koma
command fa'atonu, poloa'i
commandment poloa'iga, tulāfono *(Bible)*
commemorate fa'ailogaina, fa'amanatu
commend vi'ivi'i
comment talanoa i ai
commerce fefa'ataua'iga
commission
(payment) totogi fa'aopoopo, pasene
(task) fe'au
commissioner komesina
(high __) hai komisi
commit
(entrust) tu'uina atu
(__ adultery) mulilua
(__ suicide taupule i lona ola
committee komiti
common ta'atele, lautele, faiso'o
commoner tūfanua, tagatānu'u
commotion vāvāō
communal faitasi, tu'utele
communion
(Holy) Fa'amanatuga Pa'ia, Talisuaga a le Ali'i
community itū'āiga
(village __) faigānu'u
compact māopoopo
companion uō, soa
companionship māfutaga
company (group) aofiaga, mālō
(business) kamupanī
compare fa'atusatusa
comparison fa'atusatusaga
compass tapasā
compassion alofa'aga
compel fa'amālosi
compensation taui
compete tauvā, tausiniō
competition tauvāga, fīnauga
complain lē malie, fa'ameo, faitio, muimui
complaint tagi, fāitioga, lē maliega
complete 'ātoa, 'ato'atoa, 'uma lava, māe'a, a'ia'i
completely 'uma, matuā
complex
(involved) felefele
(building) fa'aputugāfale
complexion fōliga
complicate fa'afaigatā, fa'afelefele, lavelave
compliment 'upu fa'aaloalo, vi'ivi'iga, fa'amālō
comply (__ with) 'ioe i ai, feagai ma
compose (a song) fatu
(composed of) aofia i . . .
composer fatu pese
composition tusigātala
composure 'o le lē gāoioi, to'a lelei, to'a fīlēmū
compress 'o'omi fa'atasi
comprise aofia i . ., e i ai
compromise fetu'utu'una'iga
computer komepiuta
comrade uō
conceal natia, lilo
concede
(__ a point) fa'aui
conceited lotovi'i, lotovi'ifua,

	fa'amaualuga, fa'afiapoto
conceive	
(an idea)	afuafua
(woman)	tō, ma'itō
concentrate	ua'i, fa'asagasaga, tāula'i
concern	
(anxious)	o'otiaga, popole
(an affair)	fe'au
concerning	e uiga i
concert	koniseti
conch (shell)	pū, foafoa
conclude	fa'ai'u, fa'amotu, fa'a'uma
conclusion	i'uga, fa'ai'uga, i'ugafono, (pol.) fa'atōfāla'iga, fa'autaga
concrete	
(not abstract)	fa'atino
(mixture)	simā, vali
condemn	fa'asala, ta'uvaleaina, ta'usalaina
condensed	
(milk)	susu toto'o
(shorten)	fa'apu'upu'uina
condition	uiga
conditions	tu'utu'uga
condole	fa'amaise, tigā fa'atasi
conduct	
(behaviour)	āmioga, aga
(to lead)	ta'ita'i
conductor	faipese, fuataimi
confer	fono, tāupule
conference	fa'apotopotoga, fonotaga, koneferenisi
confess	fa'aali, ta'utino, konefesi (L.D.S.)
confession	ta'utinoga, kofesio (R.C.)
confidence	talitonuga, talisapaia
confidential	fa'alilolilo, natia i fatualavai
confine	e gata i, e pau mai i, puipuia
confirm	fa'amausalī, fa'amāonia
confiscate	'ave mea i luga o le tulāfono
conflict	fete'ena'iga, taua
confuse	fa'avevesi, fenumia'i
congratulate	fa'amālō
congregation	'au lotu, fa'apotopotoga, (L.D.S.) uarota
congress	fono
connect	soso'o, lavea, 'auai, feso'ota'i
connexion	feso'ota'iga
conquer	fa'ato'ilalo
conscience	lotofuatiaifo, loto fa'amaoni
conscientious	loto fa'amaoni
conscious	
(be aware)	mālamalama, lagona, iloa, mautinoa
consecrate	fa'au'u, fa'apa'ia
consent	loto i ai, 'ioe i ai, malie, (pol.) finagalo i ai
consequence	'o le i'u, mea'ua mulimuli i ai
conservative	faufaumau, fa'autauta
considerable	matuā, tetele
considerate	manatu i isi
consideration	māfaufauga, manatu
consist (of)	e i ai ma . . .
consistent	tutusa
(__ with)	talafeagai
console	fa'amaise, fa'amāfanafana
consolidate	māopoopo, fa'atūmau
constable	leoleo
constipated	mamau (le manava)
constant	pea lava pea
constitution	tusi fa'avae
constraint	'o'ono
construct	fau, fausia, ati
consul	konesula
consult	tālatala ma, tāupule-pule
consume	fa'aaogā, 'ai
consumption	mea 'ua fa'aaogāina
contact	fetaui, feiloa'i, pipi'i
contagious	
(illness)	pipisi
contain	o lo'o i ai
(__ water)	sua
container	mea e teu ai isi mea
contaminate	pīsia
contemporary	fa'aneionapō, tupulaga fa'atasi
contempt	manatu fa'atauva'a

contend (with) tau, tauvā
content loto malie, pāgamālie, (pol.) finagalo malie
contention finauga
(__ between orators) 'o le fa'atau
contentious fa'afitāuli
contents 'o mea o i totonu
contest pāga
continent konitineta
contingent vāega, vasega
continual faiso'o, lē utuvā, fa'alausoso'o
continuation fa'asologa, so'oga
continue fai pea, fāifaipea
contract
(shrink) māui, meme'i
(work __) konatelate
contrary
(be __) fa'atuga'ese
(on the __) peita'i
contradict fa'atu'i'ese, tete'e
contrast fa'ailoa mea ua 'ese'ese ai, fa'atusa
contribute
(money) lafo, totogi
contribution lāfoga, togiga, monotaga, fa'atua
contrite
(heart) loto salamō
control pule, ta'ita'i
controversial
(subject) matā'upu fa'afitāuli, fefeu
convalesce sā'ili matagi, fa'apelepele
convenient aogā, avanoa
converge fetāula'i
conversation talanoaga
conversion fa'aliliuga
convert fa'aliliu
convey momoli, fa'ao'o, fa'ataunu'u
convict nofo sala, pāgotā
convince fa'atalitonu, fa'a mautinoa
convulsion ma'alili, tafiti vale
coo (dove) olo
cook (to __) kuka, tao, fa'avela, (pol.) fa'amālū, tuna, gāsese
(a __) tagata fai mea'ai, tūvaiaso, kuka
cook-house umu falekuka
cool mālū, fa'amālū, fa'ama'alili, fa'asavili
co-operate 'aufa'atasi, gālulue fa'atasi
cope (w. s.th.) mafaia
copper 'apamemea, kopa
copy ata, kopi, lōmiga
coral 'amu, puga, lapa
cord mānoa, maea tuaiti, uaea o mea fa'aeletise
(umbilical __) uso
cordial
(conduct) agafiafia
(drink) vai suamalie
core (centre) 'autū, fatu, fune
cork momono
(__ screw) vilimomono
corm (plant) 'i'o
corn (food) sana
corner tulimanu, vāimea
(__ of eye) si'u mata
(__ of mouth) si'u gutu
coronary fatu ma'i
coronation fa'au'uga o le tupu
corporal 'o le tā'ailua (fitafita)
corpse tinooti
corpulent tino'ese, putā
correct sa'o, tonu, fa'asa'o, fa'atonu
correspond
(meet, match) feagai, fetaui
(write to ea. other) fetusia'i
correspondence
(letters) fetusia'iga
(__ school) a'oga fetusia'i
cosmetics vali o mata
cost tau
costly taugatā
costume
(women's) pea, puletasi
cotton vavae, filo
couch sofa
cough tale, (pol.) male
(whooping __) tale vivini
(__ medicine) vai tale
council fono, pule
counsel fautua, faulalo
count faitau, mātau
counter laulau fa'atau

counterorder	gāupule
countless	manomanō
country	atunu'u, fanua, i tuā
couple (two)	se lua, taulua, to'alua
(married __)	ulugālii
(__ of birds)	ulugāmanu
(to __)	soso'o
courage	lototele, toa
course	gāsologa, ala, alāva'a
court (law __)	falefa'amasino
(__ a woman)	aumoe (pol.) tu'ualaala
(tennis __)	malae tenisi
(__ case)	fa'amasinoga
courtesy	fa'aaloalo
courting party	aumoega, (pol.) falegāfuafua
courtyard	lotoā
cousin(s)	tauusoga
covenant	feagaiga
(make a __)	osi le feagaiga
cover	tao, ufi, ufitaga, fa'amalu, fa'apulou, ufiufi
(face __, mask)	ufimata
(__ of book)	fa'ava'a
covet	losivale, mānumanu, mana'o vale, tu'inanau leaga
cow	povi (pol.) manu papālagi
coward	tagata pala'ai, 'aiate
cowboy	kaupoe
cowrie (shell)	pule
crab (gen.)	pa'a
crack	māvae
(of brittle things)	ta'e
(skin)	māvaevae
(whip)	gapā
crackle	gapāpā
cradle	
(in arms)	sapasapai
(bed)	moega pepe
craft	va'a, va'alele, (pol.) sā
(skill)	faiva
craftsman	tufuga,(pol.) agaiotupu, mātaisau
crafty	fa'api'opi'o, fa'a'ole'ole
cram	fa'atu'i
cramp (tool)	fa'aū
(of limb)	malō, pē

crane	
(one's neck)	fālōlō
(ship's __)	siligi
crash	pa'ū, pā'ō
(__ helmet)	pūlou malō
crater	ano, gutu o le maugamū
crave	naunau tele
(__ water)	gālala
crawl	tolo, sosolo
crayfish	ula, ulātai
crazy	valea
creak	'ō'ī
cream	kulimi
(medical __)	ga'o, vai malū
(coconut __)	pe'epe'e
crease	ma'anumi
create	fai, fa'atupu, fatu, gaosi, foafoa
Creator	Lē na faia mea uma, 'o le Atua
creature	tagata, manu, meaola
credit (on __)	fa'a'aitālafu
(__ balance)	tupe mamā
(take __)	ta'uleleia
creek	ālia
creep	totolo, sosolo, gāsolo mālie
creeper (plant)	fue, lā'au sosolo
crescent (shape)	fa'alolo'u
(street)	ala fa'alo'ulo'u
crest (bird)	to'ē
(hill)	tumutumu
crew	'auva'a
cricket	
(insect)	'ālisi
(game)	kirikiti
crime	solitulāfono
criminal	tagata solitulāfono
crimson	'ula'ula
cripple	pipili
criticize	fāitio, ta'uvaleaina
(__ privately)	fa'atuā'upua
crook	
(law breaker)	kuluku
crooked	pi'o
crookedly	fa'api'opi'o
crop	fuata, tausaga, fōtuga, fua
cross (ea. other)	fa'alava
(angry)	'iēina, ita
(a __)	satauro, koluse

(make a ___) fa'a'ēkisi (X)
(___ a stream) sopo'ia
(___ roads) magafā, fetaulā'igāala
cross-cut saw 'ilitutū, 'ilivavae
crossing sōpo'aga, la'asiaga
cross-legged fātai
crouch totolo, punou
crow vivini, toto'ē
crowbar kolopā
crowd motu o tagata
(to ___) fetuleni, fa'atumu, lolofi
crown paleali'i, fa'apale, fa'au'u
(coin) kalauna
crucifix koluse
crucify fa'asātauro
cruel sāuā, agaleaga, fa'a taūtala, fa'atāugā, fa'asāunoa
cruise folauga
cruiser (warship) manuao
crumb momoi mea
crumple fa'ama'anuminumi
crunch pa'agugu, pagugu
crunchy matolutolu, ma nutinuti
crush 'o'omi, nuti, sōlipala
crutch to'oto'o (i lalo o'ao'ao)
cry 'alaga, tagi, (pol.) tutulu
cubit kūpita
cuckoo (bird) 'āleva
cucumber kukuma
cuff tapulima, tapuvae, afega
cultivate fa'ato'a, totō, fa'afa'ato'aga
culture aganu'u
(S. ___) 'o le faaSamoa
cumbersome valea, lē pulea
cunning atamai, agapi'opi'o, faitogafiti
cup ipu, iputī, ipuniu
cup-bearer tautū, solialofi
cupboard pusatū, kāpoti
cure (heal) fofō, fa'amālōlō
(dry) fa'amago, fā'asu
curfew vavao
curious fia iloa, uiga 'ese
curl migi, vi'o, ta'ai'ai, ma'epu
curly hair pi'ipi'i, migimigi le lauulu, keli
currant vine mago
currency tupe a se atunu'u
current (now) taimi nei, fa'aneionapō
(water) au, tafega
(electric) paoa, uila
curry kale
curse fetu'u, mālaia, palauvale
curtain 'ie pupuni, pupuni
curtains 'ie tautau, 'ie fa'amalama
curve pi'oga, fa'alo'ulo'u, vi'o, tavi'o
cushion aluga
custom(s) 'o le māsani, tū ma āmioga
customs tiute
(___ house) fale tiute
customer tagata fa'atau
cut tipi, lavea
(___ in two) vaelua
(___ down) tu'u, tatu'u, tā
(___ in pieces) soni, pena
(___ hair) 'oti ulu, (pol.) fa'afuga
cutting tipiga
cuttlefish gūfe'e
cylinder (car) 'ogāumu
cymbal la'au tagitagi, sumepalo

Dd

dab 'eu
dabble (to wet) tofutofu
daddy papa
dagger (joc.) popi, naifi suluga

daily i aso ta'itasi
dairy falesusu
(__ cow) povi taususu
dais tūlaga
dam (river) pā o le vai
damage fa'aleagaina, āfāina
damned mālaia
damp susū
(to __) fa'asūsū, sausau
dance (gen.) siva, (pol.) osiosi, pōula, sāsā, sāusaunoa
(to __) siva, sa'asa'a, sāusaunoa, tenetene, 'aiuli
(modern __) uosi
dandruff mafuga o le ulu
danger tūlaga faigatā, fa'alavelave
(no __) e lē āfāina, leai se fa'aletonu

dare lavātia, lu'i
daring 'āna'ana
dark (colour) mālosi, uliuli
(__ night) pogisā
(evil) leaga, fa'apōuliuli
(keep in the __) nātia
darken fa'apogisāina, fa'apōuliuligia
darkness pogisā, pōuliuli, 'aupōuli
darling pele, mānamea
darn (a sock) ulu, su'i, fai (se māsae)
dart (a __) ti'a
(to __) oso fa'afuase'i
dash (-) vase pu'upu'u, peni fa'asoso'o
(rush) oso loa, tamo'e saosaoa tele
(__ in pieces) momomo
date aso, taimi tuupōina
(fruit) niupiu
daub papanu
daughter
(of a man) afafine (pol.) alo
(of a woman) tamateine (pol.) alo
dawn vaveao, tafa o ata, mālama
(__ chorus) tausani
day aso, ao, mālamalama
(__ to __) i lea aso ma lea aso
(days of old) anamua
(some __) sau aso
(__ & night) pō ma ao
daydream miti ao
daylight ao, mālamalama
dazed sīoa
dazzle sesega, segasega, segaia
deacon ti'ākono
dead (people) oti, mālaia (pol.) maliu, (pl. māliliu)
(no life) lipiola
(animals) pē, mate *(also plants)* (pl. mamate)
deaf tutuli, faipē, logonoa
(turn __ ear) fa'ataligatuli
deal (a great __) e tele
(__ w. s.o.) faifaiga, lotelote, feagaiga
dear (love) alofa, pele
(cost) taugatā
dearest pele, fa'apēlepele
death oti, maliu, (pol.) tu'umalō
(put to __)
(person) fasioti, fa'a'uma
(animal) tapē, tamate
debate felafolafoa'i, taulote, liuliu
(orators' __) fa'atau
debt 'aitālafu
(in __) nofo 'aitālafu
decay pala, fāiifo
(tooth) nifo elo, nifo ma'i
deceitful fa'agutugutulua
deceive fa'ase'e, 'ōlegia, pelogia, fa'amaoina
December Tesema
decent (person) āmiolelei
decide filifili, fa'ai'u, mautonu
decimetre tesimita
decision i'uga, filifiliga, i'ugāfono, (pol.) fa'atōfāla'iga
deck fogāva'a
declaration folafolaga, ta'utinoga
declare ta'u, folafola, ta'utino
decline (go down) fāiifo
(refuse) lē talia, fa'afiti
decorate teteu, fa'amātagōfie, teuteu
decoration
(medal) fa'ailoga

(ornaments) tēuga
decrease fa'aitiiti, tauau ifo
deduct 'ave'ese
deduction
(conclusion) meaaliali, fa'auiga
deed (action) faiga
(legal) fa'aaliga saunia e se loia
deep loloto, maulalo
(__ sound) 'ō'ō
(__ rooted) maua'a
deer 'aila
default lē o'o, lē tausia se feagaiga
defeat fa'ato'ilalo, faia'ina
defecate ti'o, fe'au mamao, (pol.) tula'i, uivale, tatala le manava
defence tausiga, leoleoga, puipuiga
defend puipui, tausia, leoleo
defer (to s.o.) e'e, gaua'i
define fa'amanino, fa'amatala
definite manino, moni lava
deflect liua, seu
deflower fa'amāsei'au
deformed lē 'ātoa, pipili
(__ leg) vaesape
defy lu'i, tete'e
degree
(of an angle) tīkerī
(university) fa'ailoga, tīkerī
(by degrees) la'ala'a mālie
delay fa'atuai, fa'alevaleva
(wait) fa'atali
(without __) e lē pine ona . . . , leai se taimi māumau
delegate sui, usufono
deliberately ma le matuā loto i ai
delicacy le'ile'i
delicate fa'aeteetegatā, vāivai
delicious mānaia
(__ solid food) susua
delight fiafia tele
delirious fasa
deliver tufa, tiliva
(__ from evil) lavea'i . . .
(__ a speech) lafo, (pol.) vāgana, sāunoa, tulei, malele, fetalai
(birth) fānau
deliverance fa'aolataga, olataga
deluge lōfia
demand poloa'i, matuā mana'o
demanding fa'asaulala, tagivale, mana'o lasi
demented sipa le fāi'ai
democracy fa'atemokalasi
demolish tala, fa'amalepe
demon tēvolo, tēmoni
demonstrate fa'aali, fa'asino
demoralize fa'alotovāivai
denomination
(religious) itū'āigā lotu
(coin) lona aogā o tupe taitasi
denounce ta'uleaga
dense māfiafia
(__ forest) māoa, uluulu
dent 'omo
dentist foma'ifa'inifo
deny fa'afiti, tete'e
deodorant vailā'au manogi
depart te'a, tu'ua, fa'amāvae
department matāgāluega, 'ōfisa
depend (on) fa'alagolago
deposit (bank) teu tupe
(to place) tu'u
(payment) tupe fa'avae, tīposi
depression
(economic) pa'ū le fefa'ataua'iga
(in ground) 'omo
(of the mind) lotovāivai, loto māfatia
deprive fa'aogea, taofia
depth maulalo, loloto
deputy sui
deride fāifai, ta'ufa'atauva'a
descend
(come down) fa'aifo
(originate) tupu, tupu'aga
descendant tamafafine, tamatāne
descent tupu'aga, gafa
describe fa'amatala
desecrate solia le sā
desert toafa
deserted gaogao, tu'ulafoa'iina, tu'ufua
deserve tatau ona . . .
design mamanu, ata
desire mana'o, mana'oga, fa'a naunauga, mo'omo'oga, finagalo
desk laulau a'oga, laulau tusitusi, kesi

desolate	gaogao, fa‘alāfuāina
despair	fa‘avāivai, atuatuvale
despise	manatu fa‘atauva‘a, ‘ino‘ino
despite	e ui i . . .
dessert	puligi etc.
destination	taunu‘uga
destitute	mativa, e leai se mea e ola ai
destroy	fa‘aleaga, fa‘atāma‘ia, fa‘atāutala
details(s)	fa‘amatalaga au‘ili‘ili, tala fa‘aoti, talau
detain	tāofi
detective	leoleo nanā
detergent	vai lā‘au fufulu ipu etc.
determine	fuafua, filifili
determined	lotomau, maumaututū
detonator	ma‘a afi
devaluation	fa‘aitiitia le aogā o le tupe
devastate	tāma‘ia, fa‘alāfuā
develop	tupu, tuputupua‘e, fa‘alauteleina
(__ a photograph)	fa‘availā‘au
development	taualumaga, atiina‘e
device	togafiti
devil	tēvolo, satani, ti‘āpolo, agaga leaga
devious	fa‘a‘alo‘alo
devise	fuafua, māfaufau
devolve (upon)	pa‘u i luga o . . .
devote	tu‘utō, alofa tele, foa‘i le ola
dew	sau
diabetes	ma‘i suka
dial	mata
(__ telephone)	vili
dialect	vaegāgana, vāega o se gagana
dialogue	fetalia‘i
diameter	taiamita
diamond	taimane
diaphragm	‘afu‘afu
diarrhoea	manava tatā
diary	api fa‘aletausaga
dice	ma‘a taisi
dictate	fa‘alau
dictionary	tusi lomifefiloi, tisionare
die (people)	oti, mālaia, (pol.) maliu, tu‘umalō, usufono
(animals, fires, plants, engines)	pē, mate
diesel	tiso, suau‘u o afi
diet	mea ‘ai e tatau ai
different	‘ese‘ese
difficult (add *“gatā”*)	e.g. faigatā, mālamalamagatā
(__ work)	galuega fitā
difficulty	mea faigatā, tuano‘a, fa‘afitāuli
dig	‘eli, ‘oso, sua, suati
digest	lamulamu ma fa‘amalū (i le puta)
dignity	mamalu, māluali‘i
dilatory	faiaga
diligent	filigā, tō‘aga
dilute	sui
dim (mirror)	nefu
(eyes)	pogi
dimension(s)	fuafuaga
diminish	fāiifo, fa‘aitiiti
dine	tāumafa
dining-room	potu ‘ai
dinner	‘aiga, tāumafataga, talisuaga
diocese	matāgāluega fa‘a-epikopo
dip	fuifui, loiloi, fa‘atofu
(to go down)	fa‘aifo
diploma	tusipasi, tipiloma, tusi i‘u
direct	tonu, sa‘o
(to point)	fa‘asino
(rule, govern)	pulea, fa‘atautaia, fa‘afoe
direction	ala, itūlagi
directly	tonu, sa‘o
(immediately)	loa
(a little later)	toeitiiti ane
director	‘o le pule, fa‘atonu
dirge	auēga
dirt	‘clc‘ele, palapala
dirty	‘ele‘elea, taea, lē mamā
(__ story)	tala salatua, mulugaveve

disadvantage itūleaga, itūvāivai, fa'alētonu
disagree fa'ataute'a, lūgā, fevaevaea'i, fetineia'i
disappear mou, nimo, lilo
disappointment fa'anoanoa, fa'a meo
disapprove lē malie, lē fa'amaonia
disaster mala, puapuagā
disbelieve lē talitonu
disc tupe, ipu māfolafola
discernment poto fa'autaga, tōfā mamao
discharge fa'ate'a
(__ from jail) fa'amāgalo
disciple 'o le so'o
discipline pūlega lelei, a'oa'oina i ala sa'o, āmio pulea
discard tu'u, tia'i, lē aogā
discourage fa'alotovāivai
discover maua
discoverer lē su'e mea fou
discriminate filifili fa'apito
discretion sa'ole
discuss tālatala, tālanoa, lāfolafo, felafolafoa'i, feutana'i
disease ma'i, (pol.) gāsegase, fa'agāsegase
disembowel fa'atiau
disfigure fa'amātagā
disgrace ta'uvalea, ta'uleaga
disguise fa'afōliga'ese, suifōliga
disgust 'ino'ino
dish tānoa, 'umete, ipu, pēsini (*also bowls*)
dishcloth 'ie fufulu ipu
dishevelled failā, fa'aveveveve, mave'u
dishonest faiga leaga, lē fa'amaoni
disinter toe laga se tino oti
disinfectant vailā'au fa'amamā
disinherit lē mau tofi (i le 'āiga)
disinterested lē amana'ia, lē manatu i ai
dislike lē fiafia i se . . .
dislocate (a joint) se'e se ivi
dismantle tala
dismay fa'anoanoa
dismiss fa'ate'a, tulia
(__ the class) tu'ua le a'oga
(__ court case) solofua
disobedient fa'alogogatā, vāogatā
disobey lē usita'i, fa'ataute'e
disorder fenumia'iga, vevesi, gaogaosā
disparage ta'ufa'atauva'a, faipona
dispatch tuli ane
dispel fa'ate'a
dispensary fale talavai
disperse ta'ape
display fa'aaliga, fā'aliga
displeased fa'asiasia, fa'a'u'u, lē fiafia
dispute finauga, māseiga, tau'upuga
disregard fa'amāmāsagia, fa'agalogalo
disrespectful lē fa'aaloalo, lē migao
disrupt fa'alavelave, fa'avevesi
dissolve liusuāvaia, palu
(__ a marriage) tatala le fa'aipoipoga
(__ parliament) fa'agata le fono e fai ai pālota
dissuade fautua'ese
distance mamao, vā
distinct
(separate) 'ese lava
(sharp, clear) ma'oti
distinguished lāuiloa, (pol.) lausilafia, iloga
distort fa'asesē le uiga
distress puapuagā
distribute fa'asoa, lufilufi, tufatufa
district itūmālō, (L.D.S.) siteki, matāgāluega (C.C.C.S)
disturb fa'alavelave, fa'avevesi, fa'aatuatuvale, fa'ate'ia
disturbance vāvāō, fa'atāluā
ditch 'autū, utu, lua
dive tofu, maulu, oso
diverge ala 'ese'ese
divide vavae, vāevae, fa'avasega
(__ a pig) pena
divine fa'aleatua
division vāega, vasega
(army __) itūtauā
divorce tatala le fa'aipoipoga,

	tete'a fa'aletulāfono
(___ certificate)	tusi alei
dizzy	niniva, uea, fa'a-faufau
do	fai
(how do you do?)	'o ā mai'oe?
(___ not, don't)	'aua, 'aua ne'i
(___ again)	toe fai
(be done!)	'uma!
docile	vaogōfie, agamalū
dock (wharf)	uafu
(to ___)	'ua pipi'i le va'a
doctor	foma'i
(traditional S. doctor)	taulāsea
document	pepa
dodge	'alo
dog	maile, (pol.) ta'ifau, 'ulī
doll	pepe ta'alo
dollar	tālā
dolphin	mumua
domestic	fa'ale'āiga
dominoes (game)	tomīnō
donate	foa'i
donation	lafoga, tōgiga
done (finished)	'uma, mae'a
(exhausted)	māfatia, lē lavā
donkey	'āsini
don't	'aua, sōia
doom	mālaia, mala
(be doomed)	ōia
door	faitoto'a, avanoa
doormat	fala fa'amamā se'evae, sōloivae
dose	inumaga
dot	togi, periota
dotage	vālevale, vālevalevalea, vālevalematua
dote	alofa fa'alēpulea, alofa fa'apito
dotted	togitogi
double	fa'alua, talua
(___ barrelled gun)	fanagutulua
doubt	fa'alētonu, māsalosalo
(no ___)	e lē taumate
doubtful	fa'alētonu, 'ailoga, lē mautinoa
dough	paluga (falaoa)
dove	lupe
down	ifo, lalo
(upside ___)	fa'afaō
down (fine hair, feathers)	fulufulufiso
downhearted	lotomāfatia, lotomomomo
downpour	uaga mālosi, timu tetele, tīmuga maligi
dowry	pēlega, pelepelega, saga
doze	tulemoe
dozen	tāseni
draft	tusiga fa'ata'ita'i
drag	tolō, toso
(___ one's feet)	sasalu
dragonfly	se'emū
drain	alāvai
(___ a tank)	fa'atafe
drama (play)	tala
drank	sa inu
draught	alāmatagi
draughts (game)	mū
draw (in a game)	ua tutusa 'ai
(pull)	toso
(___ near)	sōsō
(___ a sword, raffle)	se'i
(___ water)	utuvai
(___ money)	tō'ese tupe
(___ a net)	ta'i
(___ a line)	vase
(___ a picture)	tusi
drawback	itūleaga, to'a
drawer	pusatoso
drawing (painting)	atatusi
dread	pala'ai, mata'utia
dreadful	mata'utia
dream	miti, (pol.) fa'alepō, li'a
dredge	masini sua a'e le alititai - 'o le palolo (W.S.)
dregs	'alu
dress	'ofu
(to ___)	fai lāvalava
(___ a wound)	fusi le manu'a
dried	magumagu, mamago
drift	tafetafea
driftwood	taetafe
drill (tool)	vili, vilifatafata, vili eletise
(soldiers' ___)	a'oga fitafita

drink inu (pol.) tāumafa, taute; meainu, (pol.) meatāumafa
(alcohol) ‘avapapalagi, ‘ava mālosi
drinking water vaiinu
drip sisina, sinasina, ma‘ulu, tulutulu
dripping (fat) ga‘o
drive (car etc.) uli, fa‘auli, ‘ave
(__ a nail) tu‘i, tutu‘i
(__ away) tuli‘ese
(__ way) alāta‘avale
driver ‘ave ta‘avale
driving rain ma‘ini (le timu)
drizzle ma‘ulu‘ulu
droop malo, momoe
drop (liquid) fa‘atulu, tului
(rain __) matāua
(tear __) loimata
(to __) palasi, to‘ulu, toma, pa‘ū
drought lāmala, oge
drown malemo
drowsy tulemoe, ‘ivā
drugs vailā‘au
drum tagipalau, talipalau
(oil __) kalone
drunk ‘ōnā (pl.) ‘ōnanā
drunkard ‘o le ‘ōnā
dry mago, mātūtū, mātū
(__ leaf) laumea, lausului, ‘aulama
(__ land) pa‘umātū
(to __) fa‘amago, fa‘alā
(__ season) vāito‘elau, tau mago
duck pato, toloa
(to plunge in water) lelemo, lolomi i le vai
(dodge) ‘alo
due (__ to) ‘ona ‘o
(caused by) māfua, pogai, fa‘avae
(be __) taimi e tatau ai, e o‘o i le taimi nei
(w. __ respect) vaeane, tulouna
duet e pepese fa‘atasi le to‘alua
dull (weather) tau pogisā, lagilagiā
(__ subject) e lē malie i ai, fiu ai
(__ boy) tama fa‘alēatamai, valea, vāivai
dumb gūgū
dummy (baby) matāsusu fai
dump (rubbish __) fa‘atafuna
(to __) palasi, tia‘i, lāfoa‘i
dung tae, taemanu, (pol.) otaota
dungarees tagikerī
dupe pēlogia, ‘olegia, fa‘agutugutulua
duplicate fai se kopi, ata
duplicator masini e lolomi ai kopi e tele
durable ‘anagatā
duration ‘o le ‘umi (o se faiga)
during ‘a‘o, i aso o, i le taimi o
dusk afiafi, popogi, pūnefu
duster solo, fa‘asolo, solopefu
dusty pefua, pefupefua, pūnefua
duty tiute, matāfaioi
(customs __) tiute
(be on __) tiute, faigāluega
dux kapitene a le a‘oga
dwarf sa‘a, ‘autotoe, tagata ‘āvilu
dwell nofo, mau, aumau, mafuta, (pol.) afio
dye vali
(black __) talama
dying speech māvaega
dynamite fanai‘a
dynasty augātupu, sōloga a tupu
dysentery sanatoto

Ee

each ta'itasi, ta'ito'atasi
(__ other) le isi i le isi
(two __) ta'ilua
eager naunau, olioli
eagerly fa'amoemoe i le fiafia
eagle 'āeto
ear taliga
(__ of wheat) 'aputi
earlier muamua, analeilā
early vave
(__ departure) vave malaga
earmark
(set aside a pig) 'ati, 'ati'ai
(__ for special use) fa'aleoleo, fa'apolopolo
earn totogi ua maua
earnest fa'amāoni
(__ request) fa'atauānau, pulunaunau
earnestness lotonaunau
earring tāutaliga
earth (world) lalolagi, atulaulau
(soil) 'ele'ele, palapala, lau'ele'ele
earthenware fagu'ele, ipuōmea
earthly fa'alelalolagi
earthquake māfui'e
earthy fa'aletino
ear-wax taetuli
ease filemū, faigōfie, mālōlō lelei
(of rain) ma'ama'a
easily faigōfie
east sasa'e
(__ wind) matā'upolu
Easter Eseta, Isita, Pasekate (R.C.)
(__ Day) Aso o le Toe Tu
eastwards gāga'e
easy (suffix) gōfie, e.g. faigōfie
(take it __) faifai mālie, tu'u faitalia
eat 'ai, fai'aiga, (pol.) tāumafa, tausami, talialo, talisua
eaves fa'atautau, tulutulu
ebb (low __) pē le tai, maui
(to run down) fāiifo
ebony 'anume, 'au'auli
eccentric āmio 'ese, sipa, mauaga
ecclesiastical fa'alelotu
echo si'uleo, (pol.) si'ufofoga
eclipse (of moon) gase'ele'ele, fano'ele'ele
(of sun & moon) gasetoto
edge (gen.) pito
(__ of knife) mata
(__ of forest) matāvao
edible 'aina
edit fa'atonutonu
editor fa'atonu nusipepa (etc.)
edition lomiga
editorial tala sili a le fa'atonu
educate a'oa'o (a'oa'oina = *educated*)
education a'oa'oga
eel tuna, (pol. i'a vai), pusi
eerie (of night) paū
(of sound) fa'amama'i le leo
effect taunu'uga, i'uga
effeminate fa'afāfine
efficient faimeamae'a, mā'ēlegā
effort taumafai, finafinau
egg fua, fuāmoa, fuāpato etc.
(__ on) fa'aoso, u'una'i
eight valu
eighteen sefulu valu
eighty valu sefulu
either po'o, so'o, se isi
elaborate (to __) fa'alauteleina se fa'amatalaga
elastic pa'u meme'i
elbow tulilima
elder toea'ina
(__ brother) uso matua (*also sister*)
elderly fa'amatuātagata
(__ man) toea'ina, (LDS = tamamisiona)

(__lady) lo'omatua, 'olomatua
elect filifili, pālota
election filifiliga, pālota
electric (al) uila, 'eletise
electrician fai uila
elephant 'elefane
elephantiasis o le mūmū, 'a'ao tutupa
elevate ea
eleven sefulu tasi
eliminate fa'ate'a'ese, tuli'ese
elope āvaga
else (no one __) e leai ma se isi
(if not) ā lē o lea . . .
elsewhere i se isi mea
emaciated magoivi
embalm atulalaina
embarrass fa'amāsiasi, mā, (pol.) lili'a, matamuli
emblem fa'ailoga
embrace 'a'u, opoopo, fusimau
emergency fa'alavelave, mea tupu fa'afuase'i
emetic vaifa'apua'i
emigrate 'āifanua
emotion lagona loloto
emphasize fa'amamafa
empire mālō aoao
employ fa'aogā, fa'afaigāluega
employee tagata faigāluega
employer tagata e ana le gāluega, kamupani etc.
employment gāluega, faiva
unemployment 'o le leai o ni gāluega
empty (be) tu'ufua, gaogao
(vessel, shell) atigi . . .
(__ handed) fua, samasamanoa
(to __) sa'a, sasa'a, fa'atafe
enable mafai ai ona . . .
enamel lei
encircle si'o, si'osi'o, vagavagaia
enclose puipui, si'omia
(__ in a letter) fafao
encounter fetaia'i
encourage fa'alototele, fa'amāfanafana, fa'alā'ei'au, tīma'i
end i'u, fa'ai'uga, tulu'iga, gata'aga, mūta'aga, fa'a'uma, pito
(__ of war) ola le taua
endless lē i'ua, lē 'uma, (pol.)fa'asavala
(eternal) fa'avavau
endorse saini se pepa, 'ioe i ai
endure 'o'ono, lavātia
enemy fili
energetic limamālosi, tiotio
energy tiotio, mālosi
enforce (a law) fa'ataunu'u
engagement
(marriage) fa'amau, tūsiga
(negotiate) osi se feagaiga
engine afi, masini
engineer inisinia
English Gagana Peretania, fa'aperetania, fa'aegelani, Igilisi
enhance fa'amamalu
enjoy . . . fiafia i . . .
enjoyable mālie
enlarge fa'alāpo'a, fa'atele
enormous matuā telē lava
enough lava
(__ to eat) mā'ona
(as a command) 'ua lava! sōia! 'ia 'uma!
enquire fesili
enrich fa'atamāo'āiga, fa'amau'oa
enter ulu, ulufale, afe
entertain fa'afiafia, talia
entertaining mālie
entertainment fiafia, fa'afiafiaga, tīfaga etc.
enthusiasm mā'elegā tele, fa'agae'etiaga
entire 'ātoa, 'ato'atoa, 'uma
entrails tinae
entrance faitoto'a, mea e ulu ai
entreat 'ai'oi, fa'aolo, talosaga, tauānau
entrust fa'atuatuaina
entry ulufalega
entwine vi'o, tavi'o, milosia
envelope (an __) teutusi
(to__) ufitia, āfīfī
envious matau'a, lotoleaga, lotovale, fuā
envy mo'o, tu'inanau
epidemic fa'ama'i

epilepsy ma'imāliu
epsom salts vaimāsima
equal e tusa mā, tutusa
equator ekueta
equip fa'a'ā'upega, fa'alā'ei'au
equipment mea tatau ai, mea faigāluega
erase titina, sōloi
erect (tall) 'umi fa'asa'o
(build) tō, fa'atū, atia'e, 'ava'ega
errand fe'au
error sesē, sasi
erupt (volcano) sasao, pā
escape sola, sao, sāogalemū
escort mōliga, 'āmiga, palepale, 'aulama, fa'afeaoina
especial fa'apitoa
especially aemaise lava
essay tusigātala
essence (cooking) fa'a manogi
(substance) 'a'ano, fatu
essential tāua, e ao ina
establish fa'avae, fa'atū, fa'amausalī
estate fanua, mea totino ua māvae ai
(deceased __) esetete o ē maliliu
estimate taufa'atatau, faitaulia, fuafua
estuary mulivai
eternal fa'avavau, lē 'uma
eternity i le fa'avavau lava
etiquette vāfealoa'i
European papālagi, fa'apapālagi, pālagi (colq.), fa'aeuropa
(part __) 'afakasi (pol.) totolua
evaporate liuausa
even
(__ numbers) soania
(be __) tutusa, laugatasi
(make __) fa'agatasi, fa'alaugatasi, fa'atutusa
(__ if) e ui ina, tainane fo'i
evening afiafi, afiafi pō
(this __) nānei, i le pō nānei
(__ shadow) tauafiafi
evenly (smoothly) fa'amalū
(equally) tutusa, sagatonu
event mea ua tupu, tausinioga
eventuate e i'u i . . . , e o'o ina
ever i se aso
(for - & -) e fa'avavau, fa'avavau lava
(__ since) talu ai
everlasting e fa'avavau, tūmau lava
every 'uma
(__ body) ta'ito'atasi 'uma
(__ time) i taimi 'uma lava
(__ two hours) e ta'ilua itūlā ma fai
evidence fa'ailoga, fa'amaoni
(legal __) molimau, molimau mautinoa
evil leaga, fa'atī'apolo
(__ days) asovale
ewe māmoe fafine
exactly (__ like) e pei lava, tusalava
(precisely) 'a'ato, tusa pau
exaggerate fa'a tele, talavale, talafa'afefeteina
exalt fa'asili, fa'aea
examination su'ega, iloiloga
example fa'atusa, fa'aa'oa'oga
exceedingly tele na'uā
Excellency
(His __) Lana afioga
excellent ma'eu, aupitolelei, (colq.) selau pasene
except vāganā
excess 'o le sili, fa'asilia
excessively tele, anoano, so'ona, na'uā
exchange fesuia'i, felafoa'i, fetalia'i
(telephone __) fale tali telefoni
excite fa'aoso, fa'agāoioi
excited loto fiafia, loto popole
exclusive 'ese lava, fa'apito lava, lē aofia ai
excrement tae, (pol.) otaota
excursion tāfaoga
excuse (an __) fa'amatalaga 'alo
(to __) fa'amagalo, fa'ataga, fa'atulou (pol.) fa'asolofua
execute
(carry out) faigāluega
(to __) fa'asalaoti

(to __ a document) sainia i ala e tatau ai
exempt fa‘atagaina
exercise (physical) fa‘amālositino, galuea‘iina
(__ a horse) fa‘asavali le solofanua
(__ book) ‘api
exert fai ma le mālosi
exhaust (weary) vāivaitele, māfatia, fa‘a‘iva‘ivā
(__ of car) paipa i tua o ta‘avale
exhibit mea molimau, mea fa‘aali
(to __) tu‘u fa‘aaliali
exhibition fa‘aaliga
exhort apoapoa‘i, tīma‘i, (pol.) tomatau
exile aunu‘ua (pol.) aulagia
(to __) fa‘aaunu‘ua
exist ola, tū, o lo‘o i ai
existence ōlaga, (pol.) soifuaga
expand fa‘afefete, fa‘alauteleina, fa‘asalafa
expanse (prefix) fogā (e.g. fogātai = *expanse of ocean*)
expect fa‘atalitali, fa‘amoemoe
expectorate luai, feanu
expedition malaga su‘esu‘e, ‘au malaga
expel fa‘ate‘a, fa‘atula‘i‘ese, tuli
expense(s) tupe alu, tupe fa‘aalu
expensive taugatā, totogi tele
experience poto māsani, mea ua tutupu
(strange __) mea ‘ese
experiment tofotofo, su‘esu‘e
expert poto tele i se tasi faiva, mataisau o se matātā
explain fa‘amatala, fa‘amanino, fa‘amālāmalama, fa‘apupula
explanation fa‘amatalaga etc.
explode pā, fa‘apā
explore su‘e
export la‘u ‘ese atu, fa‘atau atu i fafo
expose (to sun) atafu, lāina
express fa‘aali, fa‘a‘upu
(__ sympathy) fa‘amaise
(__ a desire) momoli le mana‘o
expression (on face) fōliga, pulapula
extend (reach to) ‘a‘u, o‘o i, pau
(add to) fa‘asoso‘o, fa‘alautele
extended family ‘āiga, ‘āiga potopoto, ‘āiga faitele
extension fa‘aopoopoga, soso‘oga
(house __) fa‘ase‘e
extensive salafa
exterior itū i fafo
extol fa‘ane‘ene‘e, fa‘asili
extra mea fa‘aopoopo
extract (teeth) fa‘i
(__ from a book) upu si‘i
extraordinary mea ‘ese lava
extreme pito mamao, matuā mamao ‘ese
extremity ‘o le pito i . . . , fa‘asi‘usi‘u, tausi‘usi‘u
extricate ā‘ili‘ili, lavea‘i
eye mata, (pol.) fofoga
eye-ball tama‘imata
eyebrow(s) fulufulumata
eyelash fulumata
eyelid laumata
eyeshade taumata
eye-shadow vali laumata
eye-specialist foma‘i mata

Ff

fable	tala fa'atusa
fabulous	fa'afāgogo, matuā manaia tele
face	mata, (pol.) fofoga, fōliga
(__ down)	faō
(__ to __)	fa'afesāga'i
(__ upwards)	taliaga
facetious	ula, fa'a'ala'ala, 'upu'atagia
facilitate	fa'afaigōfie
fact	mea moni
faction	vāega
(political __)	vāega fa'apolotiki
factor	itū, vāega
factory	fale gaosimea
fade	matafi, fāiifo, gālo atu, mata'a
faeces	tae, (pol.) otaota
fail	pa'ū, lē pasi (su'ega), pa'ela, i'uvale, lē taunu'u
faint	vāivai
(__ w. hunger)	mōlemanava
(__ hearted)	lotovāivai
(to __)	matapogia, (pol.) fofogapogia
fair (only __)	feoloolo
(i.e. just)	tonu, fa'amaoni
(__ weather)	lagilelei
(__ wind)	alafia
(__ skin)	pa'u pa'epa'e
fairly good	lelei fo'i, feoloolo lava
faith	fa'atuatua
faithful	fa'amāoni, moni
(the __)	'aufa'atuatua
fake	mea pepelo
fall	palasi, pa'ū, sulu, to'ulu
(__ ill)	ma'i
fall-out	mea 'ua leaga ai le 'ea pe ā pāpā pomuniukilia
false (wrong)	sesē
(__ teeth)	nifo fa'apipi'i, nifo fai
(unfaithful)	lē fa'amāoni
fame	lāuiloa, ta'uleleia, (pol.) lāusilafia
familiar	māsani, lata
family	'āiga
family tree	gafa
famine	oge
famous	ta'uta'ua, logologoā, vi'ivi'ia, (pol.) lāusilafia
fan	ili, 'aupolapola
(to __)	aloalo, tapili
fan (electric)	pe'a, ili eletise
fancy (thought)	māfaufau, manatu, fa'a'ite'ite
(decorated)	teuteuina
far	mamao
(__ from finished)	e le'i tāitai 'uma
(__ too much)	tele na'uā
(__ apart)	valavala, vāvāmamao
farce (play)	faleaitu
fare	pāsese
farewell	māvaega, fa'amāvaega
(goodbye!)	tofā, soifua!
farm	fa'ato'aga, fanua e ta'a ai lafu manu
farmer	faifa'ato'aga
farther	
(__ inland)	i utā
(__ seawards)	i gātai
fascinate	tepa taula'i
fashion (to __)	gaosi, tātā
(clothes)	'ofu fa'aasonei
fast (quick)	saosaoa, vave, gāsolo, masau, tele vave, tope
(secure)	mau
(hold __)	taofi mau
(__ asleep)	moegase
(to __)	anapogi, fa'molemanava
fasten	fa'amau, fa'apipi'i
fastening	'o le nonoa, noataga
faster	telelise
fastidious	fa'afāilā
fat (meat)	lololo, ga'oa
(person)	puta, tino'ese
(animal)	peti
(big)	lāpo'a

(cooking __) ga'o
fatal tau i le oti
fate i'uga, taunu'uga, 'o mea e o'o
father tamā, tupuga
father-in-law 'o le tamā o le to'alua
fathom gafa
fatigue fiu, lē lavā
fatten (person) fa'aputa
(animal) fa'apeti
fault sesē, pona, sala, uiga leaga
(find __) tio, fāitio, tilotilomāsae
(at __) pōnā
(__ in rock) tō
favour mea lelei, loto malie, alofa-fa'a'au'au, fa'apele
favourable logolelei, fiafia
favourite peleina, (lana) pele
fear fefe, popole, (pol.) mata'u, ātugalu
fearful po'epo'e, mata'utia, fefevale
fearless matatoa, toa, lēfefe
feast faigā'ai, (pol.) tāumafataga, tausamiga, tausama'aga
(funeral __) 'aitagi, lau'ava
feat faimeafitā
feather fulu
features (face) fōliga
February Fepuari
fee totogi
feeble vāivai
feed (to __) 'ai, fafaga, fa'ainu, (pol.) tausami
feeding-pen (pigs) fāgaga
feel lagona, logo
(__ w. hands) tago, tagotago, tautago, lote, lotelote
(__ sorry) alofa
(__ cold) ma'alili
(__ unwell) fa'ama'ima'i, (pol.) fa'agasegase
feeler (animals) velo, mea fa'alogo
feeling lagona, fa'alogoga, finagalo
fell (to __) fa'apa'ū (le lā'au), tutū (le lā'au)
fellow(s) tama, ali'i, aumea, 'auao
(that __) 'o le igoa lea
fellowship māfutaga
female fafine, teine
fence pā, puipui, pālā'au, āi, 'aupā
(behind the __) i tuāpā
fend off tali
ferment mafu, fa'amafu, fa'apala
fermented fa'a'a'ava
ferns(s) laugasēsē, sa'ato, 'oli'olī etc.
ferry va'a la'u pāsese, ta'avale etc.
fertile lafulemū, 'oa
(of animals) uilelei
fertilize fa'alafulēmū
fertilizer maniua, fa'alelei 'ele'ele
fervently (wish __) tālotalo
festering 'aloua
festival fiafia, tausamiga
fetch 'a'ami
fetters noataga
fever fiva, fa'avelavela
(filarial __) pu'eia
feverish fa'ama'alili
few nai, itiiti, ni nai
(__ people) to'aitiiti, ausage
fibre fau, pulu, u'a, alava
fiction tala fatu
fiddle lotelote
fidget tateme, gāoiā
field laufanua, 'ogā'ele'ele
(subject) matā'upu
fierce 'a'asa, fe'ai, ma'ama'ai
(__ heat) mūsaesae
fifteen sefulu ma le lima
fifty lima sefulu
fight misa, taua, 'avauga
(to __) tau, misa, fusu, tauvā
figure (shape) fōliga, fa'atagata, fika, fuaitino
(number) mata'inūmera, fika, nūmera
filariasis fiva mūmū
file faila, 'ili
(__ in an out) gāsolosolo
fill fa'atumu, utu, fu'e, fono
(__ a pipe) utufaga

film (thin layer) laumanifi
(photography) ata, atavili
(__ show) tīfaga
filter fa'amamā
filthy taea, fa'ainaelo
fin (fish) 'apa'apa
final (last) toe
(__ word) toe 'upu, 'upu fa'amāvae, laualuga
finally mulimuli ane
finance tautupe
find maua, tauane
(__ fault) ta'upona, fāitio, mātau pona etc.
fine (good) lelei, mānaia
(pure) mamā
(__ thread) filo tuaiti lava
(__ mat) 'ie tōga, tōfā
(__ weather) lagi lelei
(__ mesh) matalili'i
(penalty) sala, fa'asala
finger tama'ilima
(fore __) limatusi
(little __) limatama
(middle __) loaloavale
(__ nail) mai'u'u, atigilima
finish fa'a'uma, fa'amāe'a, 'uma, i'u, muta
finished (used up) ona pau lea
fire afi, mū, (pol.) mālaia
(__ a gun) fana, fa'apā le fana, 'amoti
fire-engine ta'avale fui mū
fire-extinguisher mea tineiafi, mea tinamū
firecracker fana pepa
firewood fafie, (pol.) polata
firm māua'i, tū, tūmau, māumaututū, lotomau, malō, mapo, māopoopo
(business) kamupanī
first mua, mua'i, muamua, ulua'i, lua'i
(__ time) fa'ato'ā, ulua'i
(__ place) taulāmua
(__ born) ulumatua
(__ class) tulagamuamua
(__ fruits) fa'apolopolo
(__ taro) talomua
fish (gen.) i'a
(to __) fāgota, faifaiva
(__ by torchlight) lama
fisherman tautai
fishhook mātau
fishing fāgota, faiva
(__ line) mānoa, afo, ta'ā, 'afa
(__ rod) 'ofe fāgota, (pol.) launiu
fishtrap enu, sele, pā
fissure 'o le māvae
fist moto
fit (i.e. well) mālosi lelei
(appropriate) fetaui, pāgamālie, feagai lelei, agava'a, onomea, tatau
(make to __) fa'afetaui
(try on) fa'ata'ita'i
fitful tōpu'epu'e
five lima
fix (in position) fa'apipi'i, fau, fa'atonu
(__ a day) tu'upō
fixed tumau, mautū
(appointed) atofaina
fixedly
(to look __) pūlato'a, tepataula'i
flabby 'olu'olū, gālemulemu
flag fu'a
flame 'o le mū o le afi
flank tafa
flap (pocket) ufitaga
(wings) 'apatā, palalū
flare (a __) 'aulama
flash 'emo, fa'a'emo, fa'asusulu
flat laumafola, māfolafola, sālafalafa
(__ coral) lapa
flatten papa
flatter fa'ase'e, 'upu fa'avi'ivi'i
flavour manogi, tofo
flea 'utufiti
flee sola, sōsola, sulu
fleet (ships) fuāva'a, fua
(of foot) saosaoa
flesh 'a'ano, 'anogase, manufasi
flexible vavai, meme'i, fetu'una'i
flick fiti, 'eu
flicker fe'emo'emoa'i
flight lele
flinch me'i, poi

fling ato, tia'i 'ese (mālosi)
flint ma'aafi
flipper (turtle) saga
float (for fish-net) uto
(to __) opeopea, lelea
flock (animals) lafu
(birds) taumanu
(to __) lolofi, gāsolo
flog sasa
flood tāfega, lōfia, lolovai
floor fola, fogāfale
(__ of sea) alititai, alitisami
flop fa'apalasi
(a __) mea i'uvale
florin 'afatala, felolini, luaseleni
flotilla fuāva'a
flour falaoa mata
flourish uluola
flow tafe
(of tide) fāna'e, sua mai le tai
(of years etc.) auga, gāsologa
flower fuga, fugālā'au, fua
'flu (influenza) fulū
fluctuate fesuisuia'i
fluently (speech) alu lelei lana tautala, sologāmalie le tautala
fluid sua, suāvai
flush (of face) mūmūvale
(water) fa'aalu le suāvai
flute fagufagu
flutter pepepepe, lelelele, agiagia, fa'apepepepe
fly (a __) lago
(to __) lele, fitifiti (aloiafi)
flying fish mālolo
flying fox pe'a
flyspeck taelago
fly-switch (whisk) fue
foam piapia
foetus tama fafano, fita
fog puao
foil (silver __) foli siliva
fold gaugau
(__ arms) pi'ilima
(__ umbrella, knife) fa'amoe
foliage 'o le uluulu
follow (a person) mulimuli, muli'auloa
(pursue) tatao, fa'aāfu
(__ closely) taotaotua
follower so'o
following wind matagi taumulia'i
fond of alofa i . . . , fiafia i . . .
fontanella tumua'i o le pepe fou
food 'ai, mea'ai, aso, (pol.) 'ava, avamāgalo, mea tatau ai mea tāmafa, mea tausami, mea taute
food safe sefe
fool vale, fa'asosososo, fa'aluma, fa'avalea
foolish fa'avalea, fa'avalevale
foot vae, (pol.) 'a'ao
(base) fa'avae, pito i lalo
(measure) futu
(__ print) tulagāvae
(__ wear) se'evae
for mo, ma, 'ona'o, 'auā
forage sasamu, sasau
forbear fa'apalepale
forbid fa'asā, vavao
forbidden tapu, tapui, sā
force mālosi, fa'amālosi, fa'atātā
(police __) vasega o leoleo
(__ open) talepe, vavane, laga
ford asa, āsaga
foreboding fa'ali'a
forecast valo'aga, talailetau
forefinger limatusi
forehead muāulu
foreign 'ese, mai fafo, taufafo
foreigner tagata fāimai, tagata 'ese
foreleg alagāvae
foreman pule, 'ovasia
foremost muamua, taulāmua
foresight tōfāmamao
foreskin pa'u
forest vao, togāvao, vaomatua, vaomāoa
foretell 'i'ite, vavalo
forever pea lava pea
forewarn fa'ata'imua, fa'a'ite'ite
forge (a letter) saini sesē
(a bank-note) kopi sesē tupe pepa
(a __) fale fai u'amea
forget galo, ninimo
(__ completely) galonimo
forgive fa'amāgalo, (pol.) fa'asolofua
forgiven māgalo

forgiving	lotofa'amāgalo
forgo	tutu'u
fork	tui, maga, vālalua
form (shape)	fōliga, faiga
(school)	vasega
(seat)	nofoa
former(ly)	anamua, muamua
fornicate	faita'aga
forsake	tu'ulāfoa'i, tu'utia'i
fort, fortress	'olo
forth	'i luma
(bring _ a child)	fānau
forthright	mōlitino, tausa'o
fortify	fa'amālosi
fortunate	amu'ia, manuia, taileleia, meāmanū
fortune (money)	tupetele
(goods)	'oloa
(good _)	manū
(bad _)	mala
(_ teller)	va'afa'atau
forty	fāsefulu
forward (be _)	matamuamua
(ahead)	'i luma
(look _)	fa'amoemoe ma le fiafia
(move _)	solo'i luma
foster	fa'amālosia, fa'alagolagoina
foster-father	tamā fai
foul	'ino'ino, taea, fa'atūfanua
(_ mouthed)	laulauvavale
(to _)	fa'a'inaelo
founded	fa'avaeina
foundation	fa'avae, 'auga
(raised _)	paepae
founder (boat)	goto
fountain	vaipuna, matāvai
fountain pen	peniutu
four	fā
(_ at a time)	ta'ifā
(_ legged)	vaefā
(_ sided)	tāfafā
fourteen	sefulu ma le fā
fowl	moa, moa'aivao
fox	'ālope
fraction(s)	vaegāmea
fracture (skull)	foa
(bone)	gau
fragile	ma'ale'ale, fa'aeteetegatā, mata'eta'e
fragment(s)	momoi mea, fāsimea lāiti, lili'i
frame (building)	'auivi
(picture)	fa'ava'a
(man)	tino
(_ of mind)	lagona
(_ work)	'auivi
frank	fa'aali tino mai, tautala sa'o mai
frankincense	muro lipano *(Bible)*
frantic	fitivale
fraternity	usoga
fraud	'olegia, pelogia, fa'agaoi
frayed	matalatala
freckle(s)	taelago
free	sa'oloto
(_ from)	e aunoa ma . . .
(set _	fa'asa'oloto, tatala, sao
freedom	sa'olotoga
freely	fua, noa, so'ona
freeze	fa'a'aisa, to'a i le mālūlū
freight (load)	uta
(cost)	totogi o le la'u o le uta
freighter	va'ala'u uta 'ese'ese
frequent(ly)	fai so'o
(become less _)	feto'i
fresh	fou
(_ water)	vai māgalo
(feel _)	lagona le mālosi
freshness	mālū
fret	popolevale, fa'amātagitagi
fretsaw	'ilimama
Friday	Aso Faraile
fried	falai
friend	uō, soa, 'aumea, pā'aga
(friends of bride & groom)	'aumea mamae
(favourite _)	mānamea
friendly	fa'aleuō, fa'auō, fealofani
friendship	faigāuō
fright	tete, mole le moa, segia le mauli, te'i

frighten	fa'amata'u, fefevale
frightening	fa'amatasāuā
frill	file
frivolous	tautala fa'a'ala'ala
frizzly (hair)	migimigi
frock	'ofu teine
frog	rane
from	mai, 'ai, nai, talu
front	'o luma
(in __)	i luma o
(be in __ of)	atualuma
(way out in __)	maoluma
(__ of a house)	lumāfale
frost	'o le sau 'ualiu'aisa
froth	piapia, 'oa
frown	matapaū, fa'anonou, matafa'a'ū'ū
fruit	fua, fuālā'au
fruit-bearing	mā'ave'ave
fruitless (unsuccessful)	'asa
fry	falai
frying pan	falai
fuel	meatafuafi, penisini, suāu'u
fugitive	fesūlua'i
fulfil	fa'ataunu'u
full	tumu
(complete)	'ātoa
(replete)	mā'ona
(__ score)	tapula'a
(__moon)	'ua 'ātoa le māsina
fully	matuā
fumble	'autago, tāpatapa
fumes	asu'o'ona
fumigate	fa'aasu
fun	mea mālie, tausuaga, tālasua
(make __ of s.o.)	'amusia, ulagia
function (to __)	galue, ola
(a __)	sāuniga
fund	fa'aputugātupe
fundamental	e ala mai i le fa'avae
funeral	tanuga, (pol.) falelauasiga
fungus	pa'utaliga, limu
funnel	fa'atumu
(ship)	afi
funny	malie, taufa'a'ata, sua
funny-bone	tetega, ivimutu
fur (animals)	fulufulu
furious	ita tele
furl (flag, sail, umbrella)	fa'amoe
furlong	falelogi
furlough	fa'amālōlōga
furnish	fa'ameāfale
further	sāga
(__ inland)	'i utā
(__ east)	maosasa'e etc.
furthermore	'ae lē gata i lea, 'i le ma le isi
furtive	fa'alilolilo
fuse	vavae, fiusi fa'aso'o
fuss	popolevale, fa'akolosisi
future	lumana'i
(in the __)	i aso 'o i lumana'i

Gg

gable	matāfale
gag	nonoa le gutu, fusi le gutu
gain	fa'asiliga, maua
(__ ground)	alualu i luma, lata mai
(__ access)	sao
gale	afā
gall bladder	au'ona
gallon	kalone
gallop	si'ivaelua
gamble	peti, fa'alētonu
game (be __)	loto i taumafai
(a __)	ta'aloga
gang	'au, 'aualii
(__ of thieves)	'āugāoi, 'aufaomea
gaol (also jail)	falepuipui
gap	avanoa, vā
(teeth)	nifo pū
gape	fa'amaga
garage	fale ta'avale

garden	togālā'au, fa'ato'aga, (pol.) fa'a'ele'elega, velevelega
gardener	faitogālā'au
gardenia	pua
gargle	pūpū
garland	'ula, pale, (pol.) fa'asolo
garment(s)	'ofu, lā'ei
gas	kasa
(motor fuel)	kesi
gash	manu'a leaga
gasp	māpuea, sela, fitivale
gate	faitoto'a, alatatala
gather (meet)	potopoto, aofia
(collect)	ao, aofa'i, tae, falute, putiputi, fa'aputuputu
(infer)	lagona, iloa
(__ in baskets)	tufi
(hen – chicks)	ofaofata'i
gathering	
(people)	fa'apotopotoga, saofa'iga, alalafaga
(chiefs & orators)	alofisā, (pol.) aofiaga
gauze	'ie valavala, kosi
gay	fiafia, lotofiafia
(__ colours)	felanulanua'i
gaze	pūlato'a, tepataula'i
gazelle	'aila
gazette	nusipepa a le mālō
gear	kia, tōtōga
gecko	mo'o
geld	launiu le manu
gem	ma'a tāua
genealogy	gafa
(recite the __)	talagafa
general	mea māsani
(__ election)	pālota aoao
(army __)	'ofisa pule i le vaegā'au
generate	faiga o le uila, eletise, paoa
generation	tupulaga
(rising __)	tupulaga talavou
generosity	matamau, agaalofa
generous	limafoa'i, matamau, agaalofa
genial	tu'igatā, tautalafa'afiafia
genitals	mea sā, mea,
gentle	
(__ nature)	agamalū, agavāivai, filēmū
(__ wind)	agimālie
(__ stream)	tafelēmū
gentleman	ali'i, tamāli'i
gentlemanly	fa'atamāli'i, agaali'i
gently	lēmū, mālie
genuine	māo'i, moni lava, mo'i, a'ia'i
germs(s)	siama
germinate	lā'au tupu mai le fatu
gesticulate	fe'avea'i lima
gesture(s)	tāga
get	'aumai, maua
(__ out)	alu 'ese, alu 'i fafo
(__ better)	toe mālosi
(__ up)	tū i luga, tūla'i, ala
(__ ready)	sāuni
ghost	aitu (pol.) sauali'i, agaga
giant	tino'ese, lāpo'a, toa
giddy	lili'a, niniva
gift	meaalofa
giggle	fe'atani, 'ata'ata
gill(s)	fuilauvī, pā'ō'ō
ginger	fiu
gingerly	fa'afāilā
giraffe	serafi
girdle	fusi, titi
girl	teine, tamateine, māfine, (pol.) tausala
gist	a'ano
give (__ me)	aumai (pol.) 'a'ao mai
(__ to s.o.)	avatu, 'ave, tu'u atu
(__ a gift)	foa'i, fai meaalofa
(__ outright)	tō
(__ up)	gaua'i, tu'u, lē toe faia, fa'avāivai
(__ birth)	fānau, (pol.) ola
(__ an order)	fai se fa'atonuga
(__ freely)	foa'i fua
glad	fiafia
glance	tilotilo, tepatasi
(sidelong ––)	fa'asi'usi'umata
gland	puna
glare (of sun)	susulu, segasega, sesega
(__ at o.a.)	fefa'ataupupulaa'i
glass	tioata, mālamalama
(__ marble)	toa mālama
glass (container)	ipu mālamalama
glasses	matatioata, va'aiga
gleam	ataata
glide	se'e, fa'ase'e

glider va‘alele e leai se afi
glisten ‘i‘ila, ‘ila‘ila
gloomy (person) matafa‘asiasia
(day) fa‘amālumalu
glorify vi‘i
glorious mānaia, mamalu
glossy ‘i‘ila
glove totini lima
(hand in ––) ‘au‘aufa‘atasi
glow (fire) malala le afi
(sun) pulapula
glue kelū, pipi‘i
glutinous pi‘ipi‘i
glutton ‘aifa‘apua‘a, ‘aipā
gnash (teeth) lilivau
gnat tama‘i lago
gnaw gali
go alu (pl.ō)
(__ on foot) savali
(__ on a journey) malaga, sopo
(__ about) fealua‘i, feōa‘i
(__ by way of) ui
(__ ahead) fai loa, alu i luma
(__ astray) sē
(__ away) alu‘ese
(__ on) alu loa
(__ for a walk) sāvalivali
(__ round) ta‘amilo
goad tautā, tuitui
goal tini, taunu‘uga
(score) ‘ai
goat ‘oti
go-between palepale, ‘aulama, fa‘asoa
God Atua (pol.) Tapa‘au i le Lagi
(god-like) fa‘aleatua, āmioatua
(heathen gods) atua fa‘apaupau
goggle tetē
goggles mata tioata, mata fāgota
gold ‘auro
golden fa‘a‘auro, lanu‘auro
golf tāpolo
gone
(perish, time past) fano
(used up) ‘uma
gong (wooden) patē, talua, lali, logo
good lelei
(no __) lē aogā, leaga
(__ news) tala fiafia, tala lelei
good-looking matalelei, aulelei
good-nature agalelei
goodbye tōfā soifua!
goods ‘oloa
goose kusi
goose-flesh monea
gorge (food) ‘aipā
(ravine) mato
gorgeous mātagōfie na‘uā
gorilla manukī lapo‘ā, korila
gospel Tala Lelei
gossip tala, talasalatua, faitala
got ‘ua maua
gouge (chisel) tofi lolo‘u
(to __) tātā ‘ese, una (of taro)
gourd fagu
gout gugu
govern pulea, fa‘atautaia, fa‘afoe
government pulega, mālō, faigāmālō
governor kovana
(__ general) kovana sili
grab ‘u‘u, tata, taufao, fao
grace
(__ of God) Alofa Tunoa, Kalasia (R.C.)
(meal) lotu o mea‘ai, o le fa‘afetai, fa‘amāgalo
(personal quality) onomea, onopapa‘i
gracious mamalu
grade vasega, fa‘avasega
gradual mālie
grain fatu
gram karama
grammar kalama
grand lelei tele, mātagōfie
grandchild fānau a fānau
grandfather tamā o le tamā po‘o le tinā
grandmother tinā o le tamā po‘o le tinā
grandstand fale matamata
grant (money) tupe fa‘aavanoaina fua
(__ request) malie i ai, taliaina
grapes vine mata
(grapefruit) moli lapo‘a ‘ai i le suka
grasp pipi‘i, ‘u‘u, pu‘e
(understand) mālamalama
grass mutia, vao

(__ cutting tool)	tāivai
grasshopper	sē
grate (to __)	valu, olo
(grated coconut)	penu
grateful	lotofiafia
grater	tuai, matātuai, lapa
gratify	malie, logolelei
gratitude	lotofa'afetai
grave (be __)	faigatā, tūgā
(burial)	tu'ugamau, (pol.) lāgomau, tia, 'oli'olisaga
gravel	ma'ama'a, 'ili'ili
gravely (ill)	ma'itigāina, (pol.) loulouā
graveyard	fanua oti, fanuatanu
gravy	kaleve
graze (cattle)	'ai, fa'a'a'ai manu
(touch, scratch)	pa'iane, valusi, valuvalu, ma'amulumuluia
grease	ga'o, fa'aga'o
greasy	ga'oa
great (large)	tele
(famous)	ta'uta'ua
(good)	lelei
(very __)	tetele
greater (part)	'o le tele o . . .
greed	matape'ape'a
greedy	matape'ape'a, matatu'i'ai, na'o'ai
green (colour)	lanumeamata
(raw)	mata, moto
(unripe)	moto
(new growth)	mu'a
(__ bush)	lanulauusiusi, lanulauvao, lanulau'ava
greet	fa'afeiloa'i, feofoa'i, ofoalofa, fa'atālofa
greeting	feiloa'iga
grey	
(material etc)	efuefu
(__ hair)	sinā
grief	lotomomomo, pelepelega, fa'avauvau
grill	tunu, tunupa'u, (pol.) fa'avela
grim	matapogi, matapaū
grind (axe etc.)	fa'amanifi
(teeth)	'ō'ī, 'o'i'o'ī
(cocoa beans)	olo
grindstone	foaga
grip	'u'u, 'u'uga
grit	fāsimea nini'i ma le mālō
(__ teeth)	ū nifo
grizzle (children)	limala'u
groan	ōi, ōiōi
grocery (shop)	fale'oloa mea'ai
groin	tute, puga, 'auaga
groom (bride __)	tamafa'aipoipo
(__ a horse)	tafitafi mamā
(__ a person)	failelei 'ofu, lauulu etc.
groove (hollow)	'osi'osiga, mataafi
grope	tautago, tāpatapa, tagotago
gross (__ salary)	aofa'i o tupe maua ae le'i tō'esea lafoga etc.
(__ conduct)	āmio lē migao
(one __)	kerose i.e. 144
ground (soil)	'ele'ele, lau'ele'ele, fogā'ele'ele, fanua, malae
(basis)	fa'avae
(cricket __)	malae kilikiti
group	
(__ of people)	vasega, 'au, fa'alāpotopotoga
(__ of islands)	atumotu
grove	togālā'au
grow	tupu, faia'e, ola, totō, fa'ato'a
(begin to __)	tuputupu, tātupu
growl (dog etc.)	gū, tōmumumumu
grown up	tagata matua
growth	'o le tupu, tuputupu a'e
grub	'afato
grudge	mea e ita ai, mea fa'afatu'ulu
grumble	tomumu, to'u, mulu
grunt	'ua'ua
guarantee	mautinoa, fa'amāonia
guard	leoleo, leoleoga
(__ against)	tali, puipui
(defend)	leoleo, fa'afaileleina
guava	ku'ava
guess	mate, taumate, mea taumate
guest	mālo, tagata valā'aulia, (pol.) api
(__ house)	fale talimālō

guidance	ta'ita'iga
guide	'o le ta'iala
(to __)	ta'ita'i
guile	fai togāfiti, fa'a'ole'ole
guilty	agasala, ta'usalaina
guinea	kini
gulf	fagaloa
gullible	fa'ase'egōfie
gum	pulu, somo
gummy	pa'upa'ua, somoa, u'au'a
gums	tāinifo
gun	fana, (pol.) lā'au mālosi
(__ powder)	one
(__ shot)	pulu o le ututau
gunwale	oa o le va'a
gush	puna, pipisi
guts	gā'au, tinae
(fish __)	folo
gymnastics	fa'amālositino

Hh

habit	māsani, āmio
(bad __)	uiga leaga
(Nun's __)	'ofu o Taupousā
had	sa maua
(__ it not been . . .)	'ana lē seanoa . . .
Hades	Fafā
haggard	fole
hail (s.o.)	fa'afeiloa'i
(rain)	timu 'aisa
hair	lauulu, (pol.) lauao
(white __)	sina
(body __)	fulufulu, moge
(__ cut)	'otiulu, (pol.) fa'afuga le ao
(__ cream)	fagu ga'o
hairdresser	
(barber)	pāpa, 'otiulu
hairless	ta'alaelae, ta'agaogao
hairy	fulufulua
half	vaeluaga, 'afa
(__ caste)	'afakasi, (pol.) totolua
(__ cooked)	fa'amatamata
(__ hearted)	fa'alotolotolua, fa'agēgē
(__ hour)	vaitā, 'afa itūlā
(__ moon)	māsina 'ai 'aiga
hall	potu tele, fale fai fono, koniseti etc.
(__ way)	ala i le vāipotu
hallucinations	fāsaga
halt	fa'atū, fa'alepa
halter (animals)	sele, pena
halting (speech)	tagito'ia (ana tala)
(walk)	savali fa'api'opi'o
halve	vaelua tutusa
ham	vasāsui, alagāvae fa'aasu
(leg of pork)	ālaga, (pol.) ma'oi o le ali'i, vae o le manu
hammer	sāmala, tu'ifao
hand	lima, (pol.) 'a'ao
(out of __)	e lē mavāoia, lē taupulea
(on the other __)	i le tasi itū
(shake __)	lūlū lima
(__ of bananas)	tāifa'i
(__ me s.th.)	tu'u mai
(__ ful)	lū'uga, lu'utaga
(handyman)	poto i so'o se mea
handicap	mea faigatā, mea ua lē atoa ai le tino
handkerchief	solosolo
handle (a __)	'au
(to __)	fai, fa'aaogā
(__ w. care)	fa'aeteete
(__ a subject)	talanoaina
hand pick	auau
handrail	si'o
handsome	'aulelei, lālelei
handwriting	tusilima
hang (gen.)	tau, tautau
(__ s.th. up)	fa'atautau, tāupe
(__ a prisoner)	sisi
(__ in pairs)	feti'i
hangar	fale va'alele
hanger (clothes)	uaea tautau 'ofu
happen	o'o mai, tupu
(__ suddenly)	fa'afuase'i
happiness	'oli'oli, fiafia le loto

happy fiafia, manuia
(__ arrangement) fa‘atatau e mālilie i ai tagata
harbour tāulaga
hard (not soft) malō
(difficult) faigatā, fitā
(strong) ma‘a‘a
(__ to pronounce) ta‘ugatā
(a __ hit) tā mālosi
harden fa‘ama‘a‘a
hardly tau lēmafai
hardship mea faigatā
hard-wearing tologa, ‘anagatā
hard-working lima mālosi, galue tele, tō‘aga
hare lapiti lāpo‘a
harm leaga, fa‘aleaga
(no __ done) e lē āfāina
harmless filēmū
harmonium ‘ōkeni, piano
harmonize fetaui
harmony
(be in __) talafeagai, feaugalelei
harness ‘anesi
harp kitạra *(Bible)*, nāperi
harry tulitatao
harsh sāunoa, ‘ina‘inā, ‘upu o‘o, ogoogo
harvest sēleselega, tausaga, fuata
hasten ausulu, lise, natinati, fa‘avave, fa‘anatinati
hasty ‘a‘ale, topetope, topevale
hat pulou
hatch foa (le fuamoa)
hate ‘ino‘ino
haughty fa‘asiasia
haul (pull) toso, sa‘a
(__ a canoe) talana‘i
haunch muli, (pol.) nofoi
haunted aitua, talusā
have (I __) ‘ua ia te a‘u, ‘ua i ai etc.
hay vao mago, mutia mago
hazy (vague) fa‘anenefu
he, she, him, her, it ia
head ulu (pol.) ao
(__ of school etc.) pule, ali‘i pule
(__ for) aga‘i; fa‘asaga
(__ ache) ulutigā, tigā le ulu
(__ cloth) faufautū
(__ dress) tuiga
(__ gear) pūlou
(__ land) tolotolo
(__ line(s) talatomua, ulutala
(__ long) tîtō
(__ master) pulea‘oga
(__ quarters) ‘ōfisa sili
(__ rest) ‘ali, (pol.) lalago
(__ strong) fa‘ali‘i
(__ way) alualu ‘i luma
(__ wind) matagi taumua
heal (wound) ni‘i, pē le manu‘a
(__ the sick) fa‘amālōlō
health soifua mālōlōina
heap (a __) fa‘aputuga, faula‘iga, faupu‘ega
(__ up) fa‘aputu, fa‘afaula‘i, fa‘afaupu‘e
hear fa‘alogo, lagona, (pol.) fa‘afofoga
heard sa fa‘alogo etc.
heart fatu
(enthusiasm) loto
(essential part) ‘a‘ano
(cards) ‘ata
(by __) tauloto
(broken __) lotomomomo
(__ ache) vālovalo
(__ burn) tumulemoa, tōtō‘a‘ava
hearth mūgālafu, ta‘igāfi
heart-wood (tree) taia
heat vevela, ‘a‘asa, mūsaesae
(__up) fa‘avevela, velasia
(__ leaves) fa‘amamae, lalagi
heathen fa‘apaupau,fa‘anu‘upō
heave toso
heaven lagi
heavenly fa‘alelagi
heavy mamafa
(fairly __) māfamafa
hectare hekatea
hedge pā lā‘au, āi
(to __) si‘o, ‘alo
heedlessly fua
heel mulivae
(__ over, canoe) sa‘e
height ‘o le maualuga, tumutumu

heir suli
hell sēoli
helm foeuli
helmet pulou fa‘afao, pulou malō
help fesoasoani
(cry for ___) fia ola!
(it cannot be helped) ona pau lava
helper fesoasoani, ōlaga
helpful mataalofa, mata‘āiga
helpless vāivai
hem afe, su‘iafe
hen moa, matuāmoa
hen-house falemoa
her lana, lona, (pl.) ana, ona
herb(s) laumea, laulā‘au
(___ remedy) vailaumea
herd lafu, ta‘aga
here i, ‘i, ‘i ‘ī, ‘inei, ‘i‘inei
hereafter ‘ātalī, ‘āmulī
hermit crab uga
hernia fifi pa‘ū
hero toa
herring eleni
hesitant fetōa‘i, temutemu, fa‘alotolotolua, taumatemate
hesitate fa‘alētonu, fa‘alotolotolua, po‘epo‘e
hesitation po‘epo‘evale
hew tā
hibiscus fau, ‘aute
hiccup to‘omaunu, loga
hide (skin) pa‘u o manu
(to ___) lafi, nanā, fa‘alilo, pupuni, punitia
(give s.o. a hiding) sasa
hiding place lafitaga
high maualuga
(___ tide) sua le tai
(___ school) a‘oga maualuga
highest sili
highway alatanu, auala tele
hill a‘ega, mea maupu‘epu‘e
hills, hilly maugā
hillock ‘o le pu‘e
hillside itū o le mauga
him ia
hinder fa‘alavelave, fatiātāma‘i
hind leg alagāvae
hinge fa‘amau
hint fa‘amatalaali, fa‘aataata, ta‘ufa‘atafatafa
hip suilapalapa, gaugātino
hire (a man) fa‘afaigāluega
(a bus) tautala le pasi, togi pau
his lana, lona (pl.) ana, ona
hist sisi
history tala tu‘ufa‘asolo, tala fa‘asolopito
hit tā, taisi, fasi, tu‘i, motc
(___ target) tautonu
hitch (___ up) anini a‘e, fa‘alave, fa‘asā‘au
(w.o. a ___) e aunoa ma se fa‘alavelave
hither mai
hive (bees) fa‘amoegāpī
hoard fa‘aputu
hoarse fā le leo, fāfā
hoax ‘ole, fa‘amaoina
hobble ‘etu, setu
hobby mausa, pasitaimi
hockey hoki
hoe suōtā
hoist sisi, siligi
hold ‘u‘u, tago, tāofi, vāovao
(___ up) talitali
(___ a meeting) fai le fono
(___ back) tāofi
(___ your tongue) tāpuni lou gutu
(___ tightly) palepale
(___ of ship) ana o le va‘a
(___ a title) nofo matai
(___ fast) ‘u‘umau
hole pū, ‘omo, vane
(have holes) pūpū
holidays aso mālōlō, tu‘uaga, mālōloga
hollow ‘aupū, fa‘atānoa, ‘omo
(___ sound) leo ‘ō‘ō, tagulu
holy (sacred) pa‘ia, sā, tapu
(___ bible) Tusi Pa‘ia
(make ___, dedicate) fa‘apa‘ia

home	‘āiga, nu‘u
(at __)	i le fale
home-brew	fa‘amafu
homesick	ma‘i manatu, ma‘i atunu‘u
homosexual	tauātāne
(lesbian	ulugālii fafine)
honest	fa‘amāoni
(__ opinion)	manatu moni
honey	meli
honour	mamalu, fa‘aaloaloga, āva fa‘amamalu, fa‘aaloalo
hoof	atigivae (o le manu)
hook (fish __)	mātau
(trolling __)	pā seuseu
(__ & rope)	tautauga
(hooked knife)	nifo ‘oti
hoot (loud laughter)	taliē
(call of owl)	leo o le lulu
hop	musa, oso
hope	fa‘amoemoe, fa‘atuatuaga
(__ & pray)	tālosia, tālotalo
hopeless	lē taulau, siliga
hopscotch (game)	musa
horde	manomanō
horizon	tafatafa‘ilagi
horizontal	fa‘alava
horn (animal)	nifo, seu
(musical)	pū
hornet	‘o le pī
horror	mata‘utia, maniti
horse	solofanua (pol.) manu papālagi
(wooden __)	‘ausa‘alo
hose	fagā‘au
hospital	falema‘i
hospitality	‘o le talileleia o mālō
host	tagata talimālō
hostile	te‘e, oso le lē malie tele
hot	vevela, velavela
(red __)	‘a‘asa
(of spices)	feū
hotel	fale talimālō
hot-tempered	lotoa
hour	itūlā
house (gen.)	fale, fale o‘o
(long __)	fale āfolau
(round __)	fale tele
(chief's __)	maota *(also palace)*, maota tōfā
(orator's __)	laoa
(public __)	fale ‘ava
household	‘āiga, ‘aufale
householder	taufale
hover	fa‘apepepepe, tifatifa
how	pe faapēfea?
(__ many)	e fia? pē fia?
(__ much)	e fia? pe fia le tau?
(how are you?)	o ‘ā mai ‘oe?
however	peita‘i ane, tasi le mea, ‘ae ui i lea
howl	‘e‘ē
hug	opoopo, fusimau
huge	lāpo‘ā
hull	tino o le va‘a
hum (song)	fa‘agūgū
(of engine etc.)	ū ū
human	fa‘aletagata
humble	lotomaulalo, maulalo
humidity	susū o le ‘ea
humiliate	fa‘aluma, fa‘amā
humility	lotomaulalo, agamaulalo
humour	tausua
(to __)	fa‘amālie, fa‘amālū
humpback	tuapi‘o *(also hunchback)*
hunch (have a __)	‘i‘ite, fa‘a‘ite‘ite
hundred	selau
hundredweight	‘anereueta
hung	sisi
hunger	fia ‘ai, molemanava
hunt	tūliga, tuli, tutuli, su‘e
hunter	tagata tulimanu
hurl (a spear etc.)	velo
hurricane	afā
(__ lamp)	mōlī matagi
hurried	topetope, topevale, fa‘avave, ta‘alise,
hurry	tili, masau, tiniō, tele‘a‘i, nanati, ta‘alise, fa‘avave
hurt	fa‘atīgā, fa‘aleaga, taugā
(be __)	ila, tīgā, lavea, māfatia, manu‘a
(not __)	e lē āfāina
husband	tāne, to‘alua
hush	fa‘anā
(be hushed)	ligoligoa, lologo, fa‘alologo

husk	
(dry c'nut __)	migimigi
(to __)	mele'i, o'a, soso'a
husking-stick	mele'i
husky voice	fā le leo
hustle	patiapatā, topevale
hut	fale o'o, (pol.) faletua, falelaufao, falelaupola
hydrocele	ma'ivai, ma'i o tāne, lalovasa, (pol.) gasegase o tāne
hyena	haena
hygiene	tūmamā
hymn	pese fa'alelotu
hyphen	vase pu'upu'u
hypocrite	gutupoto, fa'afiaāmiotonu
hypodermic syringe	tui

Ii

I	'ou, a'u, ta, 'ita
ice	'aisa
(__ berg)	motu 'aisa
(__ box)	pusa'aisa
(__ cream)	'aisa kulimi
idea	manatu
ideal	lelei 'ato'atoa
identical	tusa pau
identify	mātaulia, va'aia
idiom	alagā'upu
idiot	tagata valea
idle	faiaga, samanoa, nofonofovale
idol	tupua
idolatory	ifo i tupua
if (past)	'ana
(future)	'āfai, pe 'āfai, pe'ā
(as __)	e pei
(even __)	e tusa pē
(__ only)	ma'imau pē ana
ignorance	po mala ē (i se mea), (pol.); lē iloa
ignorant	pōuliuli, lē māfaufau, valea
ignore	lē amana'ia, fa'agalo, fa'asolofua
ill __ illness	ma'i, (pol.) gasegase, loulouā, pulupulusia
ill-fated	mālaia, tauvale
ill-mannered	fa'alētaupulea, āmiolēmafaufau
illegal	e lē tusa ma le tulāfono
illegitimate (child)	tama fa'apōuliuli, (pol.) tama o le pō
illtreat	sāunoa
illuminate	sulu, fa'amālamalama, fa'asusulu
illustration	
(picture)	ata
(example)	talafa'atusa
image	'o le fa'atusa
(__ of s.o.)	so'o ia te ia
imaginary	fatufua, fa'afāgogo
imagination	māfaufauga
imagine (pretend, suppose)	fa'apea
(think, suspect)	masalo
imbecile	'o le vale
imitate	fa'ata'ita'i, fa'aa'oa'o
immature (fruit)	moto, mu'a
(animals, plants)	tama'i . . .
(person)	la'itiiti
immediately	(fai) loa
immense	telē
immerse	fa'atofu, fa'avai
immoral	āmio lē tusa, āmiolētonu
immortal	tumau, ola pea pea lava pea
impartial	lē fa'a'au'au, tonu, faimeatonu
impatient	lē 'onosa'i, faifai mea vave

implicate a'afia
implore 'ai'oi, augani, talosaga
impolite lēfa'aaloalo, lē migao, tūfanua
import mea mai fafo
important tāua, mamafa
(not __) e lē āfāina, fa'atauva'a
importune fa'atauānau, vinavina
imposing (person) māluali'i
impossible e matuā lē mafai
imprison falepuipuia
improper fa'alēfeagai, fa'alēono, fa'alēonomea
improve solo 'i luma, feoloolo, au'iluma
(__ in health) fa'asolosolo manuia
impudent gutuā, tautalala'itiiti
in i, iā, a
inaccessible saogatā, lē avanoa
inadequate 'uti'uti, lē lava
inaugurate 'amataga fa'ailogaina, fa'avae, fa'aulufale
inch 'īnisi
incident se mea ua tupu, fa'avesivesi
incidentally i le ma lea
incinerator o le fa'atafuna
incise tafa
incite uluia, fa'aoso
incline malifa
(be inclined to . . .) tau . . .
include tau taulia, lavea ai, aofia ai
income tupe maua
increase fa'atele, tupu, atili, ola, uluola
incredulous lē talitonu
increment tului
indecent māsoā, mātagā, fa'anu'upō
indeed ā, lava, matuā, naunau
indefinite fa'alētonu, lē mautinoa
independent tū to'atasi
index (finger) limatusi
(list) fa'asino'upu etc.
indicate fa'asino, fa'aali, fa'ailo
indifferent fa'aleogalua
indigestion tumu le moa
indiscreet masugōfie
indiscriminately so'ona
indisposed fa'ama'ima'i, (pol.) fa'agasegase
individual ta'itasi, ta'ito'atasi
indolence fa'apaiē, faiaga
indoors i totonu o le fale
indulge (a child) fa'alolololoina
indulgent lotofa'amāgalo
industrious ma'ema'e, mā'elegā
industry gaosiga o mea
inexpensive taugōfie
inexplicable lē mafa'amatalaina
infant tama meamea
infect 'ona, pisia
infection ma'i
inferior tūlaga maulalo, māsei
infinite fa'asavala, lē ma tua'oia
inflame mū, lūgā
inflammable mūgōfie
inflammation
(__ of lymphatic glands) mūmū
(__ of eyes) matasusui
influence mamalu, paoa, pule
influenza fulū
inform ta'u atu, logo atu, logologo
informal
(__ meeting) fono e le ui i tulāfono, fono faivale
(__ dress) fai so'o se 'ofu
information fa'amatalaga
ingrowing (toenail) unālalo
inhabit 'āinā
inhabitant tagata o le nu'u/atunu'u
inherit maua mai sē ua maliu, mea e māvae ai
inhuman sāuā
initial 'āmata, muamua, mua'i
initial(s) mata'itusi e 'āmata a'i igoa
initiative (take __) solomua
inject(ion) tui, tuiga
injury lavea, manu'a
injustice fa'amasinogalētonu, āmioletonu
ink vaitusi

inland	uta
(further ___)	maouta, gāʻuta
in-laws	paolo
inlet	vaifagaloa
inn	faletalimālō
innocent	mamā, taʻumamāina
innumerable	manomanō, lē mafaitaulia
inquire	fesili mo . . .
inquiry	suʻesuʻega, fesilisili
inquisitive	naunautala, tuʻufesili
insane	valea, sipa le fāiʻai
inscription	faʻaaliga, tusiga
insect	iniseti, mea ola laiti
insert	faʻafao, faʻaofi, sulu (le pelu), sunuʻi
inside	i totonu o . . .
insight	mālamalama
insignia (war)	tagāvai
(badge)	pine, faʻailoga
insignificant	faivale, faʻatauvaʼa
insist	maumautūtū, tausisi pea
insolent	gutuā
inspect	asiasi, iloilo
(school inspector)	asiasi aʻoga
inspire	faʻalototele, (pol.) faʻalāʻeiʻau
install	faʻanofo, saofaʻi, faʻapipiʻi, faʻatū
instance (for ___)	e pei . . .
instant (now)	nei lava
instantly	fai vave, fai loa
instead	faʻasui, sui aʻi
(this ___ of that)	lenei ʻae lē o lenā
instruct	faʻatonu, aʻoaʻo atu
instruction	faʻatonuga
instructor	faiaʻoga
instrument (tool)	mea faigāluega
(musical)	lāʻau pese, pū, faʻaili
(wind)	fagufagu
insufficient	lē lava, ʻutiʻuti
insult	faʻaluma, fāifai
insurance	inisiua
intelligence	atamai, poto
intend	māfaufau
intercede	fautua
intercept	seu
interchange	felafoaʻiga
intercourse	ʻāiga, (pol.) usuga
interest (pleasure)	mea e fiafia i ai
(money)	tului, pasene
interesting	mālie
interfere	aiā fua, faʻalavelave i . . . , taelase, mulumea
interior	i totonu o . . . , utāfanua
international	i le vā o atunuu/mālō
interpret	faʻamatala, faʻaliliu
interpreter	faʻamatala ʻupu
interrogate	faʻasufi, fesilisili
interrupt	faʻamotu, lavetala, seu, faʻasalāvei
intersection	
(two roads)	māgafā, magā-ala
intertwine	fesauaʻi, fefaʻafelefeleaʻi
interval	avanoa, mālōlōga, vāitaimi
intestine	gāʻau, (pol.) taufale
(small ___)	fifi
intimate	faʻauō, māfuta, māfana
into	i, i totonu
intolerance	lē ʻonosaʻi, manatu faʻapito, lē faʻapalepale
intoxicate	faʻaʻōnā
intricate	lavelave
intrigue	tāupulepule
introduce (people)	faʻafeiloaʻi
(a speech)	faʻatomua
(a subject)	faʻamalaga
inundate	lōfia, lofitūina
invade	oso
invalid (not valid)	lē aogā, lē tonu
(sick)	tagata maʻi
invalidate	faʻalēaogā
invaluable	e le mafaʻataulia, tāua aʻiaʻi
invent (tools etc.)	muaʻi fausia
(story, song)	fatu
investigate	suʻesuʻe, iloilo, ʻauʻiliʻili, faʻamasino
invisible	e le o vaʻaia
(___ moon)	pōpōloloa
invitation	ʻo le valāʻaulia, tusi valāʻau
invite	valāʻau, (pol.) tālo
involved	aʻafia, felefele
iodine	aiotini, vaimanuʻa
iron	uʻamea
(to ___ clothes)	ʻāuli
(___ wood)	toa

irregular	vāvā'ese, fesuisuia'i
irrigate (garden)	vaita'i
irritable	itaitagōfie
irritating	soesā
Islam	Isalama
island	motu
isolate (sickness)	fale'esea
isolated (lonely)	fa'a'esea
issue (give out)	avatu, fa'asalalau, tufatufa
(the __)	i'uga, matā'upu
isthmus	'auiti
it	na, ia, lea
itch	mageso
item	mea, matā'upu
its	lana, lona (pl.) ana, ona
ivory	lei

Jj

jab	tui
jack (tool)	siaki
jacket	peleue
jagged	fa'anifonifo, ma'ama'ai
jail	falepuipui *(also gaol)*
jam	siamu
January	Ianuari
jar	fagu
(stone __)	fagu'ele, vaima'a
jaundice	fiva samasama
jaw (animal)	'aulamu
(person)	'auvae
jealous	fuā, lotoleaga, matau'a
jeans	'ofuvae
jeep	sipi
jeer	fa'atuetuē, taufāifai, fa'atauemu
jelly (food)	sieli
jellyfish	'alu'alu
jerk	se'i, lafo
jest	fa'ase'e, fa'aulaula, tausua
jet (__ 'plane)	va'alele fai afi mālolosi
(a __)	gutu la'itiiti
(__ black)	uliulipato'i
jewel	ma'atāua
jew's harp	utete
jingle	tagitagi
job	gāluega, faiva
jockey	ti'eti'e solofanua
join	so'o, soso'o, fa'atasia, 'au, auai
joist (building)	lā'au fa'alava
joke	fa'ase'e, tausua, fa'aulaula
jolly	lotofiafia
jolt	sa'alutu
jostle	fa'avāvā, taufa'aofiofi
jot (down)	tusitusiga fai fa'avave
journey	malaga, ta'amilosaga
joy	'oli'oli, fiafiaga
jubilee	iupelī
judge	ali'i fa'amasino
Chief Justice	Fa'amasino Sili
judgement	
(understanding)	fa'autaga
(to consider)	iloiloga
(Day of __)	'o le Aso Gata'aga
judo	tuito
jug	sioki
juggle	aufua
juice	sua
July	Iulai
jump	oso, puna
(__ over)	osopuna
(__ up & down)	tu'uoso
junction (road)	taula'iga o ala
June	Iuni
jungle	vaomatua, vaomāoa
junk (rubbish)	gasu
(ship)	va'a Saina
jury (court)	'au fa'amasino, (A.S.) tiuri, 'aufa'atonu
just (fair)	tonu, āmiolelei
(now)	nei lava, fa'ato'ā faia, se'i

(__ the same)	tusa lava
justice	fa'amasinoga tonu, meatonu
(a __)	ali'i fa'amasino
(__ of the peace) (J.P)	tagata tofia e saini pepa fa'aletulāfono
jut (out)	'oso'oso, tauponapona, lālā'ese

Kk

kapok	vavae
kava	'ava, (pol.) agatonu
kava (stem & root)	tugase, (pol.) mālō
kava bowl	tāusa, tānoa palu'ava, (pol.) laulau
keel	ta'ele
keen (mind)	mataala
(blade)	ma'ai
keening	lauaitu
keep (retain)	mau, tāofi
(__ guard)	leoleo
(__ in order)	tausi
(__ in mind)	teu, amana'ia
(__ on doing s.th)	fai pea, saga . . .
(__ close to)	pipi'i
(__ wickets, cricket)	talitua
keeping (in __ w.)	talafeagai, ōgatasi
keg	paelo
kerb	pito 'auala, pito alāvai
kernel	'a'ano, ta'ale
kerosene	kalasini
kettle	tītata
key	kī
kick	muāvae, tavae, a'a, kiki
kidney	fatuga'o, fatuma'a
kill (person)	fasioti, (pol.) fa'alāva'au
(destroy)	fa'aumatia
(animal)	fasi, tapē, (pol.) fa'amate
kilowatt	kilouati
kilt	'ie, lāvalava, titi
kin	'āiga, pa'u
(true __)	tōtino
kind	agalelei, alofa
(type)	itū'āiga
(__ hearted)	lotolelei
kindle	matamata (le umu)
kindling wood	alaala, matamata, (pol.) seuseu
kindness	lotolelei
king	tupu
kingdom	mālō fai tupu
kingfisher (bird)	ti'otala
kinsman	'āiga, pa'u
kiss	sogi, kisi, (pl.) feasogi
kit	mea (e fai a'i gāluega)
kitchen	umukuka, (pol.) tūnoa
kite	'o le maua
kitten	tama'i pusi
knave (person)	tagata fa'a'ole'ole
(cards)	tama
knead	lomi, palu i lima
knee	tuli, tulivae
kneecap	tupe o le tuli
kneel	to'otuli
knew	sa iloa
knife (gen.)	naifi, (pol.) polo, 'o'e, 'ofe, fa'aola fanua
(pen __)	naifi fa'amoe
(bush __)	pelu, sapelu
(hooked __)	nifo 'oti
knit	lalaga
knob	'au lāpotopoto, 'au o le faitoto'a
knock	tu'i, tu'itu'i
(__ off)	mālōlō mai gāluega, fa'i
(__ out)	tu'i oti
knot	pona
knotty	ponā, ponapona
know	iloa, (pol.) silafia
(__ by heart)	tauloto
(be known as)	ta'ua

(who knows, I don't know) ta'ilo
(who knows whether) tainane
knowledge iloa, mautinoa, poto
knuckle(s) ponāivi o tuālima
koala bear urosa la'itiiti, 'o le koala
kumara 'umala
(sweet potato) 'umala

Ll

label pepa igoa
labour gāluega
(woman's __) fānauga
(__ pains) fa'atīgā
Labour Party 'au Leipa, Leipa Pati
labourer tagata faigāluega, leipa
lace leise
lacerate māfo'e, māfo'efo'e
lack 'o le leai o se mea, lē lava, mativa i . . .
(__ of respect) fa'alēmigao
(__ of understanding) lē mālamalama
lad tama
laddie! sole!
ladder apefa'i
lade (scoop) asu vai etc.
laden 'āvega, uta mamafa
lady tama'ita'i, sa'otama'ita'i, tausala
(elderly __) tama'ita'i matua
lag (behind) taufa'avāivai, 'ua solo i tua
lagoon aloalo, taitafola
laid out (of things) folafolaina
lake vaitūloto
lamb tama'i māmoe
lame vaepi'o
lament pese aualofa, auē, tagiauē
lamentation tagisaga, laūega, auēga
lamp mōlī
(__ black) lama
(benzine __) molī penisini
lance (weapon) tao 'umi
(medical) tafa
land lau'ele'ele, fanua
(native __) atunu'u moni
(__ passengers etc.) tuta, tūlau'ele'ele
(__ of a'plane) o'o, taunu'u
(__ crab) mali'o
landlord taufanua
landslide 'o le solo
lane 'auala lauitiiti
language gagana
(bad __) 'upu palauvale
lanky 'ivā
lantern molī, molī matagi
lap (hold on __) si'i i ona vae
(sport) ta'amilosaga e tasi
lapel (coat __) fā'alo, lapela
lard ga'o
large tele, lāpō'a
(be at __) ta'a
larva 'afato
(mosquito __) tugatuga
larynx fā'a'ī
lash (beat) 'apa, sasa, sasau, tā
(bind) fusi, faufau
lass teine
lassie! funa! suga!
last mulia'i, muli, mulimuli
(__ year) tausaga talu ai
(__ day) toe aso
(__ night) anapō
(__ wish) māvaega
(to __) lava, lavātia
(__ forever) fa'avavau
(long lasting) 'anagatā, tologa
late tuai
(__ leader) ta'ita'i talu ai
(too __) siliga ona . . .
later e tuai ai, i se itūlā, mulimuli ane, nānei, sauaso

latest	aupito fou
lather	‘oa o le moli etc, fa‘a‘oa
latrine	fale‘ese, fale la‘itiiti, fale vao
laugh	‘ata (pl.) fe‘atani, toē, (pol.) soisoi, taliē
launch (to __)	tu‘u i tai
(a __)	va‘aafi
laundress	teine tā ‘ofu
laundry (clothes)	tāgāmea
(room)	potu tā lāvalava
lava (rock)	lava
law	tulāfono
lawful	e tusa ma le tulāfono
lawless	e lē tāupulea
lawn	mutia teuteuina
(__ mower)	moa
lawyer	lōia
laxative	vai fa‘atafi
lay (__ out)	fofola
(__ down)	fa‘ata‘atia, fa‘ata‘oto
(__ a trap)	lama
(__ hold of)	tagotago, pu‘e
(__ egg(s)	tu‘u fua
layer(s)	sautua (tasi) (lua) etc.
(thin __)	laumanifi
layman	puletua
layout	sāuniga, ta‘otoga
lazy	paiē, titipa
lead (metal)	pulu
(in the __)	silimusa, ta‘imua
(to __)	ta‘i, ta‘ita‘i
leader	ta‘ita‘i, ta‘imua
leaf	lau, lau lā‘au
(page)	itūlau
league (in __ w.)	‘au‘au fa‘atasi
(football __)	ta‘amilosaga
leak	mama, sisi, tutulu
lean (meat)	‘anogasea
(people, animals)	pa‘e‘e
lean (on, against)	fa‘alagolago, toto‘o
(towards)	falala, mafuli
(lean-to)	fa‘ase‘e o le fale
leap	puna, oso
learn	a‘o, a‘o a‘o
(__ by heart)	tauloto
learned	poto
lease	lisi
least	pito la‘itiiti
leather	pa‘u
leave (on __)	fa‘amālōlō

(__ out)	lē lavea
(by your __)	vāeane, vāeatu
(give __)	fa‘ataga
(let go)	tu‘u
(__ in abeyance)	tu‘u pea, ta‘atia
(__ behind)	tu‘u, tu‘una, fa‘amuli
leaven	fefete, fa‘afefete
lecture	tautalaga, lesoni, lesona
ledger(s)	tusi fa‘a-kamupanī
lee, leeward	i atea
left	tauagavale
(__ handed)	agavale
(__ overs)	toega, toe‘aiga
leg (man)	vae, (pol.) ‘a‘ao
(pig etc.)	alaga, (pol.) ma‘oi o ali‘i
(pull s.o’s leg)	tausuaga (S. = toso taliga)
legend(s)	tala mai le vavau, ‘uputu‘u
legendary	fa‘afāgogo
legislate	fa‘atulāfono, faitulāfono
legislature	fono faitulāfono
leisure	taimi pāganoa
lemon	tīpolo patupatu
lend	fa‘a‘une, ‘aitālafu
(__ an ear)	usi le fa‘afofoga
length	‘o le ‘umi
lengthen	fa‘a‘umi
lens	tioata (o le mea pu‘eata etc.)
leopard	nameri
leper	lēpela
leprosy	lēpela, ma‘i mutumutu
less	e itiiti i . . .
lessen	fa‘ala‘itiiti, fa‘aitiiti, feto‘i, fa‘amāmā
lesson	matā‘upu fa‘alea‘oga, a‘oa‘oga, lesona, lesoni
lest	ne‘i
let (allow)	fa‘ataga, fa‘aavanoa
(__ me, us, etc.)	‘ia, se‘i
(__ be)	tu‘u, sōia
(__ up, i.e. diminish)	maona ifo, maui
(__ s.o. in)	fa‘aavanoa
(to __, rent)	lisi
letter (to s.o.)	tusi
(alphabet)	mata‘itusi
(registered __)	tusi puipuia

lettuce lētisi, kapisi ‘ai mata
level laugatasi, gatasi, mafola
(make __) fa‘agatasi, fa‘alaugatasi
lever taumoa, līva, laga, sua, uati
levy saogātupe
liaison feso‘ota‘iga (o tagata)
liberal (generous) lima foa‘i, lima lelei, matamau
liberty sa‘olotoga
library fale faitautusi, fa‘aputugātusi
lice ‘utu
licence laiseni
lichen limu
lick eto, etoeto, salosalo
lid ufi, ufiufi
lie (untruth) pepelo
(__ down) ta‘oto, ta‘atia, (pol.) fa‘asa‘osa‘o
(__ awake) alapō
(__face down) faō
(__ in await) lama
(__ across) felavasa‘i
(__ evenly) sagatonu
(__ on o’s back) taliaga
(__ at anchor) tu‘utaula
life ola, ōlaga, (pol.) soifuaga
(__ buoy) poe
lift (raise) si‘i, su‘ena, afe
(__ a restriction) fa‘agafua
(elevator) potu si‘i tagata
light (colour) vāivai, pa‘epa‘e, tea
(__ weight) māmā, māmāsagia
(__ a fire) tutu, fa‘aola, fa‘amumū, tafu
(day __) ao, mālamalama
(first __) taeao sesegi
(__ for cigarette) afi, *(lighter)* afi penisini
lighten fa‘amāmā
lighter (boat) lāgisi
(cigarette __) afi penisini
light-fingered limatāgo‘ese, limavale
lighthouse fale mālamalama, molī ta‘ialāva‘a, molī o le ava
lightning uila emo
like e pe‘ī, fa‘apea, fa‘apei, pēnei, fa‘apēnei
(similar) pēlā, pēnā, fa‘apelā, fa‘apenā
(be like what?) fa‘apē‘ī?
(to __) fiafia i, mana‘o i . . .
likelihood po‘o pēnā? po‘o pēnei, semanū
likely (be __) ‘ai lava, pe mata e mafai ona . . ., ātonu, fa‘amata
likeness e pei o, fa‘atusa
likewise fa‘apea
liking for fiafia i . . .
lily lili
limb (body) itūtino, lima, vae etc., (pol.) ‘a‘ao
(tree) lālā lā‘au
lime (paint) namu
(fruit) tīpolo
lime kiln umunamu
limit tapula‘a, tua‘oi, pau
(no __) e leai se mea e gata mai ai
(set a __) fa‘agata, fa‘atapula‘a
limp (be __) gālemulemu
(walk w.a. __) savali fa‘api‘opi‘o
limpid manino
line (row) āi, laina
(fishing __) afo, ‘afa fāgota
(telephone __) uaea telefoni
(railway __) ala u‘amea
(__ of people) solo
(__ a basket) āfei
lineage ‘āiga, gafa, ma‘ave‘ese‘ese
(royal __) gafa fa‘atupu
linen ‘ie, lino *(Bible)*
liniment vaimili
linoleum kapeta
lion liona, leona
lip laugutu
lipstick valilaugutu
liquid suāvai
liquor ‘ava papālagi
(home brew) fa‘amafu
lisp laulaufaiva ‘ati
list lisi
listen fa‘alogologo, (pol.) fa‘afogafoga
listeners ‘aufa‘alogologo, (pol.) ‘aufa‘afofoga
litre līta
litter (stretcher) fata

(rubbish)	otaota
(of animals)	toloa‘i
little	itiiti, la‘itiiti, tama‘i
(a __)	sina, teisi, fa‘aleai
live (dwell)	nofo, mau
(alive)	ola, (pol.) soifua
lively	malaulau, tiotio
liver	ate, au, (pol.) veve
living (livelihood)	gāluega e ola ai
lizard	pili
load	‘āvega, uta
(carried under arm)	‘afisi, ‘afisiga
(carried from a yoke)	āmo, āmoga
(carried in arms)	opoopoga
(carried by two on pole)	tausoa
(__ a ship)	la‘u le uta a le va‘a
(__ a gun)	utu le fana
loaf (bread)	papā falaoa
(__ about)	femiomioa‘i
loan	fa‘a‘une, fa‘a‘aitālafu
lobster	ula, ulātai
local	fa‘alenu‘u
locate	mauaina, va‘aia
location	tūlaga, nōfoaga
lock	loka, fa‘amau
locust (cicada)	‘ālisi
lodge (of guest)	nofo, (pol.) api
(be caught)	‘apilitia
(__ a claim)	fa‘aulu le tagi
lodger	tagata mau totogi
log (tree)	ogālā‘au, lago
(ship's __)	api o le malaga
loin (man)	tulimanava, (pol.) tulialo
(pig)	tualā, (pol.) tua o le manu
loincloth	malo
lolly	lole
lone	ta‘anoa, ta‘atasi, to‘atasi
loneliness	fa‘avauvau
lonely (person)	fa‘a‘esea
(__ place)	ta‘aligoligoa, nofoaga tu‘ufua
long	‘umi, -loa *(suffix),* (A.S.) sa‘ō
(__ ago)	anamuā
(__ lasting)	‘anagatā, mautū
(__ time since)	leva, loa
(take a __ time)	tuai
(very __)	‘u‘umi
(__ for)	mo‘omo‘o, naunauta‘i, tu‘inanau
longing	‘o le tu‘inanau
look! (behold!)	fa‘auta!
look	‘o le pulapula
(good looks __ men)	‘aulelei
(__ serious)	matapaū
(appearance)	va‘aiga
(__ at s.th.)	va‘ai, pupula, tepa, tilotilo, pulapula, mātamata, fatua‘i, (pol.) maimoa, taga‘i, silasila
(__ after)	leo, va‘aia, tausi, fa‘amāopoopo
(it looks like)	e pei, pē‘ī, e peisea‘ī, ai lava
(__ forward to)	fa‘amoemoe ma le fiafia
(__ back)	fāliu, va‘ai i tua
(__ brave)	mata toa
(__ bad)	mata vale
(__ fixedly at)	tepa taula‘i, pulato‘a
(__ out!)	va‘ai oe!
(__ sour)	fa‘a‘ū
(__ in all directions)	tiovale ona mata, va‘ai i itu ‘uma
looking glass	mea va‘ai, fa‘aata *(also mirror),* fā‘ata
loom (over)	fa‘amālumalu
loop	futia, vi‘o, li‘o
loose	ta‘a, ta‘anoa, māgaegae, māne‘e, maveve, matagataga
(let __)	tatala, fa‘ata‘a, matala
(run __)	ta‘ata‘a
loosely (clothes)	fa‘a‘ō‘ō
(__ woven)	valavala
loosen (rope etc.)	fa‘amatagataga
loot	vete
lop	taulu, fa‘agata
lopsided	sipa
lord	ali‘i
(Lord's Prayer)	Tatalo a le Ali‘i
lordship	lana susuga, lana afioga
lorry	loli

lose (be lost) lē iloa, ʻavea, lusi
(__ a game) faiaʻina, vāivai, malolo
(__ interest) ʻuma le fiafia, fiu
(__ one's way) sē, fesēaʻi
(__ face) faʻaluma, faʻamā
loss (of money) tupe lē iloa
(be at a __) femēmēaʻi, lē mautonu
lost lēiloa
lot (the __) anoano, meaʻuma
(a __) tele, toʻatele
lotion vainini
lottery ʻo le lūlū
loud leo tele
loud speaker faʻaleotele leo, sīpika
louse ʻutu
(lousy) ʻutua
louvre (window) luva
love alofa, fiafia ʻi . . .
(__ of family) loto ʻāiga
(__of country) loto atunuʻu
(__ affair) alofa i le uō, faigāuō
lovely mānaia, mātagōfie
lover taʻa, uō
lovesick maʻi valea le uō
low māulalo
(shallow) papaʻu
(__ tide) pē le tai
lower (to __) faʻamaulalo, tuʻutuʻu ifo
(reduce) tuʻu ʻi lalo, faʻaitiiti
loyal faʻamaoni
(__ to family) lotoʻāiga
(__ to country) loto atunuʻu
luck (good __) manū, laki
(bad __) mala, lē laki, lē manuia
(have good __) ʻauamanū
(have bad __) ʻauamala
(bring bad __) talusā
lucky manuia, laki
luggage ʻato (o le malaga)
lull (to __) faʻamoemoe, faʻanānā
lullaby pese faʻamoemoe pepe
lump patu, potoi, fāsimea
lumpy patupatu, patupatuvale
lunatic ʻo le vale
lunch ʻaiga o le aoauli
lung māmā
lunge taniʻo, niʻo, oso
lure (a __) pā
(octopus __) maʻataʻifeʻe
(to __) faʻasesē, faʻaoleole, mailei, faʻatosina

Mm

machine masini
machine-gun fana taʻavili
mackerel (fish) ʻatule
mad (be __) valea
(__ on . . .) fiafia tele i . . .
madam tamaʻitaʻi
made faia, gaosia, fausia
madman ʻo le vale
magazine tusiata
maggot ili, tuga
magic mana faʻataulāitu
magician tagata fai tīfaga, faʻataulāitu
magistrate ʻo le faʻamasino
magnet maneta
magnify vivii, vīʻia, faʻatele
magnificent mātagōfie
maiden
(village __) tāupou (pol.) saʻo aualuma, saʻotamaʻitaʻi, tamaʻitaʻi faʻanofonofo
mail meli
(mail-boat) ʻo le meli
main tele, sili, silisili
(important) tāua
mainland motu tele, fanua tele
mainsail lafolā
maintain tausi
maintenance tausiga, teuteu pea
maize sana
majesty mamalu, maiesetete

majority 'o le to'atele, 'o le tele
make (to __) fai, fau, gaosi
(__ of car etc.) itū'āiga, fausaga
(__ up a quarrel) fa'alelei
(__ known) fa'ailoa
(pol.) fa'asilasila
(__ comfortable) nofo lelei, nofo sa'oloto
(__ up a story) fatu se tala
(__ water) mimi *(of children)*, pī
(__ mistake) sala, sasi
make-believe fa'afāgogo
make-up (cosmetics) 'o le vali (mo mata)
malaria malalia
male (people) tāne, tama
(animals) po'a
mallet sā'afa, samala lā'au
man (person) tagata
(male, husband) tāne
(adult __) tamāloa,
(pl.) tamāloloa
(untitled __) taule'ale'a,
(pl.) taulele'a, tama
(that __) 'o le igoa lea
(black-skinned man) tamàuli
(old __) toea'ina (pl.) toea'i'ina
(man a ship) fa'a'auva'a
manage faia, maua atu, lavātia, mafaia
management pule, faiga
mango (fruit) mago
mangrove togo
manifest (be __) tino mai
(ship's __) lisi o le uta
manifold matalasi
mankind 'o le itū'āiga o tagata
manner(s) uiga, āmio
man-of-war va'atau, mānuao
manufacture faiga, gaosiga i masini etc.
manure tae o manu, maniua
many tele, to'atele, lasi
map fa'afanua
marble mapu, toa
march (to __) savali, la'a
(the __) sāvaliga, solo
March Mati
marine malini (fitafita)
mark togi, fa'ailoga, pine, māka, ila
(question __) fa'ailoga fesili (?)
marker maka.
market māketi
(super __) supamāketi
marriage (wedding) fa'aipoipoga
married (man) fa'aipoipo, faiavā, tamāloa
(woman) fa'aipoipo, nofotāne, fafine
marsh taufusi
marvel (to __) ofo
marvellous ofoofogia
mash fa'amalū, tu'i, tu'ipala
mask ufimata
mass (R.C.) misasā
(great amount) anoano, tele naunau
(__ of people) tagatālautele
(__ of foliage) ululau
massage fofō, lomilomi
mast fanā
master ali'i, matai, faia'oga
(__ of ceremonies) fa'alau'ava, pule i sāuniga
(__ fisherman) tautai
(__ piece) gāluega aupito lelei
masticate mama, lamulamu
mat (gen.) fala
(floor __) papa, polavai
(sleeping __) fala lili'i
(fine __) 'ie, 'ietoga,
(pol.) mālō, measina, 'ie o le mālō
(food platter) laulau, pā
match (game) ta'aloga, fetauiga
(to __, compare) fa'atusatusa, fetaui
matches (box) lā'au afitusi
mate uō, soa
(ship's __) sui kapitene
(to mate, of animals) ofi, fa'a feusua'i
material mea
(cloth) 'ie
materialize fa'ataunu'u
maternity hospital fale ma'i mo failele
mathematics matematika
matter mea, matā'upu
(it does not __) e lē āfāina
(what's the __?) 'o le ā 'ea le fa'alavelave?

(i.e. substance) ʻaʻano
mattress faʻamalū
mature matua
maximum aupito tele, tapulaʻa
May Mē
may e mata, ʻānei
(maybe) ʻātonu, ʻai, e mata foʻi
mayor pulenuʻu
me aʻu, ia te aʻu
meal ʻaiga, (pol.) tāumafataga, talisuaga
mean (average) e māsani ai
(in the __ time) i lenei vāitaimi, *(also meanwhile)*
(be __) mataū, limavale
(to __) uiga
meaning uiga, faʻauiga
means tupe a le tagata
measles mīsela
measure fua
meat fasipovi, ʻaʻano
mechanic inisinia
mechanical tau masini
meddle āiā fua
medallion (R.C.) malia
mediate fautua, pupulu
mediator fautua, puluvaga
medicine vai, vailāʻau, vailaumea
(bush __) vaiaitu
(cough __) vaitale
(to get __) talavai
medium feoloolo, faʻaleogalua
meek agamalū
meet (people) feiloaʻi, fetaiaʻi
(of councils) fesilafaʻi, fono, usu
(of two things) fetaui, feagai ma . . .
meeting (a __) fono, fonotaga
melody fati
melon meleni
melt (of fat etc.) usi
(of ice) liusuāvai
member (of a society etc.) tagata, lē ʻua ʻauai
(church __) ekalesia (Meth.)
memo tusi puʻupuʻu
memorable (occasion) ʻo le taeao fou, aso faʻailogaina
memorial maʻa faʻamanatu
memorize tauloto
memory lotomanatu, māfaufau
memories māfaufauga, mānatunatuga
menace faʻamataʻu, faʻasoesā, faʻataluā
mend teu, fai, suʻi māsae, fono, timata
meningitis fiva fāiʻai
menses māʻimāsina, (pol.) ʻeleʻele
mental faʻalemāfaufau
mention taʻu, taʻutaʻu, tautalagia
menu lisi o meaʻai (i faleʻaiga etc.)
merchant faiʻoloa
mercy alofa
(divine __) alofamutimutivale
mere naʻo
merry fiafia
mesh mata (o le ʻupega, uaea valavala etc.)
mess (be in a __) gaogaosā
(officers' mess) potu ʻai mo ʻōfisa o le vaegāʻau
message feʻau, poloaʻi
messenger ʻave feʻau, sāvali
metal uʻamea, mētala
method faiga, ala, metotia
Methodist Metotisi, lotu Toga, lotu Uesilē
methylated spirits sipili
metre, meter mīta
mice isumu laiti
microphone faʻaleoteleleo, maika
middle ʻogātotonu, vaeluaga, tūlua, moa, totonugalēmū
(__ of house) lotoifale
(__ of night) vaeluāpō, valuāpō
midnight tautūluaga, vaeluāpō
midrib (c'nut leaf) lapalapa
(c'nut leaflet) tuāniu
midwife fafine faʻatōsaga
might (strength) mana, paoa
(perhaps) ʻātonu, ʻai
migrate nofu mau i fafo, tuʻua le atunuʻu
mild (manner) āmio faʻataumālie, filemū, agavāivai
(__ weather) malū, māfanafana

mildew	taetaepaloloa
military	fa'afitafita
milk	susu, suāsusu
(condensed __)	susu toto'o
(to milk)	tatau (le povi)
Milky Way (stars)	'aniva
mill	fale e olo ai falaoa mata, fale e gaosi ai mea u'amea
millilitre	mīlilīta
millimetre	mīlimīta
millipede	taetuli
million	miliona
millionaire	milionea
mind (the __)	māfaufau
(opinion)	tāofi
(be of one __)	lotogatasi, (pol.) finagalo fa'atasi
(be in two __)	fa'alotolotolua
(not to __)	lē mainiga, 'aua le amana'ia
(if you do not __)	malie lou loto/finagalo
mine (hole)	lua
(to __)	'eli
(explosive)	maina
(to possess)	o'u
minimum	aupito itiiti
minister (government)	minisitā
(church)	faife'au
minority	'o le to'aitiiti
minus	tō'ese
minute (small)	nini'i
(time)	mīnute
miracle	vāvega
mirror	fa'a'ata, fā'ata
miscalculate	tau'ese
miscarriage	ma'ifafano, fānau lē au
mischief	'avei leaga
miserable	lē fiafia, leagā
misfortune	asovale, mala, māsei
mislead	fa'asesē
mispronounce	fa'aleosesē, fa'asasisasi
miss (to __)	ela, sesē, lē maua
(to __ people)	tausa'afia
(missing persons)	tagata 'ua lē iloa
missionary	misionare, misi
mist	puao
mistake	sesē, mea sesē, 'aleu
mistletoe	tapuna
misunderstood	lē mālamalama
misuse	fa'aaogā sesē
mix	palu, seu, fa'afefiloi, filo
(be mixed up)	fenumia'i, feleilogaa'i
mixture	paluga, fefiloi
(__ of races)	totolua etc.
moan	ōi
mob	mau tagata, lafu māmoe *(sheep)*
mock	tauemu, 'a'amu
model	fa'ata'ita'iga, fa'afoliga
(new __)	faiga fou, fausiga fou
moderate	fa'afeoloolo, tāofiofi
modern	fa'aneionapō, 'o aso nei, fou
modest (manner)	āmiomaulalo, matamuli
moist	sū
moisture	'o le susū
molar	gao
mole (on skin)	ila
mollusc	figota
moment	taimi pu'upu'u lava
(in a __)	se'i toeitiiti
(for the __)	mo lenei vāitaimi
monarch	'o le tupu
monarchy	mālō faitupu
Monday	Aso Gafua
money	tupe
monkey	manukī
monotonous	pāsiā
month	māsina
(woman's monthly period)	ma'i māsina
monument	ma'a fa'amanatu
(funeral __)	tiamau
moon	māsina
moonless	pōpōloloa
moor (a boat)	fa'pipi'i
(land)	laugatasi tu'ufua
mop	solo, mopu, fufulu
moral	alatatau, āmiotatau
(__ of a story)	a'oa'oga
more	'o se mea fa'aopoopoina
(some __?)	toe avatū?
(want to know __)	fia iloa atili
(no more)	e leai se isi, 'ua lava
moreover	'i le ma le isi, 'i le ma lea
morning	taeao

(earlier this __) anataeao
(early in the __) i le taeao pō
(early this __) anataeao pō
mortal ‘o le tagata ola
(__ wound) tau i le oti
mortar palu fa‘apipi‘i piliki
mortgage mōkesi
mortise
(carpentry) vane
mosquito namu
(__ net) ta‘inamu
moss limu, limulimu
most ‘o le tele, ‘o le to‘atele
(__ difficult) aupito faigatā
motel fale talimālō
moth lelefua
mother tinā, mama
(nursing __) failele
(__ hen) matuāmoa
(adoptive __) fa‘atinā
mother-in-law tinā o le to‘alua
mother-of-pearl tifa
motion
(movement) gāoioiga
(proposal) mau, lafofa‘atū
(faeces) fe‘au mamao
motor afi
(__ boat) va‘aafi, va‘akalasini
(__ car) ta‘avale
(__ bike) uila afi, (A.S.) uila pāpā
mouldy legalegā, taepaloloa, taetaepaloloa
mound pu‘e
mount (a __) mauga
(to __) oso i luga
mountain mauga
mountainous maugā
(mountain range) atumauga
mourn fa‘anoanoa, fa‘avauvau
mouse isumu
moustache ‘avaaluga
mouth gutu, muāgutu, (pol.) fofoga
(river __) mulivai
move si‘iga, gāoioi, gāe‘e, fa‘agāe‘e
(moved emotionally) o‘otia le loto
(__ a little) sōsō ane
(__ forward) solo i luma, sōsō i luma
(__ back) solomuli, sōsō, i tua
movement gāoioiga, fegāsoloa‘iga, feōa‘iga
(a dance __) tāga
(i.e. a group of people) fa‘alāpotopotoga
mower moa
much (there is __) e tele
(too __) e tele na‘uā
(not __) lē tele, fa‘aleai
mucus vavale, isupē
mud palapala
muddy palapalā, gaepu
mudguard ‘apa‘apa (o le ta‘avale)
mulberry
(paper __ tree) u‘a
mulch nasu
mullet (fish) ‘anae
multiply fa‘atele
multitude (people) motu o tagata e to‘atele
(numerous) manomanō
mummy (mother) mama
municipality pulega fa‘aitūmālō
murder fasioti
murmur si‘uleo, magamagagū, talagū
muscle ‘ānogase, mūsele, maso
museum falemata‘aga
music musika, pese
musical
__ instrument lā‘aupese
Muslim Musalimi
mussel faisua
must tatau lava, e ao ina . . .
mustard sinapi *(Bible)*
mutiny fouvale
mutter magagū, mulu, tomumu
mutton fasimāmoe
mutual feasia‘i, ōgatasi
muzzle muāgutu
my lo‘u, la‘u, lota, lata (sing.) o‘u, a‘u, ota, ata (pl.)
mystery mea e lē mafa‘amatalaina, fa‘animonimo, misitelio (R.C.)

Nn

nag ‘iēina, saga fāitio
nail fao
(finger __) mai‘u‘u, atigilima
(toe __) atigivae
(__ down) tu‘itu‘i
(__ varnish) vali atigilima
naked telefua, (pol.) telenoa, lē lāvalava
name igoa, (pol.) suafa
(to __) fa‘aigoa, (pol.) fa‘asuafa
nap moe, miti
nape tuāua, tuliulu
napkin
(baby's nappy) napekini
narrow vāapiapi, lauitiiti, vāiti
narrowly (nearly) toeitiiti ‘ā
nasal tau le isu
(__ catarrh) isu mamafa
nasty leaga
nation mālō, tagata ‘uma o le atunu‘u
national fa‘aleatunu‘u
native tagata o le atunu‘u, tagata moni
natural tau le uiga moni
naturally ‘o lea lava
nature uiga, uiga tūmau, natura, manu ma la‘au
naughty ulavale
nausea fa‘afāufau
nauseate fa‘a‘ino‘ino
navel pute
navigate uli se va‘a poo se va‘alele, fa‘afoe, fa‘auli
navy fua, fuāva‘a, fuāmanuao
neap (tide) taimasa
near lata, latalata, i tala ane o . . ., vālatalata
nearly tāi, tāli, tau, toeitiiti ‘ā mafai, semanū
(very __) fanū, manū, toetoe‘ā
neat (dress) ‘ofu lelei, ‘ofu fetaui lelei
(__ alcohol) ‘ava 1
necessary e tatau, e ao
neck ua
necklace ‘asoa, ‘ula, ‘ulālei
necktie fūsiua
need mea ua fia maua
needle au, nila
negative ‘o le leai atu
(film) kopi, *(print)* ata
neglect tu‘ulāfoa‘i, fa‘atamala
negligence fa‘atalalē, fa‘atitipa, so‘ona fai
negotiate fetu‘utu‘una‘i
negro tamauli
neighbour lē ua tuā ‘oi
neither . . . nor e lē o lea po‘o lea fo‘i
nephew (of a man) tama a le tuafafine, atali‘i o le uso
nephew
(of a woman) tama a le uso, atali‘i o le tuagane
nervous tete, po‘epo‘e, po‘epo‘evale, lili, fefe, popole
nest ōfaga, fa‘amoega
net (gen.) ‘upega
(fishing __) ‘upega fai faiva
(to net) seu etc.
nettle ogoogo
(tree __) salato
network felavasa‘iga
neutral lē ‘auai, lē fai se tāofi
never lē faia lava, ‘aua lava ne‘i . . .
nevertheless ‘ae peita‘i, ‘ae ui i lea
new fou
(__ year) tausaga fou
newspaper nusipepa
next (__ day) ‘o le aso na soso‘o ai, ā taeao
(__ to) tua ‘oi ma, i tafatafa o, pito ane
(__ thing) ‘o le isi mea
nib nipi

nibble	‘ai‘ai la‘itiiti
nice	lelei
niece (of a man)	afafine o le uso, tama a le tuafafine
(of a woman)	tama a le uso, afafine o le tuagane
night	pō
(last __)	anapō
(tomorrow __)	pō taeao
(__ dress)	‘ofu moe
(nightmare)	mālu‘ia
nil	noa, e matuā leai lava se mea
nine	iva
nineteen	sefulu ma le iva
ninety	ivasefulu
nip	‘ini
nipple	matāsusu
nit	lia
no	e leai
(__ more left)	e leai se toe . . .
(__ more thank you)	leai fa‘afetai
noble	tamāli‘i, fa‘atamāli‘i, agafa‘atamāli‘i
nod	punou, tautulemoe, fa‘agaugau
(as a sign)	geno, lue le ulu
node	pona
noise	pisa, pa‘ō, vāvāō, maloā
(lot of __)	pisapisaō
noiseless	ta‘aligoligoa
noisy	pisaō, leoleoā
nomad	maumausolo
nominate	filifili
none	e leai se isi
noon	tūtonu o le lā, aoauli
noose	matāsele
normal	e pei o se isi, e māsani ai
North	Mātū
nose	isu
nostril	pogaiisu
not	lē, le‘i
(do __)	‘aua ne‘i
(__ yet)	e le‘i
notch	tūlaga, fa‘auaamo
note (musical)	nota

(bank __)	tupe pepa
(letter)	tusi pu‘upu‘u
(note this!)	silasila!
(__ book)	api
nothing	leai se mea
notice	fa‘aaliga, (pol.) fa‘asilasilaga
(take no __)	fa‘asolofua, e lē amana‘ia
(to __)	iloa, va‘ai, mātau, (pol.) lāusilafia
notify	fa‘aso‘oso‘o, fa‘asilasila atu
notorious	logologoā le leaga
nought	‘o, selo, leai, (colq.) fuāmoa, noa
noun	nauna
nourishment	mea tāumafa
novel (book)	tala, talafatu
(unusual)	‘ese
November	Novema
Novice	sē ua le‘i a‘oa‘oina, (R.C.) Novisia
now	nei
nowadays	i nei onapō, nei aso
nuclear	niukilia
nuisance	soesā, fa‘alavelave, fa‘ataluā
numb	pē, gase
number	numera
(opposite __)	pāga
numerous	lasi, e to‘atele
nun	taupousā, (pol.) tama‘ita‘i sā
nurse	teine tausima‘i
(to __)	tausi le ma‘i
(__ a baby)	fa‘afailele le pepe
nursery	
(children)	fale e tausi ai tamaiti
(plants)	fa‘amiliga
nut	fuālā‘au
(coconut)	popo
(coconut tree)	niu
(walnut)	lama
(chestnut)	ifi
(peanut)	pīnati
(__ for bolt)	nati
nutmeg	akone
nylon	nailoni

Oo

oar	foe
oasis	‘oase
oath	augani, tautōga, tautō
(swear an __)	tautō
(oaths, swearing)	‘upupalauvale
obedient	usita‘i, fa‘alogogōfie
obey	usita‘i, ‘ana‘ana, fa‘alogo
object	
(i.e. a thing)	mea
(aim)	sini, tini
(__ to s.th.)	fa‘atu‘i‘ese, tete‘e, te‘ena, tavale
obligation	fatu‘āiga, matāfaioi
oblige (a person)	talia le mana‘o
obscene	māsoā
obscure	
(not clear)	e lē mafa‘amatalaina, fa‘animonimo
(to __)	pupuni le vā‘ai
observe (remark)	lafo, fa‘aali atu
(study)	‘apo, su‘esu‘e, vā‘ai
(__ the law)	ui i le tulāfono
obstacle	to‘atugā, fa‘alavelave, mea e tausūai ai
obstinate	lotoma‘a‘a, loto mālosi
obstruct	fa‘alavelavea, poloka
obtain	maua
(able to __)	mafaia
obvious	manino, iloga
occasion	aso
(auspicious __)	taeao mamalu
occasionally	e fai nisi taimi
occupation	gāluega, matātā, tofiga
occupy	nofoia
(to be occupied)	fa‘alavelavea, tuagia, pisi
occur	tupu
ocean	vasa
o’clock	
(three o’clock)	‘ua tā le tolu
October	Oketopa
octopus	fe‘e
oculist	foma‘i fai mata
odd (strange)	uiga ‘ese
(i.e. not even)	lē soaina
odour	sauga, elo, ‘u‘ū, (pol.) manogi
of	a, o
off (__ the mark)	‘ela
(go __, gun)	pā
(go __ i.e. leave)	alu ‘ese
offence (an __)	solitulāfono
(to give __)	fa‘atīgā le loto o se isi
offend	fa‘atīgā, fa‘atausūai, fa‘aita
offer	ofo, tauofoga
(__ a sacrifice)	osi le tāulaga
offering (Church)	tāulaga
office (position)	tūlaga
(room)	‘ōfisa
officer	‘ōfisa, ta‘ita‘i ‘au
official	tauletofi, fa‘aiemālō
(an __)	‘ōfisa
offspring	fānau
often	so‘o
ogre	sau‘ai
oil	u‘u, suāu‘u
(to __)	fa‘asuāu‘u
(__ the body)	fa‘alala
oily	u‘ua, tāpatapa
old (aged)	matua
(ancient)	leva, loa, tausagā
(__ man)	toea‘ina, (pol.) matuāali‘i
(__ woman)	lo‘omatua, (pol.) matuātama‘ita‘i, matuātausi
(__ fashioned, people)	faufaumau
(__ fashioned, things)	fa‘aanamua
olden (times)	i le vavau
older brother /sister	uso matua
olive-tree	‘ōlive
olympics	olemipika
omega	‘omeka *(Bible)*
omen	sāsā
(ill __)	talusā
omit	lē lavea, mea ‘ua galo
omnipotent	mana aoao
on	‘i, i
(__ top of)	i luga o
once	fa‘atasi

(at __!)	fai loa!
(__ upon a time)	i le tasi aso
one	tasi
(__ who)	lē
(which __?)	‘o lē fea?
(__ by __)	fa‘asolosolo
(__ after another)	auaua‘i
(__ ea.)	ta‘itasi, ta‘ito‘atasi
one legged	vaemutu
oneself (by __)	to‘atasi
onion	aniani
only	tau, fua, na‘o fa‘ato‘ā, tasi lava, na‘ona
ooze	tafetafelemū
open (to __)	tatala
(__ a meeting)	‘āmata
(__ mouth)	fa‘amaga
opener (tin __)	tala‘apa
openhanded	matamau, maugōfie
opening	avanoa
(__ of building)	fa‘aulufalega
operate (working)	galue
(medical)	tipi, (pol.) ta‘oto
operating theatre	potu tipitipi
operation	‘o le galueai‘ina o se mea
(surgical)	tīpiga (pol.) ta‘otoga, masoe, lagimasoe
(come into __)	‘ua mamalu le tulāfono (i.e. *a law)*
operator (radio)	taliualesi
opinion	tāofi, (pol.) tōfā, tōfāmamao, fa‘autaga
(in my __)	fā te a‘u
opponent	pāga, tagata tauvā
opportune	augamālie
opportunity	āvanoa, paganoa
oppose	tete‘e, tē‘ena, fa‘atu‘i‘ese, (pol.) tālaleu, fa‘atūta‘ia, fa‘asagatau
opposite	fa‘afeagai ma . . .
opposition (gen.)	faitasiga, tete‘ega
(in government)	itūagai
oppress	luti, fa‘apologa
optician	‘o le fai tioata mata
or	po‘o
oral	tau i le gutu
(__ examination)	su‘ega tautala
orange (fruit)	moli
(colour)	lanu moli

oration	lāuga, fetalaiga
orator	tulāfale, (pol.) failāuga, fale‘upolu, tōfā *(also Talking Chief,* A.S.)
(senior __)	tu‘ua
orchard	togālā‘au aina
orchestra	fā‘aili
ordain	fa‘au‘u (le faife‘au etc.)
order (command)	poloa‘iga, fa‘atonuga
(sequence)	fa‘asologa
(discipline)	pūlega lelei
(out of __)	lē ola, lē aogā, leaga
(keep in __)	tausi, saga teuteuina
(to __)	poloa‘i, fa‘atonu
(to __ goods)	ota, oka
(in __ that)	‘ina ‘ia
ordinary	ta‘atele, e māsani ai
(__ day)	aso aunoa
organ (body)	tōtōga (pol.) taufale
(musical)	‘ōkeni
organization (society)	fa‘alāpotopotoga
(manage)	pūlega
organize	pūlea, tāupule, fai fa‘atatauga
origin (birth)	tupuaga
(source)	māfua‘aga
(__ of trouble)	māfuaga, pogai . . .
original (first)	ulua‘i, lua‘i
(unusual)	fou, lē māsani ai
originate	āfua, māfua, pogai, tupuga
ornaments	tēuga
orphan	mātuaoti
ostentatious	fia tele, fa‘alialia
ostracized	fa‘asevasevaloaina, fa‘ate‘aina
other	le isi
otherwise (differently)	‘ese, i le tasi itū
ought	e tatau, e ao . . .
ounce	‘aunese
out	i fafo, ane, atu
(__ of tune)	pa‘ulua
(__ cold)	māliu
(__ of breath)	sela
(lights out)	tapē molī
outcome	i‘uga
outdoors	i fafo
outgoings	

(expenses)	tupe alu
outline	
(summarize)	‘oto‘oto, tala fa‘a‘oto‘oto
outrigger	ama
outright	
(to give __)	tō
outstanding	
(person)	iloga, lāusilafia, ta‘uta‘u
(__ account)	‘aitālafu le‘i togia
oval	lāpotopoto
(sports __)	malae ta‘alo
oven	umu, ‘ogāumu, fa‘apusa, tagāvai
(contents of __)	(pol.) suāvai
over	i luga
(__ there)	‘i‘ilā, i tuā, i‘ō, i‘ole, iinā
(to be __)	tuana‘i, ‘uma, te‘a
overall	aoao
overalls	
(clothing)	‘ofu tali‘ele‘ele, tagikerī, ofu soloātoa
overbearing	fa‘asāusili
overcast (sky)	fa‘amālumalu, taufānu‘u
overcoat	‘ofu tele, peleue tele
overcome	
(conquer)	fa‘ato‘ilalo, ā‘ea
(__ by sickness)	mālaia, māfatia
(__ by emotion)	o‘otia, tagi
overcooked	āfulu
overcrowded	tumutele, putu
overdue	siliga
overflow	masua, lolo, oso
overgrown	
(weeds)	gaosā, vaoa
overhasty	māteletele, vavevave
overhead (sun)	pūlou tonu le lā, tū tonu le lā
overlook	lē amana‘ia, fa‘agalogalo
overpower	
(by spirit etc.)	uluitino
overrule	tāutu‘u, soloia, fa‘alēaogāina
overrun	lōfia, faoa
(__ w. ants)	lōia
overseas	i fafo, i atunu‘u i fafo
overseas news	tala i nu‘u mamao
overseer	ovasia, pule
oversleep	moeloa, moe‘umi
overstep	
(the mark)	sopo le tua‘oi, la‘asia
overtake	maua, tu‘una
(__ by daylight)	aoina
(__ by darkness)	pogia
overtime	taimi fa‘asili, ovataimi
overturn (canoe)	sa‘e, sasa‘e
(car)	fuli, fa‘ataliaga
owe (loan)	‘aitālafu
owing to	‘ona ‘o, talu
owl	lulu
own (your __)	tautino, tōtino, la ‘oe, lo ‘oe etc.
(to __ s.th.)	e ana, e ona
owner	lē e ana. . . , lē e ona
ox	povi po‘a, povi faigāluega
oxygen	‘okesene
oyster	tio, tifa

Pp

pace (to __)	savali, la‘ala‘a
(speed)	saosaoa
(one __)	la‘asaga e tasi
Pacific	Pasefika
pacify	fa‘amālū, fa‘a filemū
pack(goods)	teu, fafao
(__ up)	tapena
package	afī, āfifī
packet	afī, paketi
(__ of *palolo*)	‘ofu palolo
pad (to __)	fa‘amalū
(writing __)	api faitusi, (A.S.) api sasae
paddle (a __)	foe
(to __)	alo, (pol.) pale
paddock	lotoā

page	itūlau
paid	totogi
pail	pakete
pain	tigā
painful	tigāina, matuitui
(___ to touch)	lē atapa'ia, tūgā
paint	vali
(___ brush)	pulumu
painted *(siapo)*	tutusi
painter	'o le vali ata, tusi ata
pair	taulua, pea
(___ of people)	soa, to'alua, ulugāli'i
(to be paired)	soagia
palace	maota
pale (face)	sesega
(colour)	vāivai
(turn ___)	sesega, segavale
palm (tree)(gen.)	niu, pāma
(c'nut ___)	niu
(sago ___)	niu masoā
(___ of hand)	alofilima
pan	ulo, pani
(frying ___)	falai
pancake	panikeke
pancreas	ateali'i, atepili
pandanus (gen.)	fala, laufala, etc.
pane	tioata, vāega fa'amalama
panic	lē to'a, fefevale
pant	mapusela, selasela, ga'ega'e, saputuvale
pants (trousers)	'ofuvae
papaya (pawpaw)	esi
paper	pepa, laupepa
paperweight	ma'atāopepa
parable	fa'ata'oto, tala fa'atusa
parade	solo, sāvaliga
paradise	parataiso, (R.C.) paratiso
paraffin	kalasini, parafini
paragraph	palakalafa
parallel	fa'afeagai, paralela
paralyse	gase, pē, supa
paramount	aoao, aupito sili
parcel	āfīfī
parch	gālala, naumati
pardon	fa'amāgalo
(ask ___)	fa'ato'ese
(beg)	tulou, fa'amolemole
pare	fisi
parent(s)	mātua (pol.) tua'ā
park	malae, pāka
(___ a car)	pāka, fa'atū
parliament	pālemene
parrot	koke
parry (a blow)	tali
parson	faife'au
part	vāega
(take ___)	'auai
(portion)	tu'uga, (pol.) inati
(___ of body)	itūtino
(to ___)	fa'amāvae
(be parted)	ţe'a, tete'a
partial (incomplete)	e le'i 'ātoa
(be ___)	fa'a'au'au, fa'apito, fiafia i ai
particular	fa'apito
particularly	'aemaise lava
parting (words)	'upu fa'amāvae, māvaega
partner	soa, pāga, pā'aga
partnership	pā'aga fai pisinisi
party (political)	vāega fa'apolotiki, pati
(entertainment ___)	fiafiaga, 'aufai koniseti
(___ of travellers)	'au malaga
pass (mountain ___)	mafa
(to ___)	te'a, tuana'i, fano
(___ along)	ui ane
(___ behind)	ui i tua
(___ a law)	pasi le tulālafono, fa'atulāfono
(___ on to s.o.)	tu'u fa'asolo
(___ water)	(pol.) tūla'i
(___ examination)	pasi, manuia
pass-mark	tapula'a
passable	feoloolo
passage (reef)	ava
(book)	vāega
(opening)	ala
(journey)	malaga
passbook (bank)	tusi tupe
passenger	pāsese
passover	pāseka, (R.C.) pasekate
passport	tusi folau
past	tuana'i
(in the ___)	i aso ua mavae, aso 'ua fano
(i.e. long ago)	anamuā
(five ___ six)	e lima minute ua te'a ai le ono

paste mea fa‘apipi‘i, fa‘apipi‘i
(tooth __) mea fulunifo
pastime mausa, pasitaimi
pastor faife‘au, (pol.) feagaiga
pasty pai
pat pōpō
patch (to __) fono
(garden __) togāfa‘i etc.
(taro __) ma‘umaga
path ala, ‘auala
patience ‘onosa‘i, fa‘apalepale
patient tagata ma‘i, (pol.) gāsegase
patriotic lotonu‘u
patron saint (R.C.) sulufa‘iga
pattern (design) manu, mamanu
pause mānava, mālōloga
pavement paepae, alapae
paw (animal) alofilima, alofivae
pawpaw esi
pay totogi
(__ attention) fa‘alogo
(__ a visit) afe, asiasi
(__ respect) fa‘aaloalo
(__ back money) fa‘aola le tupe
pea pī
peace filēmū, (pol.) mālū
peaceful to‘afilēmū, to‘afīmālie
(__ sleep) moe fīmālie
peak tumutumu, fa‘auluuluga
peanut pīnati
pear pea
pearl penina
peasant tagatāvao
pebble(s) ma‘ama‘a, ‘ili‘ili
peck togitogi
peculiar ‘ese
pedal tulagāvae o le uila
(to __) vili
pedestrian tagata savali
peel fofo‘e, fisi, valu
peeler ‘asi, fofo‘e
peelings (vegetable) vālusaga
peep tilotilo, onoono
peer (to __) tilotilo, fetīlofa‘i
(a __) tamāli‘i maualuga (e.g. *a duke)*
peg pine, tautaulaga
pelvis ivino‘o
pen (enclosure) pātasi, sai etc.
(writing __) peni
penalty fa‘asalaga
pencil penitala
pending ‘ua lupe
penetrate ati
penicillin penisilini
penis ule, gā‘au, poti, (pol.) aualuma
penitent salamō
penny pene
pension penisiona
Pentecost Aso Penetekoso, (R.C.) Penekosite
people tagata, itū‘āiga o tagata
(young __) talavou, tupulaga fou
pepper pepa
perceive logo, ilo, lagona
percent pasene
perch (to __) fa‘ati‘eti‘e
perfect ‘ato‘atoa ona lelei
perform fa‘asaga e fai se mea, fai
performance (show) fa‘aaliga
perfume manogi, nāmu, sausau
perhaps ‘ātonu, mata fo‘i
period vāitūlā, vāitaimi
(woman’s __) ma‘imāsina
(i.e. full stop) periota, piriota
(school __) periota, piriota
perish fano, pala
perishable ‘anagōfie
permanent tūmau, mautū
permit tusi fa‘ataga, taga, fa‘aavanoa, pēmita
perplexing lē ‘āsino, femēmēa‘i
persecute fa‘asāuā
persevere filigā, lotulotu, sogasogā
persist ‘asosi, saga
person tagata
(__ in charge) pule, posi
personal patino, fa‘apito
perspire āfu
persuade tauānau, ‘u‘una‘i
pest, pester fa‘asoesā, vina
pestle ‘o le tu‘i
pet (animal) fāgafao
(child) pele, fa‘apele

petition tagi, tālosaga
petrify (afraid) meia
petrol pensini, (A.S.) kesi
pharisee faresaio *(Bible)*
phlegm fatutale
'phone telefoni
'phone-box potu telefoni
phosphoresence 'ālafa, taetuli
photograph ata
(to __) pu'e ata
physical tau i le tino
(__ training) fa'amālosi tino, koleni
physique fuaitino
piano pīano
pick (tool) piki
(__ up) 'ava'e, pikiapu *(car)*
(__ up rubbish) tae le otaota
(__ by hand) auau
(i.e. choose) tofitofi, filifili
(__ flowers, fruit) tau
(__ a quarrel) fa'amisa
pickle (fish) ota
picnic tāfaoga, pikiniki
pickup (car) pikiapu
picture ata, fa'atusa
(__ theatre) fale tīfaga
pie pai
piece fāsimea
(__ of soap) fāsimoli
(take to pieces) tala
(__ work) gāluega togi pau
(in one __) tūlau, solo 'ātoa
pier uafu
pierce su'i, ati
pig pua'a, (pol.) manufata, ta'iola
pigeon lupe
piglet tama'i pua'a
pigsty sai, (pol.) lo'ilo'i
pilchard pilikati
pile fa'aputuga, faula'iga, faupu'ega
(__ up) fa'aputu, fa'afaula'i, fa'afaupu'e
pill fuālā'au
pillar pou
pillow 'aluga, lago
(__ case) taga 'aluga *(also __ slip)*
pilot pailate
(__ ship) pailate
pimple fuafua
pin pine
pincers fa'aū
pinch uga, 'ini
pine (for s.o.) fa'amama'i, naunauta'i
pineapple fala 'aina
pink pīniki
pint paina
pip fatu
pipe paipa
pit lua, pū
pitch (game) pāga
(cricket __) malae simā
(to __) togi, lafo
(i.e. bitumen) tā, vali tā
pith uso o le lā'au
pitted 'omo'omo
pity fa'anoanoaga, alofa mutimutivale
(what a __!) talofa e! se pagā!
placate fa'amalie, fa'amālū
place (a __) mea, tūlaga, nofoaga
(change __) sui nofoaga
(in my __) fai ma o'u sui
(to __) tu'u, fa'anofo, fa'atū
placenta falefale, fanua
placid agamalū, malū
plague (sickness) mala, fa'ama'i tele
(worry s.o.) vina, vinavina
plain (a __) laufanua, laugatasi
(clear) mālamalama, manino
(ordinary) feoloolo
(__ paper) pepa mamā, pepa lē vasea
plait (to __) fili
(a __) filitasi
plan tonu, fuafuaga, fa'atatauga
(devise) agoago, fuafua, fa'atatau
plane (tool) tele, olo
(aeroplane) va'alele
plank papa, laupapa, laufono
plant(s) lā'au
(to __) totō, tō fa'i etc., fa'ato'a
plantation fa'ato'aga, togālā'au, (pol.) fa'a'ele'elega, velevelega
planter faifa'ato'aga
plaster vali, fa'asimā, palasitā
plate ipu māfolafola, (A.S.) ipu sālafa

plateau mauga māfolafola, laugatasi
platform tūlaga
(house __) paepae
platter (food) laulau, pā, ma'ilo, (pol.) la'o'ai
play (game) ta'alo
(theatre) tala
(cards) pelē
(piano) tā le piano
(dice) taisi
playground malae o le a'oga, malae ta'alo
plea ōlega
plead 'āi'oi, fa'aolo
pleasant mālie, tauagafau, tausala
please fa'amolemole, se'i
(__ s.o.) fa'afiafia i ai
(be pleased) fiafia
(__ oneself) faitalia
pleat (dress) numi o le 'ofu
pledge ta'utinoga
(to __) osi se feagaiga
plenty 'o le mau, tele, 'ua'ona
plexus (solar __) mauli, moa
pliable vavai
pliers fa'aū
plot (to plot) fāufauga leaga, tāupulepulega
(__ of land) lafo, ogā'ele'ele, fasi fanua
plough suōtōsina
(to __) sua fa'amalū
pluck
(feathers, hair) futi
(leaves) 'oto
plug (to __) fono, mono, puluti
(a __) momono
plum mati
plumber fai paipa, palama
plump veveni, puta, peti
plunder vete
plus fa'aopoopo, 'i le ma lea
ply (timber)
(three __) sautuatolu etc.
pneumonia fiva līmonia, niumōnia
pocket taga
poem tauloto, solo
poet fatusolo, fatupese
point pito
(in games) 'ai
(headland) tolotolo
(strong __) itūmālosi
(__ of compass) itūlagi
(__ of needle) mata
(__ out) fa'asino
(__ gun) ta'i
(__ w. finger) tusi
poison vai 'o'ona, fa'a'ona
poisonous 'ona, ogoogo, 'o'ona
poker (cards) poka
pole (of the earth) pole
(timber) lā'au 'umi, laupapa
police leoleo, 'ōfisa o leoleo
policeman leoleo
policy polisia
poliomyelitis ma'i pipili
polish fa'a'i'ila
polite fa'aaloalo
politics polotiki, fa'alemālō
(village __) faiganu'u
poll pālota
polygamy autaunonofo
Polynesia Polenisia
pond vailepa, vaitūloto
ponder feliuliua'i i le māfaufau
pony pone (tama'i solofanua)
pool vailepa, futiafu, vaitā'ele
(share) tu'ufa'atasi
(game) piliati
poor (people) mativa
(land) lāfuā, leaga, naumati
Pope Tupu Sā
popular mana'omia, tausa'afia
population faitau aofa'i o tagata
porch fa'apaologa
pork fasipua'a
porridge polesi
port taulaga
(__ side) itū tauagavale o va'a, va'alele
porter tagata feavea'i 'ato malaga
portion tufa, vāega, tu'uga, (pol.) inati
(__ out) tufatufa, lufilufi, fa'asoa
position tūlaga, tofi
possess (mea) 'ua ia te a'u, ia te ia etc.

possessions 'oa, 'oloa, mea
post (a __) pou
(__ office) fale meli
(__ a letter) lafo
(finishing __) tini
(i.e. appointment) tofi, tūlaga
postage stamp fa'ailoga tusi
postcard posikati
poster fa'aaliga matamata tetele
posterior (man) nofoaga
postmaster pule o le fale meli
postpone tolo, tolopō, tu'u i tua
posture 'o le tū o le tagata
pot 'ulo, (pol.) 'ogāumu
(earthenware __) fagu'ele
(lobster __) fagāula
(metal __) pani
potato pateta
(sweet __) 'umala
pot-hole 'omo (i le ala)
potsherd tā'ega
poultry moa 'ese'ese
(__ farm) fa'ato'aga fai lafu moa
pounce popō, pō'ia
pound (money) pauni
(weight) pauna
(to __) tu'i pala
pour (out) sasa'a, ligi, liligi
(into) utu
poverty mativa
powder efuefu, pauta, one
power (ability) mālosi
(authority) pule
(supernatural __) mana
(electric __) paoa, uila, eletise
power point palaka paoa
powerful mamana
practice
(i.e. custom) māsani, tū
practise fa'ata'ita'i
practitioner
(dental __) foma'i nifo
(medical __) foma'i
praise vi'i, vivi'i, fa'amanū, fa'ane'ene'e, vi'iga, ne'etaga
pram ta'avale pepe
prank togafiti fa'atausua
prawn ula, ulāvai
pray tatalo, tālosia
prayer tatalo, tālosaga

preach talā'i, lāuga
preacher (lay __) failāuga (Meth.)
precede muamua
precentor 'o le usu pese
precious tāua, pele
precipice mato, tofē
precise sa'o
prefect tama a'oga fesoasoani i faia'oga, leoleo, ta'ita'i
prefer fa'a'au'au, mea sili i le fa'atatau
pregnant tō, ma'itō, (pol.) ma'itaga
(__ before marriage) tōifale
premature lē au, vave
(__ birth) fānau lē au
premonition fa'a'ite'ite, fa'ata'imua
prepare sāuni, nofosāuni
(__ food) fai le mea'ai, (pol.) gasese
(__ kava) tatau le 'ava
Presbyterian (Church) Peripereane (Ekalesia)
present (__ time) taimi nei, fa'aasonei
(be __) olo'o i ai, 'auai, 'a'u, 'oe
(all __) 'ua 'ātoa
(a gift) meaalofa, (pol.) mā'au
(to __) fōa'i, (pol.) tau'a'ao
presentation (S. custom) 'o le sua, ta'alolo etc.
presently nānei
preserve tausi, fa'asao
president peresitene
press (newspapers) 'au fai nusipepa
(__ out) 'o'omi
(__ clothes) 'āuli
(__ people) fetuleni
(__ on) fa'amālosi
(i.e. urge) fa'atauānau
pressure 'ōmiga, mālosi
prestige mamalu
presume e lē taumate, masalo
presumptuous fa'afiapoto
pretend fa'atagā
pretend to be fa'a fia-(poto, mamalu etc.)
pretentious isusisi, fa'afiamaualuga

pretty	mānaia
prevail	mālō
prevalent	ta'atele
prevent	tāofi, fa'alavelave, puipui, vavao
prevention	puipuiga
previous	talu ai, muamua
price	'o le tau
priceless	e lē mafa'ataulia
prick	tui
prickle	tala
pride	fa'amaualuga, loto mitamita, mimita, mitamita
Priest	ositaulaga, (R.C.) pātele
(priest-hood)	(L.D.S.) perisitua
primary school	ā'oga maulalo
(pre-school)	a'oga fa'ata'ita'i
Prime Minister	Palemia
primer (explosive)	ma'a afi
prince	tama'āiga, perenise
princess	alo tama'ita'i, purinisese
principal	
(i.e. first)	sili, silisili
(school)	puleā'oga
principle(s)	fa'avae, ta'iala
print	lolomi
printer	tagata lomitusi
printing-press	fale lomitusi
prise (up)	uati, laga
prison	fale puipui
prisoner	pāgotā, (pl.) pāgotatā
(__ of war)	tagata o taua
private	patino, tōtino
privilege	avanoa mana'omia
(hereditary __)	igāga tō, tu'utu'uga
prize	togi, fa'ailoga
prize-giving	laugātogi
probably	'ai lava, po'o penā
problem	matā'upu, fa'alavelave, fa'afitāuli
procedure	feuia'iga
proceed	fa'aauau, fa'asolosolo, fai pea
(__ in a body)	ta'alolo
procession	solo
proclaim	'alaga, mānu, fōlafola, tāla'i
produce (of trees)	fua
(goods)	gaosi, fai
production	gaosiga
profession (work)	gāluega, faiva, tofiga
(__ of faith)	molimau i le fa'atuatua
profit	tupe mamā, fa'asiliga
profound	loloto
profuse	lasi, lava ma totoe
programme	polokalame
progress	au'iluma, sololelei, alualu 'i luma
prohibit	fa'asā, vavao
project (plan)	fuafuaga
(jut out)	'oso'oso
projector	mea vili ata
proliferate	fanafanau
prolong	fa'a'umi'umi, fa'alevaleva
prominent	lāusilafia
promiscuous	pa'umutu
promise	fōlafola
promote	si'i le tūlaga
prompt	vave mataala
(to __)	faulalo, tu'ulalo
prone	faō, fa'afaō, laveagōfie, a'afiagōfie
prong	tala
pronounce	fa'aleo
proof	fa'amaoniga
prop	te'e, palepale
propel	fa'aalu
propellor (plane)	pe'ape'a
(ship)	tāpili
proper	tatau, ono
properly	sa'o, tonu, lelei, fa'amāo'io'i
property	mea, 'oloa, fanua ma fale
prophecy	vālo'aga, vavalo
prophet	perofeta, ali'i 'i'ite
proportion	'o le fua e tatau ai
proposal	lafo fa'atū, manatu fa'atū, mau
propose	fa'atū se manatu
(intend)	fa'amoemoe
prosper	olaola
prostitute	fafine talitāne,teine pa'umutu
prostrate	fa'apa'ū faō
protect	puipui, fa'amamalu, fa'apaolo
protector	leoleo, (R.C. *Patron Saint)* sulufa'iga, fa'amālumaluga

protest	fa'aali le lē malie, tagi
protrude	patupatu, popona, fa'atalatala
proud	mimita, nene'e, fa'amaualuga, lotomitamita
(_ of s.o.)	mitamita faia'e
prove	fa'amaonia
proverb	alagā'upu, muāgagana, *(Bible, O.T.)* fa'ata'oto
provide	sāuniuni
provisions	mea'ai, oso
provoke	fa'atupu, fa'alili, fa'a'ono'ono, tofotofo
prudence	fa'autauta
prune (to _)	fa'agata lā'au, teu
(fruit)	mati mago
psalm	salamo
psychiatrist	fōma'i o māfaufau
pubic area	punialo
public	fa'alemālō, mo tagata faitele
public house	fale tālimālō, fale pia
public service	'au'auna a le mālō
public works	'ōfisa o gāluega
publican	pule o faletālimālō, *(Bible)* telona
publish	lolomi
pudding	puligi
puddle	vaivai
puff (blow)	feula
(_ up)	fefete
pull (rope)	toso, tolo, fālō
(down)	tala
(up)	se'i, lia'i, fafa'i
(_ up car)	fa'atū le ta'avale
(_ a tooth)	fa'i
(_ off, weeds, feathers)	futi
(i.e. stretch)	meme'i
pulley	polokaka
pulsate	saputu, tātā
pulse	tātā o le fatu
pulverize	tu'i nini'i
pummel (body)	tu'itu'i
pump	pamu
pumpkin	maukeni
punch (fist)	moto, pani, tu'i
punctual	tausi le taimi, a'e tonu
puncture (tyre)	pā le pa'u, tui
pungent (smell)	'a'ava, elo
punish	fa'asala
punishment (capital)	fa'asalaga oti
punt (to _)	to'o le va'a, kiki le polo
pupil (school)	tamaitiiti ā'oga
(eye)	tama'i mata
puppy	tama'i maile
purchase	fa'atau mai
pure (clean)	mamā, lē filogia
(genuine)	a'ia'i
purple	violē, pā'auli
purpose	fa'amoemoe
(to no_)	fai fua, noa
purse	'ato tupe
pursue	tulituliloa, alualu
pus	'alou
push	tulei, u'una'i
(_ back)	tete'e
put (down, place)	tu'u, fa'anofo, fa'ata'atia
(_ aside)	tu'u 'ese
(_ away, store)	teu
(_ off, delay)	tolopō
(_ on, wear)	fai lāvalava
(_ into)	utu
(_ up with)	fa'apale
(_ right)	fa'asa'o, fa'atonu
(_ to sleep)	fa'amoe
(_ together)	tu'u fa'atasi
(_ in prison)	'ave i le falepuipui
(_ out fire)	tinei le afi
putty	pate
puzzle (a _)	palo, mea lavelave
(_ s.th. out)	fa'avasega, su'e le tonu
pyjamas	'ofu moe
pylon	pou simā telē, pou u'amea telē

Qq

quack	leo o le pato
quadrilateral	fa'atāfafā
quadriplegic	tagata 'ua pepē 'a'ao uma e fā
quadruped	manu vaefā
quail (to __)	tete, tetemū
qualify	pasi, avea ma . . .
quality	uiga, uiga lelei
quantity	'o le tele, anoano
quarrel	misa, finauga, fefinaua'i, fe'upua'i
quarter	kuata, tasi vaefā, matāmatagi
quarterly	fa'alekuata
quarters	mea e api ai (pol.)
quartet	to'afā 'ua pepese, tā lā'au, etc.
quaver	tete, lūlūina
quay	uafu
queen	tupu tama'ita'i
(wife of king)	masiofo
(cards)	tama'ita'i
queer	'ese
(of people)	sipa
quench	tinei afi, fa'ainu
query	faifesili
question	fesili, fa'asufi, vā'ili'ili
(__ mark)	fa'ailoga o le fesili (?)
questionnaire	lisi o fesili
queue	laina o tagata, ta'avale etc.
quick	vave, mataala
(__ to answer)	mautali
quicken (of foetus)	tafiti le pepe
quickly	vave, saosaoa, fa'atopetope
quick-witted	mālamalama vave
quit	lafoa'i, fa'amāvae
quiet	filemū, to'afilēmū, fimālie, to'afimālie, māninoa
quietly	fimālie, lēmū
quietness	'o le māninoa
quite	matuā, lava
(__ good)	lelei fo'i
quiver(to __)	fa'atetetete
(a __)	'au
quiz	fesilisili, su'e le mālamalama faitele, su'ega
quota	vāega fa'atatauina
quotation	'upusi'i
(__ marks)	puipui
quote	si'i

Rr

rabbi	rapi
rabbit	lāpiti
race (contest)	tū'uga
(people)	itū'āiga
(human __)	itū'āiga o le tagata
(horse __)	tu'ugā solofanua
race-relations	vā fa'aatunu'u, va feiloa'i o tagata lanu 'ese'ese
rack (shelf)	talitali, fata
(__ one's brains)	fa'atigā le māfaufau
racket, racquet	pate
radar	reitā
radiation	'ave niukilia
radiator	masini e fa'amāfanafana ai le 'ea
radio	uālesi, lā'au fa'alogologo, letiō
radio station	fale uālesi

radish lakisi
raft va'a moso'oi
rafter 'aso
rag fāsi'ie'ie
(in rags) māsaesae
rage fa'ali'i, 'a'asa
(storm rages) pesi le afā
raid osofa'iga
rail(s) alau'amea *(also railway line)*, ala nofoa afi
railing (fence) puipui
rain timu, timuga (pol.) ua
(__ clouds) taufānu'u
rainbow nuanua
raincoat 'ofu fa'aua, 'ofu talitimu
raindrop matāua
rainfall timutō
raise (lift) si'i, sisi, laga
(__ eyes) ea a'e mata
(__ a question) fa'atū le fesili
(__ a family) tausi le 'āiga
(__ a stick) si'itā
(__ a corner) su'e, afe
raisin viṅe mago
raising si'itaga
(flag __) sisigāfu'a
rake salu u'amea
rally fa'alāpotopotoga, tau aofiaga
ram (sheep) mamoe po'a
(to __) tutu'i
ran sa tamo'e
random so'ona
rang sa tā (logo etc.)
range (mountain) atumauga
(of a gun) masau, mamao
(kitchen __) 'ogāumu, umu kuka
(wide __ of goods) tele itū' āigāmea
rank tūlaga
ransack sagole
rap tuma
rape toso le teine, (pol.) fa'amālosi
rapid vave tele, saosaoa
rapidly tele vave
rare seāseā maua, ta'aitiiti, mauagatā
rascal tagata ulavale
rash (be __) so'ona oso, so'onafai, mateletele
(on body) mea sasao
rasp lapa
rat 'isumu
rat-a-tat-tat patiapatā
rate (speed) saosaoa, vave
(__ of exchange) fa'atusatusaga o tupe
(charge) totogi, tau
(first __) sili lava, tūlaga muamua
rates lafoga tau fale
rather sala
(__ than) i lo le . . .
(would __) e sili pe'ā
ration vaevae fa'atatau
rattle pa'ō'ō, fa'atagitagi, lūlū
ravage fa'aleaga, fa'atāma'ia
rave tala fa'amama'i, fāsaga
ravine vanu, tofē
raw mata
ray
(of sunshine etc.) 'ave, tilo
raze (to ground) olopala, matuā tala atoa
razor tafi
(__ blade) matātafi
reach (arrive) o'o, taunu'u, tau, tūlau'ele'ele
(__ as far as) au
(__ out for) 'a'apa, fālō atu, tu'utu'u
(__ the goal) tini
reaction (his) lana tali mai
read faitau
(__ out) fa'alau
readily 'ua vave ona . . .
readiness
(hold in __) fa'atagataga
ready (be __) sāuni, māe'a
(willing) malie
(__ tongue) mau 'upu
(get s.th. __) tapena, sāuni
(__ answer) mautali
(food is __) vela
ready-made
(dress etc). māe'a ona su'i
real mo'i, moni, māo'i
realize fa'amāonia, iloatino, taulau
really matuā, lava, moni lava

ream laupepa e 500
reap selesele
rear (back) muli, i tua
(to __) tausi tamaiti, tama'i manu etc.
reason (for s.th.) ala, māfua
(commonsense) māfaufau
(to __) finau, fefulifulia'i
reasonable fetaui tonu ai, tatau
rebel tagata fa'asagatau, fouvale
rebound masagi, fiti
rebuke a'oa'i, tōtatau, tautala fa'asa'o
recall toe fafaguina, toe manatua
recede fāiifo, maui
receipt līsiti
receive maua
(__ a person) talia, talimālō
recent e le'i leva, lata mai nei
reception taliga, feiloa'iga, (pol.) fesilafa'iga, talimālō, fa'aafe
recess (cavity) āoa
(stop work) mālōlōga
recipe fa'amatalaga mea 'ai, fua o le kuka
recite fa'amalau, faifa'atauloto
reckless fai ma le lē māfaufau
reclaimed (land) fanua tanu
recline ta'oto'oto, (pol.) fālana'i
recognize iloa, toe iloa
recollect māfaufau, mānatunatu, mānatua
recommend fautua
reconsider toe filifili, fetāla'i
reconstruct toe fai
record (account) mea ua fa'amauina, tala fa'amauina
(sports __) tūlaga sili
(make a __) pu'e le leo, pese etc.
recorder (tape) teipi, lā'au pu'e leo
recount (a genealogy) talagafa
recover toe maua
(__ from illness) toe mālōlōina
recreation mausa, pasitaimi, fa'afou tino ma māfaufau, ta'aloga

red mūmū
(deep __) 'ulà
(purplish __) mūmū pā'auli
red-handed (caught) mau tāma'ia
redeemer togiola
reduce fa'aitiiti, fa'ala'itiiti, fa'amāmā
(__ price) fa'apa'ū le tau
reed ū
reef a'au
(beyond __) ituā'au
reel (wind) ta'avili
(__ of thread) tā'aigā filo
(to __) tautevateva
refer fa'asino, fa'atau atu
referee laufalī, fa'amasino
reference (letter) tusi fa'amaoni
(statement) fa'amatalaga
refine fa'amamā
reflect (to __) mānatunatu
reflection ata, ataata, fepulafi mai
reflector (car) fa'ailoga mūmū
reform toe fuata'i
refrain (from) 'alo'alo, gē, lē faia
(chorus) tali
refresh toe fa'afou
refreshing mālū
refreshment(s) meainu, vāi'aiga
refrigerator pusa'aisa
refuge lafitaga, sulufa'iga
refund fa'aola tupe
refuse (rubbish) otaota, lāpisi
(deny) te'ena, musu, fa'atu'i'ese
regain toe maua
(__ consciousness) toe mālamalama
regard (consider) manatu
(kind regards) alofa'aga
(no __) lē amana'ia
regarding e tusa ma, e uiga 'i
regiment vaegā'au
region itūlalolagi, (L.D.S.) lisone
register (a __) tusi fa'amau
(__ a letter) tusi puipuia
registrar resitara
registration (of marriage) tūsiga
(of car) laiseni

regress solo i tua
regret fa'anoanoa, sa'afi
regular tutusa, e māsani ai, pea
regulate pūlea
regulation(s) tulāfono, tu'utu'uga, aiaiga
rehearsal fa'aa'oa'oga
reign nofoa'iga
rein fa'agutu
reinforce fa'amālosia
reject mele, te'ena, tete'e, fa'atu'i'ese, fa'alēaogā
rejoice 'oli'oli, 'oa'oa, sanisani
relapse gau le ma'i
relate (tell) talā
(be related) 'āiga
relation (a__) 'āiga, tei
(connexion) feso'ota'iga
(__ ship) 'o le vā, fa'afeagaiga
relative (__ to) pe'ā fa'atatau
relatives paolo ma gafa
relax tu'ufaitalia, nofosa'oloto
(__ the body) fa'avāivai
(__ grip) fa'amatagataga
release tatala, matala, fa'asa'oloto, tu'usa'oloto, fa'asola
reliable fa'atuatuaina
relief (for needy) fesoasoani
(of mind) to'alēmū
relieve
(__ the guard) sui le leoleo
(__ the pain) fa'ate'a le tigā
(be relieved) mānava
religion lotu
relish (to __) le'ile'i
reluctant fa'atāutāu, pala'ai, temutemu, tōa'i, fa'agēgē
rely fa'alagolago, fa'atuatua
remain (stay) nofo, tu'upea, nofomau
(left over) toe, totoe
(__ at home) fa'amuli, (pol.) tomau
remainder toega, mea totoe
remains
(of a meal) toe'aiga, 'atiga
(corpse) tino oti
remark (a __) 'upu, fuai'upu, lafo
(to __) mata'i, lafo, fa'apea
remarkable iloga, ma'eu
remedy 'o le fofō, togafiti, vailā'au
remember mānatua
remind fa'amanatu
remit
(debt, punishment) ola
remnant toega
(__ of cloth) fāsi 'ie
(__ of food) momoi mea'ai, toe'aiga
remote mamao tele
remove 'ave 'ese, tafi, si'i, tō'ese
(__ prohibition) fa'agafua, taga
render 'avatu
renew fa'afou, toe fai
rent totogi se fale, lisi
repair fa'afou, fono, fai, līpea
repay taui, totogi le 'aitalāfu
repeal (law) tatala le tulāfono
repeat toe fai
repeated faiso'o, fa'alausoso'o
repent salamō
replace sui, toe sui
replete mā'ona, (pol.) laulelei
reply tali, (pol.) palepale
report tala, lipoti, fa'amatalaga, ta'u
reporter tusitala
repose ta'oto'oto, (pol.) fālana'i
represent sui (o se isi)
repress 'o'ono
reprimand fa'atonu mālosi
reproach fa'aali le lē malie tele
reprove a'oa'i
reptile manu e i ai gata, laumei etc.
republic mālō faiperesitene
repulse tete'e
reputation
(good __) igoa lelei, āmiolelei, ta'uleleia
(bad __) igoa leaga, āmioleaga, ta'uleagaina
request ole, tagi, mana'o, talosaga
(earnestly __) fa'atauānau
require mana'omia

requisition tusi tala mea
rescue lavea'i
research su'esu'e
resemble so'o i . . . , pei, pē'ī, foliga tutusa
resent tauvale, tete'e, itagia
reservation (a __) nofoa tāofi, tautalagia
reserve (__ s.th.) fa'aleoleo, fa'atagataga, fa'asaosao, fa'aagaaga, fa'apolopolo
reserved (shy) matamuli
reservoir fa'atānoa
reside nofo, (pol.) afio
resign fa'amāvae
resignation tusi fa'amāvae
resist tetee, tāofi
resolute taumau, tausisi pea
resolution
(of a meeting) i'ugāfono
resolve loto mau, tonu (ia te ia)
resort togafiti
(last __) toe taumafaiga
resouce(s) alagā'oa
respect āva, miga, migao, fa'aaloalo
(in some respects) i nisi itū
(w. __
to your letter) e tusa ma lau tusi
(w. __) vāeane, vāe atu, tulouna
respectable ta'uleleia
respected fa'aaloalogia
responsibility matāfaioi
responsible
(be __) taunapa
(he was __) na pa'ū ia te ia
rest mālōloga, mapu
(let it __) ta'atia ia le mea
(the __ of them) o isi o 'i latou
restaurant fale'aiga
resting-place mapusaga
restless tafiti, fitia, māpuitigā
(__ sleep) moefiti
restore fa'afou, fa'afo'i, toemaua
restrain tāofiofi, vavao
restrict fa'apau, fa'atuā'oia
result i'uga, taunu'uga, i'u
(__ from) māfua mai
resume fuata'i, toe 'āmata

resurrection 'o le toe tū mai
retain maù
retaliate taui, fetauia'i
retire tu'umuli, fa'amālōlō, litaea
retract (words) fa'afo'i 'upu
retreat solomuli, tu'umuli
(Ministers' __) Mafutaga a Faife'au
return fo'i, a'e, taliu mai
(election returns) i'ugāpālota
(__ s.th.) fa'afo'i
reveal fa'aali, tino mai
revelation fa'aaliga
revenge taui, taui ma sui
revenue tupe maua
reverence mīgao
reverse liliu
(__ a car) sōlomuli
review toe iloilo, toe fai
revise fa'atonutonu
revive toe fa'aola, toe mālamalama
(__ a law) toe fa'amamalu le tulāfono
revolt fouvale
revolution fouvalega, mau
(turn) ta'amilosaga
revolver fana gutuono
revulsion 'ino'ino
reward 'o le taui
rheumatism gugu
rhinocerous
beetle manu 'ainiu
rhyme fetaui leo o 'upu, solo fetaui
rib ivi 'aso'aso
ribbon lipini
rice alaisa
rich maumea, mau'oa, mau'oloa, tamāo'āiga
(__ food) lolo
(__ land) lafulēmū
riddle (a __) tupua, palo
(__ w. holes) pūpū
ride ti'eti'e, 'ave le solofanua
ridge tuasivi, taualuga
ridicule tauemu
ridiculous 'amusia, mauaga
rifle fana, (pol.) lā'au mālosi
rift tofē

right sa‘o, tonu, tatau
(put __) fa‘asa‘o, fa‘atonu
(alright) ‘ua lelei
(__ side) itū taumatau
(__ angle) tulimanu e 90°, ‘āgeli e 90°
(my __) ‘ua ia te a‘u le pule
right-handed lima taumatau
righteous āmiotonu
rim ‘augutu
rind pa‘u (o fuālā‘au)
ring mama, li‘o
(in a __) fa‘ata‘amilo, fa‘ata‘ali‘oli‘o
(__ a bell) tā, fa‘atatagi
(__ telephone) vili atu
(__ of a telephone) tagi
(__ of a bell) tatagi
(__ the bell) tā le logo
ring-bark tūtogi le lā‘au
ringworm lafa
rinse (cup etc.) fufulu
(mouth) pūpū
(in fesh water) fa‘alanu
riot fa‘anunununu
rip sasae
rip saw ‘ilitofi
ripe pula
(of bananas) otā, (A.S.) pala
ripple gagalu
rise (of moon) oso a‘e
(in road) a‘ega
(of people) nofo i luga, ala
(sun) oso a‘e
(tide) sua, fāna‘e
(dough) fefete
(waves) mapu‘e le galu
(of prices) si‘i le tau
(__ to surface) mānu
(__ before daylight) usupō
rising (generation) tupulaga talavou
risk mea lē mautinoa
rite(s) sauniga fa‘alelotu
rival ‘autauva
river vaitafe
(__ bed) ‘alitivai
road ala, ‘auala
(__ way) ‘auala
roam tafao
roar (laughter) taliē
(lions etc.) tagi
(people) fe‘ei
(guns) pāpā
roast tao i le ga‘o, (pol.) fufui
rob fao, gaoi
robber faomea
robe ‘ofu
robin (bird) tagitagi
rock papa, papatū
(to __) lue, luelue
rocky gāoā, papā
rod sasa
(dart) ti‘a
(fishing __) ‘ofe fāgota, (pol.) launiu
roll (to __) ta‘avale
(__ of mats) tā‘aiga
(__ call) tauvalā‘auga
(__ of ship) taumālua
(__ a ball) fa‘ata‘avale
(__ over) fuli, tafuli
(__ into a ball) tagai
roller lola
roller-bearings polo u‘amea *(also ball-bearings)*
rolling-stone ma‘ata‘anoa
Roman Catholic Katoliko, Pope
roof taualuga, falealuga
room (space) ava, avanoa
(a __) potu
(__ for s.th.) ofi, āvanoa
rooster toa
root a‘a
(origin) pogai, ‘auga
(edible __) ‘i‘o
(to __) sua
(rooted) maua‘a
rope maea
rose rosa
rot pala *(also rotten)*
rotate vili, ta‘avili, fa‘ata‘avili
rough lauleaga, maupu‘epu‘e
(__ cloth, skin) talatala
(__ sea) sou, galu, louā
(__ mat) papata
roughly (approximately) e tusa ma
(brutally) fa‘atūfanua
round lāpotopoto, fa‘ata‘amilo

(__ numbers)	numera tetele
(__ in boxing)	ta'amilosaga
(__ up cattle)	fa'apotopoto
(__ off a speech)	fa'apale
rousing (song)	pese fa'aosofia
route	ala
(sea __)	alāva'a
row (plants)	āi
(seats etc.)	atu, sao
(of people)	solo, laina
(a boat)	alo, (pol.) pale
rowing-boat	va'ataualo
royal	fa'aletupu, tautupu
royalty	tagata o le'āiga o tupu
rub	mili, olo, nini
(__ out)	titina
(__ off)	tafi 'ese
(__ w. oil)	u'u
rubber	pulu, pa'u
(school __)	titina
rubbing (pattern on siapo)	'ēlei
rubbish	otaota, lāpisi, gasu
(i.e. nonsense)	mea lę aogā
rudder	foeuli
rude	lē āva, fa'alēmīgao, lē 'ano'ano, fa'alēaloalo
ruffle (hair)	fa'amāve'uve'u
rug	palanikete
rugby football	lakapī
ruin	fa'aleaga, fa'amalepe
ruins	atigifale
rule (the __)	mea ua māsani ai
(authority)	pule, pūlega
(__ a line)	vase
ruler	
(one in authority)	pule
(wooden __ etc.)	vase, lula
(carpenter's rule)	futu
rum	'ava malosi
rumble	ū, gogolo, patapatatū
rummage	sagole, tagole
rumour	tala, fāfātala, talasalatua
run	momo'e, tamo'e, taufetuli
(i.e. work)	alu, ola
(water)	tafe
(__ about)	fetaufetulia'i
(__ after)	tuliloa
(__ aground)	to'a, fa'apapa'u
(__ away)	sola
(__ down)	fāiifo
(__ over s.th.)	solia
(__ a business)	fai
(__ short)	tau'uma
(__ loose)	ta'ata'a
rung (ladder)	fa'asitepu, tulaga
running	taufetuliga
rush (plant)	'utu'utu
(to __)	fa'avave, vavevave
(of people)	laga, oso loa, pati, tiniō
(of water)	tafe mālosi
rust	'ele
(rusty)	'elea
rustle	gasē
ruthless	fa'alaeō
ruts	tūlagāta'avale

Ss

Sabbath	Sāpati
sack (a __)	taga
(to __)	fa'ate'a ma le gāluega
sacrament	(R.C.) sakalameta, sauniga fa'atusa
sacred	sā, pa'ia, tapu
sacrifice	tāulaga
sacrum	ivino'o, tūlāi'u
sad	fa'anoanoa, fa'avauvau
saddle	nofoa (solofanua, uila)
safe (be __)	sao, saogālemū
(a __)	sefe
safety pin	pine fa'amau napekini
sago	saito
(__ palm)	niu masoā
said	sa fa'aali mai
sail	lā
(to __)	folau
sailor	tagata folau va'a, seila

sake (for his __)	‘ona ‘o ona āi, mo ia lava
salad	sālati
salary	totogi, fa‘aoloaga
sale	‘o le fa‘atau atu
(auction __)	fa‘atau tu‘i
(special __)	fa‘atau i le tau pa‘ū
salesman/woman	fa‘atau ‘oloa
saliva	fāua
salmon	sāmani
salt	māsima, fa‘amāsima
saltwater	suāsami
salty	māi, fa‘a‘ona‘ona, fa‘amāimāi
salute	fā‘alo
salvation	olataga, fa‘aolataga, fa‘asaoina
same (__ as)	e tusa ‘o . . .
(__ day)	aso e tasi, aso lava lea
(just the __)	tutusa lava, ui i lea
sample (to __)	tofo
sanctify	fa‘apa‘ia
sanction	malie, (pol.) fa‘atōfāla‘ia
sanctuary (refuge)	sulufa‘iga
sand	oneone
(sandy)	oneonea
sandals	se‘evae
sandpaper	pepatalatala, sanipepa
sandwich(es)	sānuisi
sap	uso (o se lā‘au), āpulupulu
sarcastic	tausuauigā
sardine	sātini
satellite	satelite
satisfaction	malie
satisfactory	‘ua lelei, fa‘amalieina
satisfy	fa‘amalie
(be satisfied)	pāgamālie
Saturday	Aso Toona‘i
sauce	sosi
saucepan	‘ulo
saucer	sasa
saunter	neva, fa‘asēlegā
sausage	sosisi
savage	fe‘ai, fa‘apaupau
save	fa‘asao
(__ money)	teu, fa‘aputuputu (le tupe)
savings	teugātupe
Saviour	‘o le Fa‘aola
saw (tool)	‘ili
sawdust	‘iligālā‘au
sawfish	sa‘ulā
saxaphone	sekisifoni
say	fai atu, tautala, fa‘apea, (pol.) afioina
saying	alagā‘upu, muāgagana
scab	pa‘upa‘u
scaffolding	fatāmanu
scald	e‘e, mū
scale (measure)	fua
(fish)	una
(to __ fish)	unafi
scandal	tausūaiga, fāfātala
scapegoat	togisala
scar	mā‘ila, tipi
(for adornment)	moti
scarce	fa‘alētele, ta‘aitiiti, oge, apiapi, mauagatā
scarcely	tau lē . . .
(__ ever)	seāseā
scarcity (of food)	laumeavale, oge
scare	fefevale
scarf	fusiua māfanafana, sikafu
scarlet	mūmūsalī
scatter	fa‘asalalau
(people)	tā‘ape‘ape
scene	va‘aiga
(part of a play)	vāega o le tala
(quarrel)	misa
scenery (landscape)	va‘aiga
(stage __)	tēuga o le tala
scent	namu
(bottle of __)	fagusausau
(__ of flowers)	manogi
(to __)	sogi
(beware of)	lagona
sceptical	māsalosalo, lē talitonu
scheme	fāufauga, togafiti
(to __, plot)	fāufauga leaga, tāupulepule
schism	fevaevaea‘iga
scholar	lē ‘ua a‘oga
scholarship	sikolasipi
school	ā‘oga
(__ house)	fale ā‘oga
(art __)	ā‘oga tusiata
(trades __)	ā‘oga matātā ‘ese‘ese
science	saienisi
scientific	fa‘asaienisi
scientist	saienitisi

scissors seleulu
scoff fa'atuetuē, taufāifai, fa'atauemu
scold 'ote, to'u
scone sikoni
scoop (water) asu
(out) sali
scorch sunusunu, mū, masunu
score (game) 'ai
(musical) nota
(full __) tapula'a
(i.e. scratch) 'o'osi, ta'osi, tosi
scorn manatu fa'atauva'a
scorpion akarava
scourge mala, sasa leaga
scout atia'iga, matamata
(boy __) sikauti
scowl fa'asiasia
scraggy pa'e'e
scramble auoso, fetaufaofa'i
scrape valu, fafai
(__ sore) lalase
scraper (shell __) 'asi, (pol.) pipi
scratch (a __) valu
(__ face) lala'u
(i.e. score) 'osi'osi, tosi
(__ of dog) valusi
(__ limb) mā'osi
(of chickens) ta'eu, sa'eu
scrawl tositosi
scream 'e'ē, uiō
screen pupuni
(cinema __) 'ie tīfaga
screw fao vilivili, sikurū
(to __) fa'aū le fao
(__ up eyes) fa'asegosego
screw pine (shrub) fala, laufala, paogo etc.
screwdriver mea tala faovili, 'o le sikurū
scribble 'osi'osiga
(to __) tositosi
scrotum laso
(enlarged __) ma'ivai, ma'iotane, lalovasa
scruple gē
scrutinize 'apo, tulimata'i, vā'ai
scrutiny mātau
scuffle gāsē
scum lala
scurf mafuga o le ulu

sea sami, (pol.) 'aupeau
(open __) vasa
(deep __) moana
sea anemone lumane
sea annelid palolo
sea cucumber loli etc.
sea rock to'a
sea urchin 'ina, tuitui etc.
seal fa'amau, fa'amaufa'ailoga
sealer vali simā, mea fa'apipi'i
seam āi, su'ifa'asoso'o
seamless sau 'ātoa
search su'e, sā'ili, su'ega, sā'iliga
(__ for food) sasamu, sasau
seashell fīgota
seasick ma'ivasa
seaside tūmatāfaga
(on the __) i tai
season tau, māsina, vāimasina, vāitausaga
(wet __) vāipalolo
(dry __) vāito'elau
seat (chair etc.) nofoa
(location) nōfoaga
(buttocks) (pol.) nofoaga
(be seated) nofo, (pol.) alala i lalo
seaward gātai
seaweed limu
second lona lua, soa
(George the __) Siaosi le lua
second (time) sekone
secret lilo, fa'alilolilo, mealilo, fa'ananā
secretary failautusi
section vāega, matāgāluega
(__ of village) 'ogānu'u, pitonu'u
secure mausalī, fa'amautū
(to __) fa'amau, fa'amautū
sedge (grass) selesele, tuisē
sediment taei'a
seductive
(of a man) avi, fa'amānaia
(of a girl) fa'ateteine
see (to __) va'ai, pupula, iloa, va'ava'ai, (pol.) taga'i, silasila
(church) matāgaluega fa'a-Epikopo

(we shall see) se'i iloa
seed fatu, fugafugāmutia
seedling bed mili, fa'amiliga
seek sa'ili
seem e peisea'ī, fa'apea
seer tagata 'i'ite
segregate fa'anofo'ese'ese, vavae
seize pu'e, fao
seldom seāseā
select fili, 'oto
selection filifiliga
self (himself) 'o ia lava
(ourselves) 'o tatou lava
selfish manatu fa'apito
self-willed fa'aali'i, sa'oloto
sell fa'atau atu
semen sī
semester (A.S.) semesa, vaitu'uaga
send 'ave,'auina atu, moli
(__ word ahead) fa'aso'oso'o
(__ away) tuli'ese
sennit 'afa
sense uiga, lagona
sensible (person) tagata māfaufau
sensitive 'ilitata *(of mind);* lē atapa'ia *(of touch)*
sentence fuai'upu
(legal) fa'asalaga
separate 'ese lava, māvae
(to __) vavae, vāevae, (pol.) tu'u 'ese'ese, fa'avasega, te'a, vā
September Setema
septic 'ona, 'o'ona, lūgā
septum pou o le isu
sepulchre loa, tia
sequence gāsologa, fa'asologa
sergeant sātini
serious faigatā, tūgā, to'aga, fa'amaoni, lotonaunau
sermon lāuga
serpent gata
servant tautua, tāvini (pol.) 'au'auna
(public __) auauna a le mālō
serve tautua, 'au'auna
(__ a meal) laulau le mea'ai
(__ a sentence) nofo sala
service tautua, gāluega
(church __) sāuniga, lotu, tāpua'iga
session vāega o le fono
(in __) 'ua usu le fono
set (of sun) goto
(cutlery) seti
(radio __) lā'au fa'alogologo
(__ free) fa'asa'oloto, tu'u sa'oloto
(__ apart) tu'u 'ese
(__ out) pae
(__ an example) fai se fa'aa'oa'oga
(__ a limit) fa'agata, fa'atapula'a
(__ on fire) fa'aola le afi, susunu, tutu le afi, fa'amū
(__ foot on land) tūvae, (pol.) tū'a'ao, tū lau'ele'ele
settle
(set up home) nofo, fa'avae le 'āiga
(of a bird) tū
(__ a quarrel) fa'alelei
(__ on, decide) mautonu
settled mautū
settlement fai'a'ai
seven fitu
seventeen sefulu ma le fitu
seventy fitusefulu
sever vavae
several nai, ni, nisi
severe tele, fitā, ogoogo
sew su'i
sewing machine lā'au su'isu'i
sewing needle nila su'isu'i
sex itū'āiga (tāne po'o fafine)
shade paolo
shadow ata, tauafiafi
shaft 'au
shake lue, gatete, lūlū
(__ one's fist) fa'alālā
(__ hands) lūlūlima, (pol.) lūlū'a'ao
shall 'o le 'ā, e ao ina
shallow papa'u
shame mā luma, māsiasi
(bring __ on) fa'amā, fa'aluma, fa'amāsiasi
shape fōliga, tino mai
(to __) fa'afōliga, tā
share (a __) vāega, tu'uga, tufa'aga, (pol.) inati
(to __) vāevae, lufilufi, tufatufa, (pol.) fa'asoa
(__ out) tufa, tofitofi

shark	malie
sharp	
(of knife etc.)	ma'ai, mātipitipi, matuitui
(of mind)	ma'ati, matapoto
(look ___!)	fai a'e!
sharpen	fa'amata, fa'ama'ai
shave	sele, tafi
shawl	'ie 'afu
she	'o ia, ia, na
shear(to ___)	sele, selesele
sheath	suluga, fa'amoega
sheathe	sulu (le pelu etc.)
shed	fale teu meafaigāluega etc.
(to ___ tears)	maligi loimata
(to ___ blood)	fa'amasa'a le toto
(to ___ leaves)	fa'ato'ulu
sheep	māmoe
sheer	matuā, tāfatō
sheet (cloth)	'ie
(paper)	laupepa
(cement)	'apa simā
(roofing iron)	'apa 'atofale
shelf	fata, talitali
shell (of s.th.)	atigi . . .
(gun)	pulufana, pulu'ō'ō
shell-trumpet	'o le pū
shellfish (gen.)	fīgota
shelter	lafitaga, fa'amālumalu, fale laufao, falelaupola
(to ___)	malu, lafi, fa'amālumalu
shelve	
(i.e. to leave s.th.)	palalau, tu'u
shepherd	leoleo māmoe
shield (a ___)	talitā
(to ___)	puipui
shift	si'isi'iane
(___ along)	māne'e
(night ___)	sifi pō
shifty	
(of character)	pi'o
shilling	seleni *(also money in gen.)*
shin	tuasivi o le vae
shine	
(of sun, moon)	susulu, pulapula
(of a surface)	'i'ila
(to ___)	fa'a'i'ila, fa'asusulu, fa'apupula

ship (gen.)	va'a, va'afolau, setima, meli
(to ___ goods)	la'u 'oloa
shirk	'alo
shirt	'ofu tino
(tee-shirt)	mitiafu meleke
shirt-less	fa'asau
shiver	ma'alili, tete, lili
shoal (fish)	'aui'a
shock	
(electric ___)	taia i le uila
(___ of hair)	foga
(be shocked)	te'i, tausūai
shoe(s)	se'evae
shoot (to ___)	fana, fa'apā
(a ___ of tree)	tātupu
shooting	fānafana
shop	fale'oloa
(to ___)	fa'atau
shore	matāfaga
(___ up s.th.)	te'e
short	pu'upu'u, sa'asa'a
(run ___)	tau 'uma
(___ of water)	naumati
(___ of food)	oge
(___ of breath)	ga'ega'e
short cut	ala fa'alava, ala pu'upu'i, ala ta loto, ala'alo
shorten	fa'apu'upu'u
shorthand	fa'afonokarafi
shorthanded	autagatā
shortlegged	
(person)	sa'a
shortly	toeitiiti
shorts	'ofuvae pupu'u
short-tempered	itagōfie
should	e tatau, e ao
shoulder	tau'au
(___ blade)	ivifoe,(pol.) ivisā
shout	fa'atāiō, 'alaga, 'avau
shove	tulei, u'una'i
shovel	suo, suo asu, (A.S.) sapelu
show (a ___)	fa'aaliga, tīfaga
(be visible)	aliali
(to ___)	fa'asino fa'ailoa
(___ off)	fa'aliavale
(agricultural ___)	fa'aaliga o mea tau fa'ato'aga
shower (rain)	mā'ulu'ulu
(sun ___)	uatea

(bathroom __) paipa
(to __) tā'ele, (pol.) fa'amālū
shred(s) penu
shrewd tōfā mamao, utamamao
shrill 'i'īvale
shrimp mosimosi
shrink
(of clothes) meme'i
(__ from s.th.) 'alo, solomuli
shrivel meme'i, magumagu
shudder maniti
shuffle (along) māne'e
(cards) tōtō
shun 'alo
shut tāpuni
(__ eyes) tapi'i mata
shy matamuli, (pol.) lili'a
(of horses) sesegi
sick (gen.) ma'i, (pol.) gasegase, pulupulusia, lagifa'atafa
(vomit) pua'i
sickly 'auma'ia, ma'ilasi, matama'i, tinovale
side itū, tafa, tafatafa, 'autafa
(on one __) itūtasi
(take sides) fa'a'au'au
sideburns talafa
sidelong (glance) fa'asi'usi'umata
siesta miti, moe pu'upu'u *(also nap)*
sift fa'amamā (falaoa etc.)
sigh mapusela, mapu ea
sight va'ai, va'aiga, (pol.) māimoa
sign fa'ailoga
(__ one's name) saini
signal (a __) fa'ailo
(to __) fa'ailo atu,(pol.) tālo
signature igoa, sainigāigoa
signpost fa'ailo
silence filēmū, gūgū, lē leoa, pāganoa
silent filēmū, lē tautala, lē pisa, ligoligoa, lologo
silk silika
silver siliva, 'ārio *(Bible)*
similar fa'apēnei, e tusa 'o . . ., fa'apēnā
(nearly the same) tālitutusa, tāi tutusa
lava
simple faigōfie
simplify fa'afaigōfie
simultaneous fai i le taimi e tasi
sin agasala
since talu, talu ai
sincere moni
sinews uaua mālosi
sing pese, lagi, (pol.) fogafoga, sāusaunoa
(of birds) tagi
singe masunu, mulu, tolo
singing pesega
single
(individual) tasi, to'atasi
(unmarried) nofofua
singlet mitiafu
sink (in water) goto, gogolo
(kitchen __) fa'atānoa fufulu ipu
sinker (fishing) maene
sinnet 'afa
sinusitis ifoaluga
sip miti
sir ali'i e
siren sailini
sister
(of a man) tuafafine
(of a woman) uso
sit nofo, saofa'i
(__ up) nofo sa'o, nofo 'i luga
(__ at night) evaeva, (pol.) alaala
(__ in assembly) alofi
(__ on chair, horse) ti'eti'e
(__ astride) fa'amāgai
site tūlaga
situation tūlaga
six ono
sixpence sisipeni
sixteen sefulu ma le ono
sixty onosefulu
size fua, lapo'a o le mea
(same __) fuapau
skeleton 'auivi
(bird w.o. wings) va'ava'a
sketch (drawing) ata, agoagoga
ski se'e i le kiona
skid se'e
skill poto, faiva, tufugālima, limalelei
skim sali, sali'ese, sasali
skin pa'u

(to __)	sae, valu
skip	osooso, temeteme
(__ w. rope)	tafue
(__ rope)	fautafue
skirt	‘ie, sakete
skite	fa‘alialia vale
skull	ulupo‘o
sky	lagi, vānimonimo, vāteatea
slack	matagataga, faiaga
slacken	
(discipline)	ma‘amulumulu
(wind)	feto‘i
(rope)	fa‘amatagataga
slacks	‘ofu vae ‘u‘umi
slam	māpuni
slander	ta‘u fa‘aleaga
slant	sipa
slap	pō, pōpō
slash	sasa, tautā, sele, sala
slate	ma‘a tusi, ma‘a ‘ato fale
slaughter	fasiga, fasi (pua‘a etc.)
slave	pologa
slay	fasi
sleep	moe, (pol.) tōfāga
(to __)	moe, (pl.) momoe, (pol.) tofā, (pl.) tōfafā
(sleep soundly)	moe gase
(__ restlessly)	moe fiti
(overcome by __)	tulemoe
sleepy	fia moe, ‘īvā
sleet	timu fa‘atasi ma kiona
slice	tipi (fa‘amanifi)
slide	se‘e, fa‘ase‘e, sulu, velo, solo
slight	la‘itiiti
slightly	feoloolo fo‘i
slim	‘aui‘a
slime	vavale
sling	ma‘atā
slip (mistake)	sesē, masei, la‘avale
(__ of paper)	fāsi laupepa
(__ of tongue)	fa‘asasisasi, sasi
(__ of foot)	masepu, se‘e
(__ out of the hand)	mamulu
slipper(s)	silipa
slippery	māse‘ese‘e
slobber	fāuā
slope	malifa, sipa
slosh	tagulugulu

sloth	fa‘apaiē
slough	atigi, laosā
slovenly	fa‘a‘inaelo
slow	telegese, tuai, lēmū, gese
(__ down)	fa‘alēmū, fa‘atelegese
slowly	lēmū, mālie, telegese
slug	gau, gaupapa
sluggish	fa‘apaiē
sly	agapi‘opi‘o
smack	misimisi, mitimiti
small	la‘itiiti, itiiti, lili‘i, tama‘i, tinoiti
(very __)	nini‘i
smart (clever)	ma‘ai, poto
(elegant)	mānaia, onomea
(of sores, cuts)	fe‘alasi, masimasi
(of eyes)	‘avasia
smash (to __)	ta‘e, malepe, nuti, talepe, lepeti
(__ in small pieces)	nuti momomo, nuti lili‘i
(a car __)	‘ua feto‘ai ta‘avale
smear	nini, papanu, panupanu
smell (to __)	sogi, lagona, nāmu
(a __)	nanāmu, manogi, sasala
(bad __)	masa, elo
(__ of urine)	sogo, sosogo
smelly	nāmuleaga, anusia, ‘u‘ū, pepe‘a
smile	‘ata‘ata, māfini
smoke (the __)	asu, ausa, pusa
(__ tobacco)	utufaga, tapa‘a
(to __)	ula, ulaula, (pol.) tāumafa
(to __ a pipe)	ifi, ula
(to __ fish, etc)	fa‘aasu
smoked	nāmuasua
smooth	molemole, lāmolemole, laulelei
(to __)	fa‘alaulelei, oloolo
snail	sisi
snake	gata
snap (to __)	motu
(to __ off)	fa‘i, momotu
snapshot (photograph)	ata
snare (fish)	sele
snatch	se‘i, segi, fao, ‘aimālō

sneak (away) fa‘agalo, totolo ‘ese
sneer ‘ata‘atafa‘atauemu
sneeze māfatuạ
sniff isumiti, sosogi, sogisogi
snob fiasili, manatu fa‘atauva‘a i isi
snore tāgulu, ta‘agulu
snout muāgutu
snow kiona
(___ ball) potoi kiona
(___ white) pa‘epa‘emā, kiona sina
sniffle isumiti
snuggle u‘u
so (in that way) fa‘apēnā lava
(___ on & ___ on) ‘ua fa‘apea ma fa‘apea
(___ & ___) ‘o le igoa lea
(___ that) ‘ina ‘ia
soak fa‘asusū, fa‘avai
soap moli
(piece of ___) fāsimoli
(toilet ___) moli tā‘ele
(washing ___) moli tā mea
(to ___) fufulu, fa‘a‘oa
soap-suds ‘oa o le moli
soar tifa
sob masūsū
sober lē ‘onā
soccer soka
social lautele
society sosaiete, fa‘alāpotopotoga, māfutaga
(old boys’ ___) sosaiete o tama tuai
sock (sox) totini
soda sota
sofa sofa
soft (pillow, ground) malū
(___ voice) mālū
(___ body, fur) vāivai, molemole, malūlū
soften fa‘amalū
softly lēmū
soil ‘ele‘ele, palapala
soiled ‘ele‘elea, ‘ola‘olā
sojourn aumau
solar plexus mauli, moa
solar power paoa po‘o uila mai le lā
sold fa‘atau atu
solder fa‘apulu
soldier fitafita
sole (only) na‘o iȧ etc.
(___ of foot) alofivae
(___ of shoe) alose‘evae, alofise‘evae
solemn paū
solid malō, mea malō
(of a wall) māopoopo
(___ gold) ‘auro māo‘i/mamā
solo (music) solo
some nai, nisi, sina
(___ one) se isi, se tasi (*also somebody)*
(___ times) i nisi aso
somersault fiti, tāgāfiti
something se mea
somewhat teisi
son (of a man) atali‘i (pol.) alo
(of a woman) tama tama (pol.) alo
song pese fa‘aletino
soon vave, vave mai, e lē pine, toeitiiti
soot ‘ele, lama
soothe fa‘amālū, fa‘amalie
sore (be ___) tigā, ‘ala, māsui
(a ___) papala, ma‘i sua, (pol.) ma‘i malū
(covered w. ___) po‘upo‘ua
sorrow tigāalofa, fa‘anoanoa
sorry fa‘anoanoa
(sorry for) alofa, tālofa
sort (kind) itū‘āiga
(___ out) tu‘ufa‘avasega
soul agaga
sound leo, logo, tagi
soundly matuā
(sleep ___) moegase
soup sua, supo
sour ‘o‘ona, mafu
source mafuaga
(___ of water) matāvai, puna
soursop sasalapa
souse fa‘avai, ota
South saute, toga
Southern Cross Sumu
souvenir suvania
sovereign (king) tupu
(coin) sēleni ‘auro
sow (pig) aumatua
(to ___) lūlū fatu
space (i.e. room) avanoa
(___ between) vā

(open __) malae laolao
(__ between villages) vā o nu‘u
(__ games) ta‘aloga sipeisi
(__ ship) va‘a-sipeisi, va‘a o le vānimonimo
spade suō, suōtipi
(cards) peti
span aga
spanner fa‘aū
spar tila
(to __) fusufusu, fusufa‘ata‘ita‘i, sipā, toleni e fusu
spare (__ time) taimi avanoa
(i.e. in reserve) fa‘atagataga, fa‘aleoleo, sīpea
(__ a life) fa‘aola
spark ‘aloiafi, sipaka
spark plug sipaka
sparkle ‘emo‘emo, ‘i‘ila
spatter pīsia
speak tautala, (pol.) fofoga, sāunoa, feganavai, tulei, malele, fetalai
(__ of, mention) ta‘u, ta‘uta‘u, tālatala
(i.e. say, thus) fa‘apea
(__ in English) nanu
(__ w. authority) fa‘amalele
(__ evil of) ta‘u ‘ese, ta‘uleaga
(__ well of) ta‘u lelei
(__ frankly) ta‘utino
spear tao
(to __) velo
special fa‘apitoa, fa‘ailogaina
specialist lē ua poto tele i se tasi faiva
(eye __) foma‘i mata etc.
specially ‘aemaise (lava)
speckle sausau
spectacle (show) tīfaga
(glasses) mata tioata, va‘aiga
spectator(s) tagata matamata, (pol.) ‘aumaimoa
speech tautala, lāuga, (pol.) malelega, sāunoaga, fetalaiga, tuleiga, vāgana
speechless lē magagana
speed saosaoa, vave
(__ s.th. up) fa‘avae, fa‘amasau, fa‘asaosaoa, fa‘atopetope
speedy televave
spell sipela
(take a __) fai se koma, (colq.) mālōlō la‘itiiti
spend fa‘aalu, fa‘aaogā tupe
sphere (round) lāpotopoto, fa‘apolo
(__ of authority) pule‘aga
spider ‘apogāleveleve
(__ web) fa‘amoega ‘apogāleveleve
spike tala
(to __) so‘a
spill sasa‘a, masa‘a
spin vili
spine ivitū
spinner (fishing) pā
spirit agāga
(ghost) aitu, (pol.) sauali‘i
(__ medium) taulāitu
(methylated __) sipili tutu molī
spiritual fa‘aleagāga
spit anu, feanu
spite (in __ of) e ui lava ina, teinane
spiteful lotovale
spittle fāua
splash pisia, fa‘apisi
(splashed) pīsia
spleen ateali‘i
splendid mātagōfie, lelei tele
splice so‘oga
splinter fāsi lā‘au
split māisi, isiisi, māvae, tofi
(of skin) mafasi
(wood) mavete, ta‘e
(__ in two) isilua
(__ a log) vete
spoil fa‘aleaga
(__ a child) fa‘apelepele
sponge (a __) omomi
(__ cake) keke māmā
spoon sipuni, (A.S.) sipunu
(tea __) sipunitī
(desert __) sipuni fa‘alēogalua, sipuni puligi
(table __) sipuni tele
sport(s) tā‘aloga
spot (place) mea, vāimea
(a mark) ila
(to __ s.th.) va‘aia, iloa
spotless āusiusi

spotted ilailā, pūlepule
spouse ‘o le to‘alua (tane po‘o fafine)
sprain mapeva, milosia
spray pipisi
spread sosolo, salalau, fe‘avea‘i
(of rash) sasao
(__ out) fofola
(__ butter etc.) fa‘apata
spring tau e fuga mai ai lā‘au, tau tutupu
(water) vaipuna, punāvai
(to jump) oso, osopuna
Spring-tide tai o‘o
sprinkle fa‘asūsū, sausau
sprout lalau
spur tala (o le toa), tui (mo solofanua)
(__ of the moment) fai fa‘afuase‘i lava
spurt (of blood etc.) oso le ‘ele‘ele
spy matamata, sipai, taulamalama
squabble fe‘avaua‘i, fe‘upua‘i
squall ‘o le ta‘uta‘u
square fa‘atāfafā, sikuea
(carpenter’s __) sikuea
squash ‘o‘omi, ta‘omi
squat (in hiding) fa‘apuga
(to __) faatū
squeak ‘i‘ī
squeal ‘e‘ē, ‘ī
squeeze ‘o‘omi
(__ a lemon etc.) tatau
squint sepa
squirm gāi‘oi‘o
squirt pipisi
stab tui
stable tū, ‘ua mau
(a __) fale o solofanua
stack fa‘aputu
staff (employees) ‘aufaigāluega
(stick) to‘oto‘o
stage tūlaga, la‘asaga
stagger tevateva
stagnant lepa
stain pīsia
stairs sitepu, alafa‘a‘apefa‘i, alasitepu
stake o‘ao‘a
(a prize) temu
stale mafu
stalk ‘au, fā
(to __) atia‘i
stallion solofanua po‘a
stammer fa‘atagito‘ia
stamp (postage) fa‘ailoga tusi
(__ the ground) tatū
stand (to __) tū, fa‘atū
(a __) lago, tūlaga
(grand __) nofoaga matamata, fale matamata
(__ up) tu ‘i luga, tūla‘i
(__ to attention) tū fa‘amalō
(__ upright) tū sa‘o
standard (level) tūlaga
(i.e. a flag) fu‘a
star fetū
(shooting __) fetūlele
(morning __) fetūao
starboard i atea (itū taumatau o va‘a)
starch masoā
stare tepataula‘i, pulato‘a, (pol.) sisila
starfish ‘aveau
starling (S.bird) fūia
start (begin) ‘āmata, ‘āmataga
startle fa‘ate‘i, laga (le manu), tē‘ia
(startled) te‘i, segia
starve oge, fa‘aoge, matelāina, lāina
state mālō, itūmālō
(condition) tūlaga
(to declare) ta‘utino
(__ an opinion) lafo le manatu
stately (of people) māluali‘i, ‘umi fa‘asasa‘o
statement tala, fa‘amatalaga
station nōfoaga
(railway __) tūlaga e tutū ai nofoa afi
stationary mautū, lē gāoioi
stationery mea tusitusi
statue fa‘atagata
status tūlaga
staunch (stop) utu le toto etc.
(__ friend) uō fa‘amaoni
stay (a prop) lago, te‘e
(to __) nofo, tu‘u pea, api

(__ at home)	fa'amuli
(__ away from school)	ta'atua
(__ away from s.th.)	taumamao ma . . .
steadfast	lotomau, māua'i
steady (wind)	taotasi
(character)	to'a
steal	gaoi, matagaoi, (pol.) limatāgo'ese, tagovale, tōtōā
(__ food)	soa'ai
(__ a glance)	fa'asi'usi'umata, tiloalalo
steam	ausa
steamer	setima, meli
steel	sila
(__ one's heart)	fa'ama'a'a loto
steep	tū, mato, tāfatō, tofē
(to __)	fa'asū, fufui, fa'avai
steeple	falelogo (i luga o falesā
steer (to __)	uli, 'ave, fa'auli, fa'afoe
(a __)	povi po'a
steering wheel	foeuli
stem	tafu'e, pogai, pogati
(to __ from)	pogai mai
stench	elo, (pol.) manogi
step	la'asaga, sitepu
(to __)	la'a, savali
(in __)	vaevae gatasi
sterile (of woman)	lē toe fānau, pā, (pol.) papā
stern (ship)	taumuli
(face)	matapaū
stew	sitiū, fa'asua
stick$_1$	lā'au, 'aumafute, to'oto'o, lou
(dry __)	alaala, lālā
(digging __)	'oso
(__ of dynamite)	fanai'a
stick$_2$ (remain fixed)	mau, 'apili, pipi'i
(__ together)	fuifui, fa'atasi
(__ into)	usui
(stuck-up person)	isusisi
stick-insect	sē
sticky	pi'ipi'i, āpulupulua
stiff	malō, ma'a'a
still (quiet)	lē gāoiā, filēmū, māninoa
(water)	lepa
(i.e. continuing)	pea
stillborn	fanauoti
stimulate	fa'agāe'e, fa'aolaola, fa'atupu, fa'alototele
sting (to __)	ū, tui, masimasi, ma'ini
(the __)	foto *(stingray)*, nila *(bee)*
stingy	limavale, mata'ū
stink	masa, elo, (pol.) manogi
(of food)	sauga, (pol.) mae
(of urine)	sosogo
stinking	namuleaga
stipend	fa'a'oloaga
stir	seu, sa'eu
(to move)	gāe'e, gāoioi
(__ up water)	fa'agaepu, fa'anefu
stirrup	vae o nofoa (solofanua)
stitch	su'iga, su'i tuāfilo
stock	'oloa
(__ taking)	su'egā'oloa
stocking	tōtini
stock-still	tūpoupou
stomach	puta, manava, (pol.) alo
stone (gen.)	ma'a
(small __)	ma'ama'a, 'ili'ili
(__ jar)	vaima'a, fagu'ele
stony	gāoā
stools	tae, (pol.) otaota
(loose __)	tatā le manava
stoop	no'utua, fa'ano'uno'u, tuano'u, tuano'o, fā'atū
stop	pau
(__ up s.th.)	pupuni, mono, puluti
(halt!)	fa'atū!
(prevent)	tāofi
(__ that!)	'aua, tu'u, soia!
(__ for a rest)	mānava
stopper	momono
store (shop)	fale'oloa
(__ up)	teu, fa'aputu
storey	fogāfale
storm	afā
stormy	loulouā, lagilagiā
story	tala
stove	'ogāumu
straight	sa'o, tonu

(__ hair) sē‘ea
straighten fa‘asa‘o
strain (stress) mea faigatā, ‘o‘ono
(physical __) gau
(clean) tatau, fa‘amamā
strainer tāuaga, fautau‘ava, fa‘amamā
straits vāinu‘u
strand (of hair) fuafuati
strange ‘ese, uiga‘ese
stranger tagata fāimai, tagata ‘ese
strangle titiva, titina
strap fusi, ‘āvei
straw vaomago
stray sesē, ta‘asē
streak
(move quickly) alamū
stream
(current) au
(river) ālia, vaitafe
street ala, ‘auala
strength mālosi
strengthen fa‘amālosi, opogi
strenuous (work) fitā
stress (to __) fa‘amamafa
stretch (of sea) ‘ogāsami
(to __) meme‘i, fālō, fa‘aloaloa
stretcher fata
strew fola, pae, tatanu
stricken mālaia, māfatia
strict lotomau, pule sa‘o
stride lala‘a
strike tā, so‘a, tu‘i, taia
(w.fist) moto
(feelings) ‘o‘otia
(__ dead) tu‘ipē
string mānoa
(__ of beads) ula
stringy ‘alavalavā, pepenu
strip (to __) sae, tala
(a __) fāsi . . .
stripe mua (o le ‘ie)
striped tusitusi
strive losi, finafinau, losilosi, naunau
stroke (of a clock) tā
(a cat) milimili
(illness) taia le tino
stroll eva, neva, sāvalivali, tafatafao
strong mālosi
(__ desire) fai ‘ese
(__ drink) ‘ava ‘o‘ona
(__ minded) fa‘auliulitō, fa‘auluulumamau
struggle tauivi, taumilo, taumafai atu pea
stub (out) titina
stubble tāgutugutu
stubborn lotomalō, lotoma‘a‘a
student tama/teine ā‘oga
study (to __) a‘o, su‘esu‘e
(a __) ‘ōfisa, potu su‘esu‘e
stuff mea, ‘ie
(to __) faotu‘i, fafao
stumble lāvea, tevateva
stumbling block tausūaiga
stump (the __) pogai, pogati, tafu‘e, tagutu
(__ of a leg) vaemutu
(cricket __) ‘olo
(to __) titina le ‘olo
stun meia
stunted (of trees) ola tagito‘ia
stupid āmiovalea, valea
stupidly fa‘avalea
stutter lē matala le tautala
sty (pig) sai
style (model) faiga, fausaga
subject (topic) matā‘upu
submarine va‘atofu, va‘amaulu
submission (a __) fa‘amatalaga, tagi
(__ to s.o.) nofo i lalo o le pule a
submit
(give in to . . .) gāua‘i, e‘e
subordinate tūlaga māulalo
subscribe fai lāfoga
subscription lāfoga
subside māui, solofa, tō
substance mea, ‘a‘ano
substitute sui
subtract tō‘ese
suburb pitonu‘u
succeed manuia, mānumālō, o‘o
(follow) auifo, auane
success mālō, manuia, mānumālō
succession sōloga, fa‘asologa, auga
(royal __) augātupu
(rapid __) saputu mai

successor	sui, suli
succinctly	fa‘a‘oto‘oto
such (___ as this)	fa‘apēnei
(___ as that)	fa‘apenā, fa‘apelā
suck	mitimiti, mimiti, susu
sucker(taro)	lauvai
(banana)	suli
suckle	fa‘asusu
suckling	tama meamea
sudden	fa‘afuase‘i
(all of a ___)	te‘i ane
sue	mōlia
suffer	māfatia, tigā, togisala
suffering	puapuagā
sufficient	‘ua lava, nanea, tofu
suffocate	mole
sugar	suka
(___ cane)	tolo
suggest	ta‘u atu, faulalo
suggestion	manatu
suicide	tōa‘i, (pol.) pule i lona ola
suit (clothes)	pea
(legal)	tagi
(of armour)	ufifatafata
suitable	ono, tatau, agava‘a
suitcase	‘atopa‘u
sulk	musu
(sulky)	musuā
sulphur	teiō
sultry (day)	a‘ava
sum (total)	aofa‘i
(figures)	nūmera
(of money)	tinoitupe
(___ up)	tu‘ufa‘atasi
summarize	fa‘a‘oto‘oto, tala ‘oto‘oto
summary	tala ‘oto‘oto
summer	tau māfanafana
summit	fa‘auluuluga, tumutumu
summon	tala‘i
summons (legal)	tusi sāmani, tusi sāisai
sun	lā
(to ___)	fa‘alā
sunbeam	‘ave o le lā
Sunday	Aso Sā
sunlight	mālamalama, susulu
sunrise	‘o le oso o le lā
supercargo	supakako
supercilious	fa‘asiasia, isusisi
superior	maoa‘e
supermarket	supamāketi
superstition	‘uputu‘u, talitonu i aitu
supervise	va‘ava‘ai
supine	taliaga
supper	‘aiga i le afiafi
(Lord’s ___)	Talisuaga a le Ali‘i. O le Fa‘amanatuga Pa‘ia
supple	vavai
supplement	tului
supplication	‘āi‘oiga
supplies	‘oloa
supply	‘avatu, maua mai
support (a ___)	te‘e, lago
(___ ea. oth.)	felagolagoma‘i
(to ___ s.th or s.o.)	te‘e, lago, tāofi, talitali, opogi, palepale, sapasapai
suppose (pretend)	fa‘apea
(believe)	talitonu, mate
supposition	mea taumate
suppress	‘o‘ono
suppurating	‘aloua
supreme	aoao, silisili, Silisili ‘ese
sure	moni, iloatino, mautinoa
(not ___)	taumate, fa‘alēmautinoa
surf	piapia o le galu
(to ___)	fa‘ase‘e
surface (prefix)	fogā e.g. fogātai = *surface of sea*
(to ___, fish)	mānu
(the ___)	salani
surfeit (of fat)	lōia
surge (of people)	gogolo, lolofi, nunu
(waves)	fefatia‘i, galu
surgeon	fōma‘i tipitipi
surpass	‘ausi, fuaao, sē a‘e lava
surplus	fa‘asili
surprise	ofo, māofa, te‘i
surrender	ifo, lolo, si‘ilima, fa‘aui
surround	si‘o, si‘osi‘o, puipui, punipuni, vagaia
survey (measure)	fuafua
(look over)	tilotilo, va‘ai solo
survive	ola
suspect(to___)	masalo, māsalosalo, lagona

(a __)	tagata masalomia
suspend	
(interrupt)	tāofi
(hang up)	fa'atautau
suspicion	masalo, māsalosaloga
suspicious	māsalosalo
swag (bundle)	ta'aiga
swagger	mamapo
swamp	taufusi, pala
swamphen	manuali'i, manusā
swarm	ga'o'i
(people)	gāsolo
(flies)	mumu
(bees)	fa'amoegāpī
swat	pō
sway (wind)	māluelue
(influence s.o.)	tā'a'ina
swear (oath)	tautō
(curse)	palauvale
sweat	āfu
sweep	salu
sweet (taste)	suamalie
sweetbread	ateali'i
sweeten	fa'asuka
(__ the air)	fa'aleleia le 'ea
sweet-smelling	manogi lelei
swell (sea)	ulu
(limb)	fula
(increase)	fa'atele
(dough)	fefete
(breasts)	popona
(filarial)	tupa
swelling	fula, patu, pona
swift	saosaoa, gāsolo
swim	'a'au, (pl.) fe'ausi
(__ w. s.o.)	'ausa'i
swimming group	'ausaga
swing (child's)	tāupega
(to __)	lue, lia'i, sasau, tāupe
switch (to__)	kī
(__ off)	titina, tapē
(orator's __)	fue
sword	pelu
swordfish	sa'ulā
symbol	fa'ailoga, pine fa'amau
sympathize	tigā alofa
sympathy	
(to express __)	fa'amaise, tāpua'i
symptom	āuga
synagogue	sunako
synod	sinoti
synonym	'upu uiga tutusa
synopsis	tala'oto'oto
syphilis	ma'i afi
syringe	tui
system (method)	faiga, metotia
(network)	felavasa'iga

Tt

table	laulau
(set of figures)	fua
table cloth	ufilaulau, 'ielaulau
tablet (medicine)	fuālā'au
(for *siapo* designs)	'upeti
(memorial __)	ma'a togitogi
taboo	tapu, sā, fa'asā
(a __)	tapui
tack (a __)	tama'i fao
(to __) (cloth)	su'ifa'amaumau
tackle (football)	tapa
(fishing __)	mea e fa'i a'i le faiva, tōtoga
tacky	pi'ipi'i
tail	si'usi'u, i'u
tailor	su'i 'ofu
(__ shop)	fale su'isu'i
take	'ave, 'avatu, moli, (pol.) tuā'a'ao, tago
(__ after, look like)	so'o, fōliga 'i . . .
(__ away)	'ave 'ese
(__ up)	laga (se mataupu etc.)
(__ care of)	tausi
(__ it easy)	faifai mālie
(__ one's life)	taupule i lona ola
(__ revenge)	tauimasui
(__ a seat)	nofo
(__ the temperature)	fua le fiva, fua le vevela o le 'ea
(__ a walk)	alu le sāvalivaliga

(__ back words) fa'afo'i 'upu
tale tala, fāgogo
(tell __) faitala, (pl.) faitatala
talent tāleni *(Bible),* tomai
talk tala, talanoa, tālatala, talanoaga, tautala, (pol.) fofoga, lāuga, malele
(__ about s.th.) fa'atalanoaina
(__ in one's sleep) moetautala
(__ too much) gutuoso
(__ to ea. oth.) fetautalatala'i
(__ against s.o.) 'upu 'ese
talker (good __) mau'upu
talking-chief (A.S.) tulāfale
tall 'umi, maualuga
(__ stories) matanana
tally fa'amau 'ai, mea ua talia etc.
tally clerk tagata siaki 'oloa
tamarind (tree) tamalini
tame lata, fa'alata
tan (colour) 'ena'ena
tangle felefele, lavelave, numi
tank tane
tanker va'a la'u suāu'u etc.
(petrol __) ta'avale la'u penisini
tantrum fā'ali'i
tap (a __) paipa, kī o le paipa, gutu o le paipa
(to __) tātā, tu'itu'i
tape mua
tape-recorder teipi
tapioca tapioka, manioka
tar tā
tardy pī'oi, telegese tele
tares titania *(Bible)*
target sini, tāula'iga, matāti'a
taro talo, (pol.) fuauli
(__ garden) ma'umaga
(__ top) tiapula
tarpaulin tapoleni
tarry fa'aleleva
tart keke pa'agugu
task gāluega, tiute, fe'au
taste tofo, mana'o
tasty manogi
tatter (clothes) penu, titi, māsaesae
tattoo tatau, pe'a, (pol.) mālōfie
(to __) tā tatau
(__ artist) tufuga·tā tatau
taunt fa'alumaina, fa'alili
taut fa'amalō
tax lāfoga
tax-collector telona *(Bible),* tagata au lafoga
taxi ta'avale la'itiiti, ta'avale la'u pasese
tea (drink) tī
(__ leaves) lautī
(afternoon __) vai'aiga
tea-kettle tītata
teach a'o, a'oa'o atu
teacher faiā'oga
teaching(s) a'oa'oga
team 'au
teapot tīpoti
tear (to __) māsae, sae, sasae
(__ skin) māfo'e, mā'osi'osi
tear (cry) loimata
tease fa'alili
teat matāsusu
technical school 'ā'oga matātā, 'ese'ese
tedious fai so'o
telegram uālesi, uaea, telekalame
telegraph telekarafi
telephone telefoni
(__ box) potu telefoni
telescope fā'ata va'ai mamao
television televise, tīvī
(__ antenna) enatena
tell ta'u, ta'uta'u, tala, logo atu
(__ tales) faitala
temper lotoita
(quick __) fulufululele, fa'aitaitagōfie
temperature 'o le vevela
temple (church) mālumalu
(head) mānifinifi, māligaliga
temporary lē tumau
tempt fa'aosooso
temptation fa'aosoosoga, tofotofoga
ten sefulu
tenant tagata mautotogi
tend
(__ towards) māfuli aga'i i . . ., tauau
tender malū, lē atapa'ia

(___ hearted)	agamalū, loto alofa
(a ___)	tauofoga
tendon	uaua i so'oga
tennis	tēnisi
tenon	fa'anifo (o le pusa)
(___ saw)	'ilimutu
tenor (voice)	ī, fa'asala
tense (grammar)	taimi o le veape
(to ___)	fa'amalō, fa'ama'a'a
tent	fale'ie
tentacle	'ave (o le fe'e)
term (school)	vāitu'uaga, kuata
terminate	fa'agata, fa'ai'u, fa'amotu, fa'a'uma
termite	ane
tern (bird)	gogo, manusina
terrace	fa'asitepu
terrible	mata'utia
terrify	fefe tele
territory	atunu'u, itūmalō, teritori
test	fa'aa'oa'oga, fa'ata'ita'iga, su'ega, tofotofo
testament	feagaiga *(Bible)*
(will)	māvaega
testicle	fuāmanava
testify	molimau, fa'amaonia
testimony	'o le mau, ta'utinoga
tether	sele
text (sermon)	matua
(of a book)	a'ano
thanks(s)	fa'afetai
that	lea, lenā, lelā, lale, lele
thatch	lau, atoga o le fale
(to ___)	ato
(___ needle)	fanalau
the	'o le, 'o se, (pl.) 'o
theatre (picture)	fale tīfaga
(operating)	potu tipitipi
theft	gaoi
their	lo latou, la latou; (pl.) o latou, a latou
(two people)	lo la, o la etc.
theme	matā'upu, 'autū
then (at that time)	i lenā lava taimi
(afterwards)	mulimuli ane
there (is)	'ua iai, e iai
(place)	lea, 'i 'ō, 'i 'inā, 'o le lā etc.
(___ you are!)	'ua ā lā!
therefore	'o le mea lea

thermometer	'o le fua fiva
these	ia, nei
thews	uaua mālosi
they	lātou
(two people)	lā'ua, lā
thick	mafia, māfiafia
(___ smoke)	tetele le asu
(of trees)	putuputu, uluulu
(liquid)	toto'o, 'a'alu
(forest)	māoa, vao matua
(rope)	tuatua
thief	faomea
thigh	'autetele, 'ogāvae, suilapalapa
thimble	atigi lima
thin	manifi, mānifinifi
(string, rope)	tuaiti
(liquid)	suāvaia
(people)	'auiti, magoivi, tinovale
(legs)	vaemimiti
(cattle)	pa'e'e
(___ out plants)	fa'avālavala
think (meditate, ponder)	māfaufau, mānatunatu
(___ out s.th.)	fuafua
(be of the opinion)	fa'apea, masalo, fa'amata
(___ alike)	lotofa'amāsaga
third	vaetoluga, o lona tolu o . . .
thirst	fiainu
thirteen	sefulu ma le tolu
thirty	tolu sefulu
this	lenei, lea, sea, sia
thorn	tala, tuitui
thorough	loloto, māe'a, au'ili'ili, faimea māe'a
those	ia, nā, lā
(___ who)	ē, ē 'ua
though	e ui ina
(as ___)	e peisea'ī
thought (meditation, reflection)	māfaufauga
(occurrence)	manatu
(I ___)	fā'i, fā'ita, fā te a'u
thoughtless	fa'alēmāfaufau
thousand	afe
thrash	sasa
thread	filo

(__ of screw)	fa'anifo
threaten	fa'amata'u, fa'amasasa
three	tolu
three-sided	tafatolu
thrifty	fa'aeteete mea
thrive	olaola, malaulau, uluola
throat	fā'a'ī
throb (pulse)	saputu
(engine)	pa'ō'ō
(w. pain)	gāoi
throne	nofoali'i
throng	malu, ga'o'i, fetuleni
throttle	titina, titina le ua
through	i
(pass __)	sao mai . . . , ui i . . .
throw	togi, ato, lafo, fetogi, (A.S.) tu'ai
(__ a spear)	velo
(__ away)	lāfoa'i, tia'i
(__ stones)	tau'ai
thrush (bird)	tutumalili
(child's sickness)	pala
thrust	sua, sunu'i, usui
thud	pātatū
thumb	limamatua
thump	tātāvale
thunder	fāititili
(i.e. loud noise)	ta'alili
Thursday	Aso Tofi
thus	fa'apea
ticket	tikite, pepa
tickle	'ene'ene
ticklish	tetega
tide	tai
tidy	tūmamā, fa'amamā, tapena, teu
tie	noa, nonoa
(pig)	oma
(horse)	sele
(neck __)	fusiua
(__ beam)	utupoto
(__ together)	fusi fa'atasi
tier(s)	fa'asitepu
tiger	taika
tight (firm)	mau
(clothes)	'afaga, fufusi
tighten	fa'amau
tight-fisted	maugatā
tile	ma'a atofale, kapeta etc.
till (until)	se'i, se'ia
(__ later)	e sau aso
(__ finished)	se'i 'uma
(money __)	pusa tupe
tilt	fa'asipa, masu'e
timber	laupapa, lā'au
time	taimi
(at the __ of)	i aso o . . .
(free __)	taimi avanoa
(ancient __)	anamuā, i le vavau
(present __)	taimi nei, 'o ona pō nei, i lenei vāitaimi
(how many times)	e fa'afia?
(three times two)	fa'atele le lua i le tolu
timely	augamālie
timid	lotovāivai
tin	'apa
(tinned, canned)	tu'u'apa
tinea	tane
tingling	tetega
tinkle	tagitagi
tin trunk	pusa 'apa
tiny	la'itiiti lava
tip	sī'ui, pito
(money)	meaalofa tupe
tire	vāivai, lē lavā
(bored)	fiu, pāsi
tireless	tāupepē, lotulotu, māua'i
tissue (dead)	'atilo
(paper)	pepa mānifinifi lava
tithe	sefulu a'i
title	igoa matai, sa'o, (pol.) suafa matai, ao, pāpā
(woman)	sa'o tama'ita'i, tausala
to	'i, 'iā, 'ia te . . .
(to do s.th.)	e fai . . .
toast (bread)	fa'apa'u
(drink)	fa'amanuia
tobacco	tapa'a, (pol.) mea namuleaga, mea tāumafa, mea taute
today	i le asō
(i.e. at present time)	i nei aso
toe	tamatama'ivae
(big __)	vaematua
(__ nail)	mati'u'u, atig'ivae
(in-growing toenail)	unālalo
together	fa'atasi, potopoto
(__ with)	'ātoa ma . . . , fa'atasi ma . . .

toil	fatu ‘atia, saga galuepea
toilet	fale‘ese, fale uila, potu tā‘ele, fale la‘itiiti
token	sāsā, fa‘ailoga
tolerate	fa‘apale
Tom Dick & Harry (colq.)	Pai ma Lafai, Tui ma Seve
tomb	tia
tombstone	tiamau, ma‘afa‘amanatu
tomorrow	taeao, ‘ātaeao
ton	tone
tongs	i‘ofi
tongue	laulaufaiva
(put out __)	fa‘aeto
tonight	nānei, pō nei
too (also)	fo‘i
(excessive)	na‘uā, tele lava
tool(s)	meafaigāluega, (pol.) tautua
tooth (gen.)	nifo, (pol.) ‘oloa
(cog-wheel)	fa‘anifo
(__ ache)	nifo tigā
(__ brush)	pulumu nifo
(__ paste)	mea fufulunifo
(__ less)	aunifoa
top	taualuga, luga, tumutumu
(toy)	moa
topic	matā‘upu
torch (S __)	‘aulama, lama, sulu, tausulu
(electric __)	molīuila
torment	fa‘asāunoa
torn	māfo‘e, māsaesae
torrent (rain)	tō uaga
(river)	lōfia
tortise shell	una laumei
torture	fa‘atāugā, fa‘atāutala, fa‘asāunoa
toss (throw)	lafo, fai le vili
(full __)	sumu
toss to-and-fro	fesoua‘iina
total	‘ātoa, ‘uma lava, aofa‘i, tau aofa‘i
touch	pa‘i, tago, taleu
(get in __)	fa‘afeso‘ota‘i
(be touched, moved)	o‘otia
tough (meat)	fefeu

(fish)	‘ata
(difficult)	faigatā
(hard to break)	ma‘a‘a
tour	ta‘amilosaga, malaga ta‘amilo, tāfaoga
tourist	tagata faimalaga, turisi
tousle (hair)	se‘use‘ua
tow	toso
towards	aga‘i i . . .
towel	solo tā‘ele, matū
tower	‘olo, fale logo
town	‘a‘ai, tāulaga
toy(s)	mea ta‘alo
trace (mark)	fa‘ailoga
trachoma	fuafuanini‘i
track	ala, alasopo
(spoor)	tulagāvae
(__ down)	su‘e, fa‘aāfu, tatao
tract (religious)	tala pu‘upu‘u fa‘alelotu
(__ of land)	‘ogā‘ele‘ele
tractable	vaogōfie
tractor	ta‘avale suafanua masini toso palau etc.
trade (to __)	fefa‘ataua‘i
(a __)	gāluega, faiva
trader	fai‘oloa, fa‘atau ‘oloa
tradewind	to‘elau
tradition	tala‘aga, tala fa‘asolopito, talatu‘u, ‘uputu‘u
traditions	tū ma māsani
traffic	feōa‘iga o ta‘avale, aluga o ta‘avale
tragedy	mala
trail (to __)	tatao, fa‘aāfu
(drag)	totoso
train (railway)	nofoa afi
(bridal)	‘aumeamamae
(to __)	a‘o, a‘oa‘o, fa‘amāsani, koleni
training	a‘oga
(physical __)	fa‘amālosi tino, koleni
traitor	fa‘alata
trample	soli, solipala
trance	sīoa
transfer	si‘itia
transfix	so‘a, velo
transgress	solitūlafono
translate	fa‘aliliu, fa‘amatala ‘upu
transparent (material)	valavala

(glass, water) manino
transport fe'avea'i
transverse fa'alava
trap mailei, faga, fa'amailei
travel malaga, sopo, folau, femalaga'i
traveller tagata malaga
trawl toso
tray pā, laulausi'i, ma'ilo, tirei
tread soli, ui
treason fa'alata
treasure 'oloa tāua, meatāua
(to __) auau, fa'afaileleina
treasurer teu tupe
treasury matāgāluega tau tupe, tu'ugā'oloa
treat
(take care of) tausi
(__ medically) fofō, togafiti, faia, (pol.) tāgofia
(__ badly) agaleagaina
(__ w. respect) fa'aaloalo
(__ lightly) māmāsagia
treatment faiga, tausiga, fofō, togafiti
treaty feagaiga
tree lā'au
(family __) gafa
tree-fern 'oli'olī etc.
tremble tete, gatete, lili, galulu
(__ w. fear, anger) tetemū
tremendous telē lava
trench lua, utu
trespass soli fanua, sopo i le tua'oi
trestle fata
trial (legal) fa'amasinoga
(test) fa'ata'ita'iga, fa'aa'oa'o, tofotofo
(preacher on __) failāuga fa'ata'ita'i (Meth.)
(ordeal) puapuagā, fa'alavelave
triangle tafatolu
tribe itū'āiga o tagata
tributary (river) magāvai
trick togafiti, vai
trickle tafe fa'amotumotu, tafetafe
trigger 'amoti
trim 'oti'oti, sasala
trip (journey) tāfaoga, malaga
(__ up) fa'asalāvei
(__ over s.th.) lāvea
triplets māsagatolu
tripod tūlaga vaetolu
triumph manumālō
troops(s) vaegā'au, 'aufitafita, 'autau, itūtaua
tropical atunu'u vevela, teropika
trot mo'emo'e, taufetulituli
trotter (pig's) tapuvae
trouble fa'alavelave, māsei
(always in __) mapuitigā
(be troubled) atuatuvale, fa'alētonu, fa'atīgāina, pagātia
troublesome
(people) agamāsesei, tāluā
(things) fa'afatiātāma'i
trough (in waves) i tuāgalu
(washing __) tānoa tā mea
trousers 'ofu vae
(shorts) 'ofu vae pupu'u
trowel (tool alofilima
truant ta'atua
truck loli, ta'avale la'u mea
true mo'i, moni, fa'amāo'i, fa'amaoni
trumpet pū
(__ shell) foafoa
truncate fa'amutu
trunk (tree) 'ogālā'au
(body) 'ogātino
(large case) pusa
(__ of elephant) isuloa
trust
(confidence) fa'atuatua
(reliance) fa'alagolago
(believe) talitonu
(__ in s.o.) fa'amoemoe, talisapaia
(a __) teugā tupe mo se fa'amoemoe
truth 'o le sa'o, mea moni, mea tonu
try (prefix = *tau*) taumafai = *attempt*
(put on trial) fa'amasino
(put to test) usi
(__ out) fa'ata'ita'i, fa'aa'oa'o
(__ to find) su'e
(__ to stand) tautū
(__ to give s.th. back) tautu'u
tub tapu
tuba pū malū

tube	fa'agā'au, paipa
tuber	'i'o, tolo
tuberculosis	māmāpala
tuck	afe, sulu (le 'ie), sulu 'ao'ao
Tuesday	Aso Lua
tuft (hair)	sope
tug (pull)	fālō, mūmūfālō
tug-of-war	tosoga
tugboat	va'atoso setima etc.
tulip	tulipe
tumour	patu, tuma
tuna (fish)	tuna
tune	fati
(__ the piano)	kī le lā'au
turkey	pīpī
turmeric	ago, lega, sama
turn	ta'amilo, ta'amilosaga, ta'avili, liliu
(__ inside out)	fela
(__ over)	fuli
(__ one's back)	fulitua
(__ pale)	sesega
(__ aside)	liliu, liua, afe
(__ upside down)	fulialo
(__ of tide)	tapa le tai
(__ over & over)	liuliu
(return)	(pol.) taliu
turtle	laumei
tusk	nifo
twelve	sefulu lua
twenty	luasefulu
twice	fa'alua
twiddle	ni'o solo
twilight (morning)	tafa o ata
(evening)	tauafiafi, pogipogi
twine	tuaia
twinkle	'emo'emo
twins	māsaga
twirl (knife)	'ailao
twist (thread etc.)	milo
(distort)	fa'asesē le uiga
(arm)	mimilo
(tobacco)	sai
twitter	valovalo
two	lua
(in pairs, two's)	soa
(__ faced)	gutugutulua
(__ sided)	tafalua
type (kind)	itū'āiga, vāega
(printing)	mata'itusi
(to type)	tā, lomitusi
typewriter	lā'au lomitusi, lomitusi
typhoid	fiva palagā'au
typical	mea māsani
typist(e)	tagata lomitusi
tyrant	tagata sauā
tyre (tire A.S.)	pa'u, fa'agā'au

Uu

udder	'au susu
ugly	matagā
(people)	'auleaga, 'aulefu, 'auvale
ukulele	'ukulele
ulcer	pala, (pol.) ma'i malū
ulna	soāivi o le lima
ulterior	fa'atilotilo
umbilical cord	uso
umbrella	fa'amalu
umpire	fa'amasino, laufalī
unable	e lē mafai
unanimous	'autasi, tafatasi, tu'ugamālie
unattached	ta'anoa
unavoidable	e lē ma'alofia
unaware	lē iloa
unbelief	lē talitonu
unblessed	nofo fa'apōuliuli
unbroken	e lē mamotusia, 'ātoa
unbusinesslike	e lē fa'apisinisi
uncertain	taumate, fa'alētonu, lē maumanatu, lē mautonu, lē mautinoa
unchaste	ta'a
uncivilized	fa'alenu'upō, lē Kerisiano
uncle	uso o le tamā, tuagane o le tinā
unclean	'ele'elea
uncomfortable	fa'agēgē, lē nofogōfie
uncommon	e lē ta'atele

unconscious e lē mālamalama, 'ua lēiloa se mea
uncooked mata
uncooperative musu, fa'atemutemu, fa'atuga'ese, lē felagolagoma'i
uncouth fa'a'āivao, fa'atūfanua
uncover
  (box, oven) su'e
uncovered (man w.o. shirt) fa'asau
undecided fa'alotolotolua, femēmēa'i
under i lalo o . . .
underneath i lalo ifo o . . .
undersized 'āvilu
understand mālamalama
understanding mālamalamaga, fa'autaga
underwear 'ofuvaeloto
undisciplined fa'alētāupulea, lē pulea
undo tala, tatala
undulate (of body) ni'o solo
uneasy li'a
unemployed e lē maugāluega, lē faigāluega
unenlightened pōuliuli
unequalled e lē fa'atusatusaina
uneven talatala, lauleaga, maupu'epu'e
unexpected e lē mafa'amoemoeina, fa'ate'ite'i
unfair fa'aitū'au, fa'a'au'au, e lē tonu
unfavourable logovale, ta'u'ese, ta'uleaga
unfit fa'alēmalosi lelei, e lē onomea
unfold tala, fofola
unfortunate taivale, lē manuia
unfortunately e leaga 'ua . . .
unfurl mātalatala
ungainly valea
unhappiness fa'anoanoaga
unhealthy 'auvale
unhitch tatala
uniform tōgiga, togitasi
uninhabited lē 'āinā
uninteresting lē mālie
union so'ofa'atasi, tu'ufa'atasiga, uni
  (association) sosaiete, fa'alāpotopotoga
  (rugby union) uni lakapī
unite tu'ufa'atasi, so'ofa'atasi
united
  (one mind) loto gātasitasi so'ofa'atasi
United Nations Organisation Mālō'Aufa'atasi
universal aoao
universe vānimonimo, vāteatea
university iunivesitē
unjust āmiolētonu
unjustly fua, lētonu, lē sa'o
unkind agaleaga, agavale, sāunoa
unless vāganā, se'iloga
unlikely 'ailoga
unlimited fa'alētuā'oi
unlucky mālaia
unmarried nofo fua
unmerciful fa'alaeō
unoccupied pāganoa
unpleasant vale, lē mālie
  (__ news) logovale
unrighteous āmiolētonu
unripe moto, mu'a, mata
unsatisfactory fa'alēlelei
unseemly fa'alēono, fa'alēonomea, fa'alētatau
unshakeable mausalī
unsightly mātagā
unstable palagatete, ta'anoa
unsteady (walk) tautevateva, temutemu
  (canoe) magotogoto, masa'esa'e
unsuccessful 'asa
untattooed pula'ū
untidy gaosā, gaogaosā
until se'i, se'ia
untilled
  (uncultivated) lāfuā
untitled (man) taule'ale'a, (pl.) taulele'a
unusual 'ese, lē māsani ai
unwell fa'ama'ima'i, (pol.) fa'agasegase, fa'alēmalosilelei
unwilling fa'atemutemu, lē loto i ai

unworthy lē onomea
unwritten
(history) talafa'asolopito, tala tu'ugutu, tu'u taliga
unyielding sogasogā
up a'e, i luga, i lugā
(i.e. awake) ala
(__ against s.th.) tuta'ia
(__ to you) tu'u ia te 'oe, pule 'oe, faitalia 'oe
uphold fa'amaonia, sapasapai
upkeep tausiga
upon i, i luga o . . .
upper i luga
upright tū sa'o, ta'uāmiotonuina
uproar vāvāō
uproot ati, fafai, lia'i, sua, suati
upset vevesi
(boat) sasa'e
(person) fa'aatuatuvale, māfatia
upside-down fa'afaō
upstairs fogāfale i luga
uptake (quick) mālamalama vave
(slow) matavalea
up-to-date fa'aneionapō, fa'aasonei

urge nanati, u'una'i, pulunaunau, tauānau, tima'i
urgent fa'avave
urinate mīmi, fe'au lata mai, (pol.) tula'i
urine miaga
us matou, tatou
(two only) ma'ua, ta'ua, ma, ta
use (the __) aogā
(to __) fa'aaogā
(be used to . . .) māsani ma . . .
(__ for) fai ma . . ., avea ma . . .
useful aogā
useless lē aogā
uselessly fua
usher tagata fa'asino nofoa
usual e māsani ai
utensils mea e fai a'i fe'au
(kitchen __) mea fai kuka
uterus fa'a'autagata
utmost pito sili
utter fai atu, (pol.) fegānavai
uvula alelo

Vv

vacant (place) mea avanoa
vacation tu'uaga, mālōloga
vaccinate fa'agata
vacuum cleaner masini fa'amamā kapeta
vagina itū sā
vagrant maumausolo
vague lē manino, fa'anenefu
vain lotovi'i, fa'alialia, lotovi'ifua
(in __) lē aogā, siliga, fua, vale
valedictory fa'amāvaega
valid mautūlaga
valley vanu
valuable tāua

valuables 'oa, meatāua
value 'o le tāua, aogā
valve paipa
van veni
vanguard muā'au
vanish mou, nimo
vanquish fa'ato'ilalo
vapour ausa
vapourizer 'apa liuausa, 'apa fanafana
varied mātalasi
variety itū'āiga 'ese'ese
various 'ese'ese
varnish vānisi
vaseline vaselini
Vatican Vatikano

veil	veli
vein	uaua
venereal disease	ma'i afi
vengeance	tauimasui
venomous	ogoogo
ventilate	fa'asavili
venture	taumafaiga
veranda	poletito
verb	veape
verdict	i'uga, i'ugā fa'amasinoga
verge (on the __ of . . .)	toeitiiti 'ā . . .
verse	fuai'upu
version	fa'amatalaga, liliuga
vertical	tū sa'o
very	tele, ā, lava, fo'i, na'uā, naunau, matuā, matua'i, ta'i, so'ona
(these __ houses)	o nei fo'i fale
(that __ school)	o lenā lava ā'oga
vessel (ship)	va'a
(dish)	ipu
vest	mitiafu, tatao afu
veto	vavao, pule fa'avavao
vex	lutia
vibrate	lūlū, lue
vice	māsani leaga, uiga leaga
(tool)	fa'a'ū
vicinity	e lata ane
vicious	fe'ai
(__ temper)	loto'a'asa
victim	tagata lavea fua, vikitimi (R.C.)
victory	mānumālō, mālō
video	vitiō, vito
view (seen)	va'aiga, (pol.) maimoaga, silafaga
(opinion)	tāofi
(in __ of . . .)	'ona 'o . . . , talu ai . . .
vigilant	mataala
vigorous	galue fa'amālosi lava
vile	leaga tele
village	nu'u, 'a'ai, (pol.) lā'o'ai, tupua
(__ affairs)	faigānu'u
(__ green)	malae

(__ maiden)	taupou, (pol.) sa'o aualuma, sa'o tama'ita'i
villager	tagatānu'u
vine	vine
vinegar	vineka, vinika
violate	soli (le sā, tulāfono etc.)
violence	āmio mālosi leaga, mālosi lē pulea, misa
violet	violē
violin	lā'au 'ili
virgin	teine, taupou
(__ forest)	vaomatua, vaomāoa
(Mary)	Maria le Taupou
virtue	uiga lelei, uiga tonu
viscous	vavale, toto'o
visible	iloaina, va'aia
(invisible)	mea lē va'aia
vision (supernatural)	fa'aaliga
(sight)	pupula mata
visit	asi, asiasi, asiasiga, usu
visitor(s)	mālō, 'aumalaga
vital	matuā tāua
vivid	malaulau
vocabulary	lisi o 'upu
vocal	leoa
(__ cords)	fā'a'ī
voice	leo, (pol.) si'ufofoga
void (empty space)	gaogao
(null & __)	sōloia ma fa'alēaogāina
volcano	volekano, mauga mū
volleyball	volipolo
volume (book)	vāega o le tusi
(noise)	fua o le pisa
(water)	fua o le tafe o le vai
volunteer	tagata ofo
vomit	pua'i
vote	si'igālima, pālota
vouch (for s.o.)	molimau lelei mo . . .
vow	ta'utino
vowel	vaueli
voyage	fōlauga, folau
vulgar	āmiotūfanua, lē mīgao
vulture (bird)	'oreva

Ww

wade	asa
wafer	masi mānifinifi
wag	tātā
wage(s)	totogi
(__ war)	si'i le taua
wagon	ta'avale toso e solofanua
wail	auē, tagiauē
wailing	lauēga, lauaitu
waist	sulugātiti
waistcoat	tao 'ofu
wait	tali, fa'atali
(__ on table)	laulau mea'ai
(lie in __)	taliala, lama, lepa
wake (up)	ala, (pol.) maleifua
(__ s.o.)	fafagu, fa'aala, fagufagu
walk (gen.)	savali, sāvalivali
(__ of life)	matātā
(__ out)	sola
(__ a horse)	fa'asavali
(__ out in protest)	teva
(__ in sleep)	moesavali
(__ on side of foot)	fa'avaesape
walking stick	to'oto'o
wall	pā, 'aupā, puipui
wallet	'atotupe
wallow	ta'afili
wall-plate (house)	amopou
wall-post	poulalo
walnut	nati 'aina
wander	fesāvalivalia'i
(of mind)	ta'a, salalau, solo le māfaufau
(__ around)	maumausolo, femiomioa'i, tafao
want (be in __)	mativa
(desire)	mana'o, fia maua, naunau, mo'omo'o, tagisia
war	taua, (pol.) tāma'i
(civil __)	vātau le atunu'u
(__ club)	uatogi
ward (hospital)	potu mo ē mama'i
(__ off)	puipui, tali

warehouse	fale teu'oloa
warm	māfanafana, vevela
(__ by the fire)	mumulu
warn	lapata'i
warrant	tusi samania *(also summons)*
warrior	toa
warship	va'atau, manuao
wart	lafetoga
warty	fe'efe'ea
wary	segisegi
wash	fulufulu, fufulu, (pol.) penapena
(__ hands)	fafano, (pol.) tatafi
(__ clothes)	tā lavalava
(__ away)	tafea
(__ off saltwater)	fa'alanu
wash bowl	'apa fafano
washer	uosa
washing (the __)	tāgāmea
(__ machine)	masinitā mea
(__ powder)	pauta tā mea
wasp	pī
waste	ma'imau, māumau
(__ land)	ta'alaelae, ta'agaogao
(to __ money, food)	fa'amāumau, lusi, tāugā
watch (clock)	uati
(observe)	va'ava'ai, tulimata'i, (pol.) silasila, taga'i
(look on)	mātamata
(be on look out)	leoleo, uati
(__ over)	leoleo, fa'amamalu
watchful	mataala, matatiotio
water (fresh)	vai, suāvai
(salt)	sami, suāsami
(birth)	lanu
(stagnant)	vailepa
(deep)	moana
(piped)	vaipaipa, (A.S.) vai kī
(holy __)	vaisā
(to __)	fui, fa'asusū
(__ animals)	fa'ainu
water bottle	vaisapai, tauluavai (*two c'nut shell containers*)

(hot __) fagupa'u
watercress kapisi vai
waterfall āfu
waterproof malu
waterspout āsiosio
watery (eyes) 'e'ela
(__ taro) susū
(__ food) suāvaia
wave (sea) galu, (pol.) peau
(__ branches) lue
(__ hands) tālo, tālotālo
(__ fan) tapili
waver vaevaelua le loto
wavy (hair) sē'ea
wax ga'o
way ala, 'auala
(make __) fa'aavanoa le ala
(custom) tū, māsani, āmio
(S. __) Fa'asamoa
(by the __) 'i le ma lea . . .
(lose the __) fesēa'i
(__ lay) lamalama
we matou, tatou
(two only) mā'ua, tā'ua, ma, ta
weak vāivai
(__ body) ausaġe, 'e'eva
weaken fa'avāivai
(__ w. hunger) lāina, matelāina
weakness (of character) pona
(gen.) vāivai
weal 'alava, ila
wealth maumea, mau'oa, tamāo'āiga
wean te'a ma le susu
weapon 'au, 'ā'upega, meatau
wear
(e.g. men's wear) 'ofu tamāloloa
(to __) fai, 'ofu, sulu, lāvalava, (pol.) lā'ei
(__ on head) pale
weary vāivai, fiu, gagase
weather (fine) lagilelei, manaia le aso
(bad) lagilagiā, leaga le aso
weave lalaga
web 'apogāleveleve
wedding fa'aipoipoga
(__ dress) 'ofu fa'aipoipo
(__ day) aso fa'aipoipo
(__ feast) 'aiga, (pol.) tausama'aga, tāumafataga
wedge tina
(to __) fa'a'ū
Wednesday Aso Lulu
weeds(s) vao, pupuvao
(to __) vele, autalu, velefuti
week vaiaso, vaiasosā
weep tagi, (pol.) tutulu, tulutulu
weigh (to __) fua le mamafa
(__ down) māfatia
(__ words) mātau 'upu
weight 'o le mamafa
weird 'ese, paū
welcome (to __) talileleia, talimālō
(a __) taliga, feiloa'iga, (pol.) fesilafa'iga, teumālō
well lelei
(__ done) mālō le galue, mālō, mālie!
(healthy) mālosi, mālōlōina
(as __ as) 'ātoa fo'i ma . . .
(be __) nofo lelei
(be __ off) mau'oloa, tāgolima
(a __) vai 'eli
(__ up) faia'e, lāgā, puna
(__ done, of meat) vela lelei
well-known iloga, lāuiloa, ta'uta'ua, (pol.) lāusilafia
well-mannered tauagafau, tausala
wench fa'alifu
west sisifo
(__ sun) taugāgaifo
westward gāgaifo
wet susū
(__ w. dew, rain) gasū
(__ season) vāipalolo
(to __) fa'asusū
whale tafolā, i'a manu
whale-boat fautasi, tulula
wharf uafu
wharfie tagata faigāluega i le uafu
what 'o le ā?
(__ about?) pe fa'apēfea
whatever so'o se mea
wheat saito
wheedle fa'ase'e, sufi
wheel (a __) uili
(to __) vili, vilivili
wheeze māsū

when ‘a, ‘ā, ina ‘ua *(past),* pe‘ā *(future),* anafea? *(past),* ā fea? *(future)*
whence mai fea?
whenever so‘o se taimi
where ‘o fea? po‘o fea? ‘āfai, ‘i fea?
(__ from?) mai fea?
wherever so‘o se mea
whether pē . . . pē, po‘o . . . pē
which (relative prn.) ai, ‘o lē fea?
whiff miti
while a‘o, ina ‘o, manū
(for a __) mo sina taimi
(in a little __) toeitiiti lava
(a __ ago) analeilā
whine (child) limala‘u
whip sasa, sapini
whirl galulu (le ulu)
whirlpool auma, vili
whirlwind āsiosio
whisk fue
whiskey uisikî
whisper musumusu
whistle fā‘aili
(w. lips) mapu
white pa‘epa‘e (pl.) papa‘e
(__ hair, surf) sina
white-haired ulusinā
White Sunday Aso Sā o Tamaiti
whitebait igaga
whiten fa‘asinasina, fa‘apa‘epa‘e
Whit Sunday Aso Penetekoso, Penekosite (R.C.)
whiz alamū
who? ‘o ai? po‘o ai? *(also whom)*
(in relative clause) i ai
(he/she, who . . .) lē ‘ua . . .
(those who) ‘o ē ‘ua . . .
(who knows?) se‘i iloa
whoever so‘o se tasi
whole ‘ātoa, ‘ato‘atoa
(swallow __) folo pa‘ō
(__ of s.th.) (‘o le mea) ‘uma
whooping cough tale vivini
whose (relative) o le tagata e ana/ona . . .
whose? ‘o ai e ana, ona . . .?

why ‘aiseā, pē ‘aiseā?
wicked agasala
wicket (cricket) ‘olo
wide lautele, vātele
(__ apart) ava, valavala
(__ open sea) vasa laolao, salafa
(__ world) ‘o le lautele o le lalolagi
widen fa‘alautele
widespread (gen.) ta‘atele
(__ tree) māfalā
widow fafine ua oti lana tāne
widower tamāloa ua oti lana avā
width lautele
wife (gen.) avā, to‘alua, (joc.) ama, (pol.) faletua, tausi, meana‘i, masiofo
(__ of paramount chief) masiofo
wig lauulu fa‘apipi‘i
wild (animal) ‘aivao, taufe‘ai
(__ bush) vao
(__ child) vaogatā
(__ weather) loulouā
(__ idea) lē fuafuaina
wilful fa‘ali‘i
will (intention) loto, (pol.) finagalo
(consent) malie
(last __) māvaega
(__ do s.th.) ‘ā, ‘o le‘ā . . .
(__ you?) pē, po‘o . . .
(be willing) malie
win (to __) mālō, manumālō
(__ a prize) maua le fa‘ailoga
wince me‘i, fa‘ame‘i
wind (gen.) matagi
(__ instrument) fagufagu
(trade __) to‘elau
(east __) matā‘upolu
(head __) matagi taumua a‘i
(following __) matagi taumulia‘i
(S.E. __) tuā‘oloa
wind (to coil) ta‘ai, i‘oi‘o
wind up kī
windbreak punimatagi, talimatagi
winding road ala fepi‘opi‘oa‘i solo
window fa‘amalama
windscreen talimatagi
(__ wiper, car) salu timu
windward i ama

wine uaina
wing (bird) 'apa'au
(aeroplane) 'apa'apa
(army) itū o le vaegā'au
wink fa'a'ivi
winter tau mālūlū
wipe solo, sālo, sōloi
(__ out) fa'a'umatia
wire uaea
(barbed __) uaea tuitui
(send a __) uaea
wireless uālesi
wiry (sinewy) u'au'ā
wisdom poto, tofā mamao, utamamao
wise poto, atamai, utamamao
wish (desire) mana'o, fia maua . . . , fia poto . . . etc., tālotalo
(__ good luck) fa'amanuia
(a __) mana'o, mana'oga, mo'omo'oga, loto, (pol.) finagalo
witch fa'ataulāitu fafine
with 'ī, ma
(fight __) fusu ma
(begin __) 'āmata i (iā)
(agree __) malie 'i ai
(together __) fa'atasi ma
(__ patience) ma le 'onosa'i
(__ which) a'i
withdraw fa'afo'i, solomuli
(__ money) tō'ese tupe
wither mae, mamae, āfu, āfulelea, magumagu, manunu, pa'a'ā
within i le, i totonu o . . .
without e aunoa ma
(outside) i fafo
(__ a result) fua
witness molimau, fa'amaonia
witty tausua
wobble māfulifuli
wolf luko
woman fafine, māfine, (pol.) tama'ita'i
(old __) lo'omatua, olomatua (pol.) tama'ita'i matua
womb fa'aautagata
wonder ofo
wonderful ofoofogia
woo aumoe
wood (timber) lā'au, laupapa
wool fulufulu, vulu
word (gen.) 'upu, (pol.) malelega
(message) fe'au
(__ of God) Afioga a le Atua
work galue, gāluega, faimea, lavalima
(__ together) gālulue fa'atasi
(__ well, machine) ola lelei
worker faigāluega
workforce 'aufaigāluega
workshop fale faigāluega, fale inisinia
world lalolagi, atulaulau
(next __) ola 'ātalī, 'āmulī
worldy fa'alelalolagi
worm (gen.) 'anufe
(__ eaten) tūgā
worry fā'atu, popole, tuano'a, lotopopole, popo'e, polepole vale
worse e leaga i lo . . .
worship tāpua'i, tāpua'iga, lotu
worst sili ona leaga, aupito leaga
worth (value) tāua, aogā, fa'atatau
worthless fua, noa, lē aogā lava
would that . . . ma'imau pe ana . . . , tau lava 'ina . . .
wound manu'a, lavea, (pol.) masoe
wounded manu'a, lagimasoe
(__ feelings) māfatia, tigāina
wrangle taua'imisa, fe'upua'i
wrap 'aui, āfīfī, ta'ui
(__ food) 'ofu'ofu
(lavalava) pulupulu, sulu (le 'ie)
wrath to'asā, to'atāma'i
wreath pale
wreck (a house) fa'amalepe, lepeti
(a ship) tu'ia
wrench (tool) fa'aū
(a bone) se'e
wrestle pi'i, mūmūfālō, tauivi, (pol.) fāgatua
wriggle femīgoia'i
wring (neck) titina le ua
(out) tatau, taufua
wringer unu, tāuaga
wrinkle fa'ama'anuminumi

wrist tapulima
write tusi, tusitusi
writer tusitala
writhe gāi'oi'o, vivili
writing tusiga, tusilima, tusitusi
(__ slab, slate) ma'atusi
(__ table) laulau tusitusi
wrong sesē, agasala, 'ese

Xx

Xmas (colq.) Kirisimasi
x-ray 'o le fā'ata
xylophone lā'au pese, lila, o le atupātē

Yy

yacht va'a failā, iota
yam (gen.) ufi
(__ seed) taiulu
(__ garden) togāufi
yard iata (3ft.), lotoā
yarn
(conversation) tala 'umi
(thread) vulu
yawn māvava
yaws (gen.) tona
year tausaga
yearn tu'inanau
yeast fefete
yell uiō, ususū, 'e'ē, 'ī, fa'ataiō
yellow sāmasama, sasama
(yellowish) memea
yes 'ioe, 'ī, 'ia, 'io, 'ō, 'ua lelei
yesterday ananafi
yet (however, nevertheless) 'ae peita'i, 'a'o lenei
(not __) e le'i . . .
yield (give in) ifo, gaua'i, fa'apalapala, tāutu'u, fa'atu'utu'u
(__ easily) tu'ugōfie
(__ w. difficulty) tu'ugatā
(__ in love) gaualofa
(__ in fear) gaumata'u
(i.e. a crop) fua
yoke amo
yolk lega (o le fuāmoa)
yonder i'o, i tuā
yorker (cricket) sumu
you 'e, 'oe
(two) 'oulua, lua
(pl.) 'outou, tou
young (people) talavou
(__ man) taule'ale'a, (pl.) taulele'a
(__ girl) teine muli
(__ animal, plant) tama'i . . .
youngest tūpito, ui'i
your lou, lau, (pl.) ou, au
yours ou, au
youth
(young people) tupulaga, talavou
(man) tama, taule'ale'a
(time) aso o le taule'ale'a, aso o le la'itiiti

Zz

zeal mā'elegā
zealous tō'aga
zebra solofanua tusitusi
zenith tumutumu
zero selo, 'ō, noa, fuāmoa
zig-zag fepi'opi'oa'i
zip-code (A.S.) numera o itumalō (setete)
zip-fastener sipi, sipa
zone vāega, sone
zoo lotoā mo manu 'ese'ese
zoology su'esu'eina o manu 'ese'ese

Grey Pages

1. Pronunciation of Samoan

There are 14 letters in the Samoan alphabet – A E I O U F G L M N P S T V. Introduced, or words of foreign origin, also make use of H K R, although R and L are sometimes inter-changed.

The "Break": There is a further "sound" known as the "break" or "glottal stop". It is represented by the symbol " ' ", and it occurs either before or between vowels in certain words –

e.g. ava – passage in the reef (no break)
'ava – beard (break before first " 'a ")

It should also be noted that the Samoan letter G is *not* the English, G as in dog; but approximates the NG as in song.

Consonants: F L M N P S T V are pronounced as in English, although the S sound is often less sibilant than in English.

Vowels: Each vowel has a "long" and a "short" form, the lengthened form being indicated by a dash (-) over the particular vowel.

A – Long, as in father
Short, as the "u" in cut

E – Long, as in "eh"
Short, as the "e" in set

I – Long, as "ee" in week
Short, as "i" in sit

O – Long, like "aw" in saw
Short, as "o" in non

U – Long, as "oo" in cool
Short, as "u" in put
(Avoid the "ew" sound as in few)

Special Note re: "I" and "U"

†When the "i" is followed by another *unaccented vowel a "y" sound appears in the pronunciation:

e.g. vaiaso (week) – vie-yah-so
iata (yard) – yah-tuh

†When the "u" is followed by another *unaccented vowel a "w" sound appears:

e.g. uō (friend) – woe
uila (bicycle) – wee-luh

* i.e. without a break before the vowel

Dipthongs: When two different vowels stand side by side in the same word, it is important to begin by giving each its own pronunciation until by practice they "run together" where appropriate.

e.g. "vae" and "vai", sound almost the same to the ear of the non-Samoan.

When correctly spoken they clearly indicate leg (vae) and water (vai).

Note also: sao and sau
toe and toi

Emphasis: In general it is the second last or penultimate syllable which is emphasized or stressed:
e.g. ma'alili (cold)
puta (fat)

Be alert however to exceptions, usually denoted by a dash (-) over the letter to be stressed or lengthened:
e.g. mālōlō (rest)
fitā (difficult)

Formal and Colloquial Pronunciation: It should be noted that there is both a formal and a colloquial form of pronunciation.

A student of the Samoan language should first acquire a knowledge of formal pronunciation which is acceptable in all situations.

Teachers, ministers of religion, members of parliament, radio announcers and other public speakers use the formal pronunciation – at least in public. Colloquial pronunciation is used by the majority of Samoans for normal communication.

It is characterized by the use of "K" instead of "T"; "G" instead of "N"; together with a nasalized pronunciation of certain syllables.

Formal Samoan however, is regarded not only as the model for foreigners who are learning the language, but also as the sign of a good education amongst the Samoan people themselves.

Even when foreigners have acquired a good knowledge of the language, they are strongly discouraged from adopting the colloquial form of pronunciation.

2. A Brief Grammar

(These are general rules which have many variants)

THE VERB: In Samoan the verb does not change its form in so far as tense is concerned.

Tense is indicated by verbal particles.

Verbal Particles or Tense Indicators :

1. *'ua* — indicates the present or recent past
   'Ua alu le tama = The boy has gone
   'Ua vevela le taeao = It is a hot morning

2. *e or te* — indicates the present or vague future
   E sau le va'a i le taulaga = The boat comes to the harbour
   Note: "te" is used when it follows a pronoun
   'Ou te alu i le maketi = I am going to the market

3. *'o lo'o* — indicates the present continuous
   'O lo'o moe le pepe = The baby is sleeping

4. *sa or na* — indicates past tense
   Sa alu le pasi i le Aso Sā = The bus went on Sunday
   Na'e sau i le va'alele? = Did you come in the aeroplane?

5. *o le ā* — indicates the immediate or definite future
   O le ā mae'a le galuega nānei = The work will be completed shortly

6. Further verbal particles are used to denote the *imperative* (i.e. commands)
   e.g. *Ia* alu loa = Go immediately

   Se'i faia e a'u = (*Just*) let me do it

Sometimes the "ia" is used *after* the verb
   e.g. Inā sau ia! = Come here! The emphatic form of the imperative is *inā*

Forms of the Verb:

1. The verbs "TO BE" and "TO HAVE" do not exist in Samoan as in certain other languages. The meaning of these two forms is obtained however by the use of certain phrases –
   e.g. "i ai", "ia te ia" etc.
   'Ua i ai = There is
   Sa i ai = There was
   'Ua ia te ia le pule = He has the authority (lit. "is to him the authority")

2. *The Negative:* The negative is indicated by the use of "lē" before the verb (sometimes "le'i")
   e.g. 'Ua lē faia le galuega = The work is not done
   E le'i 'uma le fale = The house is not yet completed

3. *The Passive* form of the verb employs one of several suffixes which must be learnt as there is no general rule. e.g. 'amata-ina, alofa-gia, nofo-ia, osofia, tafea etc.
   Some verbs change the spelling as when tete'e becomes te'ena. (The suffix "-ina" is probably the most commonly used to denote the passive).
   It should also be noted that the use of the passive does not always correspond to English usage.

4. *The Plural:* The plural form of verbs varies – some remain the same for both singular and plural –
   e.g. faitau = to read; fesili = to question
   Others change the spelling, but again these must be learnt as there are no fixed guidelines for deciding the form of the plural –
   e.g. alofa, alolofa = to love
   inu, feinu = to drink
   alu, ō = to go
   'ai, 'a'ai = to eat

5. *The Intensive or Frequentive* form of the verb in Samoan is often obtained by doubling the whole verb –

   e.g. { su'e (to examine)
   su'esu'e (to study)

   { sāuni (to prepare)
   sāuniuni (to get ready)

   { savali (to walk)
   sāvalivali (to stroll)

6. *The Reciprocal* form of the verb is usually formed by using the prefix "fe" and the suffix "a'i". There are slight variations to the suffix which must be learnt –
   e.g. fe-alu-a'i = to go back and forth (to and 'fro)
   fetusia'i = to write to one another
   fealofani = to love one another

7. *The Directive Particles – "mai" and "atu":*
   These follow the verb to give a clear indication of direction –
   i.e. "*mai*" indicates direction *towards* the speaker.
   "*atu*" indicates direction away from the speaker –
   e.g. savali mai = walk towards
   savali atu = walk away from

THE PREFIX "FA'A"

Students of Samoan will note that many words use the prefix "fa'a". It has several functions: –

(i) Probably its main use is as a "causative" prefix to a verb, having the effect of "causing something to happen" –
fa'apa'ū – to cause to fall

(ii) When prefixed to a noun it may form a verb –
fa'amasima – to salt

(iii) Used with certain adjectives it means "somewhat" –
fa'a'ena'ena – brownish

(iv) Used with the negative lē it has a qualifying effect
fa'a-lē-sa'o – hardly correct

(v) Used with numerals it indicates the number of times –
fa'alua – twice; fa'afia? – How many times?

(vi) fa'a also indicates "in the manner of"
fa'a-Samoa – in the Samoan way
fa'a-le'agaga – spiritual (way), spiritually

NOUNS:

(i) Nouns, in Samoan, (with only five exceptions) have the same spelling in both singular and plural forms.
The five exceptions are –

loomatua	= old woman	– lo'omātutua
tamaitiiti	= child	– tamaiti
tamaloa	= man	– tamaloloa
taule'ale'a	= young man	– taulele'a
toea'ina	= old man	– toea'i'ina

Some nouns indicate the plural by a change of accent –
e.g. tuafafine = sister – tuafāfine

(ii) The plural is indicated by the preceding words –
e.g. the sign of the plural article "o" or possessive pronoun

'o fale	= houses
'o ana povi	= his cows
'o a latou naifi	= their knives

(iii) A noun may be used as a verb
e.g. 'o le lāuga = the speech
'ua lāuga le tulāfale = the orator speaks

(iv) A verb may function as a noun either by standing on its own or with the addition of "ga" as a suffix.

e.g. pese = to sing; 'o le pese, pesega (song)
tautala = to talk; 'o le tautala, tautalaga

DEFINITE and INDEFINITE ARTICLES:

The definite article ("the") is indicated by "le" in sentences, but as 'o le when standing on its own –
e.g. 'ua goto le va'a = the boat sinks, 'o le va'a = the boat
In the plural form the le is omitted –
e.g. 'o va'a = boats

The indefinite article ("a", "an") is se
e.g. 'o se fale = a house
The diminutive form of the Indefinite Article is si (singular), and nai (plural)

The Particle " 'o": This particle will be seen frequently in written Samoan and heard in spoken Samoan. It has no equivalent in English although we have already noted its use with the definite and indefinite article.

It has other uses such as in the answer to the question "who are you?"

"O ai 'ea 'oe?" – " 'O a'u 'o Ioane" = I am John
also " 'ua alu 'o ia" = he has gone

(See C.C. Marsack's treatment of this subject)

THE PREPOSITION "OF" – This is translated by either "a" or "o" in Samoan and is directly related to the Possessive Pronouns. It is difficult for one learning the language to know whether a noun takes the "o" form or the "a" form.

e.g. 'O le naifi a le tama (lit.) The knife of the boy

but 'O le vae o le teine = The foot of the girl

By and large the usage simply has to be learnt, although Marsack has a useful chapter on this difficult aspect of the language.

ADJECTIVES – Adjectives almost always follow the noun in Samoan and generally agree in number with the nouns they describe. This means that while nouns rarely have a plural form, adjectives often do –
e.g. lapo'a, lāpopo'a (large)
Just a few adjectives precede the noun –
e.g. tama'i (small, young)
ulua'i (first)
Note that when used with verbal particles, many adjectives also function as verbs –
e.g. 'ua la'itiiti le va'a (lit.) is small the boat

PRONOUNS: Pronouns in Samoan incorporate an "inclusive" and an "exclusive" form as well as providing for singular, dual and plural forms.

The Possessive Pronouns are formed by using the personal pronoun together with a prefix which denotes two things: –

(i) Whether it is in the singular or plural –
e.g. la'u povi = my cow
a'u povi = my cows

(ii) Whether the noun takes the "o" form of the possessive, or the "a" form –
e.g. la'u povi, but lo'u fale

PERSONAL PRONOUNS	POSSESSIVE PRONOUNS	
(Singular – one person)	(One thing possessed)	(Several things possessed)
I, me = a'u, 'ou, ita	my, mine = lo'u, la'u	o'u, a'u
You = 'oe, 'e	your, yours = lou, lau	ou, au
He, she, him, her = ia, na	his, her, hers = lona, lana	ona, ana
(*Dual – two people*)		
We (you & I), us = tā'ua, tā	our, ours = lo tā, la tā	o tā, a tā
We (he & I), us = mā'ua, mā	our, ours = lo mā, la mā	o mā, a mā
You two, you = 'oulua, lua	lo 'oulua, la 'oulua	o 'oulua, a 'oulua
They, them = lā'ua, lā	their, theirs = lo lā'ua, la lā'ua	o lā'ua, a lā'ua
(*Plural – three or more*)		
We (you & I), us = tatou	lo tatou, la tatou	o tatou, a tatou
We (they & I), us = matou	lo matou, la matou	o matou, a matou
You = 'outou	lo 'outou, la 'outou	o'outou, a 'outou
They, them = latou	lo latou, la latou	o latou, a latou

YES and NO The normal word for "Yes" is 'Ioe with its shorter form of "i". Other words in use are 'io and 'ia with 'ō used in response when called by name.

"No" translates as leai, with the negative answer to a question being "E leai". This phrase is also used in negative statements –
e.g. E leai se mea'ai i le fale = There is no food in the house

GREETINGS "Tālofa" is a greeting used at any time of the day or night, the reply being "Tālofa lava" = Greetings indeed!

Tōfā is "Goodbye" with response "Tōfā soifua"

"Thank you" = Fa'afetai or Fa'afetai tele = Thank you very much

"No, thank you" = E leai fa'afetai

3. The Language of Courtesy

The Samoan language has certain honorific or polite aspects which lay emphasis on courtesy and respect.

This means that there are "polite" or "chiefly" words and phrases which are used in both formal and informal conversations. The language of courtesy is highly developed in traditional exchanges between orators or talking chiefs, and chiefs.

The extension of the use of these polite words requires that untitled persons should address matai (heads of families), and others in positions of influence or authority, using a polite vocabulary where appropriate. Similarly, untitled people and young people are encouraged to be courteous to each other.

This means that the ordinary word should be used when speaking of oneself, but the chiefly word when referring to others.

Not every word has both a common and a chiefly form, but words in the chiefly category are identified in this dictionary with the designation "pol." = polite.

4. Samoan Proverbs / Alagā'upu

The proverbial expressions of the Samoans listed herein are but examples of the wide range of mythological and historical sayings which, in their own way, capture some of the past as well as the present traditions of Samoa.

Wide use is made of proverbs in the utterances of the orators or talking chiefs, who endeavour to embellish their speeches with the inclusion of appropriate proverbial references.

G.B. Milner in the preface to his Samoan dictionary (1966) records that he had "collected between 1,000 and 1,500 proverbs or proverbial expressions." For a fine collection of proverbs and their explanation, reference should be made to the English translation by Brother Herman of Dr E. Schultz's work – "Proverbial Expressions of the Samoans" (Polynesian Press, Auckland.)

SELECTION OF PROVERBS

1. "E ati afi ae no masi"
   He came to fetch fire but actually wanted preserved breadfruit.
2. "E fa'asisi fua i moa ae mana'o i le pua'a"
   He merely asked for chickens but hoped for a pig.
3. "Ta te inu i Malie, ta lē malie"
   A play on words – Malie, a village, and "malie", satisfied,
   Expresses discontent when expectations are not realised.

4. "Ua mū le lima, tapa le i'ofi"
After the hand is burnt one asks for the tongs.
5. "Se'i lua'i lou le 'ulu taumamao"
First pick the highest breadfruit.
i.e. Do the hardest task first.
6. " 'Ua māi vai ae suamalie 'ava"
Water is salty but kava is sweet – an appreciation of kava.
7. "E mu'a le vao"
The bush is still immature.
i.e. An apology for one's youth and inexperience.
8. "Ia oloolo pito va'a"
Let each part of the boat be smoothed.
i.e. each to his own task.
9. "O le lā'au e tū, ae ōia"
The tree stands but is condemned.
i.e. Man is but mortal.
10. "Ua leai se manu e olo"
Not a pigeon is cooing.
i.e. There is perfect peace.
11. "E pala le ma'a ae lē pala le 'upu"
Even stones decay but words endure.
i.e. Offences are hard to forget.
12. "Ua sanisani fa'amanuao"
Singing like the birds' dawn chorus.
i.e. Joy at seeing one's friends.
13. "Ia seu le manu ae silasila i le galu"
Catch the bird but watch the breakers.
i.e. Take proper precautions.
14. "So'o le fau i le fau"
Join hibiscus fibre to hibiscus fibre.
i.e. Unity is strength.
15. "O le ala i le pule le tautua"
The way to authority is through service.
16. "Tilitili va'a goto"
Hurrying like a sinking boat trying to reach the shore.
i.e. Trying to save one's skin.
17. "E sola le fai ae tu'u le foto"
The sting ray has escaped but left its barb behind.
18. "Ua uō uō foa"
First friends, then broken heads.
19. "Amu'ia le māsina, e alu ma sau"
Blessed is the moon, it goes but comes back again –
For man there is no return from the grave.
20. "Ua fa'aselu gaugau"
Like a broken comb
Refers to those who have lost respect through quarrelling.
21. "Ua lāuiloa e pili ma sē"
It is known by every lizard and grasshopper.
i.e. Everybody knows of the matter.
22. "Ua tu'u le'upega o Pili"
Pili cast his net by himself.
i.e. A compliment to one who carries out an undertaking unaided.

23. "Se'i muamua ona ala uta"
First test the fishing line on land.
i.e. Look before you leap.
24. "Avatu ni lō, aumai ni lō"
To give lō (fish) and receive lō.
i.e. Tit for Tat.
25. "Sili le foe"
Hang up the paddle.
i.e. Take no further part, leave it to others.
26. "O le lupe o le taeao"
The early morning pigeon.
i.e. Polite reference to the first speech on a special occasion.
27. "E tasi, 'ae afe"
Only one, but worth a thousand.
28. "Ua vela le fala"
The mat is warm.
Refers to a long meeting etc.
29. "Ia fua le niu"
May the coconut tree bear a rich harvest.
i.e. May you be blessed with many children.
30. "Fa'a'ulu toli i gāoā"
Like a breadfruit picked (and fallen) on stony ground.
Disappointment at hopes unrealized.
31. "O le fuata ma lona lou"
There is a lou (harvesting pole) for every crop.
i.e. A leader will arise in every emergency.
32. "E sua le 'ava 'ae tō lè 'ata"
As the kava plant is dug up a twig is planted immediately.
The king is dead, long live the king.
33. "Fā le taeao e lē afiafi"
The morning thinks there will be no afternoon.
i.e. One who assumes there is plenty of time.
34. "Ua mana'o i le ufi, 'ae fefe i le papa"
He desires yam but fears the rocks.
The spirit is willing but the flesh is weak.
35. "Tali i lagi vai o A'opo"
A'opo waits for water from the heavens.
i.e. All blessings come from above.
36. "Ua tusa tau'au"
Both shoulders are of equal strength.
i.e. People or families of equal status.
37. "O le ti'a ulu tonu lou finagalo"
Your will is like the ti'a (dart) that flies straight for the target
i.e. Words of praise or flattery.
38. "Ia lago malū le fala"
Let the bed of mats be soft.
i.e. An apology for asking a favour.
39. "Ua tofā i vai, 'ae ala i 'ai"
Go to sleep on a drink of water but wake with the hope of a good meal.
i.e. Although the present is bad there are good times ahead.

40. "O le va'a ua mafa tautai"
The boat is full of captains.
i.e. Don't worry there are plenty of experienced people available.
41. "Ua ta'oto le 'aupeau"
The waves have subsided.
i.e. The parties are reconciled.
42. "Tali i le tualima"
To wave off with the back of the hand.
i.e. To give a cold welcome.
43. "E leai se ulu ua ala"
There is not even time to scratch one's head.
i.e. A task which keeps one's hands busy.
44. "Ua tafao taliga o le Tufugauli"
Tufugauli's ears wander about.
i.e. Beware of traitors.
45. "E lumāfale i le moana, ae tuāfale i le papa"
There is sea in front of the house, rock at the back.
i.e. An apology for the paucity of food etc.
46. "Ua feagai Vini ma Tapana"
Vini and Tapana (capes at Aleipata) lie opposite each other.
i.e. A conclusion has been reached, the matter is settled.
47. "O le vale 'ai 'afa"
Like fools eating coconut fibre.
i.e. a warning not to be foolish.
48. "Ua ala mai i pu'e o manū"
You come with the fortune you have caught.
i.e. Congratulations on someone's success, or joy at meeting friends.
49. "Se'i fono le pa'a ma ona vae"
Let the crab take counsel with its legs.
Be careful to think things out before taking action.
50. "E poto le tautai ae sē le atu i ama"
Even a skilled fisherman entangles the bonito in the outrigger.
An apology for offending someone.
51. "O lota lima e pa'ia ai lota mata"
My eye was hurt by my hand.
i.e. one who gets into difficulties through his own fault.

5. **Days of the Week** / Aso o le Vaiaso

Sunday	'O le Aso Sā
Monday	Aso Gafua
Tuesday	Aso Lua
Wednesday	Aso Lulu
Thursday	Aso Tofi
Friday	Aso Faraile
Saturday	Aso To'ona'i

6. **Seasons of the Year** / Tau Fa'aletausaga

O le Tau Māfanafana	Summer
O le Tau e Afu ai mea	Autumn
O le Tau Mālūlū	Winter
O le Tau Tuputupu	Spring

7. **Months of the Year** / Masina o le Tausaga

January	Ianuari
February	Fepuari
March	Mati
April	Aperila
May	Mē
June	Iuni
July	Iulai
August	Aokuso
September	Setema
October	Oketopa
November	Novema
December	Tesema

8. **Points of the Compass** / O le Tapasā ma ona itūlagi

North	Matū
South	Saute
East	Sasa'e
West	Sisifo

(O le itū i Matū etc . . .)

9. **Continents** / Konitineta

Africa	Aferika
America	Amerika
Asia	Asia
Australia	Ausetalia
Europe	Europa
India	Initia
Antarctic	Anetātika

10. **Countries** / Atunu‘u

Abyssinia	Apisinia
Albania	Alapania
Arabia	Arapi
Argentina	Anitenitina
Armenia	Amînia
Australia	Ausetalia
Austria	Oseteria
Belgium	Peleseuma
Bolivia	Polivia
Brazil	Pasili
Britain	Peretania
Bulgaria	Palakeria
Canada	Kanata
Chile	Sili
China	Saina
Columbia	Kolomepia
Congo	Kogo
Cook Islands	Atu Kuki
Cyprus	Kuperu
Denmark	Tenemaka
Dominica	Tominika
Ecuador	Ekutoa
Egypt	Aikupito
England	Egelani
Estonia	Esitonia
Fiji	Fiti
Finland	Finilani
France	Falani
Germany	Siamani
Greece	Eleni
Haiti	Haiti
Hawaii	Hawai‘i
Holland	Holani
Hungary	Hagakeri
India	Initia
Indonesia	Initonesia
Iran	Irana
Iraq	Irake
Ireland	Aialani
Israel	Isaraelu
Italy	Italia
Jamaica	Iamaika
Japan	Iapani
Jordan	Ioritana
Korea	Korea
Kampuchea	Kamupesia
Kiribati	Kiripati
Lebanon	Lepanona
Liberia	Laiperia
Libya	Lipia
Malaya	Meleisia
Malta	Malata
Mexico	Mekisikō
Morocco	Moroko
Nauru	Nauru
Nepal	Nepale
Netherlands	Holani
New Caledonia	Niu Kaletonia
New Guinea	Niu Kini
New Zealand	Niu Sila
Norway	Nōue
Oman	Omana
Pakistan	Pakisitana
Palestine	Palesitina
Panama	Panamā
Philippines	Filipaina
Poland	Polani
Portugal	Potukali
Roumania	Romania
Russia	Rusia
Samoa	Samoa
Scotland	Sikotilani
South Africa	Aferika i Saute
Spain	Sepania
Sudan	Sutana
Sweden	Suetena
Switzerland	Suisilani
Syria	Suria
Tahiti	Tā iti
Thailand	Taialani
Tonga	Toga
Turkey	Take
Tuvalu	Tuvalu
United States of America	Iunaite Setete o Amerika
Vanuatu	Vanuatu
Vietnam	Vietiname
Wales	Uelese
Zaire	Sā‘ia

Melanesia	Melanisia
Micronesia	Maikoronesia
Polynesia	Polenisia

11. **Christian Names** / Igoa O Tagata

Albert	Alapati	Anna	Ana
Alfred	Afereti	Anne	Ane
Andrew	Anetere'a	Caroline	Kaloline
Arthur	'Afa	Catherine	Katerina
Charles	Sale, Siale	Cecilia	Sisilia
David	Tavita	Charlotte	Salote
Edward	Eteuati	Dorothy	Tofi
Francis	Faranisisi	Elizabeth	Elisapeta
George	Siaosi	Gladys	Kilali
Henry	Enelē	Gwen	Kueni
James	Iakopo, Semi, Semisi	Hannah	Hana
John	Ioane, Sione	Isabelle	Isapela
Joseph	Iosefa, Iosefo	Jane	Sieni
Matthew	Mataio, Mikaio	Lily	Lili
Michael	Mikaele	Louise	Lu'isa
Paul	Paulo	Lucy	Lusi
Peter	Pita, Peteru, Petero	Magdalen	Makatala
Phillip	Filipo, Filipi	Margaret	Makerita
Ronald	Rano	Martha	Mareta
Robert	Ropati, Ropeti	Mary	Maria, Mele
Sam	Samu	Molly	Moli
Stephen	Setefano	Olive	Olive
Steven	Sitivi	Theresa	Tilesa
Thomas	Tomasi	Queenie	Kuini
Tom	Toma		
William	Viliamu		

12. **Numbers** / Numera

1.	Tasi
2.	Lua
3.	Tolu
4.	Fā
5.	Lima
6.	Ono
7.	Fitu
8.	Valu
9.	Iva
10.	Sefulu
11.	Sefulu tasi
12.	Sefulu lua
13.	Sefulu tolu
14.	Sefulu fā
15.	Sefulu lima
16.	Sefulu ono
17.	Sefulu fitu
18.	Sefulu valu
19.	Sefulu iva
20.	Lua sefulu
21.	Lua sefulu tasi
30.	Tolu sefulu
99.	Iva sefulu iva
100.	Selau
300.	Tolu selau
1,000.	Afe
1,000,000.	Miliona

First – Muamua
Second – O lona lua
Third – O lona tolu
etc . . .

* When *numbering* use "e" before the number; e.g. e fā fale = four houses
* When numbering people use "e to'a" before the number; e.g. e to'a fitu tama = seven boys
* How many girls are there? = E to'a fia teine o i ai?

Addition: Seven plus one is how many? = O le tasi 'ua *fa'aopoopo* ma le fitu'ua fia?
Subtract: Subtract four from ten = Ia *to'ese* le fā mai le sefulu.
Multiply: Multiply eight by three = Ia *fa'atele* le valu i le tolu
Divide: Divide one hundred by ten = Ia *vaevaeina* le selau i le sefulu

To say "in ones, twos" etc. use ta'i before the number.
Two books per child = 'E ta'i lua tusi a le tamaitiiti

but use ta'ito'a for people
Four people to each car = E ta'ito'a fā i ta'avale ta'itasi

13. Measurements / Fua'ese'ese

ounces	'aunese	**millimetre**	milimita
pound	pauna	**centimetre**	senitimita
hundredweight	'anereueta	**metre**	mita
quarter	kuata	**kilometre**	kilomita
ton	tone, tane	**gram**	kalama
inch	'inisi	**kilogram**	kilokalama
foot	futu	**tonne**	tone, tane
yard	iata	**millilitre**	mililita
chain	filifili	**litre**	lita
furlong	falelogi		
mile	maila	**hectare**	hekatea
acre	eka		
pint	paina		
quart	kuota		
gallon	kalone		

14. Common Tools / Meafaigāluega

bit	matāvili	**(cold __)**	tofi u'amea, koasisi
bolt	fao fai nati	**compass**	fai li'o
brace	vilifatafata	**drill**	vili eletise
bradawl	tui	**file**	'ili, 'ili tafatolu
brush	pulumu, palasi	**hammer**	sāmala
chisel	tofi	**level**	fuasuāvai, fuavai

nail	fao	**saw-set**	fa'api'o nifo
nail-puller	se'i fao	**screw**	sikurū, faovili
nut	nati	**screw-driver**	sikurū
pincers	se'i fao, 'oti fao, 'i'ofi	**spanner**	fa'aū
plane	tele, olo	**spokeshave**	fisi
pliers	palaea	**square**	sikuea
rule	futu	**tin-snips**	'oti 'apa
sandpaper	pepa valavala, sani pepa	**vice**	fa'aū
saw	'ili		
(cross cut __)	'ilivavae		
(rip __)	'ilitofi	**blunt**	matatupa
(tenon __)	'ilimutu	**sharpen**	fa'amata, fa'ama'ai

15. Parts of the Body / O Itutino

abdomen	manava, (pol.) laualo	**face**	mata, (pol.) fofoga
(lower __)	puimanava, punialo	**faeces**	tae, (pol.) otaota
ankle	tapuvae	**feet, foot**	vae (pol.) 'a'ao
anus	māliuga	**fibula**	soāivi
arm	lima, (pol.) 'a'ao	**finger**	tamatama'i lima
arm-pit	'ao'ao	**finger-nails**	mai'u'u
artery	alātoto	**forehead**	muāulu
		forefinger	limatusi
back	tua, papātua	**forearm**	'ogālima
beard	'ava		
bladder	tagāmimi	**gall-bladder**	au'ona
blood	toto, (pol.) 'ele'ele	**glands**	puna
bones	ivi, ponāivi	**groin**	tute,(pol.) afisāvae
bottom	muli		
brain	fāi'ai	**hair**	lauulu, (pol.) lauao
breast	susu, fatafata	**hand**	lima (pol.) 'a'ao
buttocks	nofoaga	**(palm of __)**	alofilima
		head	ulu, (pol.) ao
cheek	alāfau	**heart**	fatu
chest	fatafata	**heel**	mulivae
chin	'auvae, muā'auvae	**hip**	suilapalapa, no'o
clitoris	tila, masisi		
cranium	ulupo'o	**jaw**	'auvae
crutch	magamuli	**joints**	so'oga, fa'iga
ear	taliga	**kidney**	fatu ga'o, fatu ma'a
elbow	tulilima	**knee**	tulivae
eye	mata, (pol.) fofoga	**knee-cap**	tupe o le vae
eye-ball	i'o mata		
eye-brow	fulufulumata	**legs**	vae, (pol.) 'a'ao
eye-lash	fulumata	**ligament**	uaua
eye (pupil)	tama'i mata	**lips**	laugutu

liver	ate
lungs	māmā
mouth	gutu, (pol.) fofoga
muscle	mūsele, maso, ‘ogāgase
navel	pute
neck	ua
(back of __)	tuliulu
nipple	matāsusu
nose	isu, (pol.) fofoga
penis	poti, (pol.) mea sā, aualuma
pulse	uaua o le lima (e tātā ai le fatu)
rib(s)	ivi‘aso‘aso
saliva	fāua
scrotum	laso, lalovasa
shin	tuasivivae
shoulder	tau‘au
sinews	uaua
skin	pa‘u
skull	ulupo‘o
sole of foot	alofivae
spine	ivitū
stomach	manava, (pol.) alo
teeth, tooth	nifo
testicle	fuāmanava
thigh	‘ogāvae, ‘autele
throat	fā‘a‘ī
thumb	lima matua
toes	tamatama‘i vae
(big toe)	vaematua
toe-nail	mati‘u‘u
tongue	laulaufaiva
ulna	soāivi
umbilical-cord	uso
uvula	alelo
veins	uaua, alātoto
vertebra	ivitū
waist	sulugātiti
wrist	tapulima
womb	fa‘a‘autagata

16. Medically Related Terms / Upu Fa‘afoma‘i

abdomen	manava, (pol.) laualo
abdominal pains	to‘oala
abortion	fa‘apa‘ū le pepe
abscess	fuafua, silailalo, silailagi
(__ of foot)	to‘oma‘a
afterbirth	falefale, fanua (*also placenta*)
amputate	tipi mutu
anaesthetic	
(general)	fa‘amoe
(local)	fa‘agase
antiseptic	vaimanu‘a
arthritis	gugu
asthma	sela
autopsy	ta‘otoga o le maliu
blood	toto, (pol.) ‘ele‘ele
(blood-nose)	pāpātoto
blood pressure	
(high)	toto maualuga
boil	ma‘isua
bowel	(pol.) taufale
bruised	uno‘o
cancer	‘ailoto, kanesa
cataract	unāi‘a
chicken pox	tane susu
cold	isu mamafa
contused	totoulia
cough	tale
(hacking __)	taleū
cough medicine	vai tale
cystitis	tulitā
dandruff	mafuga o le ulu
dead tissue	‘atilo
diabetes	ma‘i suka
drugs	vailā‘au
dysentery	sanatoto
ear-wax	taetuli
epidemic	pesi le fa‘ama‘i
eye-discharge	somo

eye-specialist fōma'i mata

fever fiva, fa'avelavela
fungus disease 'utu

germ siama

heart-beat tātā
(rapid __) tātāvale
hepatitis fiva samasama
hernia fifi pa'ū
hiccup loga, to'omaunu
hydrocele ma'i o tāne

incise tafa
inflamed lugā
intestine
(large) (pol.) taufale
(small) fifi

jaundice fiva sāmasama

leukemia kanesa o le toto
linament vai mili
lotion vainini

measles mīsela
medicine vailā'au
migraine ulutigā
miscarriage fafano le pepe
mucus vavale, isupē

neuritis ma'i o neura

ointment vainini
operate tipi, ta'oto
operation tipiga, ta'otoga
organs (internal) tōtōga
osteomyelitis 'oloā

peptic ulcer papala o le puta
pill fuālā'au
pimple fuafua, tonatonafe'e
placenta fanua
pneumonia fiva līmonia, niumonia
poison vai'ona
pregnancy ma'itaga, maitō
premature-birth fanau lē au
pus alou
psychiatric illness ma'i o le mafaufau

ringworm lafa

scar tissue lupea, ma'ila
semen suāsī
septic lugā, 'ona
set a bone fa'atū le ivi
sickly ma'i lasi
surgeon fōma'i tipitipi
swelling fula

throb w. pain vanevane
thrush pala (ma'i o pepe)
tinea tane
tinea (toes) palapalaū
tumour tuma

urine miaga
(smell of __) sosogo

vaccination tui puipuia
veins alātoto
veneral disease ma'i afi

wart lafetoga
water
(childbirth) 'ua pā le lanu
whooping cough tale vivini

x-ray fā'ata

yaws tona

17. Colours / Lanu ʻeseʻese

black	uliuli, (pl.) uli	**(deep ___)**	ʻula
blue	lanumoana	**silver**	lanu siliva
brown	ʻenaʻena, (pl.) ʻeʻena	**violet**	violē
cream	kulimi, sāmasama – vāivai	**white**	paʻepaʻe, (pl.) papaʻe
gold	lanuʻauro	**yellow**	sāmasama
green	lanumeamata, lanu lauvao		
grey	lanu ʻefuʻefu, sinā	**dark (of colours)**	mālosi
orange	mūmūsesega, lanu moli	**light (of colours)**	vāivai
pink	piniki	**spotted**	pūlepule
purple	pāʻauli, violē	**striped**	tusitusi
red	mūmū		

18. Telling the Time / O Itūlā

Hour	Itūlā	**What time is it?**	ʻUa tā nei le fia?
Minute	Minute	**It is four oʻclock**	ʻUa tā le fā
Second	Sekone	**It is five minutes to six**	ʻUa toe lima minute i le ono
Hands of the clock	Vae o le uati (Literally "legs of the clock")	**It is three minutes past seven**	ʻUa teʻa le fitu i minute e tolu
		It is half past four	O le ʻafa o le fā
		It is a quarter to nine	E toe kuata i le iva